THE WAGONMASTERS

THE
WAGONMASTERS

High Plains Freighting
from the Earliest Days of the Santa Fe Trail to 1880

BY HENRY PICKERING WALKER

UNIVERSITY OF OKLAHOMA PRESS : NORMAN

Frontispiece: "Wagon Boss," from a painting in oil by Charles M. Russell. *Courtesy The Thomas Gilcrease Institute of History and Art, Tulsa, Oklahoma.*

HE
203
.W25

Library of Congress Catalog Card Number: 66-13434

Copyright 1966 by the University of Oklahoma Press, Publishing Division of the University. Composed and printed at Norman, Oklahoma, U.S.A., by the University of Oklahoma Press. First edition.

DEDICATION

This book is dedicated to
REX W. STRICKLAND AND ROBERT G. ATHEARN,
who so blithely undertook to retread an "old soldier."

ACKNOWLEDGMENTS

I T IS DIFFICULT to express my thanks to all those whose interest, support, and assistance made possible, and pleasant, the research involved in this work. Lest, because of faulty memory, I hurt someone by neglecting to name him, I shall not try to present a detailed complete list, and for this I offer my apologies. However, I do wish to acknowledge the assistance given by the personnel of the Colorado State Historical Society, the Historical Department of the State of Wyoming, the Historical Society of Montana, the Church Historian's Office of the Church of Jesus Christ of Latter-day Saints, the Utah Historical Society, the New Mexico Department of Records and Archives, the Library of New Mexico Highlands University, the Nebraska State Historical Society, the Kansas Historical Society, the Jackson County (Missouri) Historical Society, and the State Department Records and Army and Air Force Records Branches of the National Archives. Special thanks must be given to Mrs. Alys Freeze of the Western History Collection of the Denver Public Library and to Miss Lucille Fry and Mrs. Cress Taylor of the Western History Collection of the University of Colorado Libraries.

HENRY PICKERING WALKER

Tucson, Arizona
April 4, 1966

CONTENTS

ILLUSTRATIONS

"The Sentinel"
"The Jerk Line"
"The Wagon Boss"
"The Bullwhacker"

Maps

THE WAGONMASTERS

CHAPTER I

"STRETCH OUT! STRETCH OUT!"

Every morning and afternoon for fifty years or so, the cry "Stretch out! Stretch out!" rang out along the Overland and Santa Fe trails. At this order, great trains of heavy ox- or mule-drawn freight wagons uncoiled from their circular, defensive corrals and took up single-file lines of march toward the distant settlements of the Mountain West. In these slow-moving, unsprung wagons moved the life-blood of the struggling young towns and mining camps—food; clothing; machinery; furniture; even mirrors, glass showcases, and fine chinaware.

When the tide of westward-moving Americans lapped up to the line of the Missouri River, it faced a new problem in transportation—the movement of a vast bulk of freight without benefit of navigable water. Beyond the Missouri lay the Great American Desert. During their trip to the Pacific in 1804–1806, Captains Meriwether Lewis and William Clark had noted in their journals that the country from the mouth of the Yellowstone River to the foothills of the Rocky Mountains was rather arid. On Friday, May 17, 1805, Captain Lewis wrote: "The great number of large beds of streams perfectly dry which we daily pass indicate a country but badly watered, which I fear is the case with the country through which we have been passing for the last fifteen to twenty days."[1]

The first appearance of the term "Great American Desert" was on

[1] Reuben Gold Thwaites (ed.), *Original Journals of the Lewis and Clark Expedition: 1804–1806*, II, 41, 80.

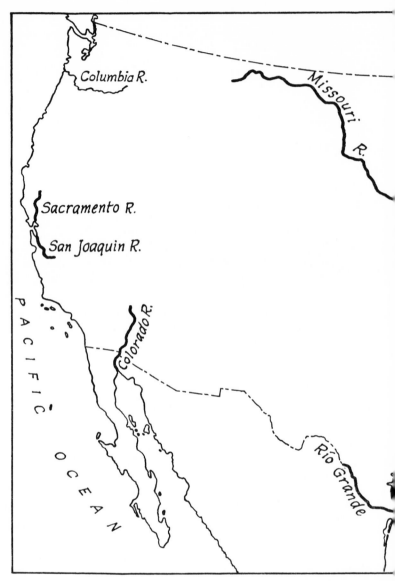

Columbia R.

Missouri R.

Sacramento R.

San Joaquin R.

Colorado R.

PACIFIC OCEAN

Rio Grande

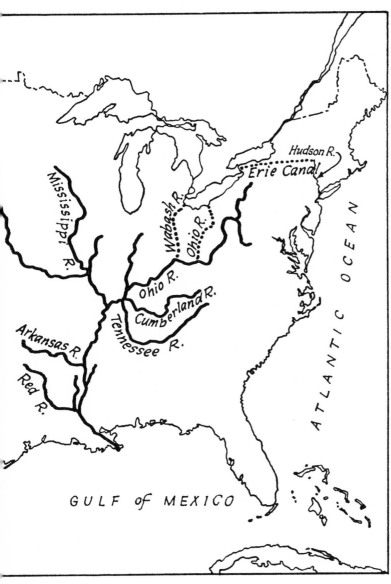

WATER-BORNE COMMERCE

the official map of Major Stephen S. Long's 1820 trip of exploration to the east face of the Rockies. In his report, Long gave his opinion that the area between the Missouri River and the Rocky Mountains "is almost wholly unfit for cultivation, and of course uninhabitable by a people depending on agriculture for their subsistence." Dr. Edwin James, a botanist who accompanied Zebulon Pike on his trip in 1806, was puzzled by the presence of wild animals in this vast region. The geography textbook published by Woodbridge and Willard in 1824 showed the desert to all schoolboys, and the idea was perpetuated in Carey and Lee's *Atlas* of 1827 and in Bradford's *Atlas* of 1833. As late as 1865, General William T. Sherman, in the St. Louis *Republican* of March 25, asked, "What are the uses to which the vast and desert regions of our country between the 100th parallel and the Pacific basin are to be applied?"[2]

The Great American Desert presented many problems to the westward-moving Americans. In the preface of *The Great Plains*, Walter Prescott Webb noted that, in *The Way to the West*, Emerson Hough had listed the ax, rifle, boat, and horse as the instruments with which the pioneers had advanced the frontier. Webb felt that this list did not apply to the plains as it did to the forested regions of the east: "The ax was not important where there were no trees, nor the boat where there was little water. The horse, to be sure, was of increased importance on the Plains, but the horseman's favorite weapon was the six-shooter and not the long rifle." Webb went on to comment that the Plains presented an obstacle that forced changes in implements and institutions. The history of the Americans on the Plains was a history of adaption, "of giving up old things that would no longer function for new things that would, of giving up an old way of life for a new way in order that there might be *a* way."[3] A noticeable omission in this great study is the problem of long-distance transportation of bulk goods and supplies, without which no civilized community can long exist.

[2] Robert G. Athearn, "The Great Plains in Historical Perspective," *Montana, The Magazine of Western History*, Vol. VIII (January, 1958), 13–29.
[3] Webb, *The Great Plains*, V, 507–508.

Up to the line of the Mississippi, water transportation had been the chief means of communication and of the movement of high-volume, low-value goods such as farm produce. The Cumberland Road, connecting Fort Cumberland on the Potomac River with the Monongahela, was but a matter of 120 miles over a prepared road that was well provided with taverns offering rest and refreshment for man and beast. Transportation companies using four-horse wagons conducted a regular business on the turnpikes, delivering freight in central Ohio one month out of Baltimore. By 1820 over three thousand wagons were in use on the run from Philadelphia to Pittsburgh, transporting an estimated eighteen million dollars worth of goods annually. The freight charge in 1817 from Philadelphia to Pittsburgh was as high as seven to ten cents per pound, but in a few years competition had lowered the charge to three cents.[4]

When the Erie Canal was opened in 1825, the cost of freighting from the old Northwest Territory to salt water at New York dropped sharply. The "Pennsylvania System" of canals, inclined planes, and railroads was opened between Philadelphia and the Ohio River in 1834. The Ohio Canal, from Cleveland on Lake Erie to Portsmouth on the Ohio River, was completed in 1823. All these man-made improvements were designed to connect one system of waterways with another.

East of the Mississippi, the country was well watered by streams that could be traveled by specially built steamboats. The upper Ohio River and its tributaries spread a net of navigable water from Olean, New York, to Malden, West Virginia, and from Zanesville, Ohio, to Lafayette, Indiana. The Tennessee and Cumberland rivers could be used by steamers as far as Knoxville and Carthage, Tennessee, respectively, while steamers could travel the Mississippi as far north as St. Paul, Minnesota.

The first steamer on western waters, the *New Orleans* of 371 tons, was launched at Pittsburgh by Robert A. Livingston and Robert Fulton in 1811. The economy of transportation by steamboat is illustrated by the experience of Nashville, Tennessee. In 1817, the

4 Frederick Jackson Turner, *The Rise of the New West*, 99.

year before steamers began operating to the city, salt sold for three dollars a bushel, but by 1825 the price had plummeted to seventy-five cents. In the same period, sugar dropped from twenty-four cents per pound to nine cents, and coffee from fifty to twenty-five.

There was hardly a point between the Appalachians and the Mississippi that was more than 100 miles from navigable water. In the whole vast region west of the Mississippi there were a few short stretches of navigable water around the perimeter. The Sacramento and San Joaquin rivers in California could handle steamers for 100 or so miles from San Francisco Bay. Steamers could, with a great deal of difficulty, make their way up the Colorado River from the Gulf of California to Callville, in extreme southern Nevada. The head of navigation of the Rio Grande was some 250 miles upstream from the Gulf of Mexico. Stretches of 150–200 miles of the lower tributaries entering the Mississippi from the west, such as the Arkansas, Red, and Black rivers, could be traveled by steamers.

Only one river in the whole Trans-Mississippi West could be used by steamboats for any great distance—the Missouri River, whose head of navigation at Fort Benton, Montana, was 3,175 miles upstream from St. Louis.[5] Steamer travel on the Missouri was a very hazardous undertaking. The outstanding peculiarity of this river was its shallowness. The annual rainfall at its mouth was about forty inches. At Sioux City it was only twenty-six inches, while at Fort Benton it was a mere twelve to fourteen inches. Steamers had to take advantage of the two annual rises of the water level. The first, from mid-March to mid-April, was caused by melting of the snow on the lower Rockies and the northern Great Plains and the early spring rain in Dakota. This rise had small effect above the mouth of the Yellowstone River. The second rise came with the melting of the snow in the high Rockies and occurred from mid-May to the first of July. The rises varied from none at all in 1863 to uncontrollable floods in 1881. Ice usually closed the river channel in late November or early December and broke up, on the upper reaches, between March 20 and April 15. An additional hazard to

5 Charles Collins, *Omaha Directory for 1866*.

navigation was the high prairie wind of twenty to thirty miles per hour that pushed the shallow draft steamers into the banks or onto sand bars. Each spring flood meant a change in the position of sand bars; in fact, the river changed beds so often that it became known as "The Harlot." In years in which the runoff was less than usual, steamers had to discharge their freight several hundred miles below Fort Benton.[6]

In addition to all the problems of navigation, the course of the Missouri River swung far to the north of any mid-continent line, and its headwaters lay in the most rugged part of the Rocky Mountains. The westward movement had to seek a line of march farther south. Bernard De Voto pointed out that the Missouri, "infinitely laborious and infinitely circuitous," was the only water route available, and "Contrary to the traditional experience of the westering Americans, most travel, the principal movement, must be by land."[7] The other western tributaries of the Mississippi and Missouri rivers have been well described as "a mile wide and an inch deep." The chief tributary of the Missouri, the Platte, caused Artemus Ward to remark that it would make a considerable river—if it were tipped on edge.[8]

The first men in the westering movement to face the problem of moving large bulk and weight of goods over long distances were the fur traders. The traders and trappers of French Canada developed, for eastern rivers and the Great Lakes, the *canot de maître*, a birchbark canoe six feet wide and thirty-five to forty feet long, capable of carrying a cargo of four tons and a crew of fourteen men. Beyond the Grand Portage, at the western end of Lake Superior, appeared the *canot du nord*, a canoe with a capacity of a ton and a half and a crew of five to eight. While the birchbark canoe was a marvel of

6 William E. Lass, *A History of Steamboating on the Upper Missouri*, 3–4; John W. Hakola, "Samuel T. Hauser and the Economic Development of Montana," Ph.D. Dissertation, Indiana University (1961), 125–26; *Fort Benton Record* (Montana), (1875–78).

7 De Voto, *The Course of Empire*, 409.

8 Charles F. Lummis, "Pioneer Transportation in America," *McClure's Magazine*, Vol. XXVI (November, 1905), 81–94.

adaptation, it was a cranky vessel. An ineptly placed, moccasined foot could punch a hole through the hull, and the pine-tar caulking had to be renewed at least daily. It took long training and great skill to pilot one of these frail craft successfully through the white water of the rivers and the high seas of a lake storm.[9]

South of the Great Lakes the most popular boat in the Trans-Appalachian region was the flatboat, a vessel that ranged from twenty to one hundred feet in length and, in construction, varied from hardly more than a raft to a fully roofed structure. The flatboat was adequate for downstream travel and was usually sold for lumber at the end of a trip.

To move against the current, a more readily handled boat was needed; the answer was the keelboat. Sturdily built on a regular keel and pointed bow and stern, the keelboat averaged some fifty feet in length and seven to ten feet in width and had a capacity of twenty to forty tons. Every available means of propulsion was used. In slack water, it could be sailed before a following wind or rowed when the wind did not favor. In shallow water, it could be poled against the current. However, there were long reaches where towing was the only answer, and the crew of twenty or so men had to slog and swear their way through mud and riverside thickets or scramble over rocks and windfalls. It was from this rugged life that there emerged the fabled "half-horse, half-alligator," Mike Fink, king of the keelboatmen.

The keelboat was a slow and wearisome means of travel and far too expensive for the movement of bulk goods. By keelboat from New Orleans to Louisville, the trip usually required three to four months, and from St. Louis to Pittsburgh, close to three months. Before 1820 keelboat rates were usually five dollars per hundred pounds from New Orleans to Louisville, and from St. Louis to Pittsburgh or St. Paul, three and seven dollars per hundred, respectively. Downstream rates were usually one-quarter to one-third of the upstream rates.[10]

9 DeVoto, *Course of Empire*, 239–40.
10 Louis C. Hunter, *Steamboats on the Western Rivers*, 22–25.

Lewis and Clark used a keelboat to carry most of their supplies as far as Fort Mandan (near the present city of Bismarck, North Dakota) in 1804. Nicholas Biddle, in his *History of the Expedition under the Command of Captains Lewis and Clark,* describes this keelboat as fifty feet long, drawing three feet of water, and carrying one square sail and twenty-two oars. It was decked over for ten feet bow and stern, and the middle section was covered by lockers which could be raised to serve as a breastwork in case of trouble with the Indians. The cumbersome keelboat was abandoned at Fort Mandan in favor of the more manageable dugout canoe or pirogue. The journals of Lewis and Clark give an excellent idea of the difficulties of keelboat navigation on the Missouri River—sand bars, snags, falling riverbanks, and mosquitoes.

The many disadvantages of keelboats, including a high rate of loss, led the American Fur Company to experiment with steamboats on the upper Missouri River. The steamer *Yellowstone,* in the spring of 1831, made the first trip above Council Bluffs, reaching Fort Tecumseh, just above the mouth of the Teton River in South Dakota, on June 19. The *Yellowstone* was 130 feet in length, 19 feet in width, and drew 6 feet of water when loaded to 75 tons.[11] This was a surprisingly deep draft when rivermen farther east were already demanding vessels of shallower draft.

When Prince Maximilian of Wied-Neuwied, a Prussian general who had fought against Napoleon I, and his artist-friend Charles Bodmer went up the Missouri in 1833, they left St. Louis on April 10 aboard the *Yellowstone.* They reached Fort Pierre (across the river from the present city of Pierre, South Dakota) on May 30 and, after a short rest, transferred to the company's second steamer, the *Assiniboin.* Leaving Fort Pierre on June 5, they reached Fort Union, at the mouth of the Yellowstone River, on June 24. They had covered about 1,800 miles in about one-third of the time that would have been required to cover the same distance by keelboat. In order to reach Fort McKenzie, near the mouth of the Marias River, for a better look at Plains Indians in the natural state, the

---

11 Lass, *Steamboating on the Upper Missouri,* 9.

travelers had to transfer to the keelboat *Flora*. The *Flora*, with a complement of forty-seven men, left Fort Union on July 6 and reached Fort McKenzie on August 9. The Prince was 34 days out of Fort Union and 109 days from St. Louis.[12]

For a comparison of speed of travel on the High Plains, it might be noted that a caravan of pack animals belonging to Sublette and Campbell, fur traders of St. Louis, had left that city about April 1, or about ten days before Prince Maximilian had sailed on the *Yellowstone*. The caravan consisted of forty men, each in charge of three pack horses, some spare mounts, twenty sheep that were to provide food until the party reached buffalo country, and two bulls and three cows that were to provide breeding stock for a new trading post to be established near the mouth of the Yellowstone River. The first goal of the caravan was the annual trappers' rendezvous to be held that year on Green River, in western Wyoming. On June 24, when Maximilian reached Fort Union, the caravan was still east of Laramie Fork, in eastern Wyoming. By August 9, when the *Flora* reached Fort McKenzie, the rendezvous had broken up and the trapping parties had scattered into the mountains.[13] For sheer speed, the pack train could outdistance the river steamer, but it could not match it for size of load or economy of operation.

In 1851 the average western steamboat measured 235 tons capacity and had a crew of 26. While canoes required about 3 men for each ton of cargo, keelboats averaged 1 man per each 3 tons, and steamers averaged 9 to 12 tons per crew member. The average trip from St. Louis to Fort Union in the 1850's was 42 days against the current, and the return trip averaged 18 days.[14]

Missing the last of the spring rise in 1834, the *Assiniboin* had to stay upriver during the winter of 1834–35, an expensive layover. It was not until 1860 that the American Fur Company's *Chippewa* reached Fort Benton, the first steamer to do so. For the next two

12 Maximilian, Prince of Wied, *Travels in the Interior of North America*, XXII, 237, 314–16, 330, 372–73; XXIII, 25–26, 86–89.

13 Bernard De Voto, *Across the Wide Missouri*, 135–37.

14 Hunter, *Steamboats on Western Rivers*, 24–25, 442–43.

years only fur-company boats pushed as far as Fort Benton. It was the discovery of gold in Montana that brought about a boom in shipping at this river port. The peak year of this boom was reached in 1867, when there were thirty-nine arrivals. The completion of the transcontinental railroad in 1869 brought about a sharp drop in steamer activity at Fort Benton, although trade with southern Canada continued for some time.[15] In 1869 there were twenty-four arrivals at Fort Benton, but in the following year there were only eight.[16] The gold strike in the Black Hills brought about a brief revival on the short stretch from Sioux City, Iowa, to Pierre and Bismarck in Dakota. This revival peaked in the years 1876–81. From May 5 to 15, 1875, there were received at Yankton, South Dakota, 841 tons of private freight and 643 tons of government freight for the upriver country.[17]

Difficulties of navigation on the Missouri River made for slow travel. As late as 1857 the record from St. Louis to Omaha (678 miles) was five days and fifteen hours. By comparison, in April, 1834 the *Tuscarora* had made the run from New Orleans to Louisville, 1,430 miles, in seven days and eighteen hours. The prolonged trips on the Missouri resulted in rates that were more than double those on other major rivers. Steamboating on the Missouri was never as important as on the upper Ohio or upper Mississippi and probably did not much exceed the business on the Cumberland or Illinois. As steamboat operation was strictly an exploitive form of business, the lack of population easily accounts for the comparatively low level of activity. Freight rates from St. Louis to Fort Benton were as high as eighteen cents per pound until 1865, but two years later competition had driven the rates down to about nine cents per pound. Insur-

15 H. A. Trexler, "Missouri-Montana Highway—Part II, The Overland Route," *Missouri Historical Review* [hereinafter referred to as *MHR*], Vol. XII (April, 1918), 155–56; Asa A. Wood, "Fort Benton's Part in the Development of the West," *Washington Historical Quarterly*, Vol. XX (July, 1929), 221.

16 T. C. Power and Brothers, "Steam Boat Arrivals at Fort Benton," *Contributions*, Historical Society of Montana [hereinafter referred to as *MHS*], Vol. I (1876), 280–87; Vol. III (1900), 351–58.

17 Harold E. Briggs, "Pioneer River Transportation in Dakota," *North Dakota Historical Quarterly*, Vol. III (April, 1929), 159–82.

ance rates were as high as 15 to 20 per cent at times, but over the whole period, they averaged 6½ per cent on side-wheelers and 8 per cent on stern-wheelers. These rates were, of course, added to the expense of moving goods on the river. For a long time stern-wheelers were thought to be less manageable, therefore less safe, than side-wheelers, and for some time insurance companies refused to take risks on them.[18]

Use of the Missouri River as a channel of trade or communications was complicated by the attitude of the Indians living along the banks of the river. The fur traders of St. Louis had long dealt with some of the upriver tribes, but certain ones sought to maintain a highly profitable position as middlemen between the traders and the tribes living upstream. They could not only take a high profit from such trade but could also control the flow of arms and ammunition to the Indians farther west—usually their natural enemies. Lewis and Clark had to bluff and threaten their way past the Sioux in the vicinity of modern Pierre, South Dakota. Word sped ahead of the explorers that these were men not lightly to be threatened, and they had no more such trouble. However, the effect of this show of force and nerve did not last long. Some three years later the Arikaras, living about fifty miles north of the Sioux, practically closed the river to the traders.[19] In 1810 and 1811 the St. Louis Missouri Fur Company had to withdraw its posts above the Mandan villages, as they could no longer supply them consistently. During the War of 1812, Manuel Lisa withdrew his upriver posts to Council Bluffs, Iowa. Referring to the Arikaras, Bernard De Voto said that it was their activities "plus the independent operations of the Blackfeet farther west" that forced the traders to abandon the trail of Lewis and Clark and to seek a new route up the valley of the Platte.[20]

[18] *Ibid.*, 163; Hunter, *Steamboats on Western Rivers*, 365.

[19] Report of Brig. Gen. Henry Atkinson, *House Exec. Doc. 117*, 19 Cong., 1 sess. (Serial 136); Hiram M. Chittenden, *The American Fur Trade of the Far West*, I, 117, 121, and Appendix B, Manuel Lisa to General Clark, July 1, 1817.

[20] De Voto, *Course of Empire*, 456; Harrison Clifford Dale, *The Ashley-Smith Explorations and the Discovery of a Central Route to the Pacific, 1822–1829*, 53; Chittenden, *American Fur Trade*, Appendix A, Pierre Menard to Pierre Chouteau, April 21, 1810.

14

As early as 1811, Wilson Price Hunt of the Pacific Fur Company, to avoid trouble with the Blackfeet, had left the Missouri at the Arikara villages with a pack train of seventy-six horses. He struck due west passing to the north of the Black Hills, crossed the Big Horns and pushed on to the North Fork of the Snake River. In 1822 and 1823, William A. Ashley suffered serious defeats at the hands of the Arikaras, while trying to pass their villages with keelboats. As a a result, he sent his partner across country to the Yellowstone in mid-1823, with supplies for the post which they had established near the mouth of that river the year before. It was probably a group from this party that first crossed the Continental Divide by South Pass, a key terrain feature of the Overland Trail. In the following year Ashley, after losing his horses to Indians on his first try, made a successful overland trip up the Platte and into Green River Valley. In September, 1827, Joshua Pilcher and a party of forty-five men and one hundred horses left Council Bluffs for Salt Lake Valley by way of the Platte and Sweetwater rivers.[21] Thus the fur traders had pioneered the Overland Trail as far as Utah long before the wave of westward migration made this one of the world's most famous highways.

While highly flexible in rough or unknown terrain, a pack train suffered from a number of serious drawbacks. The average load for a large animal in good condition was about three hundred pounds, whereas the same animal could tow as much as three times that weight in a wagon. In addition, the pack animals had to be unloaded every evening and repacked every morning, making for a great deal of handling of the cargo. All this required a number of men. In the early days of packing, it was a rule of thumb that one man was needed for each three animals, or each nine hundred pounds of cargo. This would be the same ratio of men to cargo as for the canoe. By the 1860's the operation of the pack trains running from Oregon to the Montana mines had been so systematized that one man could handle eight to ten mules, but this method was still not as efficient

21 Chittenden, *American Fur Trade*, I, 155, 188–90, 271–72; Dale, *Ashley-Smith Explorations*, 33–34, 64–82.

by half as the keelboat.[22] Only high-value goods of small volume and weight could afford the expense of pack transportation over any great distance.

The first wheeled vehicle to cross the Continental Divide seems to have been a small cannon which Ashley took through South Pass and into the Great Basin in 1825. Bill Sublette took two four-wheeled wagons to the Wind River in 1830, but since he did not repeat the operation, he apparently was not impressed by the capabilities of wagons in the fur trade.[23] In 1832, Captain Benjamin L. E. Bonneville, on leave from the United States Army and a newcomer to the fur trade, made a radical if thoroughly sensible experiment. He reasoned that, by using wagons, he could save the delays of packing and unpacking, that with fewer animals he would reduce the risk of loss of stock, and that the wagons would provide a barricade in case of attack by hostile Indians. The captain's train of twenty small wagons actually carried twice as great a load as was carried by the American Fur Company's pack train of the following year.[24]

Because no one had previously worked out the details of the trail for proper wagon operation, the best fording places were not known, stream banks had to be cut down, and streams had to be bridged. As a result, the wagon bodies, at times, had to be converted into boats by covering the beds with buffalo hides to float them across the deeper streams. These troubles caused Bonneville to fall behind the usual rate of travel of pack trains, but he did prove that wagons could be used and that they were economical.

Joe Meek and Bob Newell took families by wagon to the Whitman Mission in Oregon in 1840. Three years later the "Great Migration" of about one thousand people followed Meek's and Newell's trail, proving beyond a doubt that the high plains could be crossed

[22] James W. Watt, "Experiences of a Packer in Washington Territory Mining Camps During the Sixties," (ed. by William S. Lewis), *Washington Historical Quarterly*, Vol. XIX (October, 1928), 285–93.

[23] Chittenden, *American Fur Trade*, I, 431; St. Louis *Beacon* (Missouri) (October 7, 1830), in Nyle H. Miller, Edgar Langsdorf and Robert W. Richmond (eds.), *Kansas in Newspapers*.

[24] Washington Irving, *The Adventures of Captain Bonneville* (ed. by Edgeley W. Todd), 16; De Voto, *Across the Wide Missouri*, 51.

with wagons. As early as 1826, *Niles Register* had reported the return of General William Ashley from the Rockies and noted that the "level and open country" provided better going than eastern turnpikes. "Wagons and carriages could go with ease as far as General Ashley went, crossing the Rocky Mountains at the sources of the north fork of the Platte."[25] In view of such reports, it is hard to understand the slow adoption of wagon transport in the mid- and northern plains. By 1840 the traders to Santa Fe had been using wagons in increasing numbers for some eighteen years.

The "Great Migration" of 1843 suddenly and violently ruptured the pattern that had heretofore marked the westward movement. Before this two-thousand-mile jump from the Missouri Valley to Oregon, the movement had been more or less gradual. The new frontier areas had usually been filled by immigrants from the organized communities in the states lying just to the east of the new territory. Thus there had been a more or less orderly progression. The pattern was again disrupted in 1847 when the Mormons established an island of settlement in the Great Salt Lake Valley, some one thousand miles from the Missouri River. In the following year the Treaty of Guadalupe-Hidalgo added still another island of settlement in the Rio Grande Valley of New Mexico, a few islets in southern Arizona, and the territory of California. All these new, isolated settlements had to be provided with manufactured goods from the United States—that is, from the area east of the Mississippi River. Oregon and California could most economically be supplied by sea, but Santa Fe and Salt Lake, and later Colorado and Montana, drew mostly from the river ports on the Missouri.

Until the railroads spanned the continent and penetrated into the major mining areas, the only means of moving bulk supplies and heavy machinery across the Great American Desert was by wagon. To meet the needs of the outlying communities, there grew up a large if prosaic industry.

25 Washington and Baltimore *Niles Register*, Vol. XXXI (December 9, 1826).

CHAPTER II

TRAILS AND TRIALS

Even though the rivers of the high plains, except for the Missouri, did not provide the westering Americans with navigable waterways, the valleys of two of these rivers did provide the world's finest natural wagon roads. Along a great section of the valley of the Arkansas River ran the Santa Fe Trail, and a branch that led to Denver, Colorado. Along the Platte ran the Overland Trail, also called the Oregon Trail, the California Trail, and the Mormon Trail.

The first trading expedition from the Missouri River to Santa Fe seems to have been that of the Mallet brothers in 1739. Another French expedition, probably before 1763, is thought to have opened a "store" in the vicinity of Pueblo, Colorado. In 1804, following close on the purchase of Louisiana, a merchant of Kaskaskia, Illinois, sent one Baptiste La Lande to Santa Fe with a small assortment of goods. Apparently La Lande never returned, and one of the excuses offered by Lieutenant Zebulon Pike for entering New Mexico in 1806 was an attempt to collect the money due to the Illinois merchant.[1] In general, these expeditions were discouraged by the Spanish officials of the colonial government. The party of Robert McKnight were arrested as spies in 1812 and were not released until 1821.

It was not until Mexico gained her independence in 1821 that American traders were well received in Santa Fe. In that year Cap-

[1] Herbert Eugene Bolton, "French Intrusions into New Mexico, 1749–1752," in *Bolton and the Spanish Borderlands* (ed. by John F. Bannon), 150–71.

tain William Becknell, on his way to trade with the Comanches, met a party of Mexican soldiers who invited him to come to Santa Fe to trade. The trading was so profitable that, next year, Becknell took out another party using three ordinary farm wagons in addition to a number of pack animals. The success of this second expedition, and the first use of wagons, earned for Becknell the title of "Father of the Santa Fe Trade."[2]

Originally St. Louis was the chief entrepôt for the commerce of the Great West, but as steamboat captains and pilots pushed their vessels farther and farther up the lower reaches of the Missouri River, the eastern terminus of the trail moved slowly westward. Franklin, Independence, Westport, and Kansas City were successively gateways to the Southwest. It was from Franklin that Becknell set forth in 1821. Except for a brief period during the Civil War, Kansas City was the eastern terminus of the Santa Fe Trail after 1844.

Attempts by towns farther up the river to supersede Kansas City failed because the Kaw River (now the Kansas River) ran directly west from Kansas City and blocked the direct approaches to the Santa Fe Trail from Leavenworth and other towns to the north. Rope ferries that could handle as many as 225 wagons a day eventually were available, but the tolls would have nullified any other advantage offered by any of the upriver cities. Occasional trips by steamers up the Kaw as far as Junction City allowed some of the Santa Fe traders, generally the smaller ones, to make their purchases at that point and save a number of days of overland travel.

Thomas Hart Benton, senator from Missouri, was quick to grasp the potential commercial value of the Santa Fe trade. In early 1825 he received a detailed account of the trade from Augustus Storrs, who had gone out with the caravan of William Becknell and Meredith M. Marmaduke in the previous year.[3] In March of that year Benton pushed through Congress a bill authorizing the expenditure

2 Josiah Gregg, *Commerce of the Prairies* (ed. by Max L. Moorhead), 13–15, 15n.; Chittenden, *American Fur Trade*, II, 501.

3 Answers of Augustus Storrs of Missouri to . . . the Hon. Mr. Benton, *Sen. Doc. No.* 7, 18 Cong., 2 sess. (Serial 108).

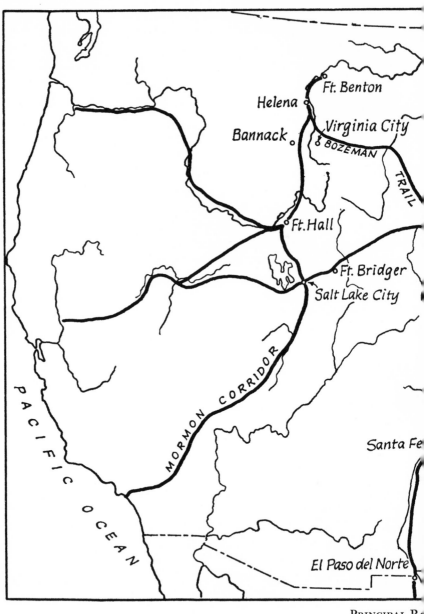

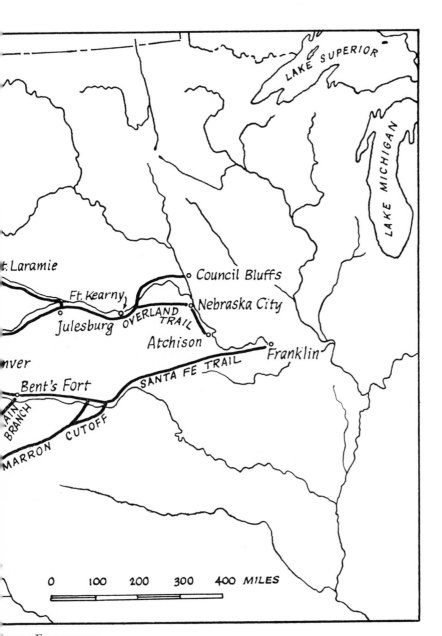

t. Laramie

Ft. Kearny

o Council Bluffs

Julesburg OVERLAND TRAIL

o Nebraska City

Atchison

o Franklin

nver

Bent's Fort

SANTA FE TRAIL

AIN
BRANCH

MARRON CUTOFF

LAKE SUPERIOR

LAKE MICHIGAN

0   100   200   300   400 MILES

AGON-FREIGHTING

of $30,000, of which $10,000 was for surveying and marking the trail, and $20,000 was for treaty gifts to the Plains Indians to allow free passage of the caravans. Two years later Benton proposed the establishment of a military post at the crossing of the Arkansas, then on the international boundary, to protect the caravans from depredations by Indians who were not parties to the treaty. The commanding general of the United States Army was not enthusiastic. He pointed out the difficulty of maintaining the necessary garrison of two companies of infantry and two of cavalry at such a distance from the nearest supply depot.[4]

Meanwhile, the Santa Fe Trail had become a subject for diplomatic activity. In 1824, Secretary of State Henry Clay had written to Joel R. Poinsett, ambassador to Mexico, to say that President John Quincy Adams regretted the reluctance of the Mexican government to agree to opening a road from Missouri to Santa Fe for purely commercial purposes of value to citizens of both countries. Clay went on to say: "In fact, an imperfect trace or road, such as it is, is now used, and the sole question is, whether it shall be rendered more convenient to the persons whose interest or inclination shall induce them to travel it."[5] The only action by the Mexican government leading toward assistance to the trade was an occasional military escort.

The surveying and marking of the Trail was, to a great extent, wasted effort. Because of the lack of timber, most of the markers were piles of sod that soon disappeared before the assaults of the weather. In addition, the commissioners did not consult with the traders who used the Trail but, in some places, marked out their own version which was never used.

From Kansas City, the trail ran westward about 41 miles to a point on the prairie where the Oregon Trail struck off toward the northwest. Beyond the forking of the trails, the first important point

[4] Act to Authorize the President . . . to Cause a Road to Be Marked out from . . . Missouri to . . . New Mexico, *United States Statutes at Large*, IV, 100; Jacob Brown to James Barbour, January 10, 1827, *American State Papers, Military Affairs*, III, 615.
[5] Clay to Poinsett, September 24, 1825, *American State Papers, Foreign Relations*, VI, 581.

on the Santa Fe Trail was Council Grove on the Neosho River, about 110 miles to the west-southwest. The importance of the point lay in the fact that it was the last place where hardwood and timber could be obtained for wagon repairs. In addition, beyond Council Grove, the Plains Indians were of uncertain temper. The traders straggled into the Grove in small groups but left in large caravans with a quasi-military organization.

From Independence or Kansas City to Council Grove, the trip was comparatively easy. Those Indians encountered were "good" ones; all travelers had to guard against was petty thievery. Grass and water were plentiful; in fact, an overabundance of the latter was at times a source of trouble. In order to complete the round trip in one season, the trains started in the spring as soon as the grass was tall enough to feed the animals, and as a result they often had to struggle through a good deal of sticky mud. On April 29, 1857, John M. Kingsbury wrote to his partner, James J. Webb in Santa Fe, to say that only two trains had started for Santa Fe and they were starving because the late spring had retarded the growth of the prairie grass. He added that he was loading wagons as fast as possible and getting them out on the plains before the roads got wet.[6]

Spring mud on the plains was such an all-pervasive element that it became a subject of the wry humor of the Westerner. One day, probably in the 1860's, Thomas A. Scott, railroad magnate, and a companion were riding on the prairie when they came across a wagon which had sunk to its axles. Scott said to the driver, "Well, my man, you are in a bad fix." "Oh, no," replied the driver, "I am all right, but there are two wagons below mine, and those fellows down there are having a h——l of a time."[7]

From Council Grove to the Great Bend of the Arkansas, a distance of 120 miles, the trail crossed a pleasant country of rolling grassy plains, cut by many streams bordered with cottonwood trees.

[6] Ralph P. Bieber, "The Papers of James J. Webb," *University of Washington Studies*, Vol. XI, Humanistic Series No. 2 (1924), 255–305.

[7] Alexander Caldwell, "Address," *Publications*, Kansas State Historical Society [hereinafter referred to as KSHS], Vol. I (1886), 259–66.

West of the Great Bend there was, and still is, a marked change in the appearance of the countryside: the green fields gave way to great reaches of short brown grass and small prickly pear. Here the summer temperature of one hundred or more degrees and the dry wind bore hard on the traveler. In his report to the Chief of Topographical Engineers, United States Army, made in 1846, Lieutenant William H. Emory noted that beyond Pawnee Fork he had entered on "that portion of the prairie that well deserves to be considered part of the great desert."[8]

Some fourteen miles southwest of Great Bend the road passed one of the most noted landmarks of the Santa Fe Trail, Pawnee Rock. This outcrop of reddish sandstone was reported to have been originally one hundred feet high, but recent quarrying has since reduced its height to about fifty feet. On this rock many of those who passed cut their names. It was at this point that Kit Carson, on his first trip west, is alleged to have shot his own riding mule, during a tour of night guard.[9]

About ninety miles up the river from Pawnee Rock one came to the lowest of the notable crossings of the Arkansas, the "Caches." At that point a party of trappers had been forced to bury, or cache, part of their load until they could return for it. The empty pits in the riverbank were visible for many years. Another crossing was located about twenty miles farther west, some twenty-six miles west of the present city of Dodge City, Kansas. Still another crossing was located fifty miles upstream, at Chouteau's Island.

At these various crossings the Santa Fe Trail split. One branch struck off southwestward across the panhandles of Oklahoma and Texas and into northeastern New Mexico; it was known as the Cimarron Cutoff or Cimarron Branch. The other part of the trail continued westward along the north bank of the Arkansas and was known as the Mountain Branch.

8 Report of Lt. W. H. Emory, Notes of a Military Reconnoissance from Fort Leavenworth . . . to San Diego, *House Exec. Doc. No. 41*, 30 Cong., 1 sess. (Serial 517).

9 "Fort Larned, Larned, Kansas," reprint from *Between the Lines*, employee magazine, Natural Gas Pipeline Co. of America.

About 130 miles up the Arkansas, on the Mountain Branch, one came to Bent's Fort, one of the best known of the western trading posts and, until 1846, the only sign of civilization between Independence and Santa Fe. The fort was founded in 1829 by the Bent brothers of St. Louis. It was laid out on a quadrangular plan with adobe walls 100 by 150 feet long and 17 feet high, with 30-foot bastions at diagonal corners. According to Susan Shelby Magoffin, the interior court measured 90 to 100 feet square with a well in the center that yielded good water. Around the square were about twenty-five rooms that included a kitchen, a dining room, a little store, a blacksmith's shop, a barbershop, and an icehouse. One large room served as a parlor. There were no chairs, only cushions on the floor against two of the walls. Adolphus Wislizenus, who had traveled widely in the West, declared that Bent's was the largest and finest trading post he had seen.[10] The post required a staff of sixty to one hundred men.

William Bent, the resident manager, lived in true baronial style, entertaining all who came his way. His Negro cook, Margaret, was known up and down the trail as the "culinary divinity." His fort even boasted a billiard table which had its own room and on which Lieutenant J. W. Abert, Topographical Engineers, seated his Indian subjects while he sketched them for his report. The joy of a traveler on reaching this haven was expressed by Thomas Jefferson Farnham in 1839: "Peace again—roofs again—safety again from the winged arrows of the savage . . . bread, ah! bread again."[11]

The fort was destroyed in 1852 by William Bent after the United States government refused to pay the price he demanded for it. Bent told his second wife, Yellow Woman, that because two of his brothers and his first wife, Owl Woman, had died there, he could not look on the place without a great feeling of depression. There was also an economic reason for his destruction of the fort: the bottom had

---

[10] *Ein Ausflug nach den Felsen-gebirgen im jahre 1839*, 105.

[11] Report of Lt. J. W. Abert of His Examination of New Mexico in the Years 1846–47, *House Exec. Doc. No. 41*, 30 Cong., 1 sess. (Serial 517), 425; Thomas Jefferson Farnham, *Travels in the Great Western Desert*, 40.

dropped out of the beaver market in the late 1830's, and the Indian trade had lost much of its value in the following decade. Bent's Old Fort was larger than was needed for the reduced trade and was too expensive to maintain. A smaller fort of stone was erected about thirty-eight miles downstream at the Big Timbers of the Arkansas, opposite the present town of Prowers, Colorado, in 1853.

At Bent's Old Fort the trail forked again. One branch continued up the Arkansas and then cut away toward Denver and the Colorado mines. The main trail crossed the Arkansas and followed up the Purgatoire to Trinidad, Colorado. From that place the trail swung sharply south and climbed the Raton Mountains to Raton Pass, considered to be the worst hazard on the Mountain Branch. Steep and rough, there were many points at which wagons had to be lowered down the slopes by rope. Lieutenant J. W. Abert, on crossing in 1846, was stopped because a trader's wagon had overturned, spilling goods down the side of the ravine. He asked the owner to have a second wagon moved so that he could pass. When the wagon was moved, the driver chocked the wheels with a piece of rotten wood and "the wagon loaded with the immense bulk of fifty-seven hundred weight of goods, rushed backwards down the hill; luckily it turned off the road, when after crushing a few trees in its course, it brought up against a sturdy pine. I was at the time riding around the wagon and just escaped."[12]

It is small wonder that the experienced traders preferred the hazards of the Cimarron Cutoff to those of the pass. In 1862 one could still see, in the pass, the remains of cabins built by the snowbound crew of a Russell, Majors and Waddell wagon train.[13] Because of a reported insufficiency of water for his army on the Cutoff, Colonel Stephen Watts Kearny marched his Army of the West over Raton Pass. The reinforcements, Colonel Sterling Price's Second Missouri Mounted Volunteers and the Morman Battalion, traveled by the Cutoff and suffered severely from lack of water.

[12] Abert's Report, *House Exec. Doc. No. 41* (Serial 517), 438.
[13] Cragin Collection, Pioneer Museum, Colorado Springs, Colorado, IV, 66.

Sometime in the 1860's, Richard Wootton, an old frontiersman, built a toll road through the pass and obtained charters from the territorial legislatures of Colorado and New Mexico. For some years this road brought its proprietor a handsome profit. In a period of one year, three months, and nine days, the only period for which a careful record exists, the receipts were $9,163.64. In 1869 the commissioners of Las Animas County, Colorado, reduced the toll rates. The answer was immediate: "Uncle Dick" raised the toll on the New Mexico end of the road by a corresponding amount.[14]

Beyond the pass the trail swung toward the west and south, keeping close to the foothills of the mountains where water and wood were available. Near the present town of Watrous, New Mexico, the Mountain Branch and the Cimarron Cutoff rejoined.

The Cimarron Cutoff was the favorite route of the Santa Fe traders, and there were a number of entrances to the cutoff at the various crossings of the Arkansas River. Getting across the river was a major problem. While much of the river bed might be dry or covered only by shallow water, there were channels in which the water ran deep enough to force the draft animals to swim for some distance. In addition, much of the bed was of quicksand that could swallow animals or wagons that stood still long enough. Before attempting the crossing, the wagons were usually repacked, putting the perishable items on top of the load. Then ten to twenty or even, on occasion, fifty yoke of oxen were hitched to the wagons in order that, when some of the animals were swimming, others were pulling from firmer footing. The trick was to keep the wagon moving after it had entered the water. Wagons that stuck had to be unloaded and, sometimes, had to be disassembled and packed to shore piecemeal. One traveler described the amusing bedlam of twenty shouting Mexicans prodding the cattle with sharp sticks as the lead oxen tried to turn back. The wagonmaster swore at both men and oxen. As one wagon climbed out of the channel, a barrel of whisky and some of the drivers' coats tumbled out into the stream. "After a deal of

14 Pueblo *Colorado Chieftain* (May 20, 1869).

excitement to the Mexicans, and diversion to those on the bank, the whiskey and clothing were saved."[15] In 1857 a train returning from Fort Union, New Mexico, crossed the Arkansas dry shod, one hundred miles below Bent's Fort, where they had forded in three and one-half feet of water about a month previously.[16]

Before leaving the river, the water barrels were filled, as the first stretch of the cutoff was a dry drive of some fifty miles, or at least two days, that started with five miles of heavy sand out of the river bed. The cutoff was pioneered by Becknell on his second trip to Santa Fe. His party nearly perished in the process. After emptying their canteens, the men killed their dogs and cut off the ears of their mules, hoping to slake their thirst with the blood. They finally were saved by meeting a buffalo fresh from a water hole with a belly distended with water. This supply was enough to allow the strongest of the party to reach the river, fill the canteens, and return to save the weaker members of the group. So serious was the water problem on the cutoff that at times wagon trains had to go into camp half a mile from the water holes and turn the animals loose, lest the smell of water stampede them, with resultant damage to the wagons or time lost in dragging them out of the mud.[17]

Finally in 1843, twelve years after the first crossing, a heavy rain swept the area as a caravan was on the move. From then on, the ruts were clearly visible and the Cimarron Branch became a permanent road leading from one water hole to another for a distance of some three hundred miles. The trace of the trail can still be seen in aerial photographs by the New Mexico State Highway Department.

From the point where the Mountain and Cimarron branches rejoined, a single trail swept through Las Vegas, New Mexico, and then turned west and northwest through the Sangre de Cristo Range to Santa Fe.

[15] Agnes Wright Spring, *A Bloomer Girl on Pike's Peak, 1858: Julia Archibald Holmes, First Woman to Climb Pike's Peak*, 24.

[16] T. C. Hall, "Personal Recollections of the Santa Fe Trail," *Kansas Magazine,* Vol. V (January, 1911), 49–55.

[17] *Ibid.,* 55; Gregg, *Commerce of the Prairies,* 50; W. B. Napton, *On the Santa Fe Trail in 1857,* 38.

Here at last was the goal: the city of romance to many an adventure-seeking American; the profitable market for some of the traders. Most travelers were keenly disappointed at their first sight of the city. There were no marble palaces; no sky-sweeping towers. Many took the single-story adobe houses for brick kilns. For the romantic, the disappointment soon wore off. Santa Fe was a distinctively foreign city, inhabited by a people speaking a strange tongue and living by different standards and customs. The weary Americans were welcomed by a friendly, gregarious people who made the most of any excuse for a *fiesta*. *Bailes,* commonly called "fandangos" by the Americans, were held almost every night, and all visitors were welcome. The picturesque dress of the men and women—especially that of the women—caught the eye of the American men. On the other hand, American women did not wholly approve of the short skirts, decolleté blouses, nor the habit of combing one's hair in the presence of male folk.

Santa Fe was a small city and could not absorb all the goods brought from the States; thus, some of the traders sought new markets. They pushed south along the Rio Grande to El Paso del Norte, the present city of Juarez, Mexico. There they left the river and passed over one of the many *jornadas del muerto* that mark the old Spanish Southwest. Gregg reported that in sixty miles there were only two "fetid springs or pools, whose water is only rendered tolerable by Necessity."[18] The distance from Santa Fe to Chihuahua was 550 miles. There the goods that could not be sold in Santa Fe found a ready market. During the period from 1822 to 1843 about 40 per cent of the goods taken from the Missouri Valley went to Chihuahua.

The Mexican War (1846–47) brought about many changes in the Santa Fe Trail. Now, in addition to the civilian population, there were several thousand soldiers garrisoned in the newly acquired territory. As a result, the volume of traffic increased greatly, and the government, especially the army, took a more lively interest in the trail.

[18] *Commerce of the Prairies,* 275.

29

During the war the post quartermaster at Fort Leavenworth had established a blacksmith shop at Council Grove to shoe animals and repair wagons, both government and private. Around this shop there soon grew up a fair-sized town that eventually became a supply point for some of the smaller Santa Fe traders.[19] Also, during the war, Fort Mann was established at a point 26 miles below the "Crossing" (about 6 miles west of present Dodge City, Kansas). This post was to serve as a halfway point between Fort Leavenworth and Santa Fe; the distances were 359 miles and 423 miles, respectively. Here was located another blacksmith shop, a wheelwright shop, and a number of storerooms. First called Fort Mackey, then Fort Atkinson, and finally Fort Mann, it was abandoned in 1854.

That was a critical area along the trail and so five years after Fort Mann was closed, a new post was established on Pawnee Fork, twenty-two miles southwest of Great Bend and nine miles from the river. First called "Camp on Pawnee Fork" and later "Camp Alert," the post received its official name, Fort Larned, a year after it was established. Because it was built of stone rather than adobe, it is the only post on the Santa Fe Trail that is well preserved. After the Civil War a small post, Fort Zarah, was maintained for a few years at Great Bend.

On the occupation of Santa Fe, a fort, named for William L. Marcy, Secretary of War, had been built to dominate the city of Santa Fe. In 1851 it was decided to move the army headquarters and main supply depot out of what Lieutenant Colonel Edwin V. Sumner called "that sink of vice and extravagance Santa Fe." As most of the troubles at this time were with the Plains Indians, a move to the east would bring the troops closer to the theater of operations and give better protection to the supply line along the Santa Fe Trail. Fort Union was established in the plains east of the Sangre de Cristos and about ten miles north of the junction of the Cimarron and Mountain branches of the trail. Besides being the supply depot for

---

[19] Clary to Jesup, July 18, 1846, Russell, Majors & Waddell Correspondence File, National Archives [hereinafter cited as NA]; Cottonwood Falls *Kansas Press* and *Council Grove Press* (1859–63), *passim*.

garrisons in New Mexico and Arizona, it served as a rest and repair point for commercial trains moving on the trail.

The Santa Fe Trail must not be pictured as a neat highway running directly across the country. It was rather a zone of beaten and scarred ground with many local, minor deviations. If a wagon bogged down in a wet spot, the following wagons detoured around that particular spot until they cut through the sod and another wagon became stuck. Thus the trail was often one hundred yards, or more, wide. The points selected for crossing the streams varied from season to season and from year to year, depending on the height of the water in the creeks. When the streams were running full, the wagon trains usually sought the buffalo crossing farthest upstream. For example, there were at least two major crossings of Pawnee Fork: one at Fort Larned, and the other, Boyd's or Dry Crossing, some three miles closer to the Arkansas. Some trains preferred to take the dry route directly west from Fort Larned to the crossing at the "Caches" rather than follow the river, a saving of twenty or thirty miles.

J. C. Hall, who made several trips to Santa Fe with wagon trains, remarked: "The one characteristic of the road was, that it kept to the highland ridges, so as to avoid the wet places and deep ruts that are found on the lowlands." He also took a matter-of-fact view of the trail, noting that there was nothing poetic about the broad, well-beaten path winding across vast stretches of wild, uninhabited country, "a mere hint of civilization, telling of a somewhence, and a somewhere whither. . . . It was a natural highway—only here and there, except in the most difficult places, had anything ever been done to develop and improve it."[20] General William Larimer, on his way to Colorado in 1859, wrote to friends in Leavenworth City that this was the world's finest natural highway, without a single heavy pull.[21]

The Overland Trail was more like a badly frayed piece of rope

[20] Hall, "Personal Recollections," *loc. cit.*, 49.
[21] Leroy R. Hafen (ed.), *Colorado Gold Rush, Contemporary Letters and Reports, 1858–1859*, 99.

than a neat highway; at each end it splayed out into a number of branches. At the eastern end, the strands originated at Independence and Kansas City, Missouri; Leavenworth and Atchison, Kansas; and Nebraska City, Plattsmouth, and Omaha, Nebraska. At the western end, strands led to Denver, Colorado; to Helena, Montana, via the Bozeman Trail; to Salt Lake City; Helena via the Malad River and Hole-in-the-Wall; to Oregon; and to California. Only from a point on the Platte River about thirty miles east of the present city of Kearney, Nebraska, to the approximate location of Julesburg, Colorado, were the strands united. The Mormon Trail originated at Omaha, Nebraska, and generally followed the north bank of the Platte for varying distances; most trains crossed to the south bank at Fort Kearny, but some clung to the north bank as far as Casper, Wyoming.

The Santa Fe Trail was essentially a route of commerce, and emigration provided a comparatively small part of the total traffic. The Overland Trail, on the other hand, was the great pathway of the westward migration, the main road of the Overland stage, and the route of a large amount of freight. The first great movement over the Overland Trail was the migration to Oregon in the early 1840's. Next came the move of the Mormons to the Great Salt Lake Valley, beginning in the mid-1840's. Still later came the gold rushes to California, Colorado, and Montana. The name applied to the trail by contemporaries depended largely on the objective of the individual traveler. During the Indian trouble of the mid-1860's, some travel followed the route of the Overland Stage from the vicinity of Julesburg, Colorado, through Virginia Dale and into the Laramie Plain of Wyoming, then over the Snowy Range via Bridger Pass, and across southern Wyoming to Fort Bridger.

At the eastern end of the trail, the towns in Missouri suffered from the same disadvantage in relation to the Overland Trail as did Leavenworth and others in relation to the Santa Fe Trail: the barrier of the Kaw River. Originally most of the travel on the Overland originated at Independence or Kansas City, but as soon as the

Kansas-Nebraska Act was passed in 1854, towns sprang up overnight farther upstream. These towns soon became important outfitting points and terminals for high plains freighting.

The northernmost feeder was the Mormon Trail which was laid out during the great trek from Nauvoo, Illinois. Crossing Iowa in a direct westerly course, the Mormons reached the Missouri River at Council Bluffs, Iowa. West from Omaha, the trail crossed a high tableland, rough and rolling and cut by the Elkhorn River which had to be ferried at a charge of fifty cents per wagon in 1864.[22] Twenty-five miles west of Omaha, the trail reached the valley of the Platte. Through fear of attack by Missourians who had caused them so much trouble in the past, the Mormons clung to the north bank of the river at least as far as the present town of Grand Island, Nebraska. This meant fording or ferrying the Loup River, a tributary of the Platte which drains most of Northern Nebraska. Captain Eugene Ware, who traveled this portion of the trail in 1863, described it as a well-beaten track four or five hundred feet wide, hard and smooth as a floor. While most trains crossed to the Overland Trail on the south bank of the river in the vicinity of Fort Kearny, some stayed on the north bank as far as Fort Laramie, or even as far as Casper, Wyoming. Because the north bank was not as heavily traveled as the south bank, the grass had not been eaten off by other trains.[23]

The trails coming out from Leavenworth, Atchison, and Nebraska City had somewhat easier traveling. They had to contend only with the upper reaches of the Blue and Little Blue rivers of eastern Kansas and Nebraska. All these feeders joined on the Platte, where the trail was described by Captain Ware as a broad, smooth, beaten track from which the sand and gravel had been swept by the prairie winds. The track was some three hundred feet wide, and the draft animals had eaten off the grass for some distance on either side.

At the forks of the Platte, about 120 miles from where the eastern

22 John S. Collins, *Across the Plains in '64*, 10.
23 John Crook, "Journal," *Utah Historical Quarterly* [hereinafter referred to as UHQ], Vol. VI (April, 1933), 51–62; (July, 1933), 110–12.

strands met, the trail followed the south bank of the South Platte River for about sixty miles to the Lower California Crossing of the South Platte. In 1866, General William T. Sherman, thinking longingly of the pine forests of the South, commented that the whole road was a dreary waste without a tree or a bush to break the endless view, "grass thin, and the Platte running over its wide, shallow bottom with its rapid current; . . . nothing but the long dusty road, with its occasional ox team, and the everlasting line of telegraph poles."[24] From the Lower Crossing, the trail traversed an eighteen-mile stretch of sand hills to the south bank of the North Platte at Ash Hollow. The approach to Ash Hollow was so steep that, about 1860, the preference for crossing points shifted to the Upper California Crossing at the site of the present town of Julesburg, Colorado, sixty miles farther west. This section came down to the North Platte by a gentle slope between Court House Rock and Chimney Rock.

The ford of the South Platte was considered to be the worst on the trail, requiring doubling or trebling of teams to drag the loaded wagons through the deep water and quicksand. John Bratt told of an experience when he was driving a team in 1866. They arrived at the crossing about five in the evening and, because the weather was threatening, the wagonmaster decided to cross at once. The heaviest wagon and the one containing the most perishable freight—sugar, coffee, salt, beans, flour, etc.—was chosen to lead. Eight yoke of oxen were hitched up. The train boss and three bullwhackers, stripped from the waist down, took position along the team on the upstream side. The assistant wagon boss and three more bullwhackers took the downstream side. They started in with a whoop and a splash, but after 150 feet, the wagon stopped in running water 3 to 4 feet deep. Another four yoke were put on. It began to rain hard, the cattle milled around, and two chains broke. The chains were doubled but then some of the oxen went down, and to save them, the oxbow keys were pulled and some of the bows cut, dropping yokes and chains in the river. They reorganized and gave another pull, and the

---

[24] Robert G. Athearn, *William Tecumseh Sherman and the Settlement of the West*, 62–63.

tongue came out of the wagon. Finally the oxen were unhooked and they at once made for the north bank. At three o'clock next morning, Bratt was up to help the wagon boss bring the oxen back.[25]

After 1858 the trail to Denver left the main trail at Julesburg and followed the South Platte to the mouth of Cherry Creek. On the main trail, just above Chimney Rock, there was a difficult passage. The trail was so narrow and steep that one wagonmaster took his wagons down at night for fear that his teamsters might refuse to hazard the descent if they could see what was ahead of them.[26]

Following up the North Platte about 175 miles, the trail reached Fort Laramie. Before Fort Kearny was established in 1847, this was the first sign of civilization to appear to the weary traveler since the Missouri Valley. The first fort at this point, near the mouth of the Laramie River, was built in 1834 by Sublette and Campbell, fur traders of St. Louis, and named Fort William in honor of William L. Sublette. In the same year the fort was turned over to the American Fur Company and renamed Fort John, popularly called Fort Laramie. Fort John was abandoned in 1846, and a new Fort Laramie was built about a mile farther up the Laramie River. The fort was described as a hollow square, about 130 feet on a side, with 15-foot adobe walls and blockhouses at opposite corners. Facing on the inner courts were shops, sheds, and rooms. Here in 1846 one could buy coffee, sugar, and tobacco for one dollar per pound and flour for one dollar a pint. Four years later prices were down to twenty-five cents per pound for sugar, and flour was eighteen dollars per hundred pounds.[27] At the fort there was a chance to rest both man and beast and to make repairs. The next place that this could be done was 394 miles away.

It was in this vicinity that Captain W. F. Raynolds displayed some ignorance of the countryside and of the Overland Trail. He asked his guide, Jim Bridger, if there was any danger of crossing the

25 Bratt, *Trails of Yesterday*, 64–65.

26 Julie Beehrer Colyer (ed.), "Freighting Across the Plains," *Montana*, Vol. XII (Autumn, 1962), 2–17.

27 Edwin Bryant, *What I Saw in California*, 112; James Abbey, *California; A Trip Across the Plains in the Spring of 1850*, 26.

trail without recognizing it. "I now understand fully his surprise, as it is as marked as any turnpike in the east. It is hard, dry, and dusty, and gave evidence of the immense amount of travel that passes over it."[28]

Seventy-five miles northwest of Fort Laramie, the Bozeman Trail branched off to the north and northwest along the eastern face of the Big Horn Mountains. It was a shortcut to the gold fields of Montana through the favorite hunting ground of the Sioux. The trail was opened in 1866 but was closed only two years later when the army, after trying to keep it open with completely inadequate garrisons, abandoned Forts Reno, Phil Kearny, and C. F. Smith. For all its short life, the Bozeman Trail was one of the bloodiest of western trails. By and large, the experienced freighter preferred to take the longer route to Montana via the north end of the Salt Lake Valley.

From Fort Laramie the Overland Trail followed the North Platte for 140 miles, until the river cut sharply south to its headwaters in the Colorado Rockies. The trail then followed the Sweetwater River, except for a waterless stretch of about 50 miles across the base of a triangle formed by the two rivers. Some 70 miles up the Sweetwater brought the traveler gradually up to South Pass on the Continental Divide. The pass was a sagebrush plain about 20 miles wide between the Wind River Mountains and the Antelope Hills. So gradual were the slopes that few people realized when they had passed from the Atlantic watershed to that of the Pacific. Almost due west from South Pass ran Sublette's Cutoff which eliminated the swing south to Fort Bridger and to Salt Lake City. The Cutoff joined the California Trail in the valley of the Humboldt River of Nevada.

The main trail swung southwest from South Pass to Fort Bridger, 123 miles away, built by James Bridger in 1843. "Old Gabe" wrote that he had built a small fort, with a well-stocked blacksmith shop, on Black's Fork of the Green River. He anticipated a fair return in business with the emigrants. "They, in coming out, are generally

---

28 Report of Capt. W. F. Raynolds' Exploration of the Yellowstone Done 1859, *Sen. Exec. Doc. No. 77*, 40 Cong., 1 sess. (Serial 1317), 70.

well supplied with money, but by the time they get there are in want of all kinds of supplies. Horses, provisions, smith-work, etc., bring ready cash. . . . The same establishment trades with the Indians in the neighborhood who have mostly a good number of beaver with them."[29]

At Fort Bridger the trail forked again. In a southwesterly direction, a trail ran down to Great Salt Lake Valley. To the northwest, another branch led to Fort Hall, 218 miles distant, the last supply point short of Oregon. This fort was built in 1834 by Nathaniel Wyeth in an attempt to break into the western fur trade. Three years later the fort was sold to the Hudson's Bay Company. It was at Fort Hall that the Oregon and California branches of the Overland Trail finally separated.

Another branch of the Overland ran from the Salt Lake Basin up the Malad River, then up the Snake, through the Bearpaw Mountains via Monida Pass and on to Bannack, Virginia City, and Helena.

The building of settlements along the Overland began at about the same time as along the Santa Fe Trail. In 1847 the army established Fort Kearny on the Platte River about three hundred miles northwest of Kansas City. This was not a stockaded fort as were the fur traders' posts but was a group of barracks, officer's quarters, stables, and warehouses sitting on the plain south of the river. Two miles west of the post, just off the reservation, there soon sprang up a settlement known as Dobytown, or Dobetown, that offered supplies and drink—strong drink—for the weary traveler. Captain Eugene F. Ware remarked that Dobytown in 1863 contained "the toughest inhabitants of the country, male and female," and that the cemetery was larger than the town.[30]

By the early 1860's, Marysville, Kansas, on the Big Blue was the most westerly town on the trail, but there were road ranches scattered along the trail at twenty- to thirty-mile intervals. These road ranches were usually built where there was a stand of timber; they

29 Chittenden, *American Fur Trade*, I, 477.
30 *The Indian War of 1864*, 31.

were not a residence, nor a farmhouse, nor a store, nor a tavern but a little of all and more. A few ran first-class eating establishments.[31] The building was usually made of sod and was connected with a large corral that included a covered way to water. The ranch was loopholed and capable of withstanding an Indian attack, as a number of them did in the years 1864–65. They usually sold liquor, canned fruit, knives, playing cards, saddlery, colored goggles, and other minor items. Practically all were equipped with large jacks so that wagon wheels could be pulled and the axles retarred. One traveler wrote that these ranches were "generally kept by mongrel French or half-breed Indians who divide their time between smoking, sleeping and playing the fiddle. They usually have from one to six squaws and papooses without number."[32]

Fort Laramie was garrisoned by the army in 1849; Fort Bridger in 1857; and Fort Hall in 1849. All these posts, and others established later, were important to the traveler. The commissaries were authorized, with the approval of the commanding officer, to sell supplies to the indigent or needy travelers at government cost. In addition, the post sutler carried goods that were not available through government channels.[33]

Sometime prior to 1859 the town of Julesburg, Colorado, was established at the Upper California Crossing. For a while it was the only settlement between Fort Kearny and Fort Laramie. The population in 1862 was about fifty, and a guidebook said that the town had "a good hotel and store." The town was burned by Indians in 1865, and shortly thereafter a passer-by reported that the town consisted of six widely scattered houses built on the old ruins. One of these was a blacksmith shop, but the most imposing was a billiard parlor.[34] Fort Sedgwick was established at a partially completed

31 Everett Dick, *Sod-House Frontier*, 104–106; James F. Meline, *2000 Miles on Horseback*, 79; St. Louis *Daily Missouri Democrat* (July 7, 1858).

32 Egbert Railley, Journal, typescript at Weston, Missouri Historical Society.

33 Ware, *Indian War of 1864*, 32; Account Books of Judge Carter, Post Sutler, Fort Bridger, in Wyoming State Historical Society, Cheyenne, Wyoming.

34 Pamphlet 341/31, Colorado State Historical Society [hereinafter referred to as CSHS], Denver, Colorado.

and abandoned road ranch in 1864, and the town of Julesburg was rebuilt on the edge of the military reservation.

During the Indian War of 1864 a number of posts were established by the army. In the fall of 1863 a two-company post was built at Cottonwood Springs, about eighty-five miles upriver from Fort Kearny. Originally called Cantonment McKean, the name was soon changed by the War Department to Fort McPherson, but the popular name was Fort Cottonwood. Other smaller garrisons were posted at ranches along the trail.

To expedite the travel of the Saints to the New Zion, Brigham Young, in 1847, opened a ferry over the North Platte at the point where the river turned south into Colorado, 140 miles above Fort Laramie. In 1858 the ferry was replaced by a bridge, and during the Indian troubles a small garrison was stationed at this important point. It was here that the Indians wiped out a small wagon train and Lieutenant Caspar Collins was killed in an attempt to rescue the train. About 1850 another obstacle on the trail had been eliminated when a toll bridge was built across the Laramie River near the fort.[35]

Despite the enthusiasm of the *Omaha City Directory of 1866*, which claimed that the valley of the Platte provided excellent wood and water, as well as excellent feed and pasturage for stock, travelers found that, at times, it was necessary to sink headless barrels in the river bed to get water.[36] Captain Howard Stansbury found "innumerable" small wells dug in the sand of the river two to four feet deep that yielded good clean water.[37] Concerning its potability, there were a number of standard quips; including, "It was good drinking if you threw it out and filled the cup with whiskey" and "It was water you had to chew."[38] Wood was generally so scarce that cook-

[35] David L. Hieb, *Fort Laramie National Monument, Wyoming*, 16.

[36] H. T. Clarke, "Freighting—Denver and Black Hills," *Proceedings and Collections*, Nebraska State Historical Society [hereinafter cited as NSHS], 2nd Series, Vol. V (1902), 302.

[37] Exploration and Survey of the Valley of the Great Salt Lake . . . by Howard Stansbury, *Sen. Exec. Doc. No. 3*, 32 Cong., Spec. sess. (Serial 608), 74.

[38] De Voto, *Across the Wide Missouri*, 35.

ing had to be done with the dry buffalo droppings, euphemistically, "*bois des vaches.*" Wind and dust were a constant harrassment.

Captain Stansbury reported:[39] "The wind in addition to its furious violence, was so very hot and dry as to render respiration, from the great rarification, quite difficult. The throat and fauces became dry, the lips clammy and parched and the eyes much inflamed from the drifting dust." William Henry Jackson, who bullwhacked a team to Wyoming in 1866, said that a hot dry wind blew continuously, choking the men with dust and burning their faces and lips with alkali dust. The older men warned the greenhorns not to wash, but nothing would keep them from moistening their lips unconsciously, and by the end of the second day all the new men had cracked and bleeding lips.[40] Dust seems to have been the particular curse of the Overland Trail; at least, there were more complaints of it than from the Santa Fe Trail. Stretches of the trail were three to six inches deep with finely powdered dust which the shuffling feet of oxen stirred into a blinding cloud, which then powdered the teamsters until they looked like workers in a flour mill. William Chandless, an English traveler who drove an ox team to Salt Lake City in 1856, said that the dust was an affliction to which one could never become reconciled.[41]

Prairie storms were always a menace. The hail could rip wagon covers to shreds and stampede the animals. Late in the season, blizzards often took their toll of men and animals. Lightning also played wierd tricks. In 1871 a bullwhacker was struck by lightning and instantly killed. There were no marks on the body, but some steps away were his clothes knotted in a pile and charred by fire. Other men near by were more or less stunned.[42] Daniel Tyler, official historian of the Mormon Battalion, has left a classic description of a prairie storm: the black cloud ripped by lightning, the continuous roar of thunder, the blast that ripped up tents and overturned

39 Stansbury Report, *loc. cit.*
40 William Henry Jackson, *Time Exposure*, 115.
41 Chandless, *A Visit to Salt Lake City*, 90.
42 *Cheyenne Daily Leader* (Wyoming) (August 12, 1871).

wagons and drove the writer twelve to fifteen rods to a clump of willows where he had to lie down, hold onto the willows with one hand, and protect his head from the hail with the other arm.

Since most travel across the plains was in the summertime, the native insect life was a constant, if minor, harrassment. A soldier writing from Fort Kearny in 1858 said: "The severe monotony of the valley is becoming disagreeable. We have also discovered to our annoyance that it swarms with mosquitos and bugs, and swelters with tropical heat."[43] Prairie fires were a source of danger to the high plains traveler. One train in April, 1864, when endangered by a fire, corraled its wagons with the stock inside. The crew then set to work and backfired between the fire and the corral, using buckets and wet grain sacks to control the backfire. Another train that was threatened by fire corraled on a small rise of ground where the grass was thin, shot a horse, and dragged the carcass back and forth until the grass was worn off of a protective strip of ground.[44]

Despite all these difficulties, Captain Ware could report that he had stood on "Sioux Lookout," near Fort McPherson, with field glasses and seen a train of wagons as long as he could definitely distinguish it, with a vast prism of dust rising either north or south, dependent on the prevailing wind. Of this traffic, three-quarters was composed of large freight wagons drawn by oxen. In 1864 there passed Julesburg some 3,574 wagons loaded with freight, driven and guarded by 4,258 men and hauled by 28,592 animals.[45]

There were other trails across the Great American Desert, but none of them reached the importance of the Santa Fe and Overland trails as routes of emigration and commerce. In 1839, Josiah Gregg, who had traveled the Santa Fe Trail four times, set out from Van Buren, on the Arkansas River, with $25,000 worth of goods in fourteen wagons. He crossed the Arkansas and followed up the Canadian almost due west to Santa Fe. In the following year, returning from

43 St. Louis *Daily Missouri Democrat* (July 8, 1858).

44 Collins, *Across the Plains in '64*, 16; Tom Rivington, "Bull Train Boss Was Doughty Man," Cheyenne *Wyoming State Tribune* (August 17, 1932).

45 John Lee Webster, "Address," *Collections*, NSHS, Vol. XVI (1911), 47–65.

Chihuahua, he retraced much the same route. He considered this route to be superior to the Santa Fe Trail but granted that his new trail would probably never break the "monopoly of the Santa Fe trade."[46] Captain Randolph Marcy scouted a route from Fort Smith, Arkansas, to Doña Ana on the Rio Grande, 265 miles south of Santa Fe, and connecting directly with the wagon road to the Pacific blazed by Lieutenant Colonel Philip St. George Cooke and his Mormon Battalion in 1846. This route carried a substantial number of gold seekers but little or no commerce to California.

Lying between the Platte and Arkansas rivers were two routes from the Missouri Valley to Denver that were somewhat shorter than the main roads. Both followed up the Kaw River to Junction City. From there one followed the Smoky Hill River and the other the Republican. Both routes suffered the same drawbacks: the western ends had long waterless stretches and an absence of timber and forage. In October the *Rocky Mountain News* of Denver summed it up: the Arkansas route was longest but firmest; the Platte route was best known but most sandy; the Smoky Hill had the most claimed for it, "but is as yet a *via incognita*." Three years later the *Council Grove Press* reported that from the Salina River to the Smoky Hill crossing, a distance of forty miles, there was, in late June, not enough water to keep a Santa Fe train for one night.[47]

Conditions were harsh on both the Santa Fe and Overland trails— long distances that produced a great feeling of isolation that "turned one's mind inward," fierce storms that swept the prairie, hostile Indians, and unfriendly nature. On the Cimarron Cutoff there was a scarcity of water. On the western end of the Overland Trail the alkali water purged the men and often killed the oxen. One man commented:

> On the stormy, rainy nights in the vast open prairies without shelter or cover, the deep rolling or loud crashing thunder, the vivid and almost continuous flashes of lightning, and howling

[46] Gregg, *Commerce of the Prairies*, 328.

[47] Denver *Rocky Mountain News* (Colorado), April 25, 1860; *Council Grove Press*, June 29, 1863.

winds, the pelting rain, and the barking of coyotes, all combined to produce a feeling of loneliness and littleness impossible to describe.[48]

The twin pulls of profit and adventure led men to defy the adverse conditions along the trails and keep the wagons rolling to carry the essential supplies and luxury goods to the communities of the Mountain West.

48 Albert Jerome Dickson, *Covered Wagon Days*, 63; Wiley Britton, "Pioneer Life in Southwest Missouri," *MHR*, Vol. XVI (July, 1922), 559.

CHAPTER III

PORTS OF THE PRAIRIE SEA

T HE GREAT PLAINS with their vast distances, unrelieved by trees or hills, the undulating surface, the absence of habitation and law, caused many people to feel that the whole region was more like the high seas than the national territory to which they were accustomed. Problems arose and had to be met by new ideas or modifications of old ones. Josiah Gregg regretted that there was no system of "Maritime Law" that would assure subordination among the traders of a Santa Fe caravan. "I can see no reason why the captain of a prairie caravan should not have as much power to call his men to account for disobedience or mutiny, as the captain of a ship upon the high sea."[1]

As early as the 1820's there were, on the western shore of this prairie sea, communities crying for the products of the States on the eastern shore. The people of New Mexico wanted cloth, dry goods, and hardware. The Morman community in Utah, numbering about 11,000 in 1850, needed the finished goods of the eastern manufacturers and machinery for its local industry. The mining communities of Colorado and Montana were almost completely dependent on the States for food and drink, clothing, hardware, and mining machinery.

On the lower Missouri River from St. Louis west to Kansas City and north to Omaha every hamlet, town, and city hoped to become the one and only port through which this great and remunerative

[1] *Commerce of the Prairies,* 58.

44

commerce would flow. Geography and the initiative of local merchants soon favored some of these river ports over others.

As early as 1787, St. Louis had been the headquarters of the fur trade of the Far West, but as population moved west along the Missouri River, the steamboat captains pushed the head of navigation westward. The Santa Fe traders were quick to take advantage of the shortened overland distance. First Franklin, then Independence, and finally Westport Landing were their points of supply and departure. William Becknell started from Franklin on his trips to Santa Fe. The later traders, the Oregon settlers, and the early Salt Lake traders left from Independence.

Although St. Louis was not a great port on the prairie sea, it was the great transshipment point, entrepôt, and wholesale market. In 1853 two parties of Santa Fe traders arrived in town with some $200,000 between them. At least one of these parties had planned to go to New York to make purchases but changed its mind and decided to fill its needs in St. Louis. The *Daily Missouri Democrat* said: "They want $40,000 worth of dry goods, $10,000 worth of groceries, as well as saddlery, hard ware, etc. As may be supposed there is some little stir among merchants."

The Santa Fe trade, which in the late 1830's averaged some $150,000 per annum, produced in the Missouri Valley a strange economic picture. Nationwide, the Panic of 1837 was marked by a shortage of specie and was felt particularly in the states of the Mississippi Basin. However, during the period of the panic, the Santa Fe traders were bringing in each year large amounts of gold and silver coin and bullion. In 1835 and again in 1839, *Niles Register* reported that the Santa Fe traders had returned with $200,000 in specie. Thus there was a strange mixture of boom and bust— a shortage of hard cash in the banks but a large supply of it in circulation.

When the Kansas-Nebraska Bill was passed in May, 1854, there was a sudden spate of founding new towns on the west bank of the Missouri River. A group of Missourians met on June 13, 1854, at Weston, Missouri, to found the town company of Leavenworth,

45

Kansas. The *Kansas Weekly Herald* in September estimated the population as "99 men, 1 woman, 0 babies, Total 100."[2] Another group of Missourians founded Atchison in July, 1854. The founders were mostly speculators who hoped to make their fortunes in real estate and then return home. By 1857, in Leavenworth, $11,000 was offered for eleven lots that had been purchased a year and a half before for $55.

The river towns, as they developed, were all much alike. At the river's edge was a levee, sometimes macadamized for all-weather use. Between the levee and the bluffs was the business district, running back for two or three blocks. Here were the warehouses and stores of the "outfitters" and the forwarding and commission merchants. Behind the business district and up the gullies that gave access to the tops of the bluffs were the small stores, saloons, and dance halls. On top of the bluffs was the residential section. Beyond the residential section were the wagon parks and corrals of the freighters who sent their wagons into town in small groups to load at the warehouse.

The towns were built almost entirely of wood and so were subject to disastrous fires such as those that wiped out much of the business districts of Leavenworth in the summer of 1858 and again in October of the next year and of Nebraska City in May, 1860. In the spring, mud was a common cause of complaint. In fact, it was so bad that large freight wagons bogged down right in the middle of town. Public accommodations were crude. Not only were there several beds to a room but, often, several occupants to a bed. The whisky sold in the saloons was hardly of the bottled-in-bond variety. Sanitation was little heeded. In Kansas City the newspaper complained of the stench from an old house used for the storage of green hides.[3] A constant source of difficulty for the freighter was the fencing in of the prairie outside the towns which forced the roads into the wet stream bottoms and over the hills. Public action to assure good access roads was slow.

After 1848 and the removal of Mexican restrictions on trade, the

2 Dick, *Sod-House Frontier*, 55, 63.
3 Kansas City *Journal of Commerce* (Missouri) (August 3, 1859).

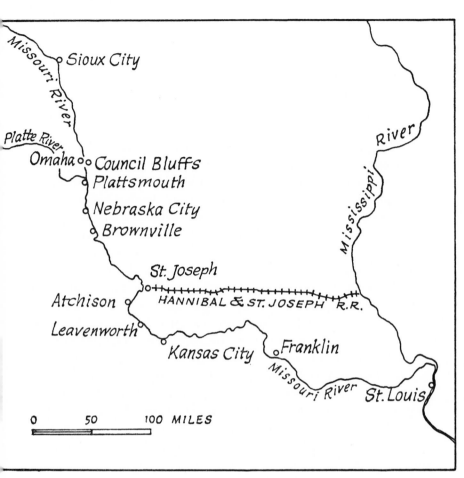

Sioux City

Missouri River

Platte River

Omaha Council Bluffs
Plattsmouth
Nebraska City
Brownville

Mississippi River

St. Joseph

Atchison   HANNIBAL & ST. JOSEPH R.R.

Leavenworth

Kansas City   Franklin

Missouri River   St. Louis

0   50   100 MILES

PRINCIPAL PORTS OF THE PRAIRIE SEA

Santa Fe trade grew apace and the army posts in the newly acquired territory had to be supplied. However, it was the Mormon War, ten years later, that really put wagon-freighting in the class of big business. The impact of the growth in freighting on the rudimentary economy of the Missouri Valley can be judged by the advertisement that Russell, Majors and Waddell inserted in the Missouri Valley newspapers. It called for 60,000 oxen and 1,500 teamsters. At the offered price of $75 per yoke of oxen, this meant $2,250,000 for the farmers and stock-raisers of the area.

Another source of income for the Missouri farmers was the winter pasturing of draft animals. In 1864 the Consolidated Gregory Mining Company of Colorado made an agreement with James N. Mills of Brown County, Kansas, to care for the animals of its train. The company was to provide the feed for 372 oxen, 2 herding ponies, and a mule. Mills was to be paid $75.00 per month for his work. In addition, Mills agreed to room and board a man free "for the privilege of the litter from corn fed said cattle." At the same time D. A. Butterfield, storage, forwarding, and commission merchant of Atchison, was to receive $2.00 per ton for storing the wagons and some machinery, until about May 1, 1865.[4]

The great tonnage that was hauled across the plains required warehouse and office space for storage and handling. In 1849 the post quartermaster at Fort Leavenworth reported that he had to have additional storehouses built. The new depot of Russell, Majors and Waddell at Nebraska City required the expenditure of $300,000 for lots, corrals, warehouses, offices, and residences.[5]

As the trade across the prairie sea grew, the business became more sophisticated. By the 1840's the traders could no longer obtain their goods from the local merchants, and it was time-consuming and expensive to travel to New York or Philadelphia to make their purchases. To serve the traders, there soon appeared forwarding and commission merchants whose business it was to receive and store the traders' goods until called for. Most houses went far beyond

---

[4] Teller Papers, University of Colorado Libraries, Boulder, Colorado.

[5] E. A. Ogden to Jesup, October 3, 1849, Record Group (hereafter RG) 93, NA; Everett Dick, *Vanguards of the Frontier*, 343.

48

this. They placed the traders' orders with the suppliers or manufacturers in the East, supervised the loading of the wagons, and often served as bankers. In Kansas City there were at least four such houses, and W. H. Chick and Company loaded as many as three hundred wagons of six-thousand-pound capacity in a single day.[6]

The relative standing of the river ports in 1860 is shown by a table compiled for the New York *Herald* by its own agent:

Port	Men	Horses	Mules	Oxen	Wagons	Lbs. Freight
Kansas City	7,084	464	6,149	27,920	3,033	16,439,134
Leavenworth	1,216	—	206	10,952	1,003	5,656,082
Atchison	1,591	—	472	13,640	1,280	6,097,943
St. Joseph	490	—	520	3,980	418	1,672,000
Nebraska City	896	—	113	11,118	916	5,496,000
Omaha	324	377	114	340	272	713,000
Total	11,601	841	7,574	67,950	6,922	36,074,159

The estimated average cost of freighting was given as $180 to $240 per ton, depending on distance, which meant that the freighting business was worth from $3,250,000 to $4,333,000. Of the above figures, the following were used to move government supplies: 1,307 wagons, 1,590 men, 232 mules, and 16,260 oxen. The total weight moved was 7,540,102 pounds, and it cost the government $890,300.[7]

The equipment and supplies needed by the freighters was another big item. In 1850 there were in St. Louis 32 wagonmakers with an invested capital of $27,275.00, employing 121 men and producing annually $146,585.00 worth of wagons of all types, including the big freight wagons. The *Atchison City Directory* for 1865 reported that "one of our enterprising citizens [*sic*] has contracted for the supply of two thousand wagons from the best factories." In 1865 the rations for twenty-eight men for sixty days cost $768.62.[8]

The mule-breeding industry of Missouri stemmed directly from the Santa Fe trade. Jacks and mules were an important part of the

6 Kansas City *Star* (Missouri) (December 14, 1906), in *Trail Clippings*, KSHS.

7 *Journal of Commerce* (December 15, 1860); T. S. Case, *History of Kansas City, Missouri*, 473.

8 R. M. Rolfe, "The Overland Freighting Business in the Early Sixties," *Kansas City Star* (December 31, 1899).

return load of the traders. By 1863 the price of a large mule, suitable to work as a wheeler, had reached $145 per head.[9]

When a new town was founded, practically the first establishment was a newspaper. Editors were enticed by gifts of buildings and lots, or by cash subsidy. Atchison donated $400 to get Dr. J. H. Stringfellow to start a paper—the *Squatter Sovereign*. As a result of these gifts, the newspaper's primary mission was to boost its own town and run down rival towns—and their papers. News seems to have been included almost by accident. The paper-and-ink war between Kansas City ("Gullytown") and Leavenworth ("Cottonwood Town") raged for years. Noting a large consignment of dry goods for Denver, the Kansas City *Journal of Commerce* crowed: "When Leavenworth loses the Colorado trade, as from present indications she is certain to do, grass will grow in her streets." In 1863 the *Journal* was careful to translate into Spanish, for the benefit of the New Mexican traders, an article from the Leavenworth *Conservative* which attacked their loyalty.[10]

All the papers pressed for local improvements that would help the town's trade. Improved levees, macadamized streets, and improved roads to the west were subjects of great attention. The *Daily Times*, in 1859, urged the merchants of Leavenworth to form a Chamber of Commerce. The *Journal of Commerce* carried advertisements and lists of current prices in Spanish. Because of the local attachments, the statistics of trade that the papers published from time to time are open to doubt. Various sources gave the following figures for freighting from Atchison in 1860:

Wagons	Men	Mules	Oxen	Lbs. Freight
1,280	1,591	472	13,640	6,007,943[11]
1,328	1,549	401	15,263	2,590,875[12]
1,713	2,010	693	18,017	8,220,883[13]

9 Leavenworth *Daily Times* (Kansas), August 8, 1863.
10 *Journal of Commerce* (June 12, August 8, 1863); *Daily Times* (1856–64), *passim*.
11 *Merchants' Magazine*, Vol. XLIV (January, 1861), 19–45.
12 Frank A. Root and William Elsey Connelley, *The Overland Stage to California*, 419n.
13 *Freedom's Champion* (Atchison) (March 11, 1860).

The figures from the local paper are by far the largest. The pound was the common unit of measurement, not only because freight rates were usually quoted as so many cents per pound per one hundred miles or per trip, but also because this produced more impressive figures for promotional material.

As the towns along the Missouri River grew, they began to ape the older towns on the Mississippi. The river boats brought in their coterie of roughnecks, gamblers, and *"femmes du pave."* In addition, these towns had a floating population of several hundred hardy men who had just completed a walk of five hundred to one thousand miles, pushing an ox team, and worrying about the security of their scalplocks. Such men would hardly be considered candidates for a Sunday-school picnic. It is small wonder that the *Journal of Commerce* could report: "A brick house of ill repute . . . was burned last evening at twilight. It is probable the house was set on fire." Later, with fine impartiality, the *Journal* reported that three houses of ill fame in Leavenworth had been cleaned out by a mob and set afire.[14] Probably the quietest town for some time was Nebraska City. When Alexander Majors selected the town as the site of the new base for Russell, Majors and Waddell, he stipulated that the city fathers agree to a local prohibition of the sale of liquor.

The freighters established a pattern of life for the ports of the prairie sea that lasted as long as wagon-freighting. In late February or early March parties of men were sent out onto the plains to round up the oxen that had been wintering there, some as far away as Denver and Fort Laramie. The animals were brought in as soon as there was enough grass, and the wagons were made ready. About April 1 the first trains were loaded and rolled out. For the next six months life was all hustle and bustle as loaded trains rolled out and empties came in to load and move out again. By early December the freighters were ready to call it quits for the season and send their stock out to winter range.

Although the pioneer had his face to the setting sun, he managed to keep a sharp eye over his shoulder, watching his connections with

14 *Journal of Commerce* (December 27, 1862; April 25, 1863).

civilization. In the Missouri river newspapers, more attention was paid to the arrival of the river steamers than to the departure of the prairie schooners. The *Rocky Mountain News* of Denver hardly let a week pass without mention of the arrivals of the trains from the States but gave slight attention to the movement of goods into the mountains. The same applies to the *Helena Herald* in Montana, and, to a lesser extent, to the *Deseret News* of Salt Lake City.

Franklin, on the left bank of the lower Missouri River, the main town of the Boon's Lick country, was the starting point of the early Santa Fe traders. The frontier storekeepers were alert to the possibilities of the Santa Fe trade. As early as 1825 one firm advertised a large assortment of goods purchased in New York and Philadelphia "expressly for the Santa Fe market."[15] Beginning about 1826, the river began to erode away the bank before the town. This became so serious that in 1828 the whole town was moved two miles inland. This move and the founding of Independence, Missouri, about one hundred miles farther west, brought about a rapid decline in the importance of Franklin as a starting point for Santa Fe. From 1822 to 1828 some $452,000 worth of goods, figured at probable cost in the eastern markets, had been shipped out of Franklin.[16]

The founders of Independence may have taken the fate of Franklin to heart; at any rate, the new town was built on the edge of the plains some six miles back from the river. It was from Independence that Captain Benjamin L. E. Bonneville, United States Army, set out in 1832, with twenty wagons for the trapping grounds of the Northwest. Francis Parkman in 1846 remarked on "the groups of piratical-looking Mexicans, employees of the Santa Fe traders, with their broadpeaked hats" and noted that every store was adapted to furnish outfits for travelers; that the public houses were full of Santa Fe men and emigrants; and there were mules, horses, and wagons at every corner.

15 Jonas Viles, "Old Franklin: A Frontier Town of the Twenties," *Mississippi Valley Historical Review* [hereinafter referred to as *MVHR*], Vol. IX (March, 1923), 269–82; F. F. Stephens, "Missouri and the Santa Fe Trade," *MHR*, Vol. XI (July, 1917), 291–94.
16 Gregg, *Commerce of the Prairies*, 332.

"The Wagon Train," painted in oil by Hollin[?] This is a Diamond
R outfit.

The owners of the Diamond R Freighting Company. Left to right:
C. A. Broadwater, Matt Carroll, E. G. Maclay, and George Steele.

A wagon train at Fort Bridger on Black's Fork of Green River.

Courtesy Library of Congress

A wagon train is corralled on Market Street, Denver, in 1866. Note
the complex mule harness.

Courtesy Denver Public Library Western Collection

Note the simple harness on this bull team in Benton, Montana.

A Diamond R freight train moves through Prickly Pear Canyon, Montana.

Freighting over Ute Pass, Colorado.

This prairie schooner is on display in the Hastings Museum, Hastings, Nebraska.

Another traveler noted that the town was a great rendezvous for trappers and freighters, "Jabbering in Dutch, higgling in Spanish, swearing in bad French, anathmatizing some refractory mule, in good, long-drawn Yankee."[17]

To the west of Independence flowed the Big Blue River of Missouri, not to be confused with the Big Blue of eastern Nebraska and Kansas. This river was at times a serious obstacle to travel. When M. M. Marmaduke went to Santa Fe in 1824, he noted that his party had to dig down the banks and lower the wagons and dearborns on ropes.[18] High water was known to hold up trains for as much as two or three weeks.

For about twenty years Independence was the eastern terminal of the high plains freighter. As Westport grew in importance, it divided the trade with Independence for some years. A few freighters continued to operate from the old base, despite its drawbacks.

The lives of Westport and Kansas City were closely interwoven until the former was incorporated into the latter in 1850. The town of Westport had been incorporated in 1833, and its steamer landing was known as Westport Landing and as Kansas. The area had two great advantages: from its location it was the natural heir of Franklin and Independence in the Santa Fe trade, and it had the best natural landing place on the Missouri River—a limestone ledge that projected into deep water and was not subject to being washed away.

In 1840 there were operating out of Westport 5 firms with 60 wagons, valued, with their teams, at $50,000. By 1841 these figures had grown to 100 and $150,000, and by 1842, to 350 and $450,000. By 1857 the value of the trade with Santa Fe reached the figure of $3,000,000.[19] The first wagon train to unload at Kansas City was that of Bent and St. Vrain which arrived from Bent's Fort in 1845 after being on the road for a month. The first train out seems to have been that of E. C. McCarty in 1847.

17 W. Z. Hickman, *History of Jackson County*, 119; Richard Lush Wilson, *Short Ravelings from a Long Yarn*, 2.
18 F. A. Sampson (ed.), "Santa Fe Trail: M. M. Marmaduke Journal," *MHR*, Vol. VI (October, 1911), 4.
19 Louis O. Honig, *Westport, Gateway to the Early West*, 108.

It was not until the California gold rush in 1849 that Kansas City really began to grow. In 1851 the population was only about 300 and four years later, scarcely 1,000; by 1860 the city could boast some 7,000 inhabitants. After 1850, Kansas City enjoyed an almost complete monopoly of the Santa Fe trade; it was threatened only briefly during the Civil War. In 1859 the *Journal of Commerce* rhapsodized: "Fair Skies, dry roads, Santa Fe trains, Pike's Peak emigrants, ox trains, mule wagons, horses, buggies, Mexicans, Indians, Mountain men, candidates and crinoline, make up the panorama of life in Kansas City at the present writing." The paper noted in April that Commercial Street was jammed with Santa Fe wagons and added: "This street seems to be entirely given up to the Mexican trade."[20] In 1854 the city's business was reported as follows:

Merchandise	$3,815,502	
Warehousing	545,000	
Livestock	2,138,200	(including $1,262,000 in draft animals)
Exports	1,767,761	
Total	$8,266,463	

The exports consisted entirely of goods brought in from New Mexico and the mountains. If no margin of profit is allowed, an equal amount of merchandise must have been shipped out across the plains. When one adds to these amounts a pro rata share of the warehousing business and, say, half the business in draft animals, it is clear that at least 50 per cent of the city's business was directly dependent on the freighter and his oxen or mules.

Standing on the steps of the Union Hotel in 1859, the editor of the *Journal of Commerce* watched a wagon train loaded with wool arriving from New Mexico and answered questions from a group of eastern businessmen. In reporting the events, he said: "There is no one thing that an eastern businessman can witness in the West so well calculated to expand his ideas of Western commerce, as these large caravans from New Mexico and the Mountains. In no west-

20 *Journal of Commerce* (March 23, April 26, 1859).

ern city can this commerce be seen to so good an advantage as in Kansas City."[21]

Until 1859, Leavenworth City had a monopoly of government freighting as Fort Leavenworth was the only supply depot for the United States Army west of the Missouri River. In that year Kansas City was made the distribution point for the supplies for the garrisons in New Mexico and Kansas. In addition to the Santa Fe trade, there was some business with the mining communities of Colorado and with the Cherokee Nation, some 200 miles to the south. There was also trade in furs and buffalo robes, as when Seth E. Ward of Fort Laramie brought in two small trainloads. However, Ward had his groceries shipped upriver to Atchison for his return trip. The total receipts from New Mexico in 1858 were reported by the *Journal of Commerce* on January 1, 1859:[22]

Mexican wool, pounds	1,051,000	$167,650
Goatskins	55,000	27,500
Dressed deerskins	60,000	175,000
Dry hides	61,857	170,107
Specie in boxes	——	1,527,789
Furs, skins (estimated)	——	50,000

The Civil War dealt a heavy blow to Kansas City. The *Journal* had to suspend publication in August, 1861. Irwin, Jackman and Company, government freighters, moved to Leavenworth City when the army moved its depot to Fort Leavenworth. Several business houses moved out of town. When the *Journal* resumed publication on March 27, 1862, it was glad to note the return of several businesses after an absence of nearly a year. Some government freighting returned with the opening of a supply depot for the "District of the Border." By July, 1862, the New Mexico trade had so far returned to normal that the paper could report the arrival of 500,000 pounds of wool, with half as much more en route. A year later it could report that, as of July 1, five business houses had loaded 1,385 wagons with

21 *Ibid.* (September 9, 1859).
22 *Ibid.* (January 1, 1859; June 13, September 2, October 7, 1860).

3,242 tons of freight. It went on to note that the so-called New Mexico trade involved a large amount of business with the Mexican states of Chihuahua and Sonora: "Indeed there was one trader who arrived here this season with a train of 10 wagons, loaded with wool from Altar, Sonora, within 35 miles of Port Liberatad [*sic*], on the Gulf of California."[23] The size, variety and importance of the trade of the plains may be gauged from the following random items taken from the *Journal of Commerce* for 1859: eight hundred sacks of sugar for one Santa Fe house; one train of fifty-nine wagons of whisky, sugar, soap, and a general assortment of goods; a boiler, a steam engine, and machinery for a flour mill.

The railroad from Kansas City to Lawrence was completed on December 22, 1864. The *Journal*, bowing gracefully to Fate, admitted that "New Mexico merchants will probably have their goods forwarded to Lawrence by rail but some will freight direct from this point."[24]

Leavenworth City started out with one great advantage: three miles to the north was Fort Leavenworth. It was from this fort that the expeditions of Major Bennett Riley, Captain Philip St. George Cooke, and Colonel Stephen W. Kearny set out. By the time of Kearny's march, in 1846, freighting had become such a big business that the post quartermaster had little trouble collecting sufficient transportation to support the first column of 1,650 men across 900 miles of the prairie sea. In addition, some 400 traders' wagons traveled with the army for protection.

On seeing the Leavenworth depot of Russell, Majors and Waddell, government freighters, in 1859, Horace Greeley was moved to say: "Such acres of wagons! such pyramids of extra axletrees! such herds of oxen! such regiments of drivers and other employees!"[25] When the company got into financial difficulties, the *Missouri Republican* pointed out that the failure of such a large company would be a severe blow to the economy of the Missouri Valley. It said: "Nearly every town, neighborhood and individual upon the Mis-

23 *Ibid.* (July 27, 1862; August 5, 1863).
24 *Ibid.* (December 22, 1864; March 27, 1865).
25 *An Overland Journey from New York to San Francisco*, 47.

ouri River is either directly or indirectly interested in their continued success."[26]

Leavenworth suffered from certain geographic disadvantages, which Atchison to the north and Kansas City to the south were not slow to point out. The military road from Fort Leavenworth to Fort Kearny passed within five miles of Atchison. To reach the Santa Fe Trail in the Arkansas Valley, several large streams had to be crossed. These facts did not bother the *City Directory* of Leavenworth: "There is no place on the Missouri River, which furnishes such good natural roads for the passing of trains to and from all points in the territories beyond us." It should be noted that Leavenworth did not get a railroad connection until the Eastern Division of the Union Pacific built a feeder line back from Lawrence in 1866.[27]

The Colorado gold rush of 1859 drew the attention of Leavenworth businessmen to the possibilities of commercial freighting. William Larimer wrote home from the Santa Fe Trail urging his friends to open their natural route to the gold fields by way of Republican Fork.[28] Freighting to Denver started in 1859, when Jones and Russell sent out at least two trains and John S. Jones announced plans for one or two trains per week during the summer. During the following year, Leavenworth shipped 2,828 tons of merchandise, including twenty quartz mills which had been built in town. The *Times* remarked: "The Denver people are rapidly providing themselves with the luxuries to which they were accustomed before leaving the East. We observe that the demand for champagne and other wines is increasing."[29]

The largest freighting firm operating out of Leavenworth was Jones and Cartwright. On October 10 the *Daily Times* reported that they sent out twenty-one trains carrying 1,783 tons at $.10 per pound

26 *Leavenworth Times* (October 26, 1860).

27 *Leavenworth City Directory and Business Mirror for 1865–66; Daily Times* (May 15, 1866).

28 Hafen, *Colorado Gold Rush*, 99.

29 *Daily Times* (June 25, September 13, 1859; July 11, 1860); Lyle E. Mantor, "Stage Coach and Freighter Days at Fort Kearny,"*Nebraska History* [hereinafter referred to as *NH*], Vol. XXIX (December, 1948), 336.

57

and grossed $356,500 on a capital investment of $208,200. Nineteen of the trains consisted of twenty-seven wagons drawn by 324 oxen and handled by thirty men. The other two trains had thirty-one wagons, thirty-three men, and 372 oxen. The capital investment was: oxen, $150,000; wagons, $39,000; yokes and chains, $7,700; mules, $5,000; camp utensils, $3,500; and wagon covers, $3,000. Their tenth train arrived in Denver about the middle of August with 780 sacks of flour, 4,200 pounds of tobacco, 48,101 pounds of machinery, 1,033 pounds of cheese, 1,200 pounds of drugs, 140 cases of boots and shoes, 11,000 pounds of crockery, 11 barrels of whisky, and other goods. One of the largest loads out of Leavenworth was a 24-stamp quartz mill for Tucson, Arizona, which required 25 four- and six-mule teams.[30]

The *Times*, in 1860, noted a large Jones and Cartwright wagon train on the levee waiting for the steamer *Omaha*. They had received advance notice of the arrival of a consignment. "Such promptness not only adds to the reputation of Messrs. Jones & Cartwright as freighters, but has a tendency to make this—as it ought to be—the greatest shipping point to the mines." As the gold from Colorado was shipped east by stagecoach, most of the wagons returned empty. But one enterprising nurseryman in Leavenworth advertised: "From the Gold Mines, 4000 Shrubery [*sic*], 1000 Balsam of Fir, 2000 American Spruce, 600 Pines, 1000 large globe cactus, all plants being one to three feet high."[31]

The opening of the Montana gold mines in 1862 gave the freighter a new port of call. The *Times*, in April, 1865, reported the departure of a mule train of twenty-six wagons for Virginia City, Montana, and, a month later, another.[32] Because of the availability of steamer transportation to Fort Benton, Montana, wagon-freighting from the lower Missouri to Montana was never an important element in the commercial life of the ports of the lower river.

Hoping that Leavenworth would capture all the Santa Fe trade,

30 *Daily Times* (August 27, October 10, 1860; February 23, 1865).
31 *Ibid.* (August 25, October 8, 1860).
32 *Ibid.* (April 10, May 10, 1865).

the *Times*, in August, 1859, made note that 17,000 pounds of wool had arrived and that another 500,000 pounds were on the road. The paper said, "This furnishes ample evidence that the immense trade of New Mexico must ultimately be carried on through Leavenworth." The Civil War seemed to offer the chance. In August, 1862, the paper reported the arrival of a train of 125 wagons whose proprietors would spend not less than $250,000. It went on: "Mexicans are almost as plenty in our streets now as in Santa Fe. The editor of the Kansas City Journal could learn to talk Spanish in about a week if he would come up here." On the other hand, the *Times* itself did not help things by referring to New Mexico as "Greaser Country."[33]

In October, 1865, the Council Grove *Kansas Press* announced the death of Leavenworth, killed by the railroads, and in the same month advertisements began to appear in the *Times* offering wagons and teams for sale.[34] General James Rusling, on a tour of inspection of the western army posts in 1866, remarked that Leavenworth was still the entrepôt for New Mexico and the plains though the railroad out of Omaha had tapped the Utah and Colorado business. Wagons were abandoned on the vacant lots around town until they were carried away piece by piece. Oxen were sold for what they would bring or were turned loose on the prairie to fatten or to die of old age.[35]

The town of Atchison had to start life without the advantages enjoyed by Kansas City and Leavenworth. In the summer of 1855 the town grew from one store and two saloons to a hotel of sorts, ten stores and shops, and probably a proportionate number of saloons. From 1858 to 1860 the population grew from 400 to 2,616.[36] The town took maximum advantage of its situation as the farthest west point on the great bend of the Missouri River and its proximity to the military road to Fort Kearny. Freighting got its start when, in June, 1855, Livingston and Kincaid, merchant-freighters of Salt

---

33 *Ibid.* (August 25, 1859; August 8, 18, 1863; June 12, 1864).

34 *Ibid.* (March 2, April 20, May 19, 1865).

35 John P. Dickinson, "On a Government Survey in the Early '70's," *The Trail*, Vol. X (December, 1917), 14–22.

36 Peter Beckman, "The Overland Trade and Atchison's Beginnings," *Territorial Kansas*, 151, 154.

Lake City, found their wagons, four days out of Leavenworth, had arrived within five miles of Atchison.[37]

To encourage the Salt Lake trade, the stockholders of the town company voted $1,500 for a 52- by 80-foot warehouse; $250 to grade Center Street; and $2,500 for a hotel, for grading the levee for 300 yards, and for fencing lots for the draft animals. Horace Greeley noted several wagons starting for Salt Lake City in 1859 and remarked, "Teamsters from Salt Lake and teamsters about to start, lounge on every corner."[38] By the end of the 1858 season, *Freedom's Champion* reported that twenty-four trains totaling 775 wagons had taken out 1,865 tons of freight. The next year was not as good: a partial failure of crops in Utah and senseless overstocking by the merchants so reduced the demand for goods that not over 150 wagons were used in the Salt Lake trade.[39]

The completion of the Atchison and St. Joseph railroad in 1860 linked the town with the east, by way of the Hannibal and St. Joseph Railroad, and the amount of freight handled increased greatly. The three commission houses reported for 1860:

Firm	Wagons	Men	Mules	Oxen	Tons Freight
Home and Chouteau	243	300	162	2,144	450
D. W. Adams	200	266	116	1,829	391
A. S. Parker and Co.	177	192	478	1,572	366
Total	620	758	756	5,545	1,207

These figures do not include any government freight. According to Walker D. Wyman, the town "Ranked second as an army depot, third or fourth in private freighting and second or third in Denver traffic."[41]

---

[37] Atchison *Squatter Sovereign* (Kansas) (June 12, 1855).

[38] *Overland Journey*, 150; *Squatter Sovereign* (February 20, March 20, 1855).

[39] Atchison *Freedom's Champion* (Kansas) (October 30, 1858); "Commerce of the Prairies," *Merchants' Magazine and Commercial Review*, Vol. XLIV (January, 1862), 19–45.

[40] James Sutherland, *Atchison City Directory and Business Mirror for 1860–61*, 8–14.

[41] "The Missouri River Towns in the Westward Movement," Ph.D. dissertation, State University of Iowa (1935).

A bad drought in 1860 sent everyone who could get a wagon and a few yoke of oxen into the freighting business. The city directory lists forty-one freighters, of whom only twelve had sufficient equipment to make up the standard train of twenty-six wagons, and eighteen had less than ten. The largest firm was Irwin, Jackman and Company, government contract freighters and successors to Russell, Major and Waddell. They sent out 520 wagons, 650 men, 75 mules, and 6,240 oxen. Altogether Atchison sent out 2,000 tons of freight, of which over one-half went to Great Salt Lake and less than one-tenth to Colorado.[42]

During the Civil War some of the freighting that was displaced from Kansas City moved to Atchison temporarily. One firm made a killing by taking advantage of that new-fangled contraption, the telegraph. With a large quantity of whisky en route, the owners learned at Fort Kearny of a new tax on whisky, passed by Congress since the train had left the Missouri. The tax was promptly added and the firm made about $50,000 additional on the shipment. With the opening of the mines in Idaho and Montana there was additional freighting. One train for Idaho, made up of 33 4-mule wagons, took out 115,522 pounds of freight, and one of 36 6-mule wagons took 113,522 pounds to the Beaverhead and Gallatin country.[43]

In 1865, D. A. Butterfield founded the Butterfield Overland Despatch. The company contracted for freight for Colorado, Utah, Idaho, Montana, New Mexico, Arizona, and Nevada, giving through bills of lading. The actual hauling was subcontracted, and from July to October handled 7,000 tons.[44] The firm was forced out of business by insufficient capital; the mining boom in Colorado had collapsed, and the company had trouble collecting for the delivery of mining machinery. In addition, there was difficulty over the delivery of some consignments for Salt Lake City.

The 1866 season started out well, but because of the westward extension of the railroads, by April wagon-freighting was almost

---

42 Root and Connelley, *The Overland Stage to California*, 419n.
43 Mantor, "Stage Coach and Freighter Days," *loc. cit.*, 336; *Freedom's Champion* (April 14, 1864).
44 Matthew Quigg, *Atchison City Directory and Business Mirror for 1865*.

dead. Thus passed the town that was credited with having dispatched more trains than any other on the Missouri River.[45]

Until 1857, Nebraska City was just another town, a product of the Kansas-Nebraska Act, of no great promise; but in that year, good fortune struck. The great freighting firm of Russell, Majors and Waddell had found conditions around Fort Leavenworth crowded and fodder scarce. When the firm signed a new contract in 1858, they stipulated for an additional starting point and Nebraska City was chosen.[46] Other freighters were prompt to follow. In November, Hawke, Nuckolls and Company. set up in the freighting business and sent their first train "to the mines." In May of the following year A. and P. Byram announced that they would send two or three heavy trains a week to Pikes Peak, each train guarded by thirty armed men.

The *People's Press* reported in 1860 the following figures, taken from a register kept by a person who had the opportunity of seeing nine out of ten of the outgoing wagons: for the week ending May 31, 93; June 7, 110; June 14, 146; June 21, 131; June 26, 152; total, 632. The paper commented that "in two days over a month, with an average load of 5000 pounds," the aggregate was 3,170,000 pounds of freight, and not one emigrant wagon was included in the count.[47]

In early November, 1862, the *Press* noted that trains were still leaving, despite the weather, the scarcity of feed on the plains, and other inconveniences, and added, "it is necessary for the comfort of the thousands of miners in Colorado, and the provisions and goods must and will be shipped." The season of 1862 was recapitulated as follows: 1,357 wagons, 1,788 men, 8,912 oxen, 1,156 mules, and 7,853,910 pounds of freight.[48]

In the spring of 1866 there were many ox and mule wagons on the streets, but freighting had fallen off. Shippers were unwilling to pay

[45] Root and Connelley, *Overland Stage*, 303; Beckman, "Overland Trade," *loc. cit.*, 157.

[46] W. S. Hancock to B. DuBarry, February 12, 1858; Hancock to Jesup, February 12, 1858, RG 93, NA.

[47] Nebraska City *People's Press* (Nebraska) (July 3, 1862).

[48] *Ibid.* (November 6, 1862; March 30, 1863).

the rates they had paid in former years, and the freighters were waiting for better prices.[49] It turned out to be a long wait.

At first glance, the town of Plattsmouth, Nebraska, would seem to occupy a perfect site for an important river port. For hundreds of miles the Overland Trail followed the Platte River, and the town was located at the point where the Platte poured its waters into the Missouri. Unfortunately, Dame Nature had treated the area shabbily. For hundreds of miles the Platte ran through a wide plain with few tributaries, but within twenty miles of the Missouri, the Platte turned at right angles and reached the Big Muddy through a valley so narrow as to force any road up into the hills. While there was an excellent ferry in operation for a number of years, the town grew slowly; by 1860 it had only 474 inhabitants, and a decade later but 2,448.

The banner year for freighting seems to have been 1866. In January trains were loading for the west, and in June not less than 250 tons of freight went out in one week, including 50 tons of machinery for a quartz mill at Bannack, Montana, claimed to be the biggest mill ever taken to the western mines. When another train of machinery went out, a week later, the *Nebraska Herald* took the occasion to say that freighters with heavy loads preferred the Plattsmouth route. The Lode Star and Ni Wot Mining Companies of Colorado had machinery shipped from Plattsmouth, and it was claimed that freighters could ship from Plattsmouth for at least $1.50 per hundred pounds less than elsewhere. Business was so good that freighters were paying teamsters $75.00 per month, and there was a perpetual man power shortage.[50]

Despite the best efforts of the *Herald*, Plattsmouth was never more than a minor port on the prairie sea.

As a freighting terminal, Brownville, Nebraska, was an example of the balloon that never quite got off the ground. As early as June, 1856, a westbound train purchased its supplies in Brownville, and

49 Julius Charles Birge, *The Awaking of the Desert*, 39–40.
50 Plattsmouth *Nebraska Advertiser*, January 31, June 21, 28, August 30, September 6, 20, 1865.

the local paper, the *Nebraska Advertiser*, urged the desirability of a public road to intersect the military road from Fort Leavenworth to Fort Kearny.[51] The unhappy facts of geography did not bother the editor. Brownville was located on a peninsula between the Missouri and Nemaha rivers, and to avoid crossing the latter, the road must pass within six or seven miles of Nebraska City, twenty-two miles to the north.

In January, 1861, a number of business houses were making preparations to send out trains in February. The *Advertiser* said, "Shippers only want to know the superiority of the route, from Brownville to adopt it, and they are rapidly finding out." By March the streets were blocked by wagons, and in June, D. J. Martin and Company was advertising for fifteen to twenty teams to freight to the mountains.[52]

Despite the "puffing" of its home town by the *Advertiser*, Brownville never rose above the status of a minor port.

Council Bluffs, Iowa, and Omaha, Nebraska, separated only by the Missouri River, were the northernmost ports of the prairie sea until the gold rush into the Black Hills in 1876, when Sioux City, which by then had a rail connection to the east, saw a short boom in wagon-freighting.

Council Bluffs, on the east bank, had been the site of various Indian trading posts until about 1850. The Morman migration of 1846, from Nauvoo, Illinois, brought an estimated 12,000 people temporarily to the vicinity. The famous "Winter Quarters" were established on the west bank on the site of the town of Florence, now part of Greater Omaha. On the Iowa side of the river, the town of Kanesville was established by the Mormons as a supply depot on their trek across Iowa and on to Utah. The name was officially changed to Council Bluffs in 1853. The United States Census of 1850 credited Council Bluffs with a population of 3,000, ten years later with only 2,011, but by 1870 it had grown to 10,020.

Omaha was described in 1855 as a town of forty finished build-

51 *Ibid.* (June 7, November 25, 1856).
52 *Ibid.* (January 10, March 14, June 20, 1861).

ings and a number of others not yet completed, including a State-house and two hotels. The population was estimated at 1,200. The Census of 1860 shows 1,853 people in the town, and in 1870 there were 16,083.

The twin cities seemed to be fortunately located on the direct road from the Midwestern states to the Platte Valley. This was important for the emigrant, but the freighter found troubles. The twenty-five miles between Omaha and the Platte Valley lead over a plateau of rough hills and required the fording of the Elkhorn River, which drained a large part of Nebraska. In addition, because of the northerly location of the twin cities, 660 miles upriver from St. Louis and 150 miles above St. Joseph, the nearest railhead required a long trip by steamer. Also, the grass required for grazing the draft animals did not mature for several weeks after it was tall enough along the southern branches of the Overland Trail, nor did the mud dry out as soon. In 1862 the Council Bluffs newspaper noted that several heavily loaded trains had left by early April, despite the almost impassable condition of the road.[53]

The Mormon emigrant trains to Utah carried some freight, goods for the church stores, and machinery for local industry, but common-carrier-type freighters did not appear until 1860 to tap the Colorado trade. The Council Bluffs paper carried a note from the Denver *Herald* to the effect that Pegram, Warner and Company's train of twenty wagons had arrived on June 16 loaded with flour, glassware, hardware, groceries, dry goods, etc. The wagons were unloaded and started back the same day. Mr. Pegram stated that "he will have a train leave the Bluffs every month for this city."[54]

Congress appropriated $50,000 in 1856 for the construction of a military road from Omaha to Fort Kearny and made a further appropriation of $400,000 for a great wagon road to South Pass. A survey was run by Lieutenant John H. Dickerson, a few small bridges were built west of Loup Fork, but the fork itself was too wide to bridge at any reasonable cost. In the dry season the road was

53 "100 Years Ago," *Omaha World Herald* (Nebraska) (April 8, 1962).
54 *Omaha World Herald* (July 3, 1960).

satisfactory, but spring freshets in the Platte made it impassable in April, May, and June. The extension of the railroads ended the wagon-freighting days of Council Bluffs and Omaha, though the latter became the headquarters of a great railroad system.

Based somewhat on geographical factors but also on the enterprise of the local merchants, the ports of the prairie sea tended to specialize. Kansas City had a practical monopoly of the New Mexico–Chihuahua trade. Leavenworth had the greater part of the Colorado trade, though sharing it with Atchison. The latter town specialized in the Salt Lake trade.

Wagon-freighting was an important element in the economic development of the Missouri Valley. Much of the equipment and livestock used and rations consumed came from the valley. What was not produced locally was handled by agents drawing commissions. The handling of the great amounts of goods passing through the river ports required a large number of men to handle them and warehouses in which to store them. The teamsters had to be equipped for the outbound trip, and those that returned needed new clothes. While only a small proportion of the teamsters returned to the valley, it was here that they spent their wages. It would appear justified to say that from sometime about 1840 on, half the business of the Missouri River towns passed through the hands of the freighter.

CHAPTER IV

A DIVERSITY OF CREATURES

THE MEN who engaged in high plains wagon-freighting were as varied a group as the American frontier ever threw together in one common field of endeavor. In general, these men fall into four categories: the entrepreneurs—the men who provided the money with which the big companies operated and who supervised the operations; the wagonmasters, who actually supervised the day-to-day operation of the trains; the teamsters—bullwhackers and mule-skinners, day and night herders, and cooks—the men who manned the trains; the clerks who staffed the headquarters of the larger companies, not greatly different from the clerks in the mercantile establishments of the Missouri Valley.

Within the group of entrepreneurs there were at least three subgroups: the promoters, the financial men, and the general super-intendents. Some of these men had practical experience in the opera-tion of wagon trains; others had no such experience.

Of the men who fall into the promoter class, William Hepburn Russell, of the giant firm of Russell, Majors and Waddell, is the perfect example. With a background in mercantile business and land speculation, Russell became interested in freighting in 1847 as a partner in the firm of Bullard and Russell, of which Bullard was the operating head. Three years later Russell and James Brown formed the firm of Brown, Russell and Company to deliver 600,000 pounds of government supplies to Santa Fe. In the same year Russell formed a partnership with John S. Jones to deliver supplies to Fort

Hall. The greatest copartnership, Russell, Majors and Waddell, was formed in 1855 and operated under several names: Waddell, Russell and Company; Majors and Russell; Majors, Russell and Company; and Majors, Russell and Waddell.[1] While the company did most of its business in contract freighting for the United States Army, it also freighted for civilian customers and branched out into retail stores, such as Bradford and Company of Denver.

Russell has been described as volatile, highly temperamental, a bundle of supercharged nerves, a man who always wore carefully tailored clothes, an aristocrat by nature. The first crisis for the giant firm came with the Mormon War of 1857. The company had the contract to freight supplies for the Army to New Mexico and posts along the Overland Trail. The trains had already been dispatched when Russell was called in by the army quartermaster at Fort Leavenworth and told that his company would be required to haul an additional 3,000,000 pounds to Utah, the supplies for General Albert Sidney Johnston's army. Russell objected to assuming the new burden although the contract set no maximum amount the firm was to haul. Unfortunately, Russell did not insist on a new contract. He mistakenly accepted the verbal statement that the quartermaster did not believe that the army would let the company suffer for assuming the additional burden.

When the company went on the market for the additional stock and equipment, they found that prices had gone up by 50 per cent. In addition, the firm had to recruit new men all up and down the frontier, taking whatever came. The firm went into debt from which it never recovered.

Although not acting as members of Russell, Majors and Waddell, Russell, John S. Jones, and others formed the Central Overland California and Pike's Peak Express Company, a stagecoach line.

---

[1] For most of this chapter dealing with Russell, Majors and Waddell, see Raymond W. and Mary L. Settle, *Empire on Wheels; ibid.,* "The Early Careers of W. B. Waddell and W. H. Russell: Frontier Capitalists," *Kansas Historical Quarterly* [hereinafter referred to as *KHQ*], Vol. XXVI (Winter, 1960), 355–82; *ibid.,* "Napoleon of the West," *Annals of Wyoming* [hereinafter referred to as *AW*], Vol. XXXII (April, 1960), 5–47; R. W. Settle, "Robert B. Bradford," *1954 Brand Book,* Denver Westerners, 49–64.

This firm was soon running in the red. Majors and Waddell reluctantly decided that they had to rescue this operation, lest its troubles reflect on the freighting firm. The stage line continued to lose money. It was also Russell who entangled his partners in the spectacular but unprofitable Pony Express. Finally it was Russell who, in a frantic effort to save the whole structure, became involved in a major scandal in Washington that brought him to jail.

Although Russell was the promoter, at least one employee said: "Major [*sic*] we knew nothing of—probably he was a sleeping partner—but 'Billy' Russell, as he was commonly called, was quite a power in the West. . . . He owned some 20,000 working cattle and about 2000 wagons."[2] Robert Aull, a noted merchant of the Missouri Valley and a Santa Fe trader who had known him for twenty years, said: "Russell is generally too sanguine."

William Bradford Waddell was the banker and financial man of the partnership. He, too, started in merchandising and, like Russell, never drove a team across the plains. He was described as phlegmatic, stolid, and inclined to sulk when crossed, "above average in education, culture, and refinement." When the crash came, Waddell stripped himself of all his assets to partially satisfy the firm's debts. Of the three major partners, Waddell was the only one not in a financially straitened condition after the crash. His wife, apparently, was a better judge of men than her husband; before agreeing to his joining the partnership, she insisted that he settle $100,000 on her and give her title to their home, saying, "Russell is a plunger, I don't like this idea."[3]

Only Alexander Majors had had practical experience in freighting on the plains. As a farmer with three daughters to educate, he decided to apply his knowledge of animals to the freighting business. Starting with six wagons, Majors made his first trip to Santa Fe in 1848, and by 1854 his capital investment was $80,000 to $100,000,

2 R. H. Williams, *With the Border Ruffians: Memories of the Far West, 1852–1868*, 104.
3 Paul I. Wellman, "The Silent Partner Who Made History and Lost Fortunes on the Great Plains," clipping in scrapbook, Leavenworth Public Library, Leavenworth, Kansas.

including four trains at $18,000 to $20,000 each. Within a few years, this notable success led other freighters to follow his general pattern of operation.

Majors was convinced that sober, industrious men made the best drivers, so he required of each new employee the following oath:

> While I am in the employ of A. Majors, I agree not to use profane language, not to get drunk, not to gamble, not to treat animals cruelly, and not to do anything else that is incompatible with the conduct of a gentleman. And I agree, if I violate any of the above conditions, to accept my discharge without any pay for my services.[4]

Majors issued to each man a Bible or Testament, which led to their being nicknamed "Bible-Backs." One of his irreverent employees remarked that the pages of these Bibles were just about the right size for rolling cigarettes. A bullwhacker with a rival train, meeting a Russell, Majors and Waddell train coming down Raton Pass in a cloud of profanity, noted that the drivers seemed to have lost "the word."[5]

William Larimer, one of Denver's early pioneers, best summed up Majors' position when he said, "Perhaps more than either of his two partners, is Majors entitled to have his name and career embodied in the lasting history of the development of our western country." Legh Freeman, editor of the *Frontier Index*, who seems to have liked very few people, said of Majors, "No man in the western country is more esteemed and universally beliked than Alexander Majors; his energy and integrity are by words, from the Missouri river to the Pacific coast. He is an honor to his race."[6]

Possibly the second largest freighting company was that of Jones and Cartwright which was formed in 1858. John S. Jones was a

4 Alexander Majors, *Seventy Years on the Frontier*, 72.

5 Rev. G. M. Darley, "The End-Gate of the Mess Wagon," *The Trail*, Vol. II (November, 1909), 17–18; George F. Vanderwalker, "Over the Santa Fe Trail in 1864," *The Trail*, II (June, 1909), 16–18.

6 William H. H. Larimer, *Reminiscences of General William Larimer*, 180; Laramie City *Frontier Index* (Wyoming) (June 12, 1868).

practical freighter at least as early as 1850 in partnership with William H. Russell and James Brown, hauling army stores to Santa Fe. The other senior partner was Dr. Joseph L. Cartwright, one of a number of trained physicians who turned to freighting, possibly a more remunerative career. It appears that Cartwright handled the general business while Jones handled the technical end. The company operated largely on negotiable paper of four to six months and, in the turmoil of the Civil War, the company went to the wall.[7]

After Russell, Majors and Waddell went bankrupt, the firm of A. and P. Byram, or Byram Brothers, emerged as a large commercial freighting concern, buying up much of the stock and equipment of the defunct company. Augustus Byram, the older brother, had served Russell, Majors and Waddell as a subcontractor, yardmaster, and confidential agent. According to the census of 1860, his three hundred oxen and three mules were valued at $11,000. He was also a partner in the freighting firm of A. Byram and Poteet. Peter Byram, the younger brother, was an active freighter from about 1852 to 1868, first freighting to El Paso and to Fort Kearny. In 1857 or 1858 he moved to Nebraska City, where he served as wagonmaster and superintendent for the great firm. He was also an incorporator of the Nebraska City, Fort Kearny, and Denver City Freight and Express Company and had an interest in a salt-making company.[8]

It is interesting to note that, prior to about 1862, high plains wagon-freighting was dominated by a "family related group." John S. Jones was a partner in both Jones and Cartwright and Russell, Majors and Waddell. William B. Waddell had married Susan Byram, sister of the Byram brothers.

Many other men who became prominent in high plains wagon-freighting served their apprenticeship with Russell, Majors and Waddell. Eugene Munn started working for them in 1858, at the age of twenty-two. In the latter part of 1864 he went into business for himself. He freighted to Denver and made at least one 1,400-

---

[7] *History of Pettis County, Missouri*, 866–68.
[8] Biographical Notes, NSHS, 407; *Nebraska City News* (Nebraska) (July 16, 1859).

mile trip to Virginia City, Montana. After nine years in the business, with the passing of the hey-day of high plains freighting, he, like many other freighters, turned to farming and was active in Nebraska politics and in insurance.[9]

One of the most colorful, and controversial, figures in the business was Ben Holladay. He started his business education as a clerk in a store at Lexington, Missouri, moving later to Weston, Missouri. At the age of seventeen he made a trip to Santa Fe as stock tender in the train of Bill Sublette. On this trip he got the idea of using wider wheels on the freight wagons to increase their floatation in sand and mud. He bought fourteen wagons, sixty mules, and some horses at an army surplus sale, equipped the wagons with ten- to twelve-inch-wide wheels, and obtained a couple of small army contracts. Using mules instead of oxen because of their greater speed, he set a record for the trip to Santa Fe and was able to make three round trips per year. He also speculated on his own account, making one shipment of 270 chests of tea which he bought for $.28 per pound and sold in New Mexico for $1.50 a pound. Adding to his equipment, Holladay entered into partnership with Theodore W. Warner of Weston and began hauling goods to Salt Lake City as the company of Holladay and Warner. Holladay stayed in the freighting business until at least 1864. In that year he had 15,000 men on his payroll, 20,000 wagons, and 150,000 draft animals—a capacity for hauling 100,000,000 pounds of freight.

It was Holladay who was credited with forcing Russell, Majors and Waddell into bankruptcy. Because of pique over what he considered personal slights at the hands of both Russell and Majors, he nursed a long-standing grudge against both. In 1858 he refused to sell out to the partners; instead, when the big firm began to get into financial trouble, he loaned them large sums until they were deeply in his debt and then called for payment of his notes. After the Civil War, Holladay went on to become one of the greatest stagecoach operators and branched out into river navigation on the West Coast. Henry Villard wrote of Ben Holladay that he was "a genuine speci-

9 *Ibid.* (1869–71), NSHS.

men of the successful Western pioneer of former days, illiterate, coarse, pretentious, boastful, false and cunning."[10]

As might be expected, a number of men who had been engaged in the fur trade, in one way or another, and who had become accustomed to hauling their goods in wagons, entered the freighting business. In 1829, 1832, and 1833, Charles Bent, of the firm of Bent and St. Vrain, was the captain of caravans to Santa Fe. In 1831, Smith, Jackson and Sublette sold out their interest in the fur trade to the Rocky Mountain Fur Company and entered the Santa Fe trade. They sent out a caravan of twenty wagons and eighty men, said to be the finest yet sent to that city. Kit Carson and Thomas Fitzpatrick also captained Santa Fe caravans. In 1863, Bent sold a train of nine wagons to his former wagonmaster, John Prowers, for $10,000.[11]

At times the freighter had to take the law into his own hands. "Uncle Dick" Wootton was much annoyed at every stopover at Fort Union in the 1850's. A gang of petty thieves operating from La Plazarota, about three miles from the post, were victimizing the freighters, and the local authorities were afraid of them. One night, after losing a wagon, "Uncle Dick" took a party of seven men, slipped into the village at night, and abducted a suspect. Riding out some distance, the party held a mock trial and made preparations for a hanging. The suspect begged for his life and was released on his promise to return the wagon and to steal no more. Next morning the missing wagon had been returned. The suspect probably kept his promise for the rest of his life. He was killed in a row at a fandango a few days later.[12]

To a great extent, the freighter and the merchants he dealt with operated on the basis of mutual trust and honesty. As one writer said, "The old-time freighter had the reputation of being honest and dependable. The frontier merchant and the ranchman knew that they could depend upon them to deliver their supplies in good

[10] Ellis Lucia, *The Saga of Ben Holladay*; James V. Frederick, *Ben Holladay, The Stagecoach King*; Frederic L. Paxson, *The Last American Frontier*, 186.

[11] Chittenden, *American Fur Trade*, I, 292; II, 552–53. George Bird Grinnell, "Bent's Old Fort and Its Builders," *Collections*, KSHS, Vol. XV (1923–25), 324–41.

[12] Howard L. Conard, *"Uncle Dick" Wootton*, 356–58.

condition." Some large outfits were bonded and drew written contracts, but the small outfits just gave their word.[13] Typical of the risks run by a freighter was the case of a train that arrived in Virginia City, Montana, from Atchison, Kansas. It was found that the consignee could not pay the freight bill of some $40,000 to $50,000. In order to get their money, the freighters took over the store and ran it until they had earned enough to pay the freight bill. Trouble developed when one of the partners bought additional goods. A fight ensued in which one man was shot and the other jailed. The surviving partner was tried and acquitted and then killed by road agents on the way home. Lewis J. Parry, who freighted from Omaha to Salt Lake City and from Corinne, Utah, to Montana, said: "Our freight was to us almost sacred."[14]

Freighting was an easy business to enter. Anyone who could raise the price of a wagon, a few head of oxen, and enough food for a couple of months could set himself up as a freighter. With luck, a handsome profit could be made. One trip was often enough to return the original investment. Majors reported that, in 1865, he and his associates had at work 300 to 350 wagons that yielded a profit of $300,000.[15] Lyle E. Mantor pointed out that anyone who stayed in the business long enough eventually went bankrupt. It might be added, from the lack of surviving business records, that, having gone bankrupt, these men seem to have used their old records to keep the home fires burning during subsequent winters. An early Colorado pioneer woman remarked that the expression "rich as a freighter" was often heard but that the high rates were justified by the high risks. A contemporary in New Mexico commented, "$10.00 a hundred weight was added for freight. As most things were hauled from Leavenworth this freight rate was not exorbitant."[16] The rates

13 R. D. Holt, "Old Texas Wagon Trains," *Frontier Times*, Vol. XXV (September, 1948), 269–72.
14 *Atchison Daily Globe* (Kansas), Pictorial Historical Edition (July 16, 1894); Jennie B. Brown, *Fort Hall on the Oregon Trail*.
15 *Denver Republican* (Colorado) (January 21, 1900) and *Kansas City Journal* (March 12, 1900), clippings in Dawson Scrapbooks, CSHS.
16 Francis C. Peabody, "Across the Plains DeLuxe in 1865," *Colorado Magazine*,

charged by the freighters became the subject of a joke that appears all up and down the Mountain West. A woman, buying a paper of needles, expostulated over the price. The trader replied, "But Madame [or Señora], the freight!"[17]

It was an easy-entrance and fast-exit sort of business. One owner, when told that raiding Indians had made off with all the mules of a train, laughed, "$40,000 worth of mules gone to the D——l."[18] He could stand this particular loss, but many of them, too close together, spelled ruin.

The capital with which the freighting companies operated appears to have been largely generated in the Missouri Valley. The Butterfield Overland Despatch seems to have been an exception. It was capitalized at $6,000,000, and the president was Chauncey Vibbard of the New York Central Railroad while the treasurer was W. K. Kitchen of the Park Bank of New York City.[19]

A study published in 1952 by Francis W. Gregory and Irene D. Neu, dealing with the social background of the industrial leaders of the United States in the 1870's, depicted the typical leader of the era as one who was native born to a New England family of English descent. He was a conservative Protestant in religion who had been raised in the city in an atmosphere of business and relatively high social standing. He took his first regular job at the age of about eighteen, "prepared to rise from it, moreover, not by a rigorous apprenticeship begun when he was virtually a child, but by an academic education well above average for the times."

Biographical data is sketchy, but the outstanding leaders of high plains wagon-freighting fit the pattern to some extent. The first and most obvious exception was the native-born freighter and trader of New Mexico who was of Spanish or Spanish-Indian descent, Roman

Vol. XVIII (March, 1941), 71; Garnet M. Brayer (ed.), *Land of Enchantment; Memoirs of Marian Russell along the Santa Fe Trail*, 118.

17 J. S. Hoy manuscript, CSHS.

18 "Freighting in 1866," *Proceedings and Collections*, NSHS, 2nd Series, Vol. I (1894–95), 47.

19 George J. Remsburg, "Gleaned from Old Files," *The Trail*, Vol. XIX (July, 1926), 16–17.

Catholic in religion, and whose education probably did not much exceed the three r's.

Among the Anglo-Americans, there is a much closer approximation. The typical boss-freighter was a native-born American of English or Scottish descent. The men of the Missouri border came more from Virginia or Kentucky than from New England. James Josiah Webb of Connecticut, Percival G. Lowe of New Hampshire, and William Hepburn Russell of Vermont are exceptions. The religious affiliation was Protestant, though Baptist rather than the more conservative sects. The family background was predominantly agricultural rather than urban. Most took their first regular jobs at age seventeen or eighteen. Formal schooling was rather spotty: only Dr. David Waldo, government contract freighter; Dr. Henry Connelley, Santa Fe trader; and Dr. Joseph L. Cartwright, all graduates of the Medical School of Transylvania University, seem to have had more than a grade-school education. Even this relatively scant amount of formal schooling was probably sufficient to make these men outstanding on the Missouri frontier of 1830 to 1860. Most of these men extended their learning by serving apprenticeships in some mercantile establishment before entering the field of trading and freighting.

Thomas Jefferson Farnham, who traveled extensively in the West in the 1840's, said, "Owners of the Santa Fe wagons were men who had seen much of life. Urbane and hospitable, they received us in the kindest manner."[20] Regardless of how well these men might have been accepted socially on Beacon Hill or at Newport, they played a vital role in the settlement of the Mountain West and in the development of the Missouri Valley.

The kingpin of the whole freighting operation was the wagonmaster, and quite a man he must have been. He had full responsibility for $18,000 to $30,000 worth of wagons, livestock, and accessories that belonged to someone else, unless he was a small operator who combined the positions of wagonmaster and owner. He had the responsibility for $25,000 to $250,000 worth of goods that did not

[20] *Travels in the Great Western Desert,* 82.

belong to him. On one occasion, Sam Pepin, wagonmaster for the Diamond R in Montana, had his pay docked by $20. He had loaned a company saddle which had never been returned. On another occasion he was charged $50 because someone connected with his train had sold two sacks of sugar from the load. The prevention of petty thievery was a constant problem. The operator of a road ranch near Fort McPherson got his start in life as a bullwhacker hauling government ammunition. He opened boxes and sold the ammunition to ranchmen along the trail. Getting into a quarrel with his wagon boss, he quit before his thievery was detected.[21] The reminiscences of former drivers are full of anecdotes relating the skill and ingenuity of the men in extracting whisky from barrels on their wagons.

The wagonmaster supervised the loading of the wagons, a job requiring considerable skill to combine the weight and bulk of a great number of articles. A sample lot might be tea, coffee, rice, sugar, tobacco, soup, candles, mustard, spices, casks of whisky, boxes of hats, shoes, and ready-made clothes, dressed leather, bags of nails and shot, sheet iron, bar iron, block tin, and stoves of all sizes and shapes. The load had to be distributed so as to keep the center of gravity as low as possible and centered in the wagon bed both longitudinally and laterally. Fragile goods such as mirrors, showcases, and picture frames had to be specially protected.

He had to be a farrier able to shoe oxen and mules and a wheelwright able to repair wagons with the simplest tools. He had to know how to get wagons out of bog holes, up and down steep hills, and across rivers. He had to know where water and grass were to be found for the noon halt and the night camp. He was expected to be a physician to his men and a veterinarian to his animals. He had to be a hunter to provide fresh game as a relief from the usual sowbelly. He had to have the magic ability to be everywhere at one and the same time—riding out a mile or so ahead, scouting for campsites or bad places in the road, watching out for Indians (small wonder they wanted good mounts!), or looking up and down the lines of wagons

21 Diamond R File, MHS; Ware, *Indian War of 1864*, 103.

stretched over a mile or more of prairie. As one wagonmaster said, "It meant pretty hard riding from morning till night."[22] Above all, the wagonmaster was expected to know how to get the best out of both animals and men. Dan Patterson, wagonmaster, was offered a bonus by some Salt Lake merchants if he would get his train to Salt Lake City before the others. Patterson drove his men hard, and because he was drunk a good deal of the time, about eight miles above Fort Laramie, nine drivers, eight Americans and one Englishman, quit.[23]

Great care was usually applied to the selection of a wagonmaster. The man had to be inured to the difficulties, hardships, and dangers of high plains freighting. Nine out of ten started as teamsters and were advanced for faithful service. By the very nature of their job, they had to be strong, brave, and tireless. They had to know how to exact obedience to their commands. On the other hand they were profane, hard drinking, fighting men who could handle a revolver or bowie knife and were "often guilty of barbarous tyranny."[24] One contemporary noted that the good wagonmaster was a great believer in the force of moral suasion and seldom resorted to knockdown personal arguments. Still another remarked, "He had shrewd knowledge of men and their limitations."[25]

Men who could fill all the requirements of a good wagon boss came high. When teamsters were drawing $25 a month, the wagonmaster was being paid $100 per month and found. By 1860 the wagonmaster received $150, his assistant $85, and drivers $70 to $75.

A composite picture of a wagonmaster, drawn from contemporary writings and reminiscences, would show a man about six feet tall, raw boned and powerfully built, with steady eyes, and a face bronzed by long exposure to the elements, scarred by youthful brawls, deco-

---

22 Williams, *With the Border Ruffians*, 105.

23 Frank H. Woody, "How an Early Pioneer Came to Montana," *Contributions*, MHS, Vol. VII (1910), 140–43.

24 "Commerce of the Prairies," *Merchants' Magazine*, Vol. XLIV (January, 1861), 38.

25 Darley, "End Gate of the Mess Wagon," *loc. cit.*, 17–18; William F. Hynes, *Soldiers of the Frontier*, 83.

rated with a drooping moustache, and framed in shoulder-length hair. He wore the usual rough trousers, shirt, and high boots of the frontier, donning a coat only in extremely cold weather. At his belt hung two revolvers and a large knife, Mexican spurs jangled at his heels as he walked, and his head was covered by a broad-brimmed hat or Mexican sombrero. Across the pommel of his saddle, or in a scabbard under his thigh, was a rifle. His customary mount was a good saddle mule, though some preferred horses. William F. Hooker, who worked as a bullwhacker in the 1870's, said that a wagon boss yelled like a Comanche. He had heard the voice of a wagonmaster above those of a train crew at a distance of a mile. Sometimes when a wagon boss lectured a bullwhacker, "he used the same key though not always the same words that he addressed to the bulls, although he might be expressing the same opinion."[26]

An interesting example of the loyalty of a good wagonmaster was related by Alexander Caldwell, concerning his man Tom Atkins. Atkins was taking a train from Fort Leavenworth to Fort Union in the spring of 1861. Most of the teamsters were from the western border of Missouri. On hearing the news of Fort Sumter, the men became restless to return and join the Confederate Army. They planned to seize the train, killing the wagonmaster if he resisted, run it into Texas, sell the contents, and then join the army. All but Atkins, his assistant, and one other were in on the plot. In Raton Pass the plot was broached to Tom, who suggested talking it over in camp that night. After camp was made, the boss got the men together around a fire, away from the wagons and their weapons. Suddenly the wagon boss and his assistant drew their guns on the teamsters while the third man rode to Fort Union for help. The teamsters were taken prisoner by a party of troops, and soldiers were detailed to bring in the wagons. Later, in Caldwell's office, while making his report, Atkins quietly drew his revolver, turned, and covered a man standing in the doorway. It was one of the mutineers, who admitted

---

26 William F. Hooker, "The Freight Train Wagon-Boss of the 1870's," *The Union Pacific Magazine*, Vol. IV (1925), 9–10.

that Atkins had the drop on him but promised to get him eventually. Some time later the wagonmaster met and shot this man and in turn died with his boots on in some Kansas town.[27]

While many of the men of the period said that the wagonmasters came from the cream of frontier society, there is no doubt that, today, most of them would be considered pretty rough characters. Hiram Vasquez and Felix Bridger joined a train for Santa Fe, in order to avoid the Civil War draft. They left the train at Fort Lyons because the wagonmaster, Fred Dodson, used his whip on both animals and men.[28] The *Daily Times* of Leavenworth said, of a report of the flogging of two teamsters by their respective wagonmasters, "If the story is true, hanging is too merciful for such wretches." On the other hand, two teamsters, who had a quarrel with their wagonmaster, enlisted in the army at Fort McPherson and turned out to be completely worthless as soldiers, winding up in the guardhouse for petty thievery.[29]

While the wagon boss had to drive his men, he was not necessarily a heartless brute. One young bullwhacker, who had trouble adjusting to the coarse fare of the plains cuisine, lost weight and became very sick. His boss, Chatham Rennick, nursed him until he had adjusted to the new life. This did not prevent the young man from causing trouble later on for Rennick. Four "Yanks," among them the sick lad, objected to driving on Sundays. When Rennick threatened to fire them, the young man told Rennick that there was "a law in regard to a train boss discharging a man over twenty-five miles from a settlement, and that the Company was responsible for the acts of a train boss." That seems to have settled the matter of driving on Sunday.[30]

As in any large group of men, there are bound to be a few bad ones, and at the height of wagon-freighting on the plains there must

---

27 Caldwell, "Address," *loc. cit.*, 259–60.

28 Hiram Vasquez, "Experiences at Fort Bridger, with the Shoshones and in Early Colorado," *Colorado Magazine*, Vol. VIII (May, 1931), 108.

29 *Daily Times* (August 24, 1859); Ware, *Indian War of 1864*, 89.

30 William Clark, "A Trip Across the Plains in 1857," *Iowa Journal of History and Politics*, Vol. XX (April, 1922), 163–223.

have been several hundred wagonmasters on the road. In 1861 it was reported that the wagonmaster of a government train with $30,000 worth of stores for Fort Buchanan had gone into Sonora, Mexico, taking all the stores with him. A Colorado freighter, five years later, sent out a train of ten wagons with thirty-six mules and four horses and twenty-five wagons with eighty yoke of oxen. After four months, during which he had no word of his train, the owner posted to Nebraska City. There he found the wagonmaster on a full-scale spree and unable to account for wagons or stock. The owner finally located the ox train, less one wagon, but of the mule train there was not a sign.[31]

The most highly publicized and infamous wagonmaster was Joseph Alfred Slade, who ended his life in a noose provided by the Vigilantes of Montana. In 1858, Slade was a wagonmaster of a train of army supplies to Camp Floyd, outside Salt Lake City. Frank A. Root told of a quarrel between Slade and one of his teamsters. Both men drew their revolvers; the driver's gun was cocked, Slade's was not. Slade remarked that their quarrel was not worth a shooting and suggested that they both throw down their guns and settle the matter with their fists. The teamster dropped his gun, whereupon Slade shot him dead and quit the train. Later, as division superintendent for a stage line, Slade did a good job in cleaning out a group of rustlers. Slade's trouble seems to have been strong drink. As time passed he took more and more to the bottle and became more and more rowdy, until Montana could stand no more of him.

Not all the violence was on one side in the quarrels between wagonmasters and their men. "Uncle Dick" Wootton had to shoot it out singlehanded with a group of Mexican bullwhackers who did not like the discipline he imposed. In 1859 a train crew was returning from Denver with a single wagon. The wagonmaster announced that no one would ride in the wagon, it being reserved for the cook and the rations. When a teamster was found in the wagon and the

---

31 Salt Lake City *Deseret News* (Utah) (April 24, 1861); J. L. Donaldson to D. C. Smith, June 23, 1861, Box 1195, RG 92, NA; *Weekly Rocky Mountain News* (February 28, 1866).

wagonmaster tried to drag him out, the teamster drew a knife and killed the wagon boss. The teamster was turned over to the authorities of Nebraska City, who released him, pleading lack of jurisdiction as the murder had taken place on the open plains. The local paper said that the town needed more federal officers so that at least one would be on duty at all times.

Except for the scattered road ranches and the army forts along the trails, the high plains were an empty space five hundred or more miles in width. As the only representative of organized society, it fell to the lot of the army to represent the law. This sometimes brought the army into unhappy contact with the freighters. Captain Eugene Ware reported that the post commander acted as justice of the peace and the post adjutant as public prosecutor. If a wagonmaster wrongfully quarreled with one of his men, the driver quit, and the wagonmaster refused to pay the wages due, the case was referred to the post commander. The commander required payment of the wages in his presence; otherwise, the wagonmaster went into the guardhouse. There was no appeal. If the teamster was in the wrong, he went into the guardhouse for ten days, until the train was well down the road, and then was turned loose to shift for himself.[32]

Occasionally a wagonmaster enforced the ban on swearing and even held church services on Sunday, but most were not that conscientious. As they were expert in running a train, so they were experts in the use of strong language. Captain Ware reported that when a train loaded with telegraph poles for emergency repair of the line to Denver arrived at Fort Sedgewick, after driving day and night from Cottonwood, they were told to rest for two hours and then push on; ". . . the profanity was terrible, especially that of the wagon-boss. His remarks had a sublimity that no unprofessional wagon-boss could hope to excel. He had a collection of compound adjectives that equalled anything I had ever heard."[33]

William Chandless, one of the most perceptive of contemporary

[32] *Indian War of 1864*, 264.
[33] *Ibid.*, 386; Colyer, "Freighting Across the Plains," *loc. cit.*, 6.

82

writers, said of his wagonmaster, Francis Carroll Hughes, that he was American by birth, of Irish ancestry, and had served in the Mexican War; a better man one could not have wished for—always a kind word for the sick and a joke or two for the rest. Hughes' assistant, a man by the name of Duncan, was quiet and undemonstrative but accomplished an incredible amount of work. Duncan had already, in 1855, made two trips to California.

One young man experienced the proudest moment of his life when, after getting his wagon through the Cimarron River unaided, the wagonmaster said, "Say, boy, even if you are from New York, you are some bullwhacker."

Nearly all wagon bosses were good sports at the end of the trail. It was not unusual for one to lead his whole crew into a saloon or dance hall, announcing them as the "best d——d lot of bullwhackers on the Wyoming trails." Bill Hooker reported, " . . . . at least once I saw Nath. Williams line up his men at Tim Dyer's in Cheyenne and inform Dyer that for half an hour he (Nath.) would pay for everything drunk on the premises."[34] This sort of thing probably accounts for some entires in the diary of John Hunton, Williams' boss:

> Sat, Dec 16 [1876]—Trying all day to adjust Nath Williams account and find him nearly five hundred dollars in my debt after allowing him liberal pay for all work. . . .
> Fri, Apr 27 [1877]—Compared accounts with Nath Williams. . . .
> Mon, Apr 30 [1877]—Give Nath Williams 50$ to get rid of him.[35]

A rough, hard-driving lot of men were the wagonmasters, but their final valedictory should be, "They got the job done."

If such a thing were possible, the teamsters were an even more mixed lot of humanity than were the wagonmasters. In one train there were men of "seven distinct nations, each speaking his own native tongue." When Lewis Garrard went to Bent's Fort in 1846, eighteen or twenty of the drivers were Canadian French from St.

---

34 Robert Bruce, *Three Old Plainsmen*, 11; Hooker, "Freight Train Wagon-Boss," *loc. cit.*, 9.
35 L. G. (Pat) Flannery (ed.), *John Hunton's Diary*, Vol. II, 163, 206–207.

Louis; "As I have ever been a lover of sweet, simple music, their beautiful and piquant songs, in the original language, fell most harmoniously on the ear as we lay wrapped in our blankets." It is related that a German boy, who worked his way from Corinne, Utah, to Helena, Montana, left Corinne without a word of English but was fluent by the time he reached Helena. "By listening to the freighter he had learned three phrases the mildest of which would sear the grass within a radius of thirty yards."[36]

Not only various nationalities but also various races were represented. Dan Patterson was a half-blood Cherokee. A half-blood Sioux dry-gulched his wagonmaster for having floored him with a spade during a quarrel. In 1849 an American bullwhacker had the poor judgment to tease one of his fellows, a Shawnee Indian. Finally the Indian shot his tormenter and had to be forcibly restrained from taking his victim's scalp, whereupon he disappeared into the hills around Las Vegas, New Mexico. Jared "Jack" Taylor, who worked for Russell, Majors and Waddell and later for himself, was described as "a huge black man in aspect a typical African, but in heart one of the whitest of men."[37] In 1864, on the McRae train, the first mess was all white, except for the cook, and the second mess was all Negro. Both races showed cool courage in a brush with the Indians some miles west of Fort Larned. About the same time another train was not so fortunate: eight white men and two Negroes were killed by the Indians.[38]

The trains originating in Santa Fe were manned almost exclusively by Mexicans, although some had "Anglo" wagonmasters. One traveler, in 1870, reported that he had taken passage on a Mexican train from Kit Carson to Trinidad, Colorado. The wagon boss, arguing with one of his drivers, knocked him down with the butt of

[36] Lewis H. Garrard, *Wah-to-yah and the Taos Trail*, 11: Bob Fletcher, "Smoke Signals," *Montana*, Vol. I (Summer, 1952), 41–45.

[37] Woody, "Early Pioneer Came to Montana," *loc. cit.*, 138–64; Colyer, "Freighting Across the Plains," *loc. cit.*, 17; Charles I. Jones, "William Kronig, New Mexico Pioneer," *New Mexico Historical Review* [hereinafter referred to as *NMHR*], Vol. XIX (July, 1944), 192; Marie Foster, undated manuscript in files MHS.

[38] William H. Ryus, *The Second William Penn; Treating with Indians on the Santa Fe Trail, 1860–66*; G. Stullken, *My Experiences on the Plains*, 32–33.

his whip. The driver quit, and the traveler took his place as far as Trinidad but refused to go farther.[39]

Chandless related that his train divided into three messes of ten men each. The number-one mess was made up chiefly of professional bullwhackers, all Americans, and it was the most useful, willing, and least quarrelsome, with the least variety of character. "Woodpecker" of this mess could sing a good song or spin a long yarn by the evening fire, making him very popular. The number-two mess was composed mostly of American mechanics, who often squabbled and railed like angry women but were handier at getting a meal and less wolflike in eating.

Number-three mess, Chandless' own, was composed of four Germans (always called Dutchmen), two Irishmen, two Americans, a Mexican, and himself, an Englishman. The Germans soon left; they were too phlegmatic. One of the Irishmen, known as the "Old Man," claimed to have been a wine-bottler in the north of England who had left home because of some trouble with the Excise. He was a man of first-rate pluck, warmhearted, with a jovial face and a sharp but never abusive tongue. The other Irishman, "Mat," had worked as a navvy and steamboat hand, had served in the army and had deserted. He had no education beyond reading and writing but was popular as a singer and storyteller. One of the replacements for the discharged Germans was a Scot who had deserted from a United States warship and who could sing Burns's songs. Landon, who was a doctor's son traveling for adventure, could make a respectable showing as a cook, confectioner, chemist, general practitioner and poisoner, painter, actor, and tailor. He was honest, honorable, and excessively good-natured but exceedingly touchy. "Little Tom" was another Irishman, a graduate of Dublin College, who had quit offices at home and in Boston and since then had been a teamster, a steamboat hand, and a hotel porter. He had been in the United States service and had left in some irregular way. "Nemahaw" was still another Irishman, a deserter from the United States Dragoons.

39 P. G. Scott, "Diary of a Freighting Trip from Kit Carson to Trinidad in 1870," *Colorado Magazine*, Vol. VIII (July, 1931), 146–54.

The train was joined by a Welsh-Piedmontese who had served as interpreter in London police courts and carried with him a violin.[40]

One musically inclined bullwhacker, who played his violin while on night guard, noted that the sound reached some prowling wolves. "The response was certainly tremendous. In a few minutes I had an enthusiastic audience in the not far distance, which might have been regarded as complimentary had it not been quite so demonstrative."[41]

Among the men Chandless met, in camp or along the trail, was a French silversmith and artist who had served seven years in the French Army, four of them in Algeria. He had a deep sense of responsibility and was handy with a musket but looked like a monkey when on horseback. His *camarade*, another Frenchman, was as lazy a man as ever breathed and was fired in a fortnight. There also showed up seven Italians, all Piedmontese, of whom two brothers had had some education and spoke good Italian; apparently Chandless preferred the Tuscan speech.

Among the bullwhackers of another train were William Henry Jackson, later a noted artist and photographer, and Bill Maddern, brother of the famous actress Minnie Maddern. Captain Ware remembered one of a group of teamsters who recited one of Vergil's *Bucolics* from memory. He continued, "As I now look back, the prominent, noticeable, rollicking dare-devils seemed to come principally from Missouri."[42]

Of the "Lords of the Lash," the stage drivers were the elite, and at times they showed their contempt for the lowly bullwhacker by running down the bull teams. The bullwhacker's response was to empty his revolver in the direction of the offending stage and its driver. Next on the social ladder were the muleskinners, who usually drew ten dollars per month more than the bullwhackers and looked down their noses at them. Again the bullwhacker's response was a

40 Chandless, *Visit to Salt Lake City*, 15–55.
41 Birge, *Awaking of the Desert*, 62.
42 Jackson, *Time Exposure*, 127; Ware, *Indian War of 1864*, 103.

resort to firearms.[43] A contemporary writer remembered that almost any boy in town would have swapped his job for that of a mule-skinner, "especially after the four-mule team and one wagon multi-plied into a sixteen-mule team and three wagons in tandem." They knew that not many kings could sit a nigh-wheeler so casually and wheel a juggernaut through the tangle of traffic of a river port.

The lowly bullwhacker also had his defenders:

> Oh! to be a bullwhacker! It meant so much! Think of it! Across the plains and back, camping all the way! . . . If the boy of the East had longings to run away and fight Indians on the Western plains, the Denver boy's ambition lay in the direction of whacking bulls across the plains and back, or, maybe, a trip to Santa Fe.[44]

By modern standards the scale of pay was not high, but a bull-whacker of 1859, who was paid forty dollars per month and his rations, remarked, "Our wages were as high as any paid at that time in the United States" and compared his wages to the eight dollars a month paid to farm help in Michigan.[45] Many young men were seek-ing a means to earn their way to the western gold camps, and freighters took advantage of this situation by paying a bonus of ten dollars per month to any teamster who would take his discharge at the far end, thus reducing the payroll. One freighter, in 1860, got his teamsters for nothing more than their rations on the promise of a Colorado mining company to employ them at the mines "if needed."[46] Such empty wagons as were not sold in the West could be hooked in tandem, three to five to a team, for the return trip.

Usually the potential muleskinner or bullwhacker arrived at the river port with little more than the city clothes he stood up in. The first thing a wagonmaster would do, on hiring a greenhorn, was to

43 James T. Rusling, *Across America or the Great West and the Pacific Coast*, 42; J. H. Beadle, *The Undeveloped West*, 226; *Daily Missouri Democrat* (July 12, 1858).
44 Larry Barsness, *Gold Camp: Alder Gulch and Virginia City, Montana*, 112–13; An Old School Boy, "School Days in Early Denver," *The Trail*, Vol. III (August, 1910), 23–24.
45 Woody, "Early Pioneer Came to Montana," *loc. cit.*, 139.
46 *Nebraska City News* (June 16, 1860).

take him to an outfitting house and oversee the purchase of the rough clothes and boots that were more suited to life on the plains—the cost to be deducted from the man's wages. Some companies required their men to buy their blankets and at least one revolver, which made the cost of an outfit run forty or fifty dollars.[47] Teamsters who ventured onto the plains in the winter were equipped with buffalo-hide overshoes, with the hair on the inside. Other companies issued blankets and firearms. Chandless received a pair of fine, thick, red blankets and at once cut a small corner from each. Soon another man claimed the blankets, but the missing corners easily proved ownership. Later he branded them by rubbing gunpowder into the nap and igniting it. Taking another's blankets was a shame but was not considered a crime as the blankets belonged to the company. The weapons provided were of a variable quality. In 1855, Majors and Russell equipped one of their bullwhackers with an old flintlock musket and required a fifteen-dollar deposit. On the other hand, during the Indian War of 1864, Henry M. Porter of Denver provided his drivers with up-to-date sixteen-shot Winchesters.[48]

Though the life was hard, and at times dangerous, some men grew gray in the service. A trip with one of the Santa Fe trains seemed so attractive that the young men of the border counties of Missouri did not consider their education complete until they had spent a season on the plains. An early Colorado settler who traveled to Denver with her father's wagon train said that many of the men were making one-way trips but others were hardened, faithful plainsmen. The driver of her wagon had made many trips with her father and would have gone through fire and water for him. The papers of the times carry many reports of drivers killed or mangled by being run over by their wagons. Joe Skelton, a Montana freighter, was hooked under the chin by a wild ox which carried him around the corral several times before he was able to lift himself off. He was carried for

---

47 Root and Connelley, *Overland Stage*; George P. Marvin, "Bull-Whacking Days," *Proceedings and Collections*, NSHS, 2nd Series, Vol. V (1902), 228.

48 Alexander Toponce, *Reminiscences of Alexander Toponce, Pioneer*, 24; Henry M. Porter, "Freighting and Merchandising in Early Denver," *Colorado Magazine*, Vol. VI (September, 1929), 172.

five days in a dead-axle wagon to the railhead and then by rail to Salt Lake City. Skelton survived his ordeal and lived for sixteen years on ground-up food fed through a silver tube in his throat.[49]

Many a youngster had to fight to gain acceptance into the fraternity of high plains teamsters. One had a fight forced on him by an older man whom he finally wounded in the thigh with a sheath knife. Thereafter, he set to work to build up his physique by wrestling and running foot races against other teamsters a few years older. Another was jumped while snoozing on night guard. The resulting uproar ended the fight. Next day his assailant refused to come out and fight when openly challenged.[50]

In spite of, or possibly because of, the roughness of the life there was a notable spirit of co-operation and mutual aid among the teamsters. In Salt Lake City three of them tried to free some of their fellows from the city jail in 1858. The attempt resulted in the fatal shooting of the policeman on guard and the arrest of one would-be deliverer. One bullwhacker reported that he suffered a severe attack of rheumatism: "The boys had to lift me on and off the wagon but I could drive all right. I soaked flannel rags in kerosene and wrapped them around my legs and soon got O.K."[51]

The sense of humor of the high plains teamster seems to have been the same broad, practical humor of overstatement that appeared on all the American frontiers. On one occasion, when asked how he managed when the brakes of his wagon broke on a steep mountain slope, a freighter merely said, "We came down as fast as the law of gravity would permit." Sometimes the humor backfired. In November, 1865, near Fort Halleck, a herder found two arrows, stuck them through his hat and coat, and rode into camp hell-for-leather. A party of soldiers was turned out to hunt down the non-existent Indians, and several were severely frostbitten. On learning that it

49 Peabody, "Across the Plains DeLuxe," *loc. cit.*, 76; *Daily Times* (July 20, 1864); *Fort Benton Record* (Montana) (September 29, 1876); Brown, *Fort Hall*, 350.
50 Wiley Britton, "Pioneer Life," *MHR*, Vol. XVI (July, 1922), 570–71; Thaddeus S. Kenderdine, *California Revisited*, 31.
51 *Deseret News* (October 13, 20, 1858); T. H. McGee, "Early Days in the West," *Quarterly Bulletin of the Wyoming Historical Department*, Vol. I (April, 1924), 13–16.

was all a joke, the commanding officer arrested the herder and the wagonmaster. The delay resulted in the train's being wintered in on the plains and losing all its stock and ultimately in the financial ruin of the owner.[52]

Majors' anti-profanity program was made sport of in a favorite song:

> I'll tell you how it is when
>   You first get on the road;
> You have an awkward team and
>   A very heavy load.
> You have to whip and holler, but
>   Swear upon the sly.
> You're in for it then, boys,
>   Root hog or die.

Apparently it was only in the actual presence of the big bosses that the men watched their tongues. On one occasion Waddell was watching the fruitless efforts of one of his bullwhackers to extricate a wagon from a mudhole. Finally, the veteran bullwhacker said:

Boss, the trouble with them oxens is that they don't understand the kind of language we're talkin' to 'em. Plain "Gee" and "Haw" ain't enough under the present circumstances. Now, if you could just find it convenient to go off on that thar hill, somewhere, so's you couldn't hear what was goin' on, I'd undertake to get them oxens out.

Waddell moved away and soon the wagon was free.[53]

Since many of the teamsters were young farmers or villagers from the western and southern states and many were immigrants, their manners and habits often left something to be desired. Lieutenant J. W. Abert, who was recovering from a serious illness at Bent's Fort in 1846, reported that the teamsters of a supply train swarmed into the patio, "and from thence commenced a minute scrutiny of every

[52] Grace R. Hebard, *Washakie, An Account of Indian Resistance*, 156; William L. Kuykendall, *Frontier Days*, 87.

[53] Dick, *Vanguards of the Frontier*, 356; Paul I. Wellman, "The Silent Partner," clipping, scrapbook, Leavenworth Public Library.

object around them, greatly to our annoyance, and unfavorable to their character for politeness." Personal cleanliness was a matter that was conditioned by one's own ideas and the availability of water. Some bathed whenever the occasion offered and were upset when they found themselves infested with "Graybacks." Others did not consider themselves complete plainsmen until their clothing was crawling with lice. A traveler reported that "the hand that piled up the dung for the fire and lit it was soon up to the wrists in the dough for the 'cakes.' "[54]

The whip was the teamster's badge of office. The muleskinner from his post astride the nigh-wheeler, with the top of the wagon close behind him, was restricted to a "blacksnake" some eight to ten feet in length. The bullwhacker from his post on the ground alongside the nigh-wheeler had room in which to swing a more magnificent instrument—a three- to four-foot stock of hickory or other tough wood, and an eighteen- to twenty-foot lash of braided rawhide, tipped with a six- or eight-inch popper of rawhide. Properly wielded, it could slash through the hide of the oldest ox, but was seldom so used. The pistol-like crack of the whip plus the oaths of the driver were usually enough to withdraw the animal from a peaceful contemplation of its cud to the business at hand. Only when a wagon had to be jerked to the top of a hill, without double-teaming or dropping the trailer, was the whip applied to the tender underparts of the ox's belly. Many teamsters boasted of having driven to Santa Fe and back without "cutting the blood" from any ox.

For the greenhorn, the whip was just one more source of trouble, constantly landing where it was not wanted, generally around the wielder's neck. One novice managed to encircle the waist of a woman driving by in an open buggy. Her scream scared her horse, which bolted, adding to the general confusion. In the hands of an expert, the bullwhip became an instrument of precision. A favorite pastime was cutting a coin from the top of a stake, driven loosely into the ground, without knocking over the stake. *Harper's* correspondent

---

54 J. S. Hoy manuscript, CSHS; Jackson, *Time Exposure*, 118; P. G. Scott, "Pioneer Experiences in Southern Colorado," *Colorado Magazine*, Vol. IX (January, 1932), 21–25.

reported a wager of a pint of whisky between two bullwhackers. One contended that, if his friend would bend over, he could cut the seat out of his pants without disturbing the flesh underneath. On putting it to trial, both men lost.[55]

A composite picture of a bullwhacker or muleskinner would not be very different from that of a wagonmaster. General James T. Rusling described them as "Outré, red-shirted, big-booted, brigand-looking ruffians, with the inseparable bowie-knife and revolver buckled around their waists, they swung and cracked their great whips like fiends, and beat their poor oxen along." The correspondent for *Harper's* painted him as a well-built, heavily tanned individual, "his hirsute and un-clean appearance indicating a cat-like aversion to water, he is more profane than the mate of a Mississippi river packet, and, we have his word for it, 'Ken drink more whiskey.' "[56]

On the other hand, another observer noted that the bullwhacker was without fear of Indians, able to stand any hardship, and generally of fine physique, "a vigorous, rollicking, devil-me-care look about him, which makes him a handsome specimen of manhood" with a magnificent beard and moustache; he was a man who made fine company when not shooting, if you could put up with some hard swearing. A British visitor noted that the conversation of some muleskinners was above expectations. Nearly all were literate and "all discussed local and national politics with a terseness and emphasis that would do credit to a professional politician."[57]

As it was with the sailors of the clipper ships, so it was with the sailors of the prairie schooners: the arrival in port was a great event. As trains approached the Missouri Valley towns, they were met, some eight to ten miles out, by runners for various hotels, stores, and saloons. Often thirty full suits were sold over one counter in an evening. After the new clothes, and presumably a bath, came the

[55] Scott, "Pioneer Experiences," *loc. cit.*, 21–25; "A Stage Ride to Colorado," *Harper's Magazine*, Vol. XXXV (July, 1867), 137–50.

[56] Rusling, *Across America*, 237; "Stage Ride to Colorado," *loc. cit.*, 138.

[57] John White, *Sketches from America*, 259; Paul F. Sharp, *Whoop-up Country*, 193.

relaxation. In Miles City, Montana, it was once noted that the town was unusually lively due to the presence of the "festive bull-whacker" who patronized heavily the "Hurdy Gurdy" or "Dance House" where he was easily cleaned out by the "girls." Meanwhile, the Old Man, the proprietor, had to wait until his men were broke before starting out on another trip.[58]

It is interesting to note that most of the derogatory remarks came from people whose contact with the teamsters was slight, such as General Rusling and *Harper's* correspondent, and Francis Parkman, fresh out of Boston, who referred to "Raw, smock-faced boys, and of sickly appearance." Richard Burton, who dashed by in a stagecoach in 1860, said, "I scarcely ever saw a sober driver." Those whose contact was closer, and who understood the conditions, generally held a higher opinion. One bullwhacker who in later life became a minister admitted that his crew was a varied lot which furnished some "droll characters," but in general they were "clever, good-natured, plucky, inclined to pull together. Occasionally we found a crooked stick, a weakling or a man with more cussedness in him than good qualities." He went on to say, "Men unaccustomed to frontier life are incompetant to judge the actions of men whose early manhood was spent amid scenes that differ so widely from all that surrounds us now."[59]

Hard as the life of the high plains freighter was, the business was not an entirely male occupation. In 1860 the *Rocky Mountain News* of Denver reported that a lady had gone into the business of freighting from Nebraska City to Denver with a train of five wagons which she owned and managed herself. "She received the freight, hired the hands, and bossed the loading of the wagons. She is said to be well posted in the business."[60]

Regardless of one's opinion of the men involved, as individuals, the high plains wagon-freighter played a vital role in the develop-

---

58 W. W. Cox, "Reminiscences of Early Days in Nebraska," *Transactions and Reports*, NSHS, 1st Series, Vol. V (1893), 76; "Bullwhackers," *Montana*, Vol. III (Autumn, 1952), 31.

59 Darley, "End-Gate of the Mess Wagon," *loc. cit.*, 17–18.

60 *Rocky Mountain News* (December 12, 1866).

ment of the Mountain West. He provided a means by which a young man, without the price of his own outfit or a ticket on a stagecoach, could travel across the plains. He hauled the necessities and luxuries of life to settlements otherwise completely isolated. He freighted out the machinery—sawmills, mining machinery, textile- and paper-making machinery, all essentials to start a community toward self-sufficiency.

CHAPTER V

HORNS, HOOFS, AND WHEELS

There was little standardization of equipment among the freighters of the high plains. The availability of material, the requirements of local markets, and the whim of the individual had more effect than theories of efficiency.

There is today a certain amount of discussion among antiquarians as to whether the "Santa Fe" or "J. Murphy" wagon, commonly used by the high plains freighter, was an entirely new wagon, designed for the Santa Fe trade, or merely a modification of the older Conestoga wagon. The Conestoga was used in freighting on the National Road and was itself an adaption of the heavy wagon common in Germany in the eighteenth century. The Conestoga had certain peculiarities of construction that made it distinctive in appearance. The floor of the wagon was built so that it was higher in front and back than in the middle, and the ends sloped outward at the top. This gave the whole wagon bed a boatlike outline that led to the nicknames of "Pitt Schooner," "Pike Schooner," and later "Prairie Schooner." The shape of the bed was deliberate, as it prevented, to some extent, shifting of the load on up- and downgrades.

The wagons used in high plains freighting varied greatly in size and appearance. Those used by Captain Becknell in 1822 were described only as being "ordinary farm wagons," and those used two years later by Marmaduke as "road wagons" and "dearborns." The first wagon in common use in the Santa Fe trade, probably Marmaduke's "road wagon," had a bed twelve feet in length, three and one-half feet in width, two and one-half feet in depth, and carried a load of approximately one thousand pounds.[1] The dearborn was smaller, drawn by two or four mules, with a front seat for the driver, and equipped with bows and a cloth cover, with or without side curtains. It was used extensively as a passenger or mess vehicle and probably carried a payload of about five hundred pounds. On this basis, Marmaduke's caravan of three road wagons and twenty dearborns would have had a capacity of thirteen thousand pounds, a small figure when compared to the capacity of later wagon trains.

When Governor Manuel Armijo of New Mexico, in 1839, imposed an arbitrary import duty of $500 per wagon, regardless of the value of the contents, the immediate response of the American traders was a larger wagon. In St. Louis there lived just the man who could meet the new requirement. Joseph Murphy had been a wagon-builder for fourteen years, and in 1841 had opened his own shop. His new wagon came as close as any to becoming the standard wagon of the high plains freighter. For its time it was a monster of a wagon: the bed was sixteen feet in length and six feet in height, and the rear wheels were seven feet in diameter. At first the wheels were not equipped with iron tires because they could not be obtained.[2]

The production of large iron tires presented a technological problem that took some time for the blacksmiths to solve. When Ben Holladay went to Santa Fe in the 1830's, he noticed how the narrow wheels then in use cut through the prairie sod or sank in the loose sand of the river bottoms. Concluding that wider wheels would provide better floatation, he experimented with wheels from ten to twelve inches wide. Since the wheels were dished to give additional strength against sideways thrust, with the rim bearing flat on the ground, the tire had to be a section of a truncated cone. With narrow wheels, exactness of shape was not too important, but when wheels from four to eight inches wide were used, an exact fit became vital. Despite the mockery of his contemporaries, Ben Holladay's

---

[1] Edwin C. McReynolds, *Missouri: A History of the Crossroads State*, 100.

[2] Emily A. O. Bott, "Joseph Murphy's Contribution to the Development of the West," *MHR*, Vol. XLVII (October, 1952), 22.

wide-wheeled wagons, drawn by fast-traveling mules, broke all records for the Santa Fe trip, making three round trips in one season. These wagons were probably built by Murphy and carried five tons each.

Prior to 1845 most wagons used on the plains were built in Pittsburgh and shipped to the Missouri River ports by steamer. In that year there were seven wagonwrights in Independence; Murphy was located at St. Louis, and in 1859, Louis Espenschied was making wagons in the same city. The Studebaker wagon did not appear in quantity until after the Civil War and was generally smaller than the big freighter. The Schlutter wagon was built in Jackson, Michigan, to take advantage of convict labor at fifty cents per day, at the same time that John Studebaker was paying twelve dollars a week to his skilled labor.[3]

One reason for the wide acceptance of the "J. Murphy" wagon was that its maker was a painstaking master craftsman. Only the best selected, seasoned woods were used. All holes were bored with a hot iron, rather than with an auger, and were drilled one size smaller than the bolt they were to take. The boring with a hot iron prevented cracking or rotting around the bolt, and the small size of the hole assured a tight fit.

When Russell, Majors and Waddell received the contract to freight supplies for General Albert Sidney Johnston's army to Utah, the demand for wagons apparently outran the supply of seasoned timber. Out of twenty-six wagons in their train number 54, only four made it all the way through, even by removing the wheels at the noon halt and soaking them in the river. The only way the train was able to deliver its load was by exchanging wagons with returning empty trains. It was noted that many of these wagons had been built in the East and shipped to Kansas via New Orleans.[4]

In the early days of freighting to Salt Lake Valley, it was thought

---

[3] H. David Condron, "Knapheide Wagon Company; 1848–1943," *Journal of Economic History*, Vol. III (May, 1943), 35; Lloyd Espenschied, "Louis Espenschied and His Family," *Bulletin*, Missouri Historical Society, Vol. XVIII (January, 1962), 89: Stephen Longstreet, *A Century on Wheels: The Story of Studebaker, 1852–1952*, 39.

[4] Thaddeus S. Kenderdine, *A California Tramp*, 35, 38.

that a round trip could not be made in one season. There was in addition a great demand in the valley for wagons that were adaptable to farm use. As a result, the Salt Lake freighters used the "Chicago" wagon with a bed twelve feet in length, three and one-half feet in width, and eighteen inches in depth, and a carrying capacity of twenty-five hundred to thirty-five hundred pounds, usually drawn by three yoke of oxen. On arriving in Salt Lake City, the freighters sold the wagons, all accessories, and the draft animals. A wagon that cost $120 in the States brought $500 in Salt Lake City. On the other hand, the trail-worn cattle sold at a heavy discount.[5]

During the great period of high plains freighting there were a number of technical improvements in the wagons. As a result of experience gained on the trek to California, the rigid tongue was replaced by one that pivoted, allowing vertical movement for negotiating the short, steep banks of prairie arroyos.

Until the late 1850's or early 1860's, braking on downslopes was accomplished by a number of devices. One was a "rough lock" brake, or hook, attached to the body by a chain, which was placed around one of the spokes of a rear wheel to prevent its turning. Another device was the "drag" or "shoe" brake—a metal skid, also attached to the body by a chain, that was placed under a rear wheel, sometimes equipped with a stud to dig into the soil. To increase the drag of a braked wheel, the rim was sometimes wrapped with a log chain. The "Mormon" brake was a log chained under the wagon bed in such a way as to lift one or both rear wheels off the ground. Eventually rough locks and drags were replaced by lever-operated friction brakes.[6]

In the early days, the bearing surface of the hub was made of several straps of iron running lengthwise on the hub. This so-called strap skein was replaced by the thimble skein, a cast-iron cup that was slipped over the end of the wooden axle. Regardless of the type

[5] George L. Strebel, "Freighting Between the Missouri River and Utah, 1847–1869," M.A. Thesis, Brigham Young University (1954); *Deseret News* (July 11, 1860; September 25, 1861).

[6] Nick Eggenhofer, *Wagons, Mules, and Men*, 42–55.

of skein, because of blowing sand and dust, the wheels had to be greased daily with a mixture of tar, resin, and tallow. Louis Espenschied of St. Louis patented a self-greasing axle, but it is not known whether this invention was adopted by the freighters.[7]

About 1845 the first iron wagon axle appeared. Solomon Houck of Westport, a Santa Fe trader, bought two new wagons with iron axles, and Josiah Webb, despite some misgivings about what might happen if an axle broke or became badly sprung out on the plains, bought one of them. He remarked, "This, I believe, was the first freight wagon with iron axles that ever went over plains. . . . Gradually they came into use for the Santa Fe trade, but not for the low country [Mexico?]."[8] Webb's first wagon for the Santa Fe trade cost him $100.00. Between 1840 and 1850, Murphy contracted to build eight wagons for "P. M. Chowteau" of Kansas City for an average price of $130.25. Another entry in his account book reads, "Richard Owens—Santafee trader—large ox wagon $130." By 1860 a large wagon cost from $800 to $1,500.[9]

The cost of wagon repairs was in line with the initial cost. The account book of a wagon-repair shop in Independence shows the following entries made in 1852:

October 10	1 tongue	$1.00
October 15	1 tongue	1.00
	1 fellow [*sic*]	.25
October 31	To riming [*sic*] & spoking 2 f wheels	5.00
November 8	for repairing wagon	6.00

Most wagons, especially those built in a hurry when the demand was high, suffered a common complaint, particularly on reaching the dry, high plains west of Fort Laramie: shrinkage of the wood. This occurred most frequently in the wheels, causing the tires to fall off. When a blacksmith shop was available, as at Fort Laramie, the tires could be cut, shortened, and reset. In 1863 the charge for

[7] Espenschied, "Louis Espenschied," *loc. cit.*, 87–103.

[8] James J. Webb, *Adventures in the Santa Fe Trade*, 129–30.

[9] Bott, "Joseph Murphy," *loc. cit.*, 21.

this service was two dollars a wheel.[10] Usually Yankee ingenuity had to devise a repair. The simplest procedure was to remove the wheels at night, or during the noon halt, and soak them in the river, but at times there was not enough water. An alternative was to drive wedges between the tire and the felly, but this had to be done carefully to avoid distorting the tire. A repair that lasted longer than either of these was to wrap the rim with cloth or green buffalo hide, expand the tire with fire, slip it in place, and then hastily quench the tire with water, before the hot iron could burn the canvas or hide. In one case, when a wagon train was smashed in a stampede and after all possible repairs had been made, it was found that one wagon was short a rear wheel. The missing wheel was replaced by a travois-like skid, part of the load was redistributed, and, by renewing the skid from time to time, the wagon reached Santa Fe.

The standard accessories for a freight wagon consisted of six or eight bows, a pair of wagon covers of osnaburg (a heavy, coarse linen cloth), a couple of water kegs, a tar bucket, a long box that hung on the rear and served as a fuel container on the trail and as a feed trough in camp, and a gunny sack for collecting buffalo chips. The Santa Fe traders found that two sheets of osnaburg gave better protection for the cargo than a single thickness. As several yoke of oxen were used for each wagon, heavy chains were needed to hitch them to the wagon. The oxen of the wheel yoke—those nearest the wagon—were placed on either side of the tongue, and the end of the tongue was attached to their yoke. The other pairs were connected by chains running from yoke to yoke and then to the end of the wagon tongue.

In order to reduce the size of their payrolls, by the late 1860s, freighters were adopting the practice of hooking two or more wagons in tandem. This resulted in a modification of the wagon; the overhang at front and rear had to be eliminated. The tongue of the wagon that was to be towed was shortened and adapted for attachment to the rear end of the reach pole of the lead wagon. Wagons so

[10] Account Book, Old Jail Museum, Independence, Missouri; Col. Samuel Ward, "Diary of Colonel Samuel Ward," *Contributions*, MHS, Vol. VIII (1917), 37–92.

hitched together were not uniformly loaded and were designated by the diameter of their skeins (the bearing surface of the hub). A "4-inch wagon," the lead wagon, carried 6,500 pounds; a "3½-inch wagon," the swing or center wagon, carried 5,500 pounds; and a "3-incher," the trail wagon, took a load of 4,500 pounds.

The opening of the western mines and the need to haul heavy machinery to them led to the development of special wagons for this work. In 1865 a letter from the Michigan Wagon Depot of St. Joseph, Missouri, to B. M. Hayes advised that the wagons furnished a year earlier at $125 were desirable only for machinery or other heavy loading; they "would not be Saleable for ordinary freighting purposes they are Stronger and more Serviceable than a wide track wagon."[11]

William Chandless remarked that as long as the wagon covers were clean and the red and blue paint of the woodwork was untarnished, a train of forty wagons, with its drivers decked out in red or blue shirts, "made really a brave show as it stretched over a mile of road." The drivers often expressed their own ideas by naming their wagons and painting the name on the wagon bed. In one train the following names were noted: Constitution, President, Great Republic, King of Bavaria, Lola Montes, Louis Napoleon, Dan O'Connell, Old Kaintuck, and many more.[12]

One man with freighting experience summed up the prairie schooner when he said that they were large clumsy wagons of 6,500-pound capacity. They were so heavily built that it was impossible to overload them or for them to break down on the trail where there were no repair shops.[13]

It is true that the importance of the horse increased as the white man emerged from the eastern forests onto the western plains. The greater distances enhanced its value as an individual mount, but as a heavy draft animal, the horse was overshadowed by the mule and the ox.

[11] Letter, Michigan Wagon Depot, St. Joseph, Missouri, to B. M. Hayes, June 26, 1865, Teller Papers, University of Colorado Libraries.
[12] Pierre Jean deSmet, *New Indian Sketches*, 79.
[13] Stullken, *My Experiences on the Plains*, 9.

Practically all the wagon-freighting east of the Mississippi was done with the famous four-horse and six-horse "bell" teams. In general, the roads were improved, forage and water were readily available, and shelter could be found every few miles along the way. Under these conditions, the big, heavy, grain-fed Conestoga horse performed excellently.

In the West, conditions were radically different. The fur trappers and early freighters used horses as pack and draft animals, but it was soon discovered that they were too delicate for sustained, hard work. Cowboys and Indians who relied on horses for their livelihood worked strings of at least six or eight mounts. The horse could not keep up its strength over a long period of time on a diet of nothing but buffalo grass, and grain was not readily available. Horses were subject to a number of diseases that did not bother other draft animals, and they could not withstand the rigors of prairie heat, cold, and dust. Above all, horses always attracted the unwelcome attention of wandering bands of Indians.

Mules were better adapted to heavy work, scanty forage, and the climatic conditions of high plains freighting. Prior to the mid-1820's they were uncommon in the United States, but after the Santa Fe trade had been in operation for a few years, their availability increased greatly. In 1825 over 600 mules and asses were brought back from Santa Fe, two years later the figure had grown to 800, and by 1832 it had reached 1,300.

Mules were expensive, and as their popularity grew, so did their cost. In 1832 they could be bought in Mexico for $19 each. Nine years later, in Missouri, they cost from $200 to $400 per span. Only the United States government and the wealthier freighters who wanted to make fast trips could afford mules.[14] In addition to an initial heavy investment for a team, the equipment was expensive. Mules required a rather complex leather harness that, about 1850,

14 Lawrence L. Waldo, Chihuahua, to David Waldo, January 14, 1832, Waldo Papers, Jackson County Historical Society, Independence, Missouri; John Ashton, "History of Jack Stock and Mules in Missouri," *Monthly Bulletin*, Missouri State Board of Agriculture, Vol. XXII (August, 1924).

cost $100 per wagon. With vehicles at $100 each, ten mules at $100 apiece, harness $100, and accessories about $25, the cost of a twenty-team train, the smallest that would be secure on the plains, was about $25,000. With wages, a Chihuahua train accounted for some $29,000 at the end of the first month. In the ten years after 1859, prices advanced sharply; wagons cost from $800 to $1,500, mules from $500 to $1,000 per span, harness from $300 to $600 for a ten-mule team. The total for one wagon and team ranged from $3,600 to $7,000.

Of the three major classes of draft animals used on the plains—horse, mule, and ox—the mule had the longest average working life, about eighteen years. However, the *Journal of Commerce*, in 1860, said that a mule was just attaining his full strength at twelve years, when a horse was beginning to deteriorate, and that the average working life was thirty years. The paper continued by remarking that a mule could do as much work as a horse on one-third less food, that they were subject to fewer diseases, and that their tough hide and short hair made them more resistant to saddle and harness sores.[15]

The average freighter could not afford the time to gentle his animals slowly before introducing them to harness; as a result, the breaking of wild mules was a rough process that sometimes ended in the loss of expensive animals. The unbroken mules were roped, snubbed up close to the wagon wheels, and starved for twenty-four hours. Then a team was hitched to a heavy wagon and whipped when they would not pull and whipped even harder when they ran. After an hour or so of bewilderment, plunging, and kicking they became tractable and were ready for work. One freighter used to hitch his wild mules to an old stagecoach and give his thrill-seeking friends a wild ride around a near-by race track.[16]

Mules, like horses, would stampede at the least excuse. On one

[15] U. S. Department of Agriculture, Agricultural Research Service, Animal Husbandry Division, to author, February 27, 1962; *Journal of Commerce* (June 20, 1860).
[16] Garrard, *Wah-to-yah*, 11; Porter, "Freighting and Merchandising," *loc. cit.*, 171–73.

occasion a team bolted when the driver's hat blew off and landed among the mules' feet. When one team went, the whole train went with them. On another occasion a whole train stampeded when a group of travelers, carpetbags in hand, ran toward them. In the ensuing melee, one driver was killed. As often happened, once horses or mules were "spooked," a second stampede followed almost at once. This time a driver had his collarbone broken. A third stampede was reported in this same train, with the death of another driver. It was remarked that the operation would be an expensive one until the mules were thoroughly broken.[17] Percival G. Lowe, who, as a government wagonmaster and a private freighter, had extensive experience with mules, said that, while easily stampeded, they calmed down after a short run, whereas horses would run until exhausted. Another freighter noted that mules tended to circle back toward camp. The first few nights on the trail were always the most critical as surroundings and conditions were always new. Until they became accustomed to trail life and to looking on the wagon train as home, any animal that got loose was apt to take the back trail for its former home.

In selecting a team, there were a number of well-established rules. The largest pair, or span, was selected for the wheelers. This was the span that controlled the direction of the wagon through the wagon tongue and held back the wagon on downgrades. The nimblest and most knowledgeable span were selected for the leaders. It was they who imparted direction to the whole team. On sharp turns, they often had to leave the trail to swing wide and scramble over rocks and bushes. The nigh, or left, leader had to be particularly smart as it was he that received orders from the driver by means of the jerk line and determined the direction for the whole team.[18]

Because of the overhang at the front of the old Conestoga wagon, a team could not be properly handled from a seat on the wagon. As a result, the driver rode the nigh-wheeler. From the driver a single

[17] Charles Raber, "Personal Recollections of Life on the Plains from 1860–1868," *Collections*, KSHS, Vol. XVI (1923–25), 317; *Daily Times* (August 16, 20, 1861).

[18] Mark Trey, "Jerk Line Jockey," *True West*, Vol. V (May-June, 1958), 22–23, 40–42.

line ran forward, through the harness rings of the swing teams, to
the left end of the bit of the nigh-leader. A long, steady pull brought
the nigh-leader to the left; a series of short, sharp jerks caused him
to throw his head up and to the right, to avoid the pain of the bit,
and therefore he would turn to the right. The off, or right, leader
was connected to his span mate by a jockey stick, a piece of wood
about the size of a broom handle that was attached to the collar of
the nigh mule and to the right end of the bit of the off mule. When
the nigh-leader changed direction he pushed or pulled his companion in the same direction. One old-timer complained that modern
pictures showed all mules with bridles (with bits) whereas actually
only the leaders and wheelers wore bridles, halters being sufficient
for the rest of the team. As wagon-freighting came later to the
mining camps in the mountains, the swing teams—those between
the leaders and wheelers—had to learn to jump the chain to the
outside on sharp turns. They had to pull outward on a diagonal
to keep the chain taut and apply some pull to the wagon.[19]

One close observer of the mule noted:

> The mule is the only animal that Noah didn't take into the
> Ark. . . . the mule can be considered in a good many ways, though
> the worst place from which to consider him is directly from be-
> hind—anywhere within a radius of ten feet. . . . he can stand on one
> [leg] and wave the other three in as many different directions. . . .
> He has no more taste than a stone jug, and will eat anything that
> contains nutriment. . . . To fully appreciate a mule, one should
> listen to his voice. You never can really know whether you will like
> music or not until you have heard him sing. . . . he is surefooted,
> especially with his hind feet. . . . If I had my choice, to either work in
> a nitro-glycerine factory or to take care of a mule, I should go for
> the factory.[20]

The rivalry that naturally arose between bullwhackers and mule
skinners led to unfavorable opinions of the other's animals. As one

[19] Marion Beckler, "He Could Crack a Bull-Whip," *Desert Magazine*, Vol. XIII
(August, 1950), 27–29; H. A. Hoover, *Early Days in the Mogollons*, 28.
[20] *Benton Record* (Montana) (September 7, 1877).

old bullwhacker remarked: "Think of adopten [sic] a mule into your family. The nearest I ever come of tryin it was after I was married when I took my mother-in-law to live with me."[21] Certainly there must have been grounds for the myriad of tales, tall and otherwise, that involve the mule, "without pride of ancestry or hope of progeny," as the central character.

The ox was introduced to high plains freighting by Major Bennett Riley of the United States Army in 1829. Because of troubles with the Plains Indians in the previous year, Riley was ordered out with four companies of the Sixth Infantry to escort the annual caravan of the Santa Fe traders to the crossing of the Arkansas River, then the international boundary. Riley reasoned that if he used oxen, instead of horses or mules, they could graze for their subsistence and so reduce the amount of forage that would have to be carried. In addition, as the loads were reduced, the oxen could be used as a source of beef for the troops. On reaching the Arkansas, Riley loaned one yoke of his oxen to William Bent, who wanted to experiment with them over the whole route. On returning to the river from Santa Fe, Bent reported that the oxen had performed well all the way. Riley's only comment was that the animals' feet became tender from so much walking.[22]

In the following year Charles Bent took an ox-powered team to Santa Fe. Thomas Forsyth, writing from St. Louis, said that if Bent succeeded with his teams, the animals would serve three purposes: "1st, drawing the wagons; 2nd, the Indians will not steal them as they would horses and mules; and 3rdly, in cases of necessity part of the oxen will answer for provisions."[23]

Besides the advantages enumerated by Forsyth, oxen had certain other advantages. For one thing, they were considerably cheaper than horses or mules. In 1844 oxen cost $28.00 per yoke; the price fell two years later to $21.67. In 1866, when mules cost from $200.00

21 Sam P. Ridings, The Chisholm Trail, 399–400.
22 Bennett Riley to Leavenworth, October 24, 1829, 74-R-1829; Journal of Maj. Riley—Santa Fe Trail in 1829, NA.
23 Thomas Forsyth to Lewis Cass, October 24, 1831, Appendix E; Chittenden, American Fur Trade, II, 936.

to $400.00 a span, working cattle were selling for $75.00 to $145.00 per yoke, and unbroken steers for $100.00 to $120.00 per yoke. One exceptionally fine yoke of oxen sold, in 1864, for $219.00. They weighed 4,300 pounds each but were not fat, were a full eighteen hands (six feet) tall, five feet, ten inches long, and eight feet around the girth.[24]

The oxen were not, in general, the massive beasts bred in the northeast but were range cattle from Texas or the Cherokee country. While they should be large and at least four years old for best performance, they actually varied greatly. One man said that they were "of every character and description—some of them very small, but having horns of such immense size, that we boys used to say that the meat of the steer could be packed in his horns."[25] According to a merchant of Nebraska City who had done some freighting, the Texas steer made the best leader; quick on his feet, he could, and at times did, outrun a horse. Horace Greeley described the oxen that he saw in the Russell, Majors and Waddell corrals at Leavenworth as "lean, wild looking oxen (mainly of the long-horned stripe, which indicated Texas as their native land, and which had probably first felt the yoke within the past week)."[26]

The harness equipment for oxen was much cheaper than that for mules. A yoke of pine, or other light wood, a pair of hickory bows that passed under the ox's neck, and metal keys or wooden pins to hold the bows in the yoke were all that were needed. The yoke had an iron ring hanging from the center to which was attached the tongue of the wagon or the draw chain. It was the American custom to place the yoke on the neck of the oxen so that the hump of the shoulders gave a full purchase against the yoke. The Spaniards and Mexicans lashed the yoke to the horns of the oxen. This tended to lift the animal's head, preventing a full thrust with its weight.

In mud or sand the cloven hoof of the ox gave a better purchase

24 Webb, *Adventures in the Santa Fe Trade*, 46; *Journal of Commerce* (March 2, 1860); *Omaha Daily Republican* (May 17, 26, 1866).

25 T. C. Hall, "Personal Recollections of the Santa Fe Trail," *Kansas Magazine*, Vol. V (January, 1911), 50.

26 Rolfe, "Overland Freighting Business," *loc. cit.*; Greeley, *Overland Journey*, 23.

for heavy pulling than the small hoof of the mule. About the mid-century another advantage of the ox was discovered. It was found that he could be wintered on the free grass of the western ranges and would fatten in the process. This discovery is attributed to different people by different authors. It is pretty well established that one of the early discoveries came in the winter of 1854–55 when an ox train was wintered in on the Laramie Plains. The oxen were turned loose to die, but when they were found in the spring, they were in better condition than they had been when turned out in the fall. Alexander Majors made it a regular practice to winter much of his stock on the Laramie Plains or along the Chugwater River in central Wyoming. The loss averaged only about one-half of one per cent. John Wesley Iliff of Denver is credited with being an early discoverer of the food value of range grass when, about 1860, he began buying up footsore cattle as they came off the plains, putting them on the range for a few months, and then selling them to the local abatoir.[27]

There soon developed a trade in cattle that was an offshoot of high plains freighting. Ben Holladay, in 1850, bought up a good-sized herd of cattle in the Salt Lake Valley and drove them to California where he sold them at a good profit. Nine years later Russell, Majors and Waddell suffered a heavy loss when they tried to drive 3,500 head of oxen to California. The herd was caught in a blizzard in Ruby Valley, Nevada, and in the spring there were only 200 survivors.[28]

One important line of business of the road ranches that grew up along the Overland Trail was to buy up footsore oxen and herd them on the prairie until they had recuperated and then sell them to following trains.

Oxen were not without shortcomings. Sometimes their hoofs became so tender that they had to be shod. The blacksmith shop at Council Grove made quite a business of this operation. Because the

---

[27] John K. Standish, "A Pioneer Freighter," *American Cattle Producer*, Vol. XXIX (March, 1948), 11–12, 30–31; E. W. Milligan, "John Wesley Iliff," *Denver Westerners Monthly Roundup*, Vol. VI (August, 1950).

[28] Lucia, *Ben Holladay*, 62–63; Majors, *Seventy Years*, 144.

beast objected to the process it was, for him, very undignified. Each ox was driven into a special stall, hoisted off his feet, and his legs lashed to the side rails, allowing the blacksmith safe access to his hoofs. Out on the plains, the operation was more abrupt. The ox was roped and thrown and then his feet were tied together; the shoeing was done by cold hammering. When metal shoes were not available, buffalo hide made a good makeshift. Sometimes the hoof was so badly cracked that a pad had to be inserted between the hoof and the shoe, and what better material was apt to be close at hand than a piece from the brim of the bullwhacker's hat?[29]

Oxen were also subject to disease. In 1863 a train belonging to Irwin, Jackman and Company was struck by the fatal disease "murrain" (any of a number of infectious diseases of cattle). In the 1870's, Texas fever caused a great deal of trouble. A Kansas pioneer said, "I knew one man who drove into Dodge City with over a hundred head of fine work oxen, and in less than six weeks he did not have enough stock left to pull the empty wagons out of town."[30] Teams were also victims of alkali poisoning. The heavy losses of 1860, between the Missouri River and Denver, were ascribed to this cause. It was a very dry year, and the water of the Platte had a higher alkali content than usual. In addition, the trail was deep in dust, and the grass for three miles on either side of the trail was covered with dust. The oxen took in alkali with every swallow of forage or water and with every breath they drew. Some wagonmasters found that lard or fat bacon stuffed down the animal's throat, if done soon enough, produced a cure. In 1865 a herd got into a patch of wild parsnips and, in an hour, fifteen to twenty were down, poisoned. Fat bacon saved them all.[31]

Oxen, in addition, often froze to death in the arctic blizzards that

29 Robert S. Roeschlaub, "The Pioneer Trail," *Sons of Colorado*, Vol. I (May, 1907), 33–34; William E. Connelley, *History of Kansas: State and People*, I, 136; Ed Blair, *History of Johnson County*, 70.

30 Dennis Collins, *The Indian's Last Fight or the Dull Knife Raid*, 14.

31 Robert G. Athearn (ed.), "From Illinois to Montana in 1866, The Diary of Perry A. Burgess," *Pacific Northwest Quarterly*, Vol. XLI (January, 1950), 47–53; *Rocky Mountain News* (October 20, 1860); Frank M. Case, "Experiences on the Platte River Route in the Sixties," *Colorado Magazine*, Vol. V (August,, 1928), 147.

swept the prairies. In 1850, Dr. David Waldo, making a trip to Santa Fe late in the season with urgently needed army supplies, was caught by a winter storm and lost 800 head.[32] Lieutenant Abert reported in 1846 that oxen seemed to suffer more from lack of water than did mules, and Lieutenant Abraham R. Johnston, traveling with the Army of the West, noted that oxen got along very well and seemed able to go as far as mules, but not in the heat of the day. The cattle had to be brought up at night, and this rendered them unfit for hauling the camp equipment of troops on the march.

Despite their seeming lethargy, oxen could be stampeded. They greatly feared snakes, and on one occasion when a whiplash came loose from the stock and fell across the road in front of the leaders, up went the heads and tails, and away went the whole team on a dead run.[33] On another occasion, a bullwhacker, having caught an estray some miles from camp, was driving him back to the train. It was a hot morning so the man took off his coat, which was lined with red and had yellow sleeves, and hung it on the steer's horns. As they approached the camp, where all was hitched and ready to roll, the ox let out a bellow of recognition and started to join his team on the trot. The other oxen took one look at the approaching apparition and started for parts unknown. All that finally stopped them was an arroyo into which they crashed. It took nearly a week to collect the cargo and repair the wagons. When oxen panicked, even rough locks could not prevent a run of a mile or so.[34]

The breaking of new steers brought about a period of excitement, hard work, and frustration for all hands. The first step was usually branding, which did nothing to endear mankind to the animal. Then came the job of yoking the wild steer. He was lassoed and snubbed up close to a post or wagon wheel, one end of a yoke was placed on his neck, and then he was turned loose to buck and bawl

[32] Daniel [David] Waldo and Co., Committee of Military Affairs, *House Report No. 56*, 35 Cong., 2 sess. (Serial 1018).

[33] Ethel M. Withers (ed.), "Experiences of Lewis Bissell Dougherty on the Oregon Trail," *MHR*, Vol. XXIV (April, 1930), 359–78.

[34] R. M. Wright, "Personal Reminiscences of Frontier Life in Southwest Kansas," *Transactions*, KSHS, Vol. VII (1902), 48–83.

to his heart's content. All in good time, the ox calmed down, and then the other end of the yoke was placed on an already broken steer.

In a letter to his parents, written in 1866, William H. Jackson well described the uproar, confusion, and bafflement of assembling a team:

> It was no easy task for us green hands to go into that corral—the bulls ramming and crowding about, pick out our "wheelers," then our "leaders," "swing" and "pointers" and make no mistake. But that's not the worst of it. After half an hour's chasing through the mass after a wild fellow, you corner him & manage to fasten the bow by working very carefully—some other steer, having a grudge, probably, against the one you are gently urging up to the wagon wheel to fasten—gives him a punch in the ribs with his horns and sends him "kiting" into the herd again. You hang on manfully and are snaked around "right smart" & get into a jam probably, and you have to jump on some of their backs to escape being squeezed to a jelly—then take all the kicks you will get.[35]

For the first few days, many drivers marked their team in some special way so that they could spot them in the melee of an early morning yoke-up. One driver tied bits of black cloth to the tails of his team. Often the oxen were not unyoked for the first few nights on the road. This was considered a bad practice if carried on too long; however, particularly wild steers might not be unyoked for several weeks. Some wagonmasters even forbade the use of fires for the first night lest the wavering shadows send the animals into a panic. When the danger of stampede was particularly acute, the lead yoke might be circled around and attached to the wheelers by an extra length of chain. Thus they could graze in a circle, but found themselves at odds when it came to running very far or fast.[36]

Getting the oxen under the yoke was only the beginning; then came the problem of getting them to pull in unison. Until the

---

[35] Clarence S. Jackson, "Roll Out, Roll Out, The Bulls Are Coming," *1954 Brand Book*, Denver Westerners, 6.

[36] Birge, *Awaking of the Desert*, 21; Julie Beehrer Colyer, "Freighting Across the Plains," *Montana*, Vol. XII (Autumn, 1962), 8; Withers, "Experiences of Lewis Dougherty," *loc. cit.*, 359–78.

cattle were accustomed to working together, "each wagon became a unit of disorder." Despite the best efforts of all hands, with the old-timers helping the greenhorns, it might take until midafternoon to get the animals yoked and hooked, and three miles would be a good day's march for the first day. Chandless said that the first attempt to drive was ludicrous; every ox had his feet over the chain, and yokes were turned upside down. No one in his train could do any better until they changed the leaders. A train that covered twenty miles in the first week was doing well.

The selection of oxen for a team was described by one bull-whacker: "Kindly, trim and biddable cattle for leaders, being sure that they know something about the yoke—and then for the wheelers we sought out the heavy sturdy fellows, for they had not only to carry the wagon tongue, but to hold the wagon back going down the hills.[37] When there was a large selection of oxen, and a wagonmaster with something of an artistic taste, the oxen were teamed up according to color—blacks, browns, whites, and brindles. An experienced, trail-broken ox could be identified by a bald spot on its left rump, where the hair had been worn away by the bullwhacker's whip. Once on the road with a train, it was found that a few horses were always useful when it came to crossing a river. The oxen would follow a horse into the water when no amount of whipping would drive them in.[38]

The ruggedness of the ox is attested to by a story from the *Cheyenne Leader*. A six-bull team stopped in front of the newspaper office, and the editor remarked to the driver that one of his animals was a walking skeleton. The driver agreed and said:

> Goin' up to Deadwood las' trip I got stuck on Hat creek an' the critters couldn't budge the load. I'd 'bout give up, and war goin' ter wait fur some other teams ter come up an' help me out, when I thought I'd try jes' once more. I got beside ole Bruiser, ther, an' when all was ready, gin a yell an' ye jes' ought to a seen thet cuss straighten out. He stood as straight ez that whip-stock, an his eyes

37 Hall, "Personal Recollections of Santa Fe Trail," *loc. cit.*, 51.
38 Olive K. Dixon, *Life of "Billy" Dixon*, 20.

hung clar down to his nose. All to once I heerd a kind o' a "tear-r-r" so help me pard, thet cuss went rite through the yoke, leavin' his hide layin' quiverin' beside the tongue of the wagon, an he stood thar without hair or hide on him ahind o where the yoke sot. I got the skin open an backed him inter it, but he hasn't been the same steer since.[39]

In 1861 the *Merchants' Magazine and Commercial Review* noted that oxen were the draft animals in most common use. It also noted that the animals were grass fed and unaccustomed to shelter, "two most essential qualities while doing freighting service on the Plains," and added that two seasons of work were all that was expected of the oxen.

American inventors were not slow to accept the challenge of high plains wagon-freighting. In 1853 and again in 1859 there appeared on the streets of Westport a "Wind-Wagon," a wagon described as a prairie schooner that had been decked over and equipped with sails. It had been designed by one "Wind-Wagon" Thomas and built by the Westport and Santa Fe Overland Navigation Company. On a trial run, with the designer at the helm and the stockholders for crew, disaster struck. As the wind picked up and the wagon gained speed, the crew, one by one, noticed that they were outdistancing a galloping mule, and abandoned ship, leaving Thomas alone on the deck "whence all but him had fled." Just exactly what happened is not clear, but the wagon went out of control and smashed in an uncharted arroyo where it lay until carted away piece by piece.[40]

There were at least two attempts to adapt steam power to high plains transportation before the railroads were built. In 1861, Thomas L. Fortune of Mt. Pleasant, Kansas, built a steam wagon to operate on the open prairie. Thirty feet in length, twelve feet in width, with wheels eight feet in diameter, the machine was powered by a thirty-horsepower steam engine geared up to sixty horsepower.

---

[39] *Cheyenne Leader* (November 2, 1876).

[40] Edmund C. Field, "A Wind Wagon," *MHR*, Vol. XXXI (October, 1936), 85; "Do You or Don't You?" *MHR*, Vol. XXXIV (October, 1939), 96; "Wind Wagon of Westport," *MHR*, Vol. XXV (April, 1931), 528–29.

It was estimated to weigh ten tons and to be capable of pulling twenty-five loaded wagons or of hauling ten tons. With a crew of six, it was to run day and night and make three round trips to Denver per month. Someone figured that at 360 tons per year and a rate of $160 per ton, the gross would be $57,600 for a machine that cost $2,500. The saving in loss of cattle and other expenses would pay the cost of wood and water. The Overland Steam Wagon added to the excitement of the Fourth of July celebration when it failed to navigate a street corner in Atchison, Kansas, and had to be backed out of a store. On the second trial, made in the safety of the open prairie, the Steam Wagon bogged down in a convenient mudhole—and that ended that experiment.[41]

About a year later there was landed at Nebraska City, Nebraska, a "Prairie Motor," or steam tractor. It was more roadworthy than the Steam Wagon, but it broke a crankshaft in the hills outside the town. The pressure of war orders in the machine shops of New York precluded the production of a new crankshaft. The machine was abandoned on the Morton farm and eventually was broken up.[42]

Thus the high plains freighter was left with the mule and the ox to draw his wagons, despite the shortcomings of both animals.

[41] *American Railway Times* (September 14, 1861); *Journal of Commerce* (July 2, 1861).

[42] Nebraska City *Peoples' Press* (July 17, 21, September 1, 1862; February 23, 1863); Paul Morton, "Early Freighting Days in the West," *Santa Fe Employees' Magazine*, Vol. III (August, 1909), 1013–16; D. E. Allen to Bulger, June 5, 1861, in Arbor Lodge Nebraska City, Nebraska.

CHAPTER VI

KEEP THEM ROLLING

The WAGONMASTER, or train boss, was almost absolute master of his train. While he may not have had the *de jure* powers that Gregg would have given the captain of a Santa Fe caravan, he had *de facto* powers that were fully as strong. The daily routine of a wagon train was just whatever the wagonmaster saw fit to establish. The large-scale freighter, operating more than one train, might set certain standards, such as Majors' rule against marching on Sunday. His wagonmasters seem to have violated this rule more than they observed it. Surprisingly often the Sunday campsite did not have good pasturage, adequate water, or other desiderata for a good place to stop.

Since most wagon trains operated under similar conditions of climate and terrain, it is only natural that a fair degree of uniformity developed in the routine of train operation. The goal of all freighters, and their wagonmasters, was the highest possible rate of travel commensurate with maintaining the strength of the draft animals. At times the desire of a particular wagonmaster to build a reputation for speed became evident, but the strength limits of the animals held this ambition within limits, or assured the ruin of the train.

The Santa Fe trade was the great training school for high plains wagon-freighting. Many of the prominent freighters got their first training and experience along the Santa Fe Trail: Dr. David Waldo, Alexander Majors, and Ben Holladay, to name just a few. As might be expected with any new operation being carried out under strange conditions, there was a striking lack of uniformity in the early days. There was no standardization in equipment, and there was as much variation in dress, equipment, and arms as there was in men, animals, and wagons. A writer in the Missouri *Intelligencer* called the Santa Fe trade "one of the most curious species of foreign intercourse which the ingenuity and enterprise of American traders ever originated."[1] In the early days especially, a caravan might have, in addition to the traders and their drivers, invalids (Gregg), scientists (Wislizenus), adventurers (Garrard), fugitives, and drifters.

At first there were many appeals to the government in Washington for assistance of various sorts, but the tardiness of response, or the complete lack of sympathy, soon showed the traders that they could rely only upon themselves. As a result they adopted a technique that, with only minor modifications, answered, with a high degree of success, for fifty years or so. As indicated earlier, the Santa Fe caravans collected at Council Grove in Kansas. Here they formed a quasi-military organization with a captain, a lieutenant for each division of approximately 25 wagons, and a sergeant of the guard for each relief of the guard. The men of the caravan were divided into reliefs—usually eight in number—and each relief stood guard for a quarter of every other night. All members of the caravan, including the tourists and loafers, were expected to stand guard.

The caravans soon learned to form a corral with their wagons at night. Alternate wagons swung out to left and right and moved in a curving course until the leading wagons met and halted. The following wagons closed up so that the front wheel of one wagon was opposite the rear wheel of the wagon ahead. The wheels were chained together, and the openings at both ends of the eliptical space were closed by chains. A train of 41 wagons made a corral about 50 by 30 yards, not too much room for 420 head of cattle and 40 drivers seeking their animals in the melee. A well-trained crew could corral in five minutes.[2] The corral made an excellent defense

---

[1] Robert Glass Cleland, *This Reckless Breed of Men*, 142.
[2] Chandless, *Visit to Salt Lake City*, 52; Toponce, *Reminiscences*, 107.

in case of attack by hostile Indians and a convenient enclosure for holding the animals during the harnessing or yoking process. When the Indian threat was slight, the wagons were corralled with the tongues to the outside of the enclosure so that the animals were close to water and grass. When the threat was acute, the wagon tongues were turned inward so that the animals were protected by the wagons and could not easily be driven off.

As indicated by Gregg's figures for the first twenty-one years of the Santa Fe trade, there was considerable variation in the proportion of proprietors, men, and wagons. The proportion of about two men per wagon was rather consistent. But there was a slow yet steady increase in the average number of wagons per proprietor. Even so, by 1843, this average was only seven to eight wagons for each owner. Considering the amount of merchandise involved, almost half a million dollars, at East Coast prices, this was big business conducted on a small scale.

Following the occupation of New Mexico, in 1846, and the removal of the Mexican restrictions on the trade, the business grew by leaps and bounds, and a better organization was needed. The merchant-freighters began to separate the functions of freighting and merchandising. James Josiah Webb, who made his first trip to Santa Fe in 1844, settled down as a merchant in Santa Fe about 1860 and hired out his freighting. On the other hand, Charles Raber, after being caught a couple of times with loads of merchandise in a glutted market, decided to forego the hazards of the market place and concentrate on the hazards of the plains as a professional freighter.

Majors entered the freighting business in 1848 and was so successful that shortly he was setting the pattern for most high plains freighters. Majors said that a standard train consisted of twenty-five wagons, but many of his contemporaries set the figure at twenty-six: twenty-five cargo wagons and a mess or supply wagon. The latter carried the rations for the crew, the cooking utensils, and some pioneer tools: axes, shovels, carpenter's tools, and, in some cases, a small forge. Some companies provided a medicine chest stocked

chiefly with calomel, laudanum, and Epsom salts.[3] The investment
in a single train might range from $18,000 to $35,000. At times the
large trains, essential for protection from the Indians, were made up
of several smaller trains. In 1862 one train under Tom Fitzwater
was composed of six wagons of A. and P. Byram, six of John D. Clay-
ton, and one belonging to Steve Lyons.[4]

The crew for a train of twenty-six wagons ranged from about
thirty-two to thirty-six men: a wagonmaster, an assistant wagonmaster, twenty-six bullwhackers or mule skinners, a night herder,
two day herders, and three or four spare hands to take the place of
deserters or casualties. It was as night herder that Ben Holladay
signed on for his first trip to Santa Fe. Some freighters provided a
cook for the whole crew, and occasionally the owner of the goods or
one of his clerks accompanied the train in the capacity of supercargo
and may have had the use of an "office wagon." Many freighters sent
with each train a herd of thirty to forty extra oxen as replacements.
This herd was referred to as the "calf-yard," a corruption of the
Spanish word *caballada*; hence, the need for day herders.

As word of the profit to be made in freighting spread, the competition grew. Some operators, seeking to reduce the size of their payroll, eliminated the extra hands and extra oxen and required the
regular drivers to perform the night guard duties. Night herd was
the most heartily detested duty a teamster could be called on to perform. One of them said, "It is impossible for anyone who has never
had the experience, to realize the overpowering sense of sleepiness
that comes over one after midnight, particularly after a strenuous
day of yoking and unyoking the animals of his team, driving them
to water, and walking beside them on the road when the train was
moving."[5] Herders were sometimes provided with rubber coats and
leggings to protect them from heavy dew or the occasional rain-

[3] Bratt, *Trails of Yesterday*, 50, 59; "Commerce of the Prairies," *Merchants' Magazine*, Vol. XLIV (January, 1862), 37; William Clark, "Trip Across the Plains," *Iowa
Journal of History and Politics*, Vol. XX (April, 1922), 180; Kenderdine, *California
Tramp*, 18.
[4] Francis Withee, Letters, 1899–1900, NSHS.

storms. There was, however, no protection from the mosquitoes that could make life very uncomfortable for the night herder. An experienced man on night herd would pick out a reliable old ox and lie down against him; thus, anything that disturbed the animal would rouse the man. On a cold night the body heat of the ox kept the man more comfortable.[6]

Once on the road, the crew usually divided into "messes" of eight to twelve members. One man was elected cook and thereby relieved of all other duties except handling his team. The other members of the mess had their regular duties: gathering fuel, fetching water, etc.

Each mess had two or three camp kettles, a fry pan, a skillet or bake pan, a Dutch oven, a coffee mill, an ax, a spade, and two or three six-gallon water kegs. Rations were usually issued in the evening and were based on the government ration: food for one man for one day. Basically this ration consisted of one and one-quarter pounds of flour, three-quarters to one pound of bacon, and one and one-quarter ounces of coffee, and two and one-half ounces of sugar. Most freighters were a bit more liberal—a little more bacon and a few beans and dried apples. With the emphasis on flour and bacon, it is small wonder that the men looked forward with great anticipation to reaching buffalo country and a supply of fresh meat. The supply of beans usually allowed one meal of beans per week, and the dried apples were enough for a dish once in two weeks. The supply of sugar never lasted a full trip.

To eke out the supply of bacon, William Bent usually sent two hunters with his trains, and the church trains from the Mormon settlements in Utah to the Missouri Valley were each provided with a hunter. When no professional hunter was provided, the first choice of meat went to the mess whose member had killed it; the excess was divided among the other messes.[7] About 1865 the rations for a crew of twenty-eight men for sixty days were:

5 Britton, "Pioneer Life," *loc. cit.*, 559.
6 *Ibid.*, 558–59; Herman R. Lyon, "Freighting in the '60's," *Proceedings and Collections*, NSHS, 2nd Series, Vol. V (1902), 296–97.
7 Chandless, *Visit to Salt Lake City*, 21.

30 sacks flour, 98 lbs. ea.	$5.00	$150.00
2500 lbs. bacon, 20 sacks	.18	450.00
1 sack 50c coffee, 125 lbs.	.38	48.00
2 sacks $1 sugar, 250 lbs.	.18	46.00
1 sack 75c beans, 2 bushels	3.50	7.75
1 sack dried apples, 103 lbs.	.15	15.45
10 lbs. soda	.20	2.00
6 boxes matches	.12½	.75
1 sack 50c salt, 100 lbs.	.03	3.50
20 lbs. soap	.15	3.00
Sheet and Lariat rope 321½ lbs.	.28	8.82
1 keg $1.50 vinegar, 5 gal.	.60	4.50
3 10-gal. water kegs	2.50	7.50
1 lb. candles		.35
4 boxes ground pepper	.25	1.00
24 qt. cans wagon grease	.50	12.00
1 lb. ground mustard		.75
2 lbs. ox nails	.75	1.50
1 oz. shoeing hammer		1.25
1 oz. shoeing rasp		2.00
1 oz. shoeing pincers		2.50
		$768.62[8]

One teamster said that the men were poor cooks and that baking bread while on the move was a science which required much experience. "No matter how much or how little soda, salt or saleratus and shortening we used, the yellower, more sodden and the heavier the result.... flapjacks ... a scurvy, dispepsia-breeding, muddled mess." He went on to remark that if the employer "Had a stomach like an ostrich, we got the worse" and that sowbelly had a unique place among food products: "It was indestructible. Neither heat, cold, damp nor arid conditions made it better or worse."[9]

While the buffalo was a source of fresh meat to supplement the ration, it could also be a source of danger to a wagon train. "Buffalo Bill" Cody told of one case in which the train of which he was acting

8 Rolfe, "Overland Freighting Business," *loc. cit.*
9 J. S. Hoy Manuscript, *loc. cit.*

as wagonmaster was overwhelmed by stampeding buffalo. The train was strung out along the trail near the foot of some sand hills and about two miles from the river. Between the road and the river there was a herd of buffalo quietly grazing. Suddenly a party of returning Californians spotted the herd and charged toward it. About five hundred of the animals, hotly pursued by the hunters, dashed into the train. In an instant all was confusion; some of the wagons were turned clear around and the oxen tried to drag them into the hills; wagon tongues were snapped; oxen became entangled in their gear; some oxen broke their yokes and dashed off among the buffalo. "One big buffalo became entangled in one of the heavy wagon chains, and it is a fact that in his desperate efforts to free himself, he not only snapped the strong chain in two, but broke the ox-yoke to which it was attached, and the last seen of him he was running toward the hills with it hanging from his horns."[10]

The daily routine of a wagon train varied with the ideas of the wagonmaster and with climatic conditions. On most trains the working day began before first light when the night herder routed out the crew. On some trains it was the cook who summoned the crew with:

> *Bacon in the Pan*
> *Coffee in the Pot*
> *Get up and get it—*
> *Get it while it's hot*[11]

On other trains the outfit rolled out on empty stomachs, at least as far as the men were concerned, for breakfast was not eaten until the noon halt. The occasional farsighted individual might have saved a snack from supper to help him through the morning.[12]

At first light, the animals were driven into the corral and the teamsters began the search, through a whirling mass of 250 to 300 restless beasts, for the 10 or 12 that comprised their teams. After some time on the trail, many of the animals would move quietly to the proper place by the correct wagon and wait patiently to be

10 William F. Cody, *Life and Adventures of "Buffalo Bill,"* 48–50.
11 William F. Hooker, *The Prairie Schooner,* 36.
12 Jackson, "Roll Out, Roll Out," *loc. cit.,* 7–8.

harnessed or yoked.[13] Majors insisted on good discipline in his crews. On one occasion he timed a crew, and in sixteen minutes they yoked six pair of oxen apiece and hooked them to the proper wagons. One of Majors' bullwhackers reported that once his outfit had yoked up and was ready to roll in five minutes. But Percival G. Lowe, a civilian wagonmaster in the employ of the army, once came across a Russell, Majors and Waddell outfit that had stalled completely because the drunken wagonmaster could not enforce any discipline.

Colonel James F. Meline remarked:

> This word "outfit" is on duty night and day, without relief, from the Missouri River to California. To cross the plains, or go to the mountains, every one must get an outfit; and, having outfitted, you become yourself an outfit. . . . A train of wagons is an outfit; a man on a mule is an outfit; a squadron of cavalry is an outfit. . . . So is a man with a cane, or a woman with a parasol.[14]

The first drive usually lasted until about ten in the morning. Then the train halted, the animals were unhitched, driven to water, and allowed to graze until about two in the afternoon. This noon grazing was important in order that the animals would rest all night and not spend the time wandering around in search of food. If the animals rested at night, it made life easier for the night herders and there was less chance of a stampede caused by the Indians as the herd was more compact.

It was during the noon halt that the crew got its chief meal of the day—for some crews it was breakfast, for others dinner. While the animals might rest, this was a busy time for the men. There was always plenty to do besides eat: wheels to be greased, repairs to yokes or harness to be made, sores on the animals to be medicated, new poppers to be fitted to the whips, and a dozen other items of maintenance to be done. If there were no herders in the outfit, the drivers had to take turns herding the animals during the noon halt.

---

[13] William H. Jackson, "The Most Important Nebraska Highway," *NH*, Vol. XIII (July-September, 1932), 137–59; "Commerce of the Prairies," *loc. cit.*, 28–39.
[14] *2000 Miles on Horseback*, 74–75.

This was also a time for hunting, though this was looked on more as a sport than as a means of procuring food. On occasion, noon halt was enlivened by the settlement of a dispute between a pair of teamsters. Occasionally a train was fortunate to have in the outfit a carpenter or cabinetmaker, who might be excused from extra duties in order to devote full time to keeping the wagons in good repair.[15]

The second drive lasted from two in the afternoon until about six o'clock, at which time the train went into camp for the night. In periods of excessive heat, the noon halt might be extended by some hours and the second drive continued into the night, especially if there were a full moon. After the evening meal came the one period of relaxation for the crew: a time for smoking, singing, telling tall tales, or playing cards on the tail gate of the mess wagon. A good singer or storyteller was always a welcome addition to any mess. Particularly in the early days of a trip, many of the greenhorns were too exhausted to join in the social hour but crawled into bed, even without waiting for supper. One traveler noted, "One of these camps, seen at sundown, with nightfires kindled, and from five hundred to a thousand head of animals feeding nearby, is well worth a long visit to behold."[16]

A constant concern of a good wagonmaster and a source of extra work for the teamsters was the danger of alkali poisoning, which seems to have been particularly acute from the forks of the Platte River westward. A conscientious wagonmaster would have his animals driven to the North Platte for water rather than rely on nearer water holes. One train drove their animals as much as five miles to water every day. They lost time by this but they saved all their animals.[17]

The order of march of a train varied with the whims of the wagonmaster and with the terrain. When in hostile Indian country, the train marched in two columns, making it easier to corral. During the

15 Pamphlet 344/21, CSHS.

16 George F. Vanderwalker, "The Bull-whacker or Prairie Sailor," *The Trail*, Vol. I (February, 1909), 26; Jackson, "Roll Out, Roll Out," *loc. cit.*, Demas Barnes, *From the Atlantic to the Pacific, Overland*, 23.

17 Percival G. Lowe, *Five Years a Dragoon*, 323.

Indian troubles of the 1860's, the trains were consolidated into large caravans that marched in four columns. Henry M. Porter of Denver combined his trains into a single caravan of 126 wagons and provided extra men to serve as scouts and pickets. In such a consolidated caravan, the captain was usually chosen from the most experienced wagonmasters of the component trains.[18]

When attack by Indians was possible, it was vital that a train stay well closed up. In one case, in 1852, a train of ten-mule teams was attacked near Pawnee Rock. The last wagon in the column was drawn by seven small mules and three burros. It was overloaded and slow and had fallen behind. When the Indians appeared, the train corralled without the last wagon. The driver of the laggard hid his ten-year-old son under some blankets and prepared to do what he could alone. Fortunately some Dragoon skirmishers saw the attack, formed in line, and charged, driving off the Indians. The driver had suffered nothing more than a slight arrow wound and a good scare. After this attack Troop "B," Second Dragoons, collected the wagons and escorted them via the Cimarron Crossing to a point sixty miles southwest of Fort Atkinson.[19]

In some trains, once they had begun to move, the position of each wagon in the column was fixed for the rest of the trip. The majority of wagonmasters realized how undesirable the rear position was because of the dust and therefore established some sort of a rotation plan. Some rotated messes in the lead position; others divided their train into "wings," which took turns leading. The best driver usually held the lead position, as it was he who set the pace. If the train marched in wings, the two best drivers were numbers one and fourteen. The greenest driver usually started off with the mess wagon and brought up the rear. This was probably based on the idea that interest in the fate of the rations would assure the driver of assistance from the more experienced hands. When a cook was provided, it was he who drove the mess wagon.[20]

[18] Henry M. Porter, *Autobiography*, 28; A. W. Haygood, "The Freighting Business," *Annals of Wyoming*, Vol. III (July, 1925), 85–86.

[19] Lowe, *Five Years a Dragoon*, 104.

[20] Toponce, *Reminiscences*, 103; *Atchison Daily Globe* (July 16, 1894).

The wagonmaster, who was usually mounted on one of the four or five saddle mules provided for each train, generally rode ahead of the train to select the next campsite, to spot bad places in the road and the best stream crossings, and to scout for Indians. The assistant wagonmaster could usually be found near the rear of the train pushing along the laggard wagons and helping the greenhorns to learn their business.[21]

The length of the day's march varied with the availability of water and grass for the stock. On the *jornada del muerto* of the Cimarron Cutoff, long marches had to be made between water holes. The average day's march for oxen was twelve to fifteen miles per day, at a rate of one and one-half to two miles per hour. A mule train would usually cover fifteen to twenty miles in a day.[22] Majors said that the distance covered in a day depended on the skill of the wagonmaster. When Horace Greeley noticed the oxen of a train kept under yoke all day while waiting to cross a river and then whipped when they tried to drink, he blamed this cruel treatment on the wagonmaster.

Most freighters acknowledged that their animals should rest for about one day in seven. Few went as far as Alexander Majors, whose book *Rules and Regulations for the Government of Russell, Majors and Waddell Outfit* stated: "We expect our trains to observe the Sabbath, and whenever an opportunity occurs to hear preaching, embrace it."[23] While some wagonmasters ignored such rules and thereby got into difficulties with some of the more conscientious of their drivers, the majority took the rest in the form of two half-days. Because of the scarcity of water and forage, companies having several trains on the road ordered that they march at two- to ten-mile intervals and keep that distance between camps.

It was an almost invariable rule with experienced wagonmasters to cross any stream encountered when it came time to make camp for the night. It sometimes happened that a rainstorm miles away

21 Majors, *Seventy Years*, 143; Kenderdine, *California Tramp*, 39.
22 "Commerce of the Prairies," *Merchants' Magazine*, Vol. XLIV (January, 1862), 40.
23 *Rules and Regulations for the Government of Russell, Majors & Waddell Outfit*, 7.

would cause a creek to rise during the night, thereby delaying the train for several days. Also, the animals would pull better in the evening. In the morning, those with sore shoulders were reluctant to lean into the collar or yoke for a heavy pull until they had warmed to their work.[24] Whenever possible, a trail-wise wagon-master would pick a campsite on some elevation where the wagons would be safe from a flash flood. This put extra work on the men because water for drinking and cooking had to be carried up from the river in kegs.

Dragging a mired-down wagon out of a mudhole called for the use of two or three teams, the efforts of all available hands, and some ingenuity. When the extra teams were hooked on, they were positioned at right angles to the tongue, forming a rough letter S. Thus as the teams moved out, they picked up some momentum before the chain was straightened and the weight of the wagon was felt. Either the wagon moved or the wagon tongue came out under a pull like this.

A boggy spot in the trail that could not be bypassed always presented serious problems. First, any wagon stuck in the mudhole had to be pulled out. Then all hands went to work cutting prairie grass with their knives and collecting it in their blankets. The grass was dumped on the mud until it made a carpet thick and strong enough to bear the weight of the succeeding wagons of the train.[25]

About 1860 the idea of coupling two or more wagons in tandem and pulling them with one team came into vogue. This step reduced the number of drivers needed to move a given weight of freight. In the later period of wagon-freighting in Montana, three and even four wagons per team became common. When wagons and trailers were used, the lead wagon carried a heavier load than the trailer. In one train, the lead wagon was loaded with four thousand pounds while the trail wagon carried three thousand pounds. When a bad place in the road was encountered, the trail wagon was uncoupled,

---

[24] Spring, *Bloomer Girl*, 19; Collins, *Indian's Last Fight*, 17.
[25] Kenderdine, *California Tramp*, 39–40; Withers, "Experiences of Lewis Bissell Dougherty," *loc. cit.*, 370.

the team dragged the lead wagon through, and then returned for the trail wagon. The coupling of empty wagons returning to the Missouri Valley was common—as many as five or six to a team, the surplus drivers having been discharged and some of the animals sold at the far end.[26]

At times there was considerable rivalry between ox trains and mule trains. One bullwhacker related, with a touch of pride, that a mule train left the Missouri at the same time as his bull train but that his train beat the mules into Fort Laramie, a distance of 667 miles, by two weeks.[27] "Buffalo Bill" Cody related that, in 1858 or 1859, his wagon boss, Lew Simpson, then working for Russell, Majors and Waddell, insisted that a carefully selected bull train could beat any mule outfit. His employers gave Simpson his chance—the pick of the herd and a head start of one week. After about 150 miles the mules passed the oxen, but at the crossing of the Platte, the oxen took the lead again. Before reaching the North Platte, the mules again took the lead but could not hold it. From then on the oxen continued to hold their lead. Cody makes it clear that this was a hand-picked lot of oxen, capable of covering twenty-five miles per day, compared to the normal fifteen miles a day. Another telling factor was the skill of Simpson in selecting the point of crossing the Platte. There is no doubt that average mule trains traveled faster than average ox trains. The average time from the Missouri River to Denver was stated by several authorities as being three weeks for mules and five weeks for oxen.

Mexican-operated trains do not seem to have been quite as efficient as those operated by Americans. The animals used were generally smaller, requiring one more span of mules or oxen per wagon. Generally two drivers were needed with each wagon, and they were armed with goads, long sharpened sticks, rather than the long-lashed whip that was the trade-mark of the American bullwhacker. It was reported that some wealthy Mexicans did not give their employees

26 *Deseret News* (August 25, 1860); Clarke, "Freighting—Denver and Black Hills," *Proceedings and Collections*, NSHS, 2nd Series, Vol. V (1902), 305–306.
27 McGee, "Early Days in the West," *loc. cit.*, 13–16.

a knife or fork to eat with. A butcher knife and a spoon in their belt was all they needed. The spoon was for *tole*, a kind of mush of parched Mexican corn, and knife and fingers were enough for any meat they might have. Most of the Mexican teamsters did not understand English, so Prowers and Hough of Las Animas, Colorado, a forwarding and commission house, had to hire an interpreter from Trinidad. Their warehousemen had a hard job getting a reasonable load on the wagons as the Mexicans never seemed to learn to load in such a way as to protect the goods and to get a good, paying load properly stowed. The warehouseman also had to inspect the wagons and send those that needed repair to the blacksmith or carpenter. The amount of any repairs was entered on the bill of lading as an advance charge to be paid by the owner of the goods.[28]

A man who claimed twelve or thirteen years' experience connected with the business of freighting on the plains presented a novel idea in 1866.[29] He claimed that a small wagon of 2,500 pounds' capacity, drawn by one yoke of good oxen, would be more economical than the large wagon in common use, carrying 6,000 pounds and drawn by six yoke of oxen. The figures which he presented were based on two trips of three months each, hauling 250,000 pounds each time at $.10 per pound. For the small wagons, the investment in rolling stock, animals, rations for the crew, and incidentals amounted to $28,580, while the payroll came to $4,200. At the end of the first trip, the freighter would be in the red by $8,230. The writer assumed a 20 per cent loss of cattle on the first trip, and these were replaced. At the end of the second trip all animals and equipment would be sold at a discount approximating 40 per cent. It was concluded that the freighter would clear about $24,700 on an investment of about $28,000. In considering the large wagons, the figures showed an investment of $39,350 and a payroll of $5,750. The deficit at the end of the first trip was $18,120. After buying fresh oxen for the second trip and selling off the equipment

28 James Hobbs, *Wild Life in the West*, 61; Personal statement by P. G. Scott, H. L. Pickett Collection, University of Colorado Libraries.
29 *Leavenworth Times* (March 7, 1866).

and animals at the end of the trip, the profit was $22,090 on an investment of $39,350.

At first glance these figures appear to present a profitable method of operation. However, on closer examination, there are a number of flaws in the reasoning. In the first place, the "Chicago" wagon as used in the Salt Lake trade, carrying 2,500 pounds, was usually drawn by three yoke of oxen, not one. For the train of one hundred small wagons, our economist employed only one assistant wagonmaster, but for the train of forty-two large wagons he provided two assistants. Finally, it was claimed that one teamster could handle two small wagons as well as one large one. The nearest thing to this small-wagon type of operation that was extensively used was the "brigades" of Red River carts that operated between Pembina and St. Paul. Here one driver tended three or four carts of nine-hundred-pound capacity, each drawn by one ox or cow. It would appear to be more strain on the bullwhacker to have to run back and forth to keep two wagons moving and closed up than to keep one in place.[30]

In 1864, Henry M. Porter of Denver made the only known trial of this small-wagon type of operation. With the Montana boom in full swing, Porter sent an agent east to buy 100 two-horse wagons and 100 yoke of fine, well-broken cattle. Each wagon was to be loaded with 2,500 pounds of groceries and some feed for the oxen. The drivers of the train were each to manage two teams. The entire operation was a success. The train arrived in Denver in April. The light wagons and teams sold "like hot cakes" to Montana-bound Coloradans, and Porter cleared some $16,000, net.[31]

A number of travelers observing wagon trains at a distance waxed lyrical over the spectacle. One compared them with Biblical caravans, another said that the effect was "poetic, grand, beautiful," while still another compared them to "lines of white cranes trooping slowly over the prairie, or in more mysterious evening resembling dim sails crossing a rolling sea." One might note that these comments were made by stagecoach passengers; few bullwhackers

---

30 Joseph K. Howard, *Strange Empire; A Narrative of the Northwest*, 55.
31 Porter, "Freighting and Merchandising in Early Denver," *loc. cit.*, 171–73.

or mule skinners were touched with such beautiful sentiments toward their job. One farmer-turned-freighter, in 1875, was caught in a plains blizzard that buried all the sleeping men in snow so tightly packed that they had to be rescued, after two days, by soldiers from Fort Dodge. His advice was: "So much for freighting on the frontier. My advice to farmers is to attend their farms and let freighting alone."[32]

Because of the similarity of conditions, terrain, weather, Indian hostility, and above all the single mission, there developed among high plains wagon-freighters a pretty complete standardization of the techniques of wagon train operation. This applied whether the trains were powered by mules or oxen and almost regardless of size. Although Indian attacks received a lot of publicity, the trains that suffered the heaviest damages were the immigrant trains, not those of the professional freighter.

Without such a standardized technique, losses to Indians and nature probably would have been much greater, and the wagon-freighter might not have been able to support the growth of the Mountain West.

[32] Samuel Bowles, *Our New West*, 34; Barnes, *From the Atlantic to the Pacific*, 23; Sir Richard F. Burton, *The City of the Saints*, 27; "Freighting on the Frontier," *KHQ*, Vol. XX (May, 1953), 452–54.

CHAPTER VII

TO THE LAND OF ROMANCE

Fᴿᴼᴹ ᴛʜᴇ ᴇᴀʀʟɪᴇsᴛ ᴅᴀʏs of its settlement, Santa Fe had been supplied by wagon over the great distance from Mexico City. About 1609 a regular supply service was established, and the supply trains were subsidized by the Spanish royal treasury. The plan called for a wagon train every third year from Mexico City to Santa Fe—six months to reach Santa Fe, six months to distribute the supplies to the missions, and six months to return. As with all operations in the Spanish colonies in which the government took any interest, the organization of the train was spelled out in detail. A caravan was to comprise thirty-two wagons of two-ton capacity, each drawn by eight mules. It was to operate in two sections under four *mayordomos* and to have a military escort of twelve to fourteen soldiers. The edict went so far as to specify that each group of eight wagons was to carry 16 spare axles, 150 extra spokes, and 500 pounds of tallow. By the middle of the seventeenth century, the edict was modified to require a supply train every year.

Originally the caravans were supposed to carry only supplies for the missions, but before long they were also carrying a certain amount of commercial freight. The city of Chihuahua, lying some 550 miles south of Santa Fe and on the direct road from Mexico City, had about twice as large a population as Santa Fe and its merchants soon dominated the commercial life of Santa Fe. New Mexico was a poor province with little to export to pay for imports.[1]

[1] Max L. Moorhead, "Spanish Transportation in the Southwest; 1540–1846,"

The one exception to the lack of exportable goods was copper from the Santa Rita mines. About 1800 a friendly Apache chief showed an outcropping of native copper to Lieutenant Colonel José Manuel Carrasco. Production began in 1804, and three years later Lieutenant Zebulon Pike reported the output to be 20,000 mule loads annually. This seems to be an improbably high figure. If the mules were loaded to their capacity of two hundred to three hundred pounds, this would mean an annual production of two to three thousand tons. Apparently Colonel Carrasco had sold his interest to Don Francisco Elguea in 1804. The latter contracted with the Spanish colonial government to provide copper for its small coins at sixty-five cents per pound, and it was said that there was enough gold in the copper to pay the cost of transportation.

Because of the hostility of the Apaches, operation of the mines was sporadic. They were leased to various operators, including Sylvester Pattie in 1825 and Robert McKnight from 1826 to 1834. About 1855 or 1860 the miners began shipping high-grade ore and 100- to 120-pound pigs of copper to Indianola, Texas, a distance of some 1,000 miles, and again the gold in the copper paid for the transportation. The mines and their machinery were destroyed by the Confederate force under General Henry Hopkins Sibley in 1862, and the mines were apparently not reopened until about 1869.[2]

It can be suspected that the merchants of Chihuahua forwarded to Santa Fe only those goods that would not find a ready local market. Before the American traders came on the scene, common calicoes and bleached and domestic goods sold for two to three dollars a *vara*, the Spanish yard of thirty-three inches. William Becknell advised American traders to "Take goods of excellent

---

NMHR, Vol. XXXII (April, 1957), 112–15; Moorhead, *New Mexico's Royal Road*, 28–35, 55, 64.

2 John R. Bartlett, *Personal Narrative of Explorations*, I, 227; T. A. Rickard, "The Chino Enterprise . . . Beginning of Mining at Santa Rita," *Engineering and Mining Journal*, Vol. CXVI, (November 3, 1923), 752–56.

quality and unfaded colors."[3] This in itself is a commentary on the goods available in Santa Fe. It is small wonder that the New Mexicans received the American traders, with their cheaper goods of better grade, with enthusiasm. By 1843 calicoes were selling for twenty-five to fifty cents per yard.

It was in 1821, the first year of Mexican independence, that Captain William Becknell set out from Boon's Lick, Missouri, with a small train of pack animals to trade for fur with the Indians of the southern Rockies and to catch wild animals. On the plains he met a party of Mexican soldiers who urged him to go to Santa Fe instead. This venture was so successful that Becknell went out to Santa Fe again during the next year, taking with him three ordinary farm wagons as well as some pack animals. On this trip, Becknell scouted the Cimarron Cutoff, soon to be the most heavily traveled branch of the Santa Fe Trail. Becknell's second venture was also highly successful; one Miss Fanny Marshall, who had invested $60, pocketed $900 as her share of the profits.[4]

The publicity attending Becknell's success led to three expeditions in 1823, and for the next ten years there was an annual increase in the Santa Fe trade of 40 per cent. Year-to-year fluctuations seem to have been due to Indian depredations, as caravans seldom made a round trip without a brush with the Plains Indians.

Meridith M. Marmaduke took a party to Santa Fe in 1824, carrying about $30,000 worth of goods—mostly cotton goods but with some woolen goods and light articles of cutlery, silk shawls, and looking glasses. On their return trip, the party brought Spanish-milled dollars, some gold and silver bullion, beaver furs, and several mules. All this had an estimated value of $180,000.[5] An important consideration for the trader, in making his purchases in the Missouri Valley, was the needs of the fur-trapping companies that fitted out annually at Taos and Santa Fe.

3 Robert L. Duffus, *The Santa Fe Trail*, 107; Captain Thomas Becknell, "Journals of Becknell," *MHR*, Vol IV (January, 1910), 65–84.

4 Duffus, *Santa Fe Trail*, 78–79.

5 Answers of Augustus Storrs, *Sen. Doc. No. 7*, 18 Cong., 2 sess. (Serial 108).

As the trade continued, the merchandise carried out became more varied. When James Josiah Webb went out in 1844, he carried dry goods—black cloth, striped, plaid, and black and white calicoes, white cambric, cotton, pongee silk, fancy and blue-plaid handkerchiefs, bleached and plaid muslins, blue and brown drillings, bleached sheeting, red pongee, bonnet ribbons, plaid silk shawls, women's white cotton hose, hickory shirts, and satin jeans. Among the notions he carried were cotton thread, black sewing silk, hooks and eyes, ivory combs, coat buttons, plain and gilded vest buttons, needles, "London pins," and suspenders. In the class of hardware were brass nails, iron spoons, scissors, pocket knives, butcher knives, saw files, padlocks, tacks, hoes, and spades.[6] Other traders carried out "Quintoque Juisque." In 1857 machinery for the gold mines of Arizona began to appear in the wagon loadings, and in later years came canned goods and bottled beer.

A typical caravan of the early days might be that of 1844. When the group organized at Council Grove there were 8 traders with 23 wagons, 140 mules, 80 yoke of oxen, and 40 men. The wagons were drawn by 5 span of mules or 6 yoke of oxen, except Webb's wagon of 4 yoke. Colonel Samuel Owens had 8 mule teams; Wethered and Caldwell had 3 mule teams; N. Gentry, 2 ox teams; E. Leitensdorfer and Company, 4 ox teams; C. C. Branham, 3 ox teams; and others, 1 ox team each. Other traders apparently caught up with the train later to bring it up to 60 men, 34 wagons, and 2 dearborns.[7]

In the years from 1822 to 1828 the traders carried some $452,000 worth of goods in 281 wagons that were accompanied by 740 men. The goods were owned by 460 individuals. It is noticeable that in the early days of the trade, the proprietors averaged little more than half a wagonload of goods each. Not until 1827 did the number of wagons exceed the number of proprietors. It is also noticeable that the men outnumbered the wagons by a ratio of 2 to 1. It was not until considerably later that wagon-freighting became so systematized that fewer men were needed to operate the wagon trains.

6 Webb, *Adventures in the Santa Fe Trade*, 82n.
7 *Ibid.*, 46–47, 47n.

Practically from the beginning, a certain code of ethics was evolved concerning the operation of the various trains that made up a caravan: "On the plains or where the road is in good condition it was allowable to pass each other, but at a bad slough or in narrow or difficult passes in the mountains it was considered mean to take any undue advantage of each other in taking the road." Going out in 1844, Webb found the road on Tecolote Hill, between Las Vegas and Santa Fe, blocked by a train. He noticed that George Peacock's train was coming up as though to cut in ahead of him. Webb immediately had his oxen inspanned and moved his wagon to block the road. Peacock, seeking a way around, became so entangled in rough country that some of his wagons had to be unloaded before they could be extricated.[8]

For a number of years there was a good market in the upper Rio Grande Valley and northern Mexico for the wagons and draft animals that had come from the Missouri Valley. Fully half the wagons were sold to the Mexicans at prices four to five times their original cost, but the oxen were so worn down by the trip that they were sacrificed at ten dollars per yoke. One writer said that American wagons sold in New Mexico for better prices than secondhand wagons brought in Missouri. In 1843 there were more than one hundred American-built wagons in use by the citizens of the state of Chihuahua.[9] In 1854, Amazon Hays wrote to Webb and Kingsbury of Santa Fe:

> A small trane of wagganes to santafee 12 waggains and 80 yoke of oxen which will be for sale as soon as they git thare One of my Brothers are with them And he will be in a herry to sell as it will be giting late I wold like you wold make sum enquiry in relation to seling Them 12 waggains and 80 yoke of cattle.

Hays went on to ask Webb and Kingsbury to buy for him four or five Mexican mules for his brother's return.[10]

8 *Ibid.*, 181–83.

9 Katherine Coman, *Economic Beginnings of the Far West*, II, 87; Moorhead, *New Mexico's Royal Road*, 87.

10 Ralph P. Bieber (ed.), "The Papers of James J. Webb, Santa Fe Merchant," *University of Washington Studies*, Vol. XI, Humanistic Series No. 2 (1924), 255–305.

Largely at the urging of Senator Thomas Hart Benton, Congress in 1824 declared the Santa Fe Trail to be a highway for international commerce and, in the next year, appropriated $30,000—$10,000 for surveying and marking the trail and $20,000 for buying transit rights from the Indians. In 1825 a deputation from Santa Fe went to Council Bluffs to determine the best road from Santa Fe to the Missouri Valley, to appoint agents to handle the eastern end of their business, and to come to an agreement with the Plains Indians to secure safe passage of their caravans. This was also the year in which men began to embark seriously in the trade and to consider it their permanent business, rather than a side line to a mercantile business in some Missouri town.

Most of the early traders were speculators who left the business when they were successful and returned east, as did Webb. No wholesaler whose business was established before 1848 can be found in business in the 1860's. Generally they lacked adequate capital, suffered losses to the Indians, or lost through poor administration.[11] As early as 1826, Mexicans began to take part in the trade. In that year Don Manuel Escudero led an outfit from Franklin, Missouri. By the early 1840's, Mexicans controlled about 50 per cent of the trade and threatened to take it over completely. In 1845, Don Francisco Elguea of Chihuahua alone took out a train of forty loaded wagons. There was considerable hard feeling between the American and Mexican traders, but the latter were at such a disadvantage in dealing with the merchants in the States that their goods, laid down in Santa Fe, cost 50 per cent more than the goods brought in by their American rivals.

Gregg noted, in 1843, that some traders preferred to hire professional freighters in the Missouri Valley rather than invest in the necessary outfit to transport their own goods. Such an investment represented some 25 per cent of the total outlay for a trip. A minimum outfit would consist of a Missouri wagon at $200.00, eight to ten mules per wagon at $100.00 each, water kegs and other extras

11 William J. Parish, *The Charles Ilfeld Company: A Study of the Rise and Decline of Mercantile Capitalism in New Mexico*, 6.

at about $25.00 per wagon—an initial cost of about $1,300.00 per wagon. In addition, each member of the caravan was expected to have fifty pounds of bacon, ten pounds of coffee, twenty pounds of sugar, some salt, beans, crackers, and other luxuries.[12] The ledgers of Manuel Alvarez, Santa Fe trader and later United States commercial agent in Santa Fe, show that on his first trip east in 1838–39, his purchases in Philadelphia and New York amounted to $9,411.93, and the inventory of wagons, oxen, mules, and extras amounted to $2,500.00.[13] The usual rate charged by the professional freighter was $.10 to $.12 a pound from Santa Fe to Chihuahua. By the 1860's it was expected that a good team would earn $800.00 for each load hauled.[14]

In 1846 the St. Louis *Weekly Reveille* of March 23 carried a letter from Santa Fe which recapitulated the trade for the previous year, less two trains that wintered at Bent's Fort: 141 wagons, 21 carriages, 1,078 oxen, 716 mules, 39 horses, and 203 drivers. It set the cost of the goods at $342,530.00 and the cost of the outfit at $87,790.00. The cost of transportation from Independence at $.10 a pound amounted to $67,680.00, and the duties paid, $105,757.00. The same letter bemoaned the uncertainty of the revenue laws at the Santa Fe Custom House, "and the prohibition to retail goods, unless the person be a citizen or married in the country."

This uncertainty about the law, and its administration by the Mexican officials at Santa Fe, was a serious obstacle to the smooth flow of trade. Goods entered at the Custom House were appraised without regard to the invoice prices and usually at an advance of from 10 to 150 per cent over cost. The duties were then computed on these inflated prices. There were almost constant changes in the revenue laws. At first there was an entry tax of $10.00 per wagon; then General Manuel Armijo raised the entry tax to $500.00 per wagon, in lieu of all import duties. This tax was actually an advan-

[12] Gregg, *Commerce of the Prairies*, 332n.; Lummis, "Pioneer Transportation," *loc. cit.*, 82; Cleland, *This Reckless Breed of Men*, 140.
[13] Lansing Bloom, "Ledgers of a Santa Fe Trader," *El Palacio*, Vol. XIV (May 1, 1923), 133–36.
[14] Spring, *Bloomer Girl*, 15.

tage to the traders, as strict enforcement of the excise law would have required the payment of $1,800.00 to $2,500.00 per wagon. Armijo's successor General Don Mariano Martinez raised the entry tax to $750.00, and finally, in 1844, it went to $1,000, plus an entry tax of $50.00 on empty wagons.[15]

Another complication was the contraband list, a list of items that were completely forbidden or carried such a high duty as to amount to a ban. On the list were such items as iron, lead, gunpowder, and candlewick. Because of a government monopoly, tobacco from the States was taxed at $4.00 a pound, and the native New Mexicans were forbidden to sell even the *punche*, a poor grade of tobacco, that they grew.

The high legal tariffs, the variations in the enforcement of the law, and the existence of the contraband list invariably led to smuggling and bribery. Blankets placed between the wagon covers could be smuggled into Santa Fe. When the high entry tax was imposed, the traders stopped just short of the first Mexican settlements and repacked their loads so as to give each trader a mess wagon. Usually the loads of four wagons could be packed into three for the last few hundred miles of the trip. Any extra wagons were abandoned or burned.[16] Some traders would cache all, or part of, their goods in the mountains and then sneak them into Santa Fe at night, on pack mules. Because iron was on the contraband list and scarce, some traders, after passing the customs and unloading their wagons, would deliberately burn them and sell the scrap iron at a great profit.[17]

In 1845, Norris Colburn, a thirty-five-year-old trader from St. Louis, cached fifteen barrels of gunpowder in the Cañada de Alamos outside Santa Fe and went into the city to hire carts to bring in the powder. During his absence, the cache was found by a young boy who reported his find to the military. Colburn was arrested, tried,

---

[15] F. F. Stephens, "Missouri and the Santa Fe Trade," *loc. cit.*, 238–39, 258–59; Webb, *Adventures in the Santa Fe Trade*, 56; Ralph Emerson Twitchell, *Old Santa Fe*, 231–35.

[16] Webb, *Adventures in the Santa Fe Trade*, 71.

[17] John E. Sunder (ed.), *Matt Field on the Santa Fe Trail*, 221–25; Wilson, *Short Ravellings from a Long Yarn*, 130; Theodore S. Case, *History of Kansas City*, 31.

and fined fourteen pesos, four reals, and had the powder confiscated. The only defense offered was that Colburn had brought in the same type of goods, in the same manner, two years before and did not know that there was anything illegal about the whole process.[18]

Once the caravans had reached the first Mexican settlements and the Indian menace had abated, they began to break up, each trader trying to outstrip his competitors in the race for the Santa Fe market. The trader himself would usually race ahead with a small party to make arrangements for the prompt passage of his goods through the Customs. This might require as much as a week of negotiations with the officials. It was said that one-third of the tax paid went to the treasury, one-third to the governor and other officials, and the remaining one-third was rebated to the trader.[19]

According to Webb, an American merchant in Santa Fe overheard a conversation between Armijo and Martinez during which the former admitted that there had been corruption during his administration and that he and his secretary had taken financial advantage of the situation. Webb himself bought a fine pair of sorrel horses in Missouri for $175 and carefully nursed them across the plains. After giving time for word of his fine animals to get around town, he sold them to Armijo for the tariff on one wagonload of merchandise, though he had to pay $750 per wagon on the balance of his goods. It was rumored in Santa Fe that General Martinez, when he was replaced as governor, had departed with $100,000, "the proceeds of *a single year of extortion*."[20] Webb noted that Thomas Caldwell had earlier met Martinez in Chihuahua and used this connection to corner the retail market for that year.

Discrimination against the American traders began to appear as early as 1828, in the form of a per diem tax levied for keeping a retail store. Most traders preferred to sell their goods at retail rather than share the profits with a storekeeper. A commercial treaty with

18 File Number 8247, Mexican Archives of New Mexico, State Records Center and Archives, Santa Fe; St. Louis *Weekly Reveille* (January 5, March 25, 1846).

19 J. Evarts Greene, "The Santa Fe Trade: Its Route and Character," *American Antiquarian Society Proceedings, New Series*, Vol. V (1892–93), 324–41.

20 *Weekly Reveille* (July 21, 1845).

Mexico in 1831 was supposed to end all unusual and discriminatory taxes, but, as events proved, it failed to eliminate corrupt officials and their interpretation of the law. In 1838 a tax on groceries and stoves was repealed, but collections continued to be made from Americans doing business in Santa Fe. Four years later the American commercial agent in Santa Fe, Manuel Alvarez, reported that two years previously, a Mexican merchant had paid $1,200 on eleven wagonloads of merchandise, or approximately $109 per wagon. At the same time, an American had paid $1,286 on three wagonloads of comparable goods, or about $429 per wagon. The agent was in a difficult position to press for equitable treatment as neither the Mexican nor the American had paid the full import duties as set forth by law. Alvarez was convinced that Armijo was trying to drive the Americans out of the trade, in which he seems to have had a large interest through Don Christoval Armijo, his nephew. Alvarez went on to say of Armijo: "He is positively the ruler and regulator of duties and Customs House affairs, as he is in every thing else in this Department."[21]

It became apparent, soon after the opening of the trade, that Santa Fe could not absorb all the merchandise that the traders brought across the plains. The population of New Mexico in 1825 was estimated at not far from 40,000, of which 10,000 were Pueblo Indians and about 30,000 were Mexicans. According to Gregg, it was in 1824 that the traders began to freight their goods south to Chihuahua. Until about 1831 this extension of the trade accounted for less than one-tenth of the total reaching Santa Fe. Thereafter it accounted for one-third to one-half, and in 1843 for two-thirds. In 1846 it was reported that most of the wagons went on from Santa Fe to Chihuahua without breaking their loads.

This extension to the south led to a number of complications. At the custom house in Santa Fe, the entire bill of lading had to be translated into Spanish and a *guia*, a sort of commercial passport, issued. Great care was necessary in drawing up the *factura*, or in-

---

[21] U.S. State Department, Consular Despatches, Santa Fe, Register 1830–46, and Despatches, August 28, 1830, to September, 1846, RG 59, Roll M–199, NA.

voice, as the slightest error or ink blot might lead to confiscation of the whole cargo. The Apache Indians of Mexico and New Mexico made something of a business of stealing mules in Chihuahua and selling them in New Mexico. On approaching El Paso del Norte, a freighter who had bought mules in Santa Fe might find himself in difficulties. An agent would appear in camp and claim all mules not bearing the sale brand of the hacienda whose identification they bore. In 1846, Webb lost three mules and Albert Speyer fifteen before they cleared El Paso by forced marches.

On occasion, traders into Old Mexico found loads of freight for Santa Fe. Webb, in 1846, freighted Mexican goods from Guadalajara to Santa Fe, nearly 1,800 miles, and made a profit on the transaction.[22]

Writing about 1832, *Licenciado* Antonio Barriero stated that the caravans arrived in Santa Fe in July. There they were met by Mexican and Anglo-American merchants from all over the Mexican states, from El Paso del Norte, and from Sonora. Merchandise became very cheap and many traders sold at wholesale, "at an increase of barely eighty, ninety, or one hundred per cent over Philadelphia or Saint Louis prices. Sometimes it is even sold at only a fifty per cent increase. These senseless sales have ruined many merchants."[23] Because many of the traders were operating on credit for which they had even mortgaged their homes and the credit was interest free for six to twelve months, many had to sell in a hurry and under unfavorable terms in order to get back to Missouri in time to meet their commitments. In 1853, William S. Messervy wrote to his partner Webb, "Doctor Massie sold out all his Groceries to Levi Spiegelberg and Beuthner at cost and 10¢ freight, $6,000 worth."[24]

William R. Barnard of Westport was a member of several firms that did an aggregate of $500,000 worth of business with the Santa Fe traders. He stated that their total loss was only $5,000, of which $3,500 was caused by the death of a trader at the hands of the Indians and the loss of his stock and merchandise. The merchant

22 Webb, *Adventures in the Santa Fe Trade*, 191–94, 284.
23 Pedro P. Pino, *et al.*, *Three New Mexico Chronicles*, 108.
24 Bieber (ed.), "Papers of James J. Webb," *loc. cit.*

through whom the trader bought his goods often served as a factor; he bought the wagons and teams, if they were not brought in from New Mexico, received the goods, attended to loading the wagons and the preparation of waybills and bills of lading, and also advanced money to the trader.

Occasionally a train from far afield appeared in the Missouri Valley. In 1863 the *Council Grove Press* noted the passage of one E. Agueirre, with a large mule train for "Tuscan, Arazonia [*sic*]."[25]

The long period of time involved in a round trip to Santa Fe or to Chihuahua or Durango apparently was not always understood by the eastern merchants who supplied many of the traders. In May, 1830, James Aull of Lexington, Missouri, wrote to C. S. and T. W. Smith of Philadelphia, "The Santa Fe caravan is about setting out. My sales for that trade will be from 8 to $10,000 at 25 per cent advance on cost and carriage with interest after six months at 10 per cent until paid." In October of the following year Aull wrote to Siter, Prince and Company, also of Philadelphia, to report that his goods had all been sold but that he had received only $1,200, and that the remainder would not arrive for twelve months but that he hoped for a good profit. He pointed out that cash was very scarce so the merchants were delaying their purchases from January until April or May.[26]

An additional source of trouble was the absence of any sort of a clearinghouse of information; as a result, there was often a glut in some goods and a shortage in others. It was reported, in 1848, that all the stores in Santa Fe were overstocked and many merchants had failed. Calico sold at its cost price in St. Louis, and the high duties on goods taken into Chihuahua made that outlet very precarious. It was this problem of getting the right goods to the right market at the right time that in 1863 caused Charles Raber to give up hauling his own goods and to become a professional freighter. In that year he had to store three wagonloads of merchandise for later sale.

---

25 *Council Grove Press* (October 5, 1863).

26 Ralph P. Bieber (ed.), "Letters of James and Robert Aull," *Collections*, MHS, Vol. V (June, 1928), 267–310.

The most successful traders were those who set up shop in some Mexican city, kept traveling themselves, and employed partners or agents to sell the goods in an orderly manner and keep track of the local market. James Josiah Webb is an excellent example. Starting in 1844 with $600 of his own, $600 worth of goods, and $612 worth of transportation on credit, he opened a store in Santa Fe after the Mexican War, and in 1851 the firm of Meservy and Webb required a train of sixty-three wagons to haul their goods for one year. In 1861, Webb retired from business after crossing the plains eighteen times in seventeen years. He retired with a competency that kept him in comfort on his Connecticut farm. An Albuquerque resident, writing to his brother in the States in 1853, said that James, apparently another brother, "has heretofore owned a 'train,' and been what is called a Santa Fe trader, out of which business he has saved $30,000, but he says that his farming is so lucrative that he shall abandon trading."[27]

The hazards of the prairies and of the market place were not the only risks a trader had to run; there were man-made risks as well. Those presented by the Indians will be discussed later, but white men also created dangers. In the summer of 1842, Don José Antonio Chavez, wealthy Mexican trader and brother of a former governor of New Mexico, who was known to be well disposed toward Americans and the Republic of Texas, was waylaid on the Santa Fe Trail, well within the territorial limits of the United States, robbed of $12,000 and some bales of furs, and murdered. The deed was performed by a band of some fifteen Missourians commanded by one "Captain" John McDaniel. On being captured by United States troops, McDaniel claimed to hold a Texas commission, received from Colonel Charles Warfield. Apparently no such commission was ever produced, and several members of the gang were hanged, including "Captain" McDaniel.

In February of the following year, the Republic of Texas issued a sort of letter of marque and reprisal to Colonel Jacob Snively of the Texan Army. Snively was authorized to raid the Santa Fe cara-

27 *New York Daily Times* (November 19, 1853).

vans and seize the property of the Mexican members, the booty to be divided fifty-fifty between the members of the expedition and the treasury of the Republic. At the request of the Mexican minister to Washington, Captain Philip St. George Cooke was ordered out with four companies of the First Dragoons to escort a caravan to the Arkansas River, where a Mexican escort would take over. Before the caravan reached the river, Snively had defeated and driven off the Mexican escort under Governor Armijo. When Cooke reached the river he crossed into what was generally considered to be Texan, or Mexican, territory, though Cooke insisted that it was United States territory and disarmed Snively's band.[28]

While the Texans were supposed to seize only Mexican property and let the Americans pass, many American traders had Mexican partners. If the Americans had stood by and watched the pillaging of the Mexicans, it would have ruined their business for many years to come. Cooke noted in his report that the Mexican traders expressed many fears of robbers and that the American traders were anxious to please them, "the guests of whose country, they are soon in their turn, to become.[29] It seems clear that Cooke's action avoided a bloody clash.

As a result of these attacks, President Santa Anna of Mexico issued a decree in August, 1843, closing the ports of entry at Taos, El Paso del Norte, and El Presidio del Norte, thus cutting off all overland trade. Evidently this decree worked such hardships on New Mexico and the northern states of Mexico that the embargo was raised in the following year. Because of the uncertainty created by these acts, not over 4 companies with 92 wagons, 200 men, and $200,000 worth of goods crossed the plains in 1844.[30]

---

[28] H. Bailey Carroll, "Steward A. Miller and the Snively Expedition of 1843," *Southwestern Historical Quarterly*, Vol. LIV (January, 1951), 261–86; William C. Binkley, *The Expansionist Movement in Texas, 1836–1850*; William E. Connelley, "A Journal of the Santa Fe Trail," *MVHR*, Vol. XII (June, 1925), 72–98, (September, 1925), 227–55.

[29] Connelley, "Journal of the Santa Fe Trail," *loc. cit.*, (Cooke lists 10 American owners and 5 Mexican; armed Americans 68, Mexicans, about the same; American wagons, large and small, 24; Mexican wagons, large, 32.)

[30] *Niles Register*, Vol. LXVII (November 2, 1844); C. P. Deatherage, *Early History of Greater Kansas City, Missouri and Kansas*, 359–60.

The Mexican War of 1846 was a great turning point in the Santa Fe trade. It was no longer an international trade; only the extension to Chihuahua crossed the new boundary with Mexico at El Paso del Norte. For some years the bitterness arising from the war cut heavily into this part of the trade. In 1848 the firm of Webb and Doan invested $30,000 in goods, of which amount they took only $10,000 worth to Chihuahua. The postmaster of Santa Fe said that, in 1851, some 544 wagons went south but that the high ad valorem duties collected at El Paso del Norte discouraged the Chihuahua trade.[31] Merchants tended to settle in some New Mexican town and hire out their freighting, as did Webb. The great movement of supplies to the army posts in the newly acquired territory brought the professional freighter to prominence. In 1857, the freighters found that they could make two round trips in one season, thus returning a greater profit on their initial investment.

The slavery issue in Kansas in 1856 brought trouble to the wagon-freighter. Abolitionists attacked trains from Kansas City and Westport, two towns presumed to be proslavery in sentiment. Colonel S. L. McKinney lost about sixty oxen and ten loaded wagons to a band led by one Captain Cutter.

The amount of money invested in transportation in the year 1858 for the Santa Fe trade was computed to be:

1,510 wagons	at $200	$302,000.00
361 horses	at $100	36,100.00
3,707 mules	at $100	370,700.00
14,515 oxen	at $37.50	554,312.50
	Total	$1,263,112.50

When wages and incidentals were added, the total figure reached $1,400,000.00.[32]

While the American traders tended to separate the functions of merchant and freighter, the Mexican merchants, especially the larger ones, continued to furnish their own trains, though there

---

31 Walker D. Wyman, "Freighting: A Big Business on the Santa Fe Trail," *KHQ*, Vol. I (November, 1931), 17–27.

32 Cottonwood Falls *Kansas Press* (July 25, 1859).

were some New Mexican freighters who made a business of hauling for the smaller firms.

The New Mexican merchant who ran his own trains always faced a serious problem: how many wagons to send out in order to assure a full load and no wasted space in the wagons. A. Letcher and Company of Taos often requested forwarding houses with which they dealt to hold enough general freight to fill their wagons to capacity. Government freight was preferred, as it was paid for in eastern exchange that could be used to settle accounts contracted on the East Coast, without loss through discount. In addition, government freight eliminated the problem of collecting the freight charges from civilian customers.

The independent freighters were as reliable a group of "boomers" as could be found in the West. They were highly paid specialists, with no permanent home base, who went wherever a job offered. In the books of the Charles Ilfeld Company, from 1867 to 1883, there appear the names of some forty major-domos, wagon bosses, yet there are only two or three cases where the same name appears twice. Most of these men were Mexicans who proved themselves completely reliable. There is no record of theft in the Ilfeld books for the whole period, though other merchants were not as fortunate. This is in contrast to the employees of a railroad who opened a case of champagne, removed a couple of bottles, and noted on the case that they had drunk to the owner's health.

Of course, things did not always go smoothly with the freighters. A train from Silver City, New Mexico, en route to the railhead, was delayed for several days near Las Vegas while the freighter dallied with some of the local "soiled doves." Another train was delayed because the major-domo, Manuel Barela, left a saloon in Las Vegas, shot two men without provocation, and was hanged the next morning by the Vigilantes.[33]

The account books of A. Letcher and Company show an excellent example of the cost of doing business in New Mexico in 1865, the

---

[33] Parish, *Charles Ilfeld Company*, 71–73.

last year before the westward extension of the railroads produced a radical change in the business of high plains wagon-freighting:

Expenses on $12,769.84 from New York at 15%	1916.48
10,895 lbs. from St. Louis to Leavenworth	
at 75¢ per 100 pounds	81.71
Storage, commission and drayage at Leavenworth at 17¢	18.52
Insurance from St. Louis to Leavenworth of $1065.00 at 1¢	10.65
Freight from Leavenworth to Santa Fe, 10,895 pounds at 14¢	1525.30
Total	3552.66
Cash paid on above from Santa Fe	351.00
	3903.66

Thus, freight, drayage, insurance, and storage commissions from New York to Santa Fe added slightly more than 30 per cent to the cost of the merchandise as delivered in Taos.[34] It might be noted that the freight charge amounted to just under 11 per cent of the cost price of the merchandise, considerably less than the cost of an outfit, set by Gregg as being some 25 per cent of the total outlay.

The contract between the professional freighter and the merchant was a simple affair:

> Received of W. H. Chick & Co. the following goods marked "Webb & Kingsbury, Santa Fe, N.M." in good order, which I promise to deliver in like good order, without delay (unavoidable dangers of the plains only excepted) at Santa Fe, N.M., to said Webb & Kingsbury, they paying freight on same at the rate of Nine cents pr. pound.... CHARLES W. KITCHEN.[35]

As the rails extended westward across the plains after the Civil War, the cost of wagon-freighting went down:

1865	from Leavenworth, Kansas	14¢	per pound
1868	from Ellsworth, Kansas	8¢	per pound
1869	from Sheridan, Kansas	2–3¢	per pound
1871	from Kit Carson, Colorado	1½¢	per pound

34 *Ibid.*, 13.
35 Bieber (ed), "Papers of James J. Webb," *loc. cit.*, 303.

The usual rule of thumb for computing freighting costs was one cent per pound per one hundred miles. The standard time allowance was twelve days for each one hundred miles. The freight bill was not always paid in cash; some freighters preferred to take part, or all, of their payment in trade.[36]

Until the 1850's the freighter could not make the most efficient use of his equipment and stock for lack of a return load from New Mexico to the Missouri Valley. In the early days of the Santa Fe trade the return load consisted of mules, jennets, or horses that needed no transportation, and specie or bullion, furs, and deerskins—items of high value and small bulk requiring little wagon space.[37] Gregg stated that the returning wagons carried only one to two thousand pounds because the teams were unable to haul heavy loads "on account of the decay of pasturage at this season" and because the traders wanted to travel fast to avoid the winter storms on the plains. The return trip was usually made in about forty days. He also noted that wool barely paid a return freight for wagons that would otherwise return empty.

In 1834 a quantity of wool had been shipped east, but apparently this speculation was not profitable as it was not repeated for twenty years.[38] In 1844, Webb noted that wool was one of the products of New Mexico but that it would not pay for transportation to the Missouri Valley. About 1854 someone who had not Webb's pessimistic point of view tried again. Several wagonsloads of wool were brought into Westport, and the Independence *Dispatch* noted this was a new feature of the Santa Fe trade. If properly carried out, it should be a profitable bit of business for the sheep ranchers, if they found a regular outlet. The paper went on to note that the traders would find it more profitable to bring back loads of wool than to return with empty wagons. Wool could be bought very cheaply in New Mexico, and in St. Louis it would always command a good

36 Parish, *Charles Ilfeld Company*, 14, 74–75.
37 *Niles Register*, Vol. IL (November 21, 1835); Vol. LVII, (October 26, 1839).
38 Bieber (ed.), "Letters of James and Robert Aull," *loc. cit.*, 286n.

Alexander Caldwell

Courtesy The Kansas State Historical Society, Topeka

William H. Russell

Courtesy The Kansas State Historical Society, Topeka

James J. Webb

From University of Washington Studies, XI, Humanistic Series No. 2 (1924)

This water-color self-portrait was made by William H. Jackson on his arrival in Salt Lake City in 1866.

Main Street, Helena, Montana, about 1869.

Courtesy Historical Society of Montana, Helena

A rare sight—this woman bullwhacker freighted to Deadwood, South Dakota.

Courtesy Nebraska State Historical Society, Omaha

These deep ruts were part of the Santa Fe Trail at Fort Union,
New Mexico.

Bulls of the Woods freighting train leaving Nebraska City for
Denver in the early 1860's.

Courtesy Nebraska State Historical Society, Omaha

price. Three years later Kansas City received 865,000 pounds of wool from New Mexico. By 1859 the importation of wool had reached such proportions that agents from Boston and New York appeared in Kansas City to buy up the wool as fast as it arrived. As of August, 1862, there had been received in Kansas City, 687,960 pounds of wool, and there were another 265,00 pounds on the road according to the bills of lading.[39]

The New Mexicans soon became unhappy about being merely a supplier of raw material. The Albuquerque *Press*, in 1863, pointed out that wool sold in Kansas City for twelve to fifteen cents per pound and that the first cost did not exceed four cents per pound, leaving eight to eleven cents for the freighters. The wool of New Mexico was coarser than States wool and was usually used in blankets, carpets, and other heavy goods. As a result of this coarse grade, New Mexico wool selling in Kansas City was appreciably cheaper than the average price of common wool on the eastern markets.

While the greatest period of growth of the American wool industry was from 1830 to 1850, it is apparent that it was not an increase in the price of wool that made it profitable to begin freighting wool to Kansas City. The annual average price in 1834, 1844, and 1854 was almost identical.[40] It seems rather that the supply of bullion and specie was nearly drained from New Mexico, and the diminution of the trade to Chihuahua had reduced the flow of silver from the Mexican silver mines. Webb stated that the gold mines of New Mexico produced only about two hundred thousand dollars per year, when in bonanza, and after the Mexican War the trade grew until it involved goods to the value of millions of dollars. The traders and merchants had to accept wool when they could no longer get gold and silver. *Merchants' Magazine* noted, in 1861, that this return load, accepted at a rate of four to five cents per pound, gave to the Santa Fe freighters "an advantage not enjoyed by the overland

[39] *Daily Missouri Democrat* (April 7, 1859); "The New Mexico Wool Trade," *Merchants' Magazine*, Vol. XLVII (October, 1862), 356–57; *Journal of Commerce* (August 5, 1859).

[40] *Journal of Commerce* (July 27, 1862; March 10, 1863).

freighters to any other portion of the country west of the great Plains."[41]

In the 1870's base metals began to appear in the return loads. The first shipment of copper seems to have been made to Sheridan, Kansas, when that town was the railhead of the Kansas Pacific Railroad. The charge for wagon freight from Fort Union to Sheridan was one and one-half cents per pound and two and one-half cents from Santa Fe. In 1873 the Las Animas, Colorado, *Leader* noted that a shipment of 29,000 pounds of lead from New Mexico had been forwarded by rail from that town. In the following year it reported shipments of 200,400 pounds of copper, as well as 25 bars of bullion weighing 1,487 pounds, plus 7,122 pounds of copper ore.[42] It is this development of a return load that makes the business of freighting into Santa Fe unique in the field of high plains wagon-freighting.

With the opening of the mines in Colorado in 1859, a good many freighters went through Denver to trade provisions for stock. One paper claimed that Denver was almost directly on the line from Taos and not far out of the way from Santa Fe. In addition there was, for a few years, a brisk trade with the mining camps in New Mexican flour, which was regularly quoted in the *Rocky Mountain News* at a dollar to two dollars per sack lower than States flour.[43] Taos Lightning, New Mexican whisky, was also freighted to Denver. This trade brought to New Mexico badly needed money with which to pay for purchases made in the East.

The Civil War was a period of crisis on the Santa Fe Trail which passed without serious complications. The interdependence of Missouri and New Mexico and the politico-economic bond between the two was early recognized. In May, 1861, the editor of the *Mesilla Times*, in southern New Mexico, wrote that a correspondent in

41 " Commerce of the Prairies," *Merchants' Magazine*, Vol. XLIV (January, 1862), 22, 28.

42 Rossiter W. Raymond, Statistics of Mines and Mining . . . West of the Rocky Mountains, *House Exec. Doc. No. 207*, 41 Cong., 1 sess. (Serial 1424), 404; Las Animas *Leader* (Colorado) (February 13, October 8, 1874; August 6, 14, October 15, November 26, 1875).

43 *Daily Missouri Democrat* (April 7, 1859); *Rocky Mountain News*, Prices Current, 1859–61.

Santa Fe thought that the influential citizens had decided to await the decision of Missouri in the difficulties between the North and the South. "The closest commercial relations exist between New Mexico and Missouri and probably induces the above line of action." When Colonel Edward Richard Sprigg Canby took command of the Department of New Mexico in June of the same year, he noted that the citizens of New Mexico had closer relations with Missouri than with Texas or Mexico. As a result, he did not anticipate any immediate political trouble.[44]

Fearing action by guerillas from Arkansas or Texas, Canby in the same month wrote to the commanding officer of Fort Union that he had requested the commander at Fort Larned to "advise trains passing through that post to keep up the Arkansas and come into New Mexico by the Raton route." Of thirteen trains arriving at Fort Union in July and August following that request, the first seven came via the Cimarron route, the next six by the Mountain route.[45]

This was to lead to a change in the flow of traffic on the Santa Fe Trail. Percival G. Lowe noted in 1854 that the Mountain Branch had been abandoned at Raton Pass: "Trees had fallen across the trail, mountain torrents had made great gullies, and it took Lieutenant Craig's pioneer party—details from 'B' and 'D' troops—several days to make the road passable." Prior to 1861 the Cimarron Cutoff had carried the bulk of the traffic, but in 1866, Colonel Meline noted, "The usual route is by the Raton Pass and the Arkansas River." In 1865, "Uncle Dick" Wootton had improved the road through the pass, and freighters were apparently willing to pay the toll and use the improved road.[46] With the westward extension of the rails, the Mountain Branch became the shorter route from the railhead to Fort Union.

44 Edward Steere, "Fort Union: Its Economic and Military History," unpublished manuscript, Fort Union National Monument; *Official Records of the War of the Rebellion* [*OR*], Series 1, I, 606.
45 Robert M. Utley, "Fort Union and the Santa Fe Trail," unpublished manuscript, Fort Union National Monument, 7, 7n.
46 Lowe, *Five Years a Dragoon*, 387; Meline, *2000 Miles on Horseback*, 261; Bess McKinnon, "The Toll Road over Raton Pass," *NMHR*, Vol. II (January, 1927), 83–89.

Because of the guerilla activity in Kansas and Missouri and the Confederate invasion of New Mexico, there was very little traffic on the trail in 1861. With the defeat of the Confederates at Glorieta Pass, in New Mexico, in the spring of 1862, the trains began to roll again, to fill the shortage of supplies that had developed. In May, 1863, Brigadier General James H. Carleton, who had relieved Canby, reported that more trains had left for the States than ever before and that nearly all available capital had been invested in transportation. Carleton went on to mention the threat to the trail by the rebels in Arkansas and Texas who knew as well as he what would be on the road and "just how poorly they may be guarded."[47] Fortunately for the freighters, the threat was greater in the minds of the military commanders than it was in actual fact. The Council Grove, Kansas, *Press* remarked in April, 1863, "Large trains are passing in to the river daily now. The trade to New Mexico promises to be much larger than ever this season."

The end of the Civil War did not bring peace to the Santa Fe Trail. The Indian War of 1864 spread death and destruction from the Rio Grande to Montana. The Apaches in the Guadalupe Mountains of southern New Mexico and around Fort Davis, between San Antonio and El Paso, killed twenty men in a six-week period in the spring of 1866. In the previous May the commanding officer of Fort Union advised all trains traveling east to organize themselves so that they would have at least forty armed men, each supplied with twenty-five rounds of ammunition. Small trains were to be consolidated to meet these requirements or be obliged to take the Raton route. A sergeant was stationed at Koenig's ranch, where the two branches of the trail forked. It was his duty to see to it that trains were organized in accordance with Paragraph 2, General Orders Number 29, Headquarters Department of the Missouri, dated 25 February 1867. Trains not fully armed bought weapons at Las Vegas and ammunition at Fort Union.

All freighters did not take kindly to the army's concern for their welfare. The sergeant had some trouble with the major-domo of a

[47] *OR*, Series 1, XV, 724.

train of ten wagons. Instead of camping where he was told, the major-domo moved farther out and the sergeant had to go out and bring him back, attach him to a larger train, and appoint a captain for the consolidated train.[48] In time the railroad eliminated the Indian menace.

As the western territories became more settled, there appeared another problem for the freighter—the law. About 1870, Morris Wise was freighting to New Mexico. Near Bent's Fort, on the Indian Reservation, someone in his train traded 5 gallons of whisky to an Indian for a pony. The local Indian agent complained to the territorial authorities, who seized the train. The records of the territorial District Court, in the case of "The United States vs 93 oxen and other property," list 93 oxen, 10 large freight wagons, 4 ponies, 1 mule, 1 Rockaway carriage, 80 boxes of soap, 70 boxes of candles, 334 sacks of sugar, 10 sacks of coffee, and 50 barrels of whisky, all appraised at $8,550, as the cargo of the train. Unfortunately there is no record of the disposition of the case.[49]

The high plains freighter who tried to extend the season, by leaving one end or the other early in the spring or late in the fall, ran a constant risk in the winter. Animals, and sometimes men, were lost to prairie storms. In 1840, Albert Speyer lost 400 out of 750 mules. In 1841, Alvarez lost 2 men and all of his mules. In 1844 a party lost 300 mules in an October storm. In 1848 a government contractor lost 800–900 oxen and had to abandon his wagons. In 1848 a party wintered in on the *jornada,* and lost all animals. In 1850, 1,000 head of cattle were lost between Cimarron and San Miguel. And in 1851, 1 man and 300 mules were frozen 37 miles west of Council Grove, Kansas.[50] The above is only a partial list of the losses to the whims of Dame Nature, but it is enough to emphasize the fact that anyone who stayed in the business long enough was bound to meet serious reverses. Certainly the life of the trader or freighter

48 James H. Carleton to John Pope, April 26, 1866; W. B. Lane to Gonzalez, May 23, 1867; Quartermaster Sgt. McLoughlin to W. B. Lane, June 22, 28, 1867, Arrott Collection, New Mexico Highlands University, Las Vegas, New Mexico.
49 Forbes Parkhill, *The Law Goes West,* 50.
50 Duffus, *Santa Fe Trail,* 136; Hobbs, *Wild Life,* 59.

was not one of ease. In 1844, Colonel Samuel C. Owens wrote from the Caches that there had been sickness among his hands that had delayed him for ten days. "I have been mule driver, ox driver, and every thing else, from Council Grove to this place."[51] No matter how strenuous the life on the plains, there was always the lure of the exotic city at the end of the trail to maintain a supply of men for the trains.

Not all the freighting from New Mexico went over the Santa Fe Trail. The output of the copper mines in south-central New Mexico was for years hauled to the coast of the Gulf of Mexico. In 1860 the *Mesilla Miner* noted that the local merchants were divided concerning the best route for obtaining their supplies. About fifty wagons had gone to Kansas City, and freighters were quoting nine cents per pound. Other goods came from Indianola and San Antonio, Texas. "We believe the freight is about the same on both routes." It might be noted that, at this time, Mesilla was a stronghold of Southern sympathy.

The arrival in Santa Fe might mean a busy time for the traders, but for the bullwhackers and mule skinners it opened a period of pleasant relaxation from the hard work and constant tension of the plains. One bullwhacker recalled that during his stay of four days, his crew of Missouri boys danced every night, and added, "Those Mexican girls were not such good lookers when seen on the street in the day time, but they were dolls when rigged out in the dancing costumes." Another traveler wrote that the Mexican girls were more beautiful than those of like social rank in the States, "their jetty black eyes, slender and delicate frame, with unusual small ankles and feet, together with their gay winning address, make you at once easy and happy in their company." Marian Russell, who traveled to Santa Fe with her mother in 1852, noted that Santa Fe seemed to come to life with the fall of darkness. "As soon as our freight was delivered at the customs house, our drivers began eagerly to sign up and draw their wages. They washed their faces and combed their hair. Pierre even drew the comb through his croppy moustache.

[51] *Weekly Reveille* (October 12, 1844).

There was a great hunting for clean shirts and handkerchiefs . . . a *baile* was forming."[52] It is small wonder that Santa Fe drew many adventure-seekers as well as profit-seekers.

The importance of the overland freighter was recognized in 1864 by the *New Mexican* of Santa Fe:

> THE FREIGHTERS—The enterprise of this portion of our fellow citizans is worthy of warm commendation. They run many risks and are full of energy. Their profits, when they have no bad luck, are said to be fair. The present month has been extremely cold, and the snows have fallen heavily. Yet our townsman, Charles Parker, Esq. has come in with his mules in good condition. Mr. Allison also came in with his ox train.—Don Teodoro Baca of Las Vegas also arrived here with his train. These three trains have made two trips, each, to Kansas City, and returned since early last spring. Freighting for the government, traders, and merchants from the States, is a very heavy business.[53]

The *Topeka Record* in 1860, noting the preparations for the freighting season about to open, remarked that only those who had seen the wagon trains rolling out could realize the magnitude of the Santa Fe trade, "every one of the hugh 'prairie schooners' . . . being laden with from fifty to eighty hundred pounds of merchandise, sometimes of the richest fabrics that find their way to the West."[54]

Not only did Santa Fe trade serve as the training ground for many of the freighters who later hauled to other points, but it served as the life line that lifted New Mexico from a pastoral existence, barely above the subsistence level, to the position of an active producer of raw materials to feed the growing industry of the United States. In addition, the trade had a great effect on the economy of the Missouri Valley—in the demand for wagons, draft animals, and supplies; in the need for warehousing, banking, and forwarding and commission houses; and in man power, arms, and all sorts of supplies for the trains.

52 Toponce, *Reminiscences*, 25; *Niles Register*, Vol. LXI (December 4, 1841); Russell *Land of Enchantment*, 30.
53 *Journal of Commerce* (January 7, 1864).
54 *Daily Times* (February 2, 1860).

CHAPTER VIII

TO THE CITY OF THE SAINTS

Freighting into Salt Lake City from 1849 to 1869 was dominated by the merchant-freighter. The common-carrier-type freighter did not play the important role that he did in freighting into Denver and the Montana gold fields.

The first migrants to the Great Salt Lake Basin in 1847 and 1848 took with them sufficient clothing, tools, and food to sustain the settlement for a year or so, but after that, a great demand for goods of all sorts grew up. Throughout the period of migration, there was a certain amount of what has been called "incidental freighting." Migrants arriving in the Missouri Valley often converted any spare cash into merchandise which they carried along, with their personal possessions, for possible sale in Utah.[1] This, however, was hardly enough for a population that exceeded 80,000 souls by the time the transcontinental railroad was completed in 1869.

A small amount of property belonging to the Church of Jesus Christ of Latter-day Saints was carried in the very early emigrant trains. In 1849 some five tons were carried: a carding machine, a printing press, type, a box of cases, glue, stationery, printing ink, and 872 bundles of paper—most of this needed to start the *Deseret News*.[2]

The first great influx of goods into Salt Lake City, and the first saving boon to Utah's economy, came not from the merchants but

---

[1] Strebel, "Freighting Between the Missouri River and Utah," 60.
[2] Wendell Ashton, *Voice in the West: Biography of a Pioneer Newspaper*, 17–18.

from the California-bound forty-niners. Many individuals, to expedite their travels to the New El Dorado, traded large wagons for small, or even for pack animals. Some offered as many as three or four large wagons complete with oxen for one light "Yankee" wagon. Pack mules and horses, ordinarily worth $30, were selling for as much as $200. Some persons, because of losses on the trail, had to buy or barter for additional food or draft animals or for the services of blacksmith, wheelwright, or wagonmaker. One traveler noted, "We can trade groceries for anything that they have, but they will not sell for money, for they have plenty and cannot buy what they want with it." Another wrote, "One lady begged a handful of coffee, saying that in two years she had not tasted that beverage. Another asked for as much as would make a cupful for a sick friend."[3]

Among the early travelers were a number of California-bound merchants with stocks ranging in value from $2,000 to $10,000. While they were in Salt Lake City, word was received that ships had arrived in San Francisco with similar merchandise and the market was overstocked. A party from Missouri, whom the Mormons believed to have had a hand in the troubles that led to their expulsion from that state, had a stock valued at $50,000, and the *Frontier Guardian* of Kanesville, Iowa, said, "they found it indispensibly necessary to sell out in the Valley." While the earliest gold seekers, in June, 1849, found prices very high—tea, $5.00–$10.00 per pound; coffee, $2.00–$3.00 per pound; and sugar, $1.00–$1.50 per pound—with the arrival of more migrants and the Missouri train, prices came down. In July coffee was down to $.50 per pound and sugar to $.37 per pound.[4]

With such a demand for goods, Captain John Grant, Indian trader from Fort Hall, was able to sell a small amount of sugar and coffee at $1.00 per pint (less than a pound) and $.25 calico at $.50

3 Willaim Mulder and A. Russell Mortensen (eds.), *Among the Mormons: Historic Accounts by Contemporary Observers*, 235: J. Cecil Alter, *Utah: The Storied Domain*, I, 102.

4 Journal History [hereinafter referred to as JH], Church Historian's Office, Church of Jesus Christ of Latter-day Saints, Salt Lake City, Utah, December 11, 1849; Gustavus G. Pearson, *Overland in 1849* (ed. by Jessie H. Goodman), 26; Mulder and Mortensen (eds.), *Among the Mormons*, 235–36.

to $.75 per yard. In November, 1849, Louis Vasquez, also an Indian trader, brought in a small amount of sugar which he sold at the rate of three pounds for $2.00.[5]

In the spring of 1849, James M. Livingstone and Charles A. Kincaid, of St. Louis, decided to gamble on the needs of the Mormons in far-away Utah, and hauled $20,000.00 worth of goods to Salt Lake City. The *Frontier Guardian* in September predicted that, because of the boom set off by the forty-niners, Livingstone and Kincaid would be ruined by the time they got to Salt Lake City; common domestic sheeting was selling for $.05 to $.10 per yard, good spades and shovels for $.50 each, and $1.50 vests for $.37½ each. "Indeed, almost every article, except sugar and coffee, is selling on an average fifty per cent. below wholesale prices in the Eastern cities."[6] As it turned out, Livingstone and Kincaid found such a ready market that they did business at the rate of $2,000.00 to $3,000.00 a day until their stock was exhausted.

Conditions were so bad that many women were wearing burlap and many men were wearing buckskin. For lack of metal, many pioneers were using wooden utensils such as spoons and wash basins. Four months later another correspondent of the *Frontier Guardian* pointed out that the California migration was essentially a bachelor affair and that most of the goods unloaded in Utah had been men's ready-to-wear clothing. When Livingstone and Kincaid, followed by J. and E. Reece of New York, arrived with balanced assortments, their sales were good. " . . . the cry of the people is goods, Goods, GOODS." William Chandless, visiting Salt Lake City in 1855, said, "The Mormans bought freely—nay, fiercely: the first stores were besieged from morning till night, and in ten days or a fortnight all was sold and paid for in specie; for the merchants *must* pay in the States for their goods in gold."[7] He also remarked that most of the

---

[5] JH, September 28, 1854; Strebel, "Freighting Between the Missouri River and Utah," 67.

[6] JH, September 3, 1849.

[7] *Ibid.*, December, 1849 (N.B.: Often clippings in the Journal appear not under the date of publication but under the date to which they apply); Chandless, *Visit to Salt Lake City*, 216.

goods were "what we should consider necessaries, some few luxuries." In the spring of 1850 the church erected a large store on the southeast corner of the Council House lot, for the "temporary" accommodation of Livingstone and Company.

As nothing succeeds like success, 1850 saw more merchant-freighters enter the Utah trade. Ben Holladay, who had been a successful contractor for Kearny's Army of the West in 1845, went into partnership with Theodore Warner of Weston, Missouri. Holladay was to provide fifty wagons and teams and Warner to provide $70,000 in merchandise. The *Deseret News* of Salt Lake City noted on June 22, 1850, "Mr. Holladay comes highly recommended by our old friend, Gen. Doniphan, and others."

By October there were four firms established in Salt Lake City, and all were doing a profitable business. Livingstone and Kincaid and Holladay and Warner were by far the largest commercial houses, but Williams and Blair and J. and E. Reece were sharing in the market. In addition, Elders Heywood and Wooley brought in goods for the church, and Elder Wilford Woodruff brought in ten wagonloads of goods for his brother-in-law Ilus F. Carter.[8]

Some idea of the service rendered to Utah by the merchant-freighter can be gained by scanning the advertisements appearing in the *Deseret News* on the arrival of the season's trains. Holladay and Warner, in July, 1850, offered, "Ladies' and Gent's Boots and Shoes; Men's and Boys' Hats and Caps; Ladies' Bonnets, Parasols, &c., Also Oysters, Sardines, Pepper Sauce, Lemon Syrup, Tobacco, Teas, Rice, &c." They also announced that they would receive by the train due on August 1: "Groceries, Hardware, Glass, Nails, Oil, Paints, Leather, Stationery, &c." A year later T. S. Williams opened a new store stocked with tea, coffee, sugar, saleratus, raisins, currents, figs, candies, nutmegs, spices, olive oil, lemon syrup, pickles, mustard, pepper, salt, crockeryware, hardware, stationery, domestics, shirting, printed calicoes, delaines, Orleans cloth, alpacas, shawls, ribbons, artificials, gloves, stockings, pins, needles, kerseymeres, and jeans.[9]

8 JH, October 31, 1850.
9 Salt Lake City *Deseret News* (July 6, 1850; November 29, 1851).

As late as 1864 one sharp-eyed young man trading in Utah noted that many of the housewives were cooking at open fireplaces. In the following year he freighted a trainload of stoves from Des Moines, Iowa, to Salt Lake City. Single stoves costing $24.00 sold readily for $125.00 to $175.00. Somewhat later, in 1865, one wagon train took to Utah two threshing machines at a charge of $.25 a pound, making the total cost, laid down in Utah, $3,000.00 to $3,500.00 each. Also on the train were twelve combined "Buckeye" harvesters and mowers costing, laid down in Utah, $1,000.00 each. In 1859, Cyrus H. McCormick was selling a two-horse mower-reaper combination for $140.00 and a four-horse model for $155.00. In 1865 his two-horse self-rake reaper sold for $190.00 cash.[10]

The *American Railway Times* pointed out, in January, 1861, that the Salt Lake trade was less profitable, though more varied, than the Santa Fe trade because of the high cost of transportation and the interest on the invested capital that was lost during the long overland trip. The Utah trade was largely in cheap dry goods and clothing, boots and shoes, groceries and liquors. Most foodstuffs except pork were locally raised. The *Times* expressed doubt that, because of heavy overstocking during the last years, the trade for 1860 exceeded half a million dollars.[11]

In the first years of freighting, not only the goods but also the wagons and draft animals were sold, thus adding to the profit of the venture. Wagons that cost $120 in the Missouri Valley were worth $500 in the Great Salt Lake Valley. To suit the Utah market, the freighters used wagons that were adaptable to farm use, the 2,500- to 3,500-pound capacity "Chicago wagon." As most of the bullwhackers were bound for California, the freighter could also close his payroll at Salt Lake City. This sometimes led to complications, as witness a complaint lodged in 1864 with Squire Miner by

[10] Joseph G. McCoy, *Historic Sketches of the Cattle Trade of the West and Southwest*, 409; Eugene Munn, "Early Freighting and Claim Club Days in Nebraska," *Proceedings and Collections*, NSHS, 2nd Series, Vol. V (1902), 313–17; William T. Hutchinson, *Cyrus Hall McCormick; Harvest, 1856–1884*, 80 n., 94.

[11] "Commerce of the Prairies," *American Railway Times* (Boston) (January 26, 1861).

two teamsters who claimed breach of contract by Buckmaster and Company in refusing to take them to California. Judgment was granted the plaintiffs in the amount of $20 each.[12]

These local conditions added to the length of the trip, some 1,000 miles or more, probably account for the predominance of the merchant-freighter. He could stay in Utah to supervise his sales without worrying about getting his wagons back to Missouri or about the overhead of an empty return trip. Holladay was the first to extend his trade to the Pacific Coast. He bought up good Mormon cattle in the Salt Lake Valley and drove them to California, where beef was in great demand.

It was these early traders that set a price policy that lasted with only minor fluctuations until the mid-1860's. The *Deseret News* noted in 1854 that Livingstone and Kincaid had established the prices "and based them on first cost, interest, and expenses, until sales could be made." The paper went on to say that they never raised prices when they had a monopoly of a certain item. Year in and year out, coffee and sugar sold for forty cents a pound. There was one break in these prices for about three months when J. H. Horner and Company drove coffee down to three pounds for a dollar, sugar to thirty cents a pound, and twenty-five cent calico to eighteen and three quarters cents per yard.[13]

The first serious break in the uniform price policy came in late 1858, when the so-called Mormon War disrupted the trade. At that time both coffee and sugar rose to sixty-five cents a pound. By mid-1859 prices were back to normal. The second, and much more serious, break came in 1864–65. The Civil War drove prices in the Missouri Valley markets up by 300 to 400 per cent. An early settler in Iowa remembered that coffee became so expensive that his father had to serve unadulterated coffee on Sunday afternoon only.[14] In addition to the general nationwide price rise, the Plains Indian War of 1864 made freighting more hazardous and expensive; in Utah,

12 Abbey, *Trip Across the Plains in the Spring of 1850*, 39; Strebel,, "Freighting Between the Missouri River and Utah," 50, 115–18; *Deseret News* (August 3, 1864).
13 *Deseret News* (September 28, 1854).
14 Charles A. Ficke, *Memories of Fourscore Years.*

sugar soared to a dollar a pound and coffee to a dollar and a quarter. The general price stability in Utah was in marked contrast to the annual rise and fall in the price of bacon, flour, and coffee on the Denver market. There prices dropped when the wagon trains began to arrive in the spring and began to climb when the last trains of the fall had come in.

Economic warfare was not unknown in the mid-nineteenth century. General Daniel Hanmer Wells of the Nauvoo Legion, Mormondom's militia, on the outbreak of the Mormon War, passed orders to his subordinates to treat C. A. Perry's train as one of those of the government but to let pass those of Livingstone and Kincaid. On the other side, General Albert Sidney Johnston ordered that no trains be passed through government lines.[15]

It was the same issue of *Deseret News* that had remarked on the uniformity of prices that set afloat the canard that Livingstone and Kincaid had agreed to trade in Salt Lake City for five years, to realize a certain net profit, "and then return to Egypt, which they have done."[16] Apparently the gentlemen in question changed their plans, as they were still in business in 1862. Could it be that at the end of the five-year period they had not realized their goal?

When Sir Richard Francis Burton was making a short visit to the City of the Saints in 1860, he noted that sugar, selling in the States for six cents a pound, cost thirty-seven and one-half cents in Salt Lake City and that coffee, at ten cents per pound in the States, cost forty to fifty cents. He also remarked that freight was reckoned at fourteen cents per pound coming from the east and twenty-five cents per pound when coming from the west. Burton seemed to imply that the Salt Lake merchants were first-class gougers. A little arithmetic may make the picture a little clearer. In the first place, fourteen cents per pound for freight was low; the going rate until the railroads came was seventeen to twenty-five cents a pound.[17]

---

15 JH, October 25, 1857; Edward D. Tullidge, *History of Salt Lake City*.

16 *Deseret News* (September 28, 1854).

17 William Fulton, "Freighting and Staging in Early Days," *Proceedings and Collections*, NSHS, 2nd Series, Vol. V (1902), 263.

Using the ruling rate and allowing 10 per cent interest on the capital that was tied up for almost a year, we get the following:

100 pounds coffee at St. Louis	at $.10	per lb.	$10.00
Freight	at .17	per lb.	17.00
Interest, one year	at 10%		1.00
			28.00
Sold in Salt Lake City	at $.40	per lb.	40.00
		Gross Profit	$12.00

It is impossible to assess against this one-hundred pound sack of coffee the normal overhead of a retail business. It is known that Livingstone and Kincaid paid an annual rent for their store of $1,000 per year until about 1859 and thereafter $2,400. By 1853 a man with special qualifications could earn $2,000 a year and expenses as a clerk in Salt Lake City.[18]

It is equally impossible to assess against this one sack of coffee the random losses that were incidental to the business. In 1850, on his first trip, Ben Holladay had to buy oxen in Salt Lake City and send them back to bring in his wagons. Three years later the train of J. and E. Reece, coming from California, lost fifty to sixty horses out of a total of ninety, a loss of $15,000 to $20,000.[19] The hard winter of 1856 struck the pastured herds of both Gilbert and Gerrish and of Livingstone and Kincaid, each company losing six or seven hundred head of cattle. One train, under government contract, loaded chiefly with flour, was eleven months on the road from Fort Leavenworth. In the summer of 1864 it was so harrassed by Indians that it was caught on the plains by winter weather, and the thaw of 1865 was late. The mule skinners ate most of the flour and some of the mules, leaving the contractor to pay for the flour, stand the loss of his animals that had cost from $100 to $125, meet the payroll, and still receive no payment for his efforts. Even the act of traveling on busi-

18 Account Book, Livingstone and Kincaid in Account with Governor Brigham Young, 1853–62, Church Historian's Office, Church of Jesus Christ of Latter-day Saints, Salt Lake City; William K. Sloan, "Autobiography," *Annals of Wyoming*, Vol. IV (July, 1926), 248–49.

19 *Deseret News* (June 22, 1850); William B. Rice, "Early Freighting on the Salt Lake–San Bernardino Trail," *Pacific Historical Review*, Vol. XI (March, 1942), 73–80.

ness had its hazards. In 1854, Charles A. Kincaid, on his way east by stagecoach, was wounded in a skirmish with Indians and lost $10,150. Certainly the return to the freighter had to be good if he were to sustain the inevitable losses that he would suffer if he stayed in business long enough.[20]

Conditions in Utah in October, 1853, are described by William K. Sloan, who arrived with a train of goods of L. Stewart, a Mormon merchant:

> The Mormons had plenty of money, obtained by supplying the California emmigration [sic] with their surplus produce, cattle and horses, and were very destitute of clothing and groceries consequently when they heard of our train they flocked in from all parts of the Territory to purchase our goods; the farm was completely covered with campers, some of them being there a week before we came in.[21]

A serious problem for the Salt Lake merchant was the long-range planning required. As only one trip per year was feasible for an outfit, the merchant had to plan ahead for a full year. When he went east in January or February to make his purchases, he had to think of Christmas some ten or eleven months away. The *Deseret News* was often embarrassed by nonarrival of supplies. In 1853, Reece's train was supposed to pick up a supply of newsprint in southern California but could find none, and so the *News* had to fall back on half-sheets and locally made rag paper. Five years later the *Valley Tan* noted that there was much excitement at Gilbert and Gerrish's because they had just received a large stock of cotton yarn, an item that had been in short supply for some months.[22] In 1860 the *Valley Tan* was driven out of business by a shortage of paper. The term "valley tan" was originally applied to locally tanned leather but soon was applied to anything produced in the Salt Lake Valley.

The account books of Livingstone and Kincaid with Brigham

[20] Brownville *Nebraska Advertiser* (September 21, 1865); Strebel, "Freighting Between the Missouri River and Utah," 44, 292.

[21] "Autobiography," *loc. cit.*, 248–49.

[22] Salt Lake City *Valley Tan* (November 8, 1858; February 29, 1860).

Young, over a nine-year period, show clearly the effects of the arrival of the wagon trains. In August and September the transactions required a number of pages, but for the four months preceding the arrival of the year's trains there were few, if any, entries. The reporter for the *Deseret News* complained in July, 1855, "We did not call on the first day [at Livingstone and Kincaid] . . . because the store was so full of greedy customers, we could get no chance."[23]

The size of the early trade may be seen from the following table which appeared in the *Deseret News* in November, 1855:

Firm	*Tons Freight*	*Cost at 17¢/lb.*	*Wagons*	*Oxen*	*Oxen Died*
T. S. Williams	185	$62,900	87	1,000	300
Livingstone and Kincaid	160	54,400	102	1,000	210
Gilbert and Gerrish	75	25,500	54	600	75
Snow and Company	50	17,000	35	234	110
Blair and Company	35	11,900	21	336	20
W. S. Godbe	8	2,720	5	49	7
Total	513	$174,420	304	3,219	722

The table shows the magnitude of a year's trade and reveals one of the random hazards of freighting, the loss of animals on the trail. The losses range from 6 per cent for Blair and Company to 47 per cent for Snow and Company.[24] The load per wagon was 1.68 tons, or 3,360 pounds each; obviously these were the "Chicago" wagons. If the population can be assumed to have had a steady rate of growth between the censuses of 1850 and 1860, the population in 1855 would have been about 26,000, and dividing this into the weight of goods imported to Salt Lake Valley, the average would have been a little less than forty pounds per person, not a great deal for a life of comfort.

The single greatest freighting effort to Utah was that of the United States Army during the Mormon War in 1857. The prime

---

23 Account Book, Livingstone and Kincaid with Governor Young; Pass Book, B. Young and Council in Account with Livingstone and Kincaid, Church Historian's Office, Church of Jesus Christ of Latter-day Saints, Salt Lake City; JH, July 9, 1853.
24 JH, November 21, 1855.

contractor was the firm of Russell, Majors and Waddell, who sent out 59 trains of 25 wagons each to haul 18 months' supplies for an army of some 2,500 men. In the following year an additional 3,000 soldiers were to be sent to Utah, and the firm built up their equipment to 4,500 wagons, 50,000 oxen, and 4,000 mules and employed 5,000 teamsters, wagonmasters, clerks, and other employees. Eventually this freighting operation was a boon to the Mormon economy. The "J. Murphy" wagons were too large for farm use, and it would not have been economical to send them back empty to the Missouri Valley. As a result, the freighter sold thousands of these wagons, which had cost $175.00 to $200.00, to the church authorities for $10.00 each. The wagons were broken up to salvage their ironwork.[25] When the army garrison was reduced in 1859, huge stocks of supplies, wagons, and animals were sold at great discounts. Six-mule government wagons, complete, sold at auction for $6.50.[26]

The success of Livingstone and Kincaid in their first trip spurred a group of Mormons, including Shadrach Roundy, Jedidiah M. Grant, Abraham O. Smoot, and others, to form the Great Salt Lake Valley Carrying Company. This company offered to freight to Utah for twelve cents a pound, well below the customary seventeen cents. In the summer of 1850, Grant brought out one train of goods for John Reece, and Smoot brought out one for Livingstone and Kincaid plus some goods for the church store. For reasons that are not clear, this was the whole effort of the Great Salt Lake Valley Carrying Company. There was a great drive by the church authorities to attain self-sufficiency, and it may be that the operation of this company, bringing in goods from outside, was considered inimical to this goal.[27] On the other hand, it may be that the company found that its advertised rates were uneconomical.

The drive for self-sufficiency took many forms. In 1851 equipment for a woolen mill was brought in, despite the fact that the territory could not supply enough raw wool to meet its own needs.

[25] Leonard J. Arrington, *Great Basin Kingdom*, 198.
[26] Toponce, *Reminiscences*, 39.
[27] Arrington, *Great Basin Kingdom*, 79–80; Orson F. Whitney, *History of Utah*, 418–19; Leland H. Creer, *Founding of an Empire*, 352.

The United States Censuses for 1850, 1860, and 1870 show fewer sheep than people and a production of wool of less than two pounds per person. In the following year machinery was brought in for a sugar-beet mill. The machinery was bought in France, and the estimated cost of transportation from France to Utah was twenty-five cents per pound. To transport the machinery from the Missouri Valley, the agent of the church bought fifty-two light wagons, suitable for farm use. When a number of these broke down under the weight of the machinery, he had to buy forty large "Santa Fe" wagons. The new wagons and the oxen to draw them called for a cash outlay of $40,000. The attempt to produce sugar failed, apparently because of a lack of technical know-how.[28]

In the early 1860's an attempt was made to grow cotton in the southwestern part of the state, the area still known as "Utah's Dixie." With the Civil War in full swing, in 1862, some 74,000 pounds of cotton were shipped east where it sold for $1.00 a pound. Despite the best efforts of the church authorities, it was a hard fact that the estimated cost of production of Utah cotton never went below $1.19 per pound. With the end of the Civil War, the price of cotton at St. Louis dropped to $.50 a pound, and cotton-raising in Utah was doomed.[29]

In addition to supporting the many efforts leading toward local production, the church kept up a drumfire of preaching against the purchase of nonessential items, all to no avail. Edward D. Tullidge, Mormon historian, said, "A fresh opening of a season's stock of States' goods by our merchants, for instance, was quite sufficient to kill a whole year's preaching on home manufactures."[30]

In an attempt to keep the money paid for freighting in the community and to provide assistance to the handcart companies of immigrants, the Brigham Young Express and Carrying Company was formed in 1856. The plan called for the establishment of villages every fifteen to thirty miles along the route from Omaha to Salt

28 Creer, *Founding of an Empire*, 352; Arrington, *Great Basin Kingdom*, 117–20.
29 "The Cotton Mission," *UHQ*, Vol. XXIX (July, 1961), 201–21.
30 Tullidge, *History of Salt Lake City*, 670.

Lake City. Each village was to provide a resting place, to raise sufficient wheat and forage to support the trains, and to provide fresh
draft animals. The success of the entire enterprise depended on the
contract to carry the United States mail. When this contract was
secretly canceled at the beginning of the Mormon War, the project
was doomed. When word was received of the approach of Johnston's
army, the parties already in the process of setting up villages in western Wyoming were recalled.

A major problem faced by the church was the transportation of
the poorer Saints from the Missouri Valley to Zion. In 1859 experi-
ments were made looking to a round trip in one season, an operation heretofore considered impossible. It was soon apparent that
this could be done, if the draft animals were properly cared for. The
first train of forty-three wagons brought back, besides the baggage
of the immigrants, seven tons of paper; two tons of cotton yarn; four
tons of tea, coffee, and tobacco; three tons of sugar; ten tons of dry
goods; two tons of axes, scythes, shovels, and spades; several carding
machines; a button-making machine; and several tons of miscellaneous items such as black pepper, raisins, files, candles, type, ink,
anvils, steel, madder, and liquor.[31]

In the following year Joseph W. Young left the valley in the
spring with thirty wagons and returned in the fall with newly purchased machinery and merchandise. When the train was ready to
start back, the men said that they could use two or three girls to cook
and wash for them. "The girls would get their food and a wagon to
sleep in, but they would have to walk the entire distance, except
when crossing streams, they could ride."[32] This is one of the few
examples of a mixed company in a freight train.

As a result of the successes in 1859 and 1860, the first of the so-
called Church trains rolled out in 1861. During the previous winter
an estimate had been made of the number of wagons that would be
required for that year's immigration, and they were apportioned to
the wards of the church. Personnel and equipment for the train

[31] Arrington, *Great Basin Kingdom*, 159-69, 207, 239.
[32] Kate B. Carter, *Our Pioneer Heritage*, IV, 74.

were credited to tithing to the amount of services rendered or goods donated. Flour sufficient to feed the train crew and the immigrants, plus any surplus to be sold in the Missouri Valley, was loaded out. Extra oxen were taken along for sale to the wealthier immigrants. The trains left Utah in May and returned in October.

In January, 1862, Brigham Young remarked that there had been complaints about the loading of the past year's trains. Some teams took only six or eight travelers and their baggage, while others handled a ton of merchandise, in addition to the same number of immigrants. He had given orders that, in the future, the loading was to be more equitable. The 1863 train, in addition to flour, carried east 4,300 pounds of cotton, which were exchanged in St. Louis for cotton cloth.[33]

Over the nine years from 1859 to 1868 seven annual trains were sent out, and they brought back an average of fifty tons of merchandise, in addition to specialized equipment. The 1862 train brought in twenty-five carding machines, one hundred cotton gins and spinning jennies, a number of nail-making machines, several circular saws, and many boxes of "Mill fixings."

It should be noted at this point that practically all the Utah trade was in the hands of Gentiles, non-Mormons. Leonard J. Arrington explains this phenomenon. Any Mormon who did not readily extend credit to a fellow churchman was not a good brother, and if he pressed for payment of an overdue bill, he was worse. On the other hand, the Gentile merchant could not be expected to know any better, and he insisted on payment in coin. It was also a fact that the Missouri Valley suppliers insisted on payment in cold cash.[34] There was as yet no bank in Utah on which drafts could be drawn. The first bank, the Miners National Bank, was not founded until 1866.[35]

Lacking a bank in Salt Lake City, the merchants had a serious problem in transmitting their funds to the Missouri Valley. In 1854, L. Stewart had the problem of transferring $40,000, two hundred

33 Arrington, *Great Basin Kingdom,* 207, 209, 239; JH, January 30, 1862.
34 Arrington, *Great Basin Kingdom,* 209.
35 *Bankers' Magazine,* New Series, Vol. X (May, 1866), 11.

pounds of gold. His clerk, William K. Sloan, dreaded crossing the plains in February or March in a light wagon. Finally, Livingstone and Kincaid, who had been in the Salt Lake business for three years and were well known back east, suggested that Stewart put the money in their safe; one of the Kincaids would be going east in the party with Sloan and would vouch for Stewart's credit until the latter could bring the money east later in the season.[36]

Because of the great distances and long time involved in getting supplies from the Missouri Valley, considerable attention was given to alternate routes of supply. In 1855, Brigham Young sent out a party to investigate the possibility of operating steamers on the Missouri, Yellowstone, and Bighorn rivers, which it was thought would reduce the land carry to something like three hundred miles.[37]

In 1853, J. and E. Reece opened an alternate supply route when they sent a wagon train to southern California via Provo, Cedar City, Las Vegas, and Cajon Pass. Within two years this trade had grown so that several California merchants were moving 15-wagon trains, carrying merchandise worth $20,000.00, into Utah. This soon became a two-way trade. One young man who came to Utah as a bullwhacker in 1853, and served as a clerk for Livingstone and Kincaid for eight months, left for California in a train of 125 wagons loaded with flour. Ten years later, $12,000,000.00 was paid for freight between California and Utah at rates of $.05 to $.10 per pound. Valuable clothing material, musical instruments, fine china, and even farming implements came in this way. An approximate count indicates that 7,000 teams made the trip in one year.[38]

In March, 1859, the Los Angeles *Vineyard* reported that since the first of January, sixty wagons of one-ton capacity, carrying $60,000 to $70,000 worth of goods, had left for Salt Lake City and that there were en route to Los Angeles another hundred tons for Utah. A week later the *Valley Tan* reported, "The shelves of the merchants present a beggarly account of emptiness, all having sold out," and

36 Sloan, "Autobiography," *loc. cit.*, 249–50.
37 JH, November 21, 1855.
38 C. G. Coutant, "Dwight Fisk, Early Freighter," *Annals of Wyoming*, Vol. IV (October, 1926), 305–308; Kate B. Carter (comp.), *Heart Throbs of the West*, X, 53–103.

that Gilbert and Gerrish and Radford, Cabot and Company, rather than wait for the trains from Missouri, had taken time by the fore-lock and ordered goods from California.[39] Trade with California had one great advantage over that with the Missouri Valley: by using the southern route, trains could get through all winter long. When General James F. Rusling interviewed Brigham Young in 1866, he asked why the Utah trade was with the Missouri Valley instead of with California. Young admitted that it was largely a matter of habit.[40] In the over-all view, the trade with California seems never to have been more than a source of emergency supplies. Whether it was habit or not, one factor that helped keep the Utah trade turned to the east must have been the efforts of Atchison, Kansas, to encourage the trade. It may be that attention to the customer had a lot to do with maintaining the Missouri habit.

A variant of the California route was established by ship from San Francisco to the mouth of the Colorado River and thence by river steamer to Callville, at the great bend of the Colorado, some thirty-five miles east of Las Vegas.[41] Over this route, freight was only ten cents per pound from San Francisco, compared to seventeen cents from the Missouri. This route never carried much freight, presumably because of the difficulty of navigating the river. A further complication arose when a survey placed the Mormon villages along the Muddy River in Nevada and the inhabitants moved into Utah.

The greatest boon to Utah's economy came with the great mining strikes in the mountain west—the Comstock and Colorado strikes in 1859 and the Idaho and Montana strikes in 1862 and 1863. These mining communities were entirely dependent on the outside world for everything—tools, food, clothing, and above all whisky. In 1860 there developed a regular trade from Utah to Denver in flour and other farm produce. In August, Edward Milo Webb bullwhacked on a train of 22 wagons loaded with 7,500 pounds each of flour, and drawn by 6 oxen. The trip required 15 days. In the following year

39 *Valley Tan* (March 8, 13, 1859).
40 Rusling, *Across America*, 175.
41 Message of Governor James Duane Doty, December 7, 1864, Utah State Archives, Salt Lake City, Utah.

he went again to Denver with a train of 10 wagons loaded with flour, butter, and vegetables.[42]

In October the *Rocky Mountain News* noted the arrival of great quantities of fresh eggs, butter, onions, barley, oats, etc., only fifteen days from the City of the Saints. The paper also reported rumors of 12,000 sacks of flour, 5,000 bushels of corn, plus barley, onions, and other produce, on the road in the train of Miller, Russell and Company. For eighteen months the market reports of the *News* carried a separate quotation for Salt Lake flour, usually one to two dollars per sack lower than States flour. Lieutenant Caspar Collins observed in 1862 a continual passing of freight trains from Utah, bound for Denver along the North Platte.[43] Freighting from Salt Lake City to Denver was a great help to the commercial freighter as it gave him a pay load for the first half of his return trip to the Missouri Valley, an otherwise profitless run.

It was in June, 1862, that the *Deseret News* first noted that some Gentile merchants were doing an extensive business freighting flour and butter to Carson and to the Humboldt Valley in Nevada Territory. It noted that in the last two weeks forty to fifty wagons had left town, and the newspaper deprecated the export of so much flour in the light of past troubles with drought and grasshoppers. Many of the trains to the Comstock, after unloading, crossed the Sierra Nevada and picked up merchandise in California for the Utah market. Six months later the *News* had changed its mind: "This class of enterprise is a decided improvement upon the old style of our merchants."[44]

It was also in 1862 that J. Woodmansee and Brother made a trip to the newly opened Idaho mines and were reported to have done very well. At the same time a Mr. Mendenhall took six wagons north, to take advantage of the current prices along Grasshopper Creek or Beaver Head: flour, $20.00 per hundred pounds; bacon, $.50 per pound; sugar, $.75 per pound; and coffee, $1.00 a pound.

[42] Carter (comp.), *Heart Throbs*, X, 69.
[43] *Ibid.*, 88; *Rocky Mountain News* (1861–64), *passim.*
[44] *Deseret News* (June 18, November 12, 1862).

In May, 1866, the *News* reported that 40,000 sacks of flour had been shipped to Montana during the past season. This item alone meant an income to Utah Territory of nearly $500,000.00. The *Montana Post* referred to a shipment of 2,000 pounds of apples as "Salt Lake luxuries." Utah also gained, if less directly, from the services rendered to freighters passing through en route to the Montana mines from both California and the Missouri Valley. While the Bozeman Trail was opened in 1864, it never was popular with freighters because of the strenuous resistance of the Sioux Indians. They preferred the longer, quieter trail north from Utah to Virginia City and Helena. When the army abandoned its posts in 1868, it advised travelers to Montana to go by way of Corinne, Utah, at the northern end of Great Salt Lake.[45]

With the driving of the Golden Spike in May, 1869, Salt Lake City lost its position as the great transshipment point for the Montana mines. The Gentile town of Corinne took its place. Laid out in February, 1869, the town had a month later five hundred frame buildings and tents for a population of 1,500. Many non-Mormon merchants moved there from Salt Lake City, large warehouses were built, and a bank was opened. Within a year most freighters serving Helena and Virginia City changed their base from Fort Benton, at the head of navigation of the Missouri River, to the Union Pacific Railroad at Corinne. Death came to Corinne in the late 1870's when the Northern Utah Railroad pushed north from Ogden to the valley of the Snake River and intersected the road from Corinne to Montana.[46]

Throughout the period of wagon-freighting into Utah, the freighters rendered to the community an additional aid in a form of passenger service. Holladay and Warner's first train in 1850 took a few families of Saints to Utah, and in 1855 thirty-three immigrants traveled with Livingstone and Kincaid's train.[47]

45 *Ibid.* (November 26, 1862; March 22, May 17, 1866; September 16, 1868).
46 Bernice G. Anderson, "The Gentile City of Corinne," *UHQ*, Vol. IX (July-October, 1941), 141–54; Jesse H. Jameson, "Corinne; A Study of a Freight Transfer Point in the Montana Trade," M.A. Thesis, U. of Utah, 1951, *passim.*
47 JH, August 28, 1850; August 22, 1855.

Another random service rendered by the freighter was the occasional carrying of the United States mail. In 1854 the *Deseret News* noted the arrival of sixteen sacks of old newspapers, books, wrapping paper, and letters written in 1852. They had been accumulating for a long time at different points along the trail from Independence to Fort Laramie. Finally they were hauled in by a freight train at freight rates.[48]

As early as 1852 the importance of Utah was recognized. A correspondent of the New York *Times* said, "Already this Territory has grown into a place of vast importance to the trade and travel between the valley of the Mississippi and the Pacific coast."[49] As Arrington says, "In the face of Mormon resistance, Salt Lake City did become the entrepôt of the Mountain West. Its central location, the abundance of skilled and professional labor, and, above all, its supply of raw materials and consumer goods, all contributed to that end." He goes on to point out that Utah was the most economical source of food for nearly all the mines between the Rockies and the Sierra Nevada.[50]

As with the Santa Fe trade, it is very difficult to separate the roles of merchant and freighter. It seems clear that the Mormon War had somewhat the same effect on freighting to Utah as did the Mexican War on freighting to Santa Fe: the introduction of the professional freighter. Part of the difficulty lies in the lack of precision on the part of newspaper editors in designating the name of the owner of the transportation. In general, the Utah editors designated the wagon trains by the name of the owner of the goods—i.e., Livingstone and Kincaid, Gilbert and Gerrish, Hooper and Eldridge, etc. On the other hand, the papers of the Missouri Valley tended to name the owners of the wagons and animals when referring to a wagon train.

In 1854, William K. Sloan contracted with Barnes Brothers to haul his goods to Salt Lake City for twelve and one-half cents per

48 *Deseret News* (August 17, 1854).
49 October 16, 1852.
50 *Great Basin Kingdom*, 196, 204.

pound. In the following year, because of Indian troubles on the plains, Sloan could not find a freighter willing to risk the trip except at exorbitant rates, so he decided to ship nothing. "I think only two trains of merchandise succeeded in getting through that season to Salt Lake, both suffering heavy losses in cattle." Actually at least eight to ten trains made the crossing that season, as reported by the *Deseret News.* During the winter of 1855–56, Sloan decided to do his own freighting, in conjunction with Gilbert and Gerrish. They bought two trains of twenty-six wagons each, loaded out six to seven thousand pounds per wagon, and started from Atchison. The Indian War of 1864 caused the freight charges to nearly double. A correspondent for the New York *Times* reported in the spring of 1865 that "Twenty-five to thirty cents per pound from the Missouri River to this city, is the usual charge this year." He also remarked that a number of people were rushing into the freighting business.[51]

It is likewise difficult to arrive at any firm figures for the quantity of goods freighted into Utah. While the valley newspapers noted the arrival of wagon trains, the editors were not statistically minded; usually they failed to mention the number of wagons involved. In 1854 an advertisement reported the arrival of a J. M. Horner and Company train of thirty-six wagons; six weeks later the paper noted the arrival of Horner's second train of twenty-seven wagons; and two weeks after that, the arrival of their third and last train of eighteen wagons—a total of eighty-one wagons, which presumably hauled some 243,000 pounds. However, there is no mention of the number of wagons in the trains of the other merchant-freighters. In the following year the arrival of Livingstone's first train of forty-six wagons, and their second of fourteen, was reported, but nowhere does the paper give the number of wagons in their third and last train.[52]

The appearance of the bullwhackers and mule skinners in Salt Lake City created social problems. The teamsters of Gilbert and

---

51 Sloan, "Autobiography," *loc. cit.,* 253, 257; New York *Times* (April 23, 1865).

52 *Deseret News* (September 7, October 26, November 9, 1854; August 22, October 24, November 7, 1855).

Gerrish's train of 1855 arrived in Salt Lake City in a destitute condition and could find no winter jobs. As a result, they broke into the store of S. M. Blair and Company at various times, stealing provisions and groceries. The townspeople were not the only ones victimized by the ruffians who came in on the heels of the army. In 1860 the herdsmen of Miller, Russell and Company had to beat off a raid on the herd. In another case, two teamsters stole twelve revolvers from a train and tried to sell them in Salt Lake City. In 1858 the *Deseret News* warned the inhabitants that many transient persons, teamsters, etc., were planning to leave for California. During the winter they had been unemployed and had sustained themselves by petty thievery. When getting ready to depart, they might try to equip themselves in the same manner.[53]

One of Russell, Majors and Waddell's bullwhackers remarked in 1858 that Salt Lake City turned the heads of men just freed from the prison of the plains. In that rendezvous of the vicious, they squandered both money and soul. "Within three days, three of my train comrades were dead. Antonio was stabbed in an affray over a bar-maid. Johnny Bull was shot at a gaming table; and Red, the Missourian, was murdered in a saloon brawl."[54]

A number of Salt Lake City merchants were caught in the collapse of the bubble of the Butterfield Overland Despatch. The *News* complained that Butterfield's had handled the freighting to Utah very badly in 1865, leaving much merchandise at Fort Bridger and Denver and even some at the starting point, Atchison, and claimed it to be the greatest failure to fulfill a freighting contract since the settlement of Utah. Eventually representatives of Butterfield and his subcontractors arrived in Salt Lake City to make arrangements for the delivery of the goods. In June the subcontractor completed his shipment. Some 106 wagonloads of goods had been stored for the winter in Denver and were hauled out in the spring. Butterfield

53 Strebel, "Freighting Between the Missouri River and Utah," 247, 255–56; *Deseret News* (November 24, December 1, 1858; March 9, 1859); Colyer, "Freighting Across the Plains," *loc. cit.*, 2–17.

54 Colyer, "Freighting Across the Plains," *loc. cit.*, 2–17

was reported to have paid damages to the Salt Lake City merchants for the delay.[55]

It was probably the trouble with Butterfield that caused the *News* to ask, "Can we not do our own freighting?" It pointed out that the freight bill for the past season had amounted to about half a million dollars. "We freight from the east and the west; we freight to the north."[56] Nothing seems to have come from this renewal of efforts by the Mormons to do their own freighting.

That freighting was a profitable following, if one avoided the pitfalls so bountifully provided by nature, there can be no doubt. In the mid–1860's a traveler to New Mexico noted that many American professional freighters made large fortunes. "One freighter, an American, residing in this Territory, realized last year from a single trip with eighteen wagons, from Kansas City, Mo. to Salt Lake, the sum of $12,000." In 1859, L. J. Randall was so successful with a large train of merchandise for Utah that he wrote his agents, Ashton and Tait of Atchison, to prepare more trains for the next year. Hooper and Eldridge of Salt Lake City paid $80,000 in freight charges on an order of over $150,000 worth of goods from eastern cities. Samuel Bowles noted in 1865 that freights were enormous and that sometimes goods were as much as a year on the road: "One firm has just received [in June] a stock of goods, costing one hundred thousand dollars, that was bought in New York last June." The shipment had been snowed in on the plains. He went on to say that another large house had, in the last year, paid $150,000 for freight. "One lot of goods, groceries, hardware, dry goods, everything, was found to have cost on reaching here, just one dollar a pound, adding to original purchase the cost of freighting, which from New York to this point averages from twenty-five to thirty cents a pound."[57]

Tullidge pointed out that one limitation on home manufacture

---

55 *Deseret News* (March 15, April 19, June 14, 21, May 10, 1866); *Rocky Mountain News* (July 18, 1866.)

56 *Deseret News* (November 30, 1865).

57 Spring, *Bloomer Girl*, 15; Nebraska City *Peoples' Press* (February 3, 1860); Tullidge, *History of Salt Lake City*, 77–78; Bowles, *Our New West*, 100–101.

was the weight limitation imposed on machinery by wagon transportation. That this limitation was well recognized is shown by the advertisement of a commission merchant stating that he could have heavy machinery—steam engines, carding machines, planing machines for wood and iron, looms, spinning machinery, and reaping and mowing machines—built with special reference to wagon transportation.[58]

If it had not been for the wagon-freighter, the attempt to colonize the Great Salt Lake Basin might have failed, or might at least have been much slower and more expensive. Home manufactures could not compete, in most cases, with eastern goods, even with the freight charges added. Also some of the home manufactures could not compete in quality with eastern products. The *News* pointed out, in 1865, that flour freighted from the States commanded a higher price in Montana than flour from Utah and added that this was due to poor milling policy.[59]

[58] Strebel, "Freighting Between the Missouri River and Utah," 52.
[59] *Deseret News* (November 30, 1865; March 22, 1866).

CHAPTER IX

SLOW FREIGHT TO DENVER

THERE was not much excitement in the Missouri Valley when the first rumors of gold began to trickle in from the area that is now Colorado. Three or four prospecting parties traveled west in the summer of 1858 and settled, some two hundred strong, at the junction of Cherry Creek and the South Platte River. Before winter had set in, it was conceded that there was not enough gold in the South Platte to be worth working. During the winter of 1858–59, a few of the more persistent prospectors pushed into the mountains to the west, and there the first paying strike was made in the Gregory Diggings.

During the late winter and spring stories of great strikes and small amounts of gold reached the East and touched off a gold rush that has been called one of the greatest fiascoes of frontier history. During the summer of 1859, it has been estimated, 100,000 people set out from the Missouri Valley towns. As many as three trains a week left Omaha, Nebraska, and this was but one of the outfitting points.[1] It was "Pike's Peak or Bust" for many of the hopefuls. Probably half of those setting out became discouraged and turned back before they even saw the mountains. Now it was, "Busted, By Gosh!" Of those who reached the foothills, probably half were back in the States before the first snow flew. So great was the excitement that Horace Greeley, editor of the *New York Tribune*, made the trip from New York to verify the presence of gold or to explode the rumor.

[1] Walker D. Wyman, "Omaha; Frontier Depot and Prodigy of Council Bluffs," *NH*, Vol. XVII (July-September, 1936), 148.

Alfred D. Richardson, who traveled with Greeley, described Denver in the spring of 1859 as "a most desolate and forlorn-looking metropolis." During the summer, the growth of the city was so rapid that, when Richardson returned in November, he found it "Wonderfully changed . . . frame and brick buildings were going up and two theatres were in operation." He found the place uncomfortably crowded.[2] By the census of 1860, Denver had a population of 4,749, but there were 34,277 persons in the Territory of Colorado. During the next ten years Denver grew by only 10 persons, but the population of the Territory had grown by almost 5,600. Though the Cherry Creek Gold Fields did not pan out, Denver became the distribution point and recreation center for the mining camps in the mountains.

While the first prospectors brought their own supplies, it was not long before men arrived to trade rather than to prospect. The first trader was John Smith, an agent for Elbridge Gerry of Fort Laramie, who brought in a small stock of supplies. He was followed, in October, 1858, by Charles H. Blake and Andrew J. Williams, who arrived with four wagonloads of merchandise and opened a store in a large tent, moving later to a large double cabin.[3] On Christmas Eve, Richens Lacy "Uncle Dick" Wootton came in with four wagons loaded for the Indian trade—three wagons of New Mexico flour and one of "Taos Lightning," described as the world's worst whisky. On his arrival, "Uncle Dick" unloaded the whisky, opened one barrel, set pans on the heads of the others, and invited everyone to help themselves. A jolly good time was had by all. In the following April, "Uncle Dick" brought in another load of flour. These shipments were barely enough to meet the requirements of the first handful of settlers. William Larimer, writing to the Leavenworth *Times* in March, 1859, reported that the people of Denver wanted for nothing but that provisions were very costly.[4]

Some of the early traders, such as Blake and Williams, made no

2 *Beyond the Mississippi*, 117, 279.
3 Percy S. Fritz, *Colorado; The Centennial State*, 171; Alonzo E. Ellsworth, "Early Denver Business," *Denver Westerners Monthly Roundup*, Vol. VI (November, 1950), 1.
4 Andrew Sagendorf, "History of Auraria—Narrative of Andrew Sagendorf," *Com-

effort to renew their supplies and were soon out of business as other merchants began to bring in large stocks. In December, 1858, one of the settlers wrote: "Prices here are exorbitant and will be higher in the spring. Good clothing, provisions, medicines, building hardware, sheet iron, books, stationery, and such articles will sell readily." During the winter, immigrants from New Mexico brought in supplies of flour, onions, and beans. The onions were especially in demand as there had been a few cases of scurvy. By April, 1859, it was reported that some 500 or 600 sacks of flour had come in but were then almost expended.[5] Two months later another settler wrote that disappointed "Pike's Peakers" were selling their supplies at ruinous discounts—flour for $9.00 a sack and bacon for $.12 per pound. At the same time he predicted $30.00 flour and $.40 bacon by the next spring. It was reported that "go-backers" were selling flour, at Fort Kearny, for $1.50 to $2.00 per hundred-pound sack and bacon for $.04 to $.05 a pound.[6]

This was hand-to-mouth existence for Denver, but back in the Missouri Valley, alert merchants were making plans for a more systematic supply. As early as November 24, 1858, William H. Russell wrote to his partner, William B. Waddell, suggesting that they send a train of supplies to Denver in the following spring. Their first train left Leavenworth, Kansas, in the following July. Meanwhile, a train of twenty-five six-mule teams belonging to Russell and Jones arrived in Denver in early June and was greeted as "a real godsend." In the previous October some Mexicans had packed a small supply of flour into Denver but could not sell it for $12.00 per hundred; yet in the following April flour sold for $16.00 a hundred, right out of the wagon. A Denverite wrote in May that provisions were very scarce and high, that New Mexico was not able

monwealth *Magazine* (Denver), Vol. I (April, 1889), 58; Larimer, *Reminiscences*, 118; Hafen, *Colorado Gold Rush*, 249.

[5] Hafen, *Colorado Gold Rush*, 181; Leroy R. Hafen, "Supplies and Market Prices in Pioneer Denver," *Colorado Magazine*, Vol. IV (August, 1927), 136–42.

[6] Leroy R. Hafen, *Reports from Colorado: The Wildman Letters, 1859–1865, with Other Related Letters and Newspaper Reports, 1859*, 35; "Letters Home," *NH*, Vol. XVII (July-September, 1936), 159.

to meet all the requirements of the growing community, and that trains from the Missouri were urgently needed.[7]

A month later the trains began to roll in, and the correspondent of the *Missouri Republican* could write that large shipments by Russell and Jones had driven prices down sharply in four weeks. The local situation was helped somewhat by the fifty-niners, who brought in more than their own needs, on speculation, and indeed they glutted the whisky market.[8]

In August, 1859, Robert B. Bradford entered into partnership with Russell, Majors and Waddell to operate a store in Denver on a salary and one-third of the profits. The first train of supplies for the new store arrived in September or early October. By the end of the year the freighting company was bankrupt, but Bradford was able to continue in business and in May, 1860, announced that he would receive 800 wagonloads of goods during the coming season, at three tons per wagon.[9]

As the community grew, its needs increased. Early in 1859 two steam-powered sawmills were freighted in. While the mills drove down the price of lumber, they created a great demand for building hardware, paint, glass, and house furnishings, all of which had to be imported. William Larimer wrote in March, 1859, "I have heard of 75 cents a pound for nails, and none here. . . . Glass and paints, in fact everything in the building line is wanted." A year later it was reported that a train of three wagons had come in laden with butter and nails. This arrival drove the price of butter down from $1.25 to $.65 a pound, but the demand for nails was so great that prices stayed at $.60 for shingle nails, and 8's, 10's, and 20's ranged down to $.35.[10]

In the same spring a small quantity of locally raised vegetables began to appear on the market, adding some variety to the pioneer's

[7] Hafen, *Colorado Gold Rush*, 144, 359, 367; Larimer, *Reminiscences*, 155.

[8] Hafen, *Wildman Letters*, 128.

[9] Settle, "Robert B. Bradford," *loc. cit.*, 53; Hafen, "Supplies and Market Prices," *loc. cit.*, 138n.

[10] Hafen, *Colorado Gold Rush*, 249; Libeus Barney, *Early-Day Letters from Auraria*, 54, 61.

diet but not affecting the price of staples. Luckily, in the first year, abundant game "was a blessing."[11]

The *Rocky Mountain News* of Denver reported in May, 1859, the arrival of Fisher's and Dunn's trains and added that many more were on the road. The paper went on, somewhat optimistically, " . . . there is every prospect of abundant supplies henceforth." The continuing influx of settlers during the summer gave the lie to the *News.* By February, 1860, Thomas Wildman was writing: "One wagon has made its arrival from the States and created quite a sensation, being the first one of this season." The stagecoach reported that a few more were on the road but that the full flow would not start until March. In April the newspaper stated "Flour is getting very scarce, and we fear will be scarcer before a supply arrives. We do not believe there is [*sic*] two hundred sacks in the city for sale."[12]

The movements of the high plains freighters were controlled by the seasons, especially in the early days of the Denver trade. The 650-mile stretch from the Missouri Valley to Denver was almost devoid of human habitation, and if the freighters were to feed their stock off the country they had to wait on the spring grass, which was usually high enough for feed by March or early April. By about 1865 there were road ranches and stage stations every 15 to 20 miles along the Platte River where hay could be obtained. However, the price of three cents per pound, or fifty dollars per ton, discouraged much reliance on this source of fodder. In 1864 one freighter had to pay one dollar per day for each span for stabling and hay at the road ranches and one dollar a day for the use of the cookstove.[13]

The freighters always hoped to avoid the problem of rivers swollen by the spring thaw and the problem of spring mud. One train left Nebraska City on February 18, 1865, loaded largely with pork sausage in twenty-five-pound cans. At the Blue River in Nebraska there was a long delay because the river was in flood. At Beaver Creek the wagons stuck in the mud and had to be entirely unloaded

[11] Barney, *Early-Day Letters,* 82.
[12] Hafen, "Supplies and Market Prices," *loc. cit.,* 136; *ibid., Wildman Letters,* 245; *Rocky Mountain News* (April 4, 1860).
[13] *Rocky Mountain News* (February 6, 1866); Jonathan Shinn, *Memoirs,* 71.

before they could be moved. The train finally reached Denver fifty-six days out from the Missouri.[14] Because of the danger to man and beast presented by the winter storms on the plains, most freighters tried to be off the plains by November.

About 1859 or 1860 some freighters began wintering in Denver, taking advantage of the free buffalo-grass range on which their oxen could rest and fatten, despite the rigors of the climate. These freighters could leave the Missouri Valley later in the season and still be in winter quarters by early November. As a result of this wintering in the West, Denver had a period of about six months in which it could receive a year's supplies.

The dependence of Colorado on the high plains wagon-freighter is clearly illustrated by a study of the "Prices Current" published in the *Rocky Mountain News*. In November or December of each year, when the last trains came in, the prices of staples began to rise, reaching their peak in April or May, when the first trains of the new freighting season arrived from the Missouri. In the winter of 1860–61 flour failed to follow the annual rise. As late as the last of November over 100 wagons per week were still rolling into Denver. A local merchant estimated that there were 28,937 sacks of flour in Denver, and half as many more in the mining camps. In the following May the trains began dumping more flour, before the winter's supply had been consumed, further depressing the price. The *Nebraska City News*, carrying a report that an eastern company had contracted for the shipment of 35,000 sacks of flour to Denver, noted:

	Pounds
Amount of flour here [Denver], Oct. 4, 1860	2,500,000
Expected from Salt Lake	1,600,000
Alex. Majors from Nebraska	1,200,000
New York and Boston company	3,500,000
	8,800,000

and concluded that this amount of flour would completely flood the

14 William Dunn, "Diary of William Dunn, Freighter," *NH*, Vol. IV (April-June, 1921), 31. (This item consists of extracts from the original, which has disappeared.)

market.[15] From the spring of 1864 to the fall of 1865, all staples failed to follow the annual trend. The uprising of the Plains Indians in 1864 and 1865 practically closed the trails. The advantage of the completion of the railroad to Denver in 1870 is seen in the fact that the fluctuating prices that held during the days of wagon-freighting tended to level off at the summer low, and the annual rises and falls tended to fade into insignificance.

While the prices of foodstuffs were sensitive to the movement of the wagon trains, certain items were in such good supply that the price remained steady throughout the year. For example, common whisky sold for $3.00 to $4.00 a gallon, year in and year out. Most nonperishable items likewise showed little or no fluctuation: shoes sold for $2.00 to $2.50 a pair, woolen shirts for $1.00 to $2.00, and heavy pants for $2.00 to $3.00. A man could put up with a ragged shirt but he had to eat, regardless of the cost.

The needs of Colorado were many and varied. In 1859 it was reported that Dr. John Lee of Denver was in Kansas City with a large order for freight, one item of which was 500 chairs "in Bundles" (knocked down?). Next year the *Rocky Mountain News* reported that the one firm of A. and P. Byram had brought in, from Nebraska City, during the past summer and fall, over 3,000,000 pounds of freight, and this was only one of a number of freighters, though probably the largest. The paper added that an immense item in the trade was the freighting done by individuals, many of whom used horses or mules rather than oxen.[16] For sheer volume of a single commodity in a single shipment it would be hard to beat the 80-wagon train to Denver in 1864. The single consignment occupying the whole train was alcoholic: 1,600 barrels of liquor and 2,700 cases of champagne. As the *Rocky Mountain News* said: "That's a 'train what is a train.' "[17]

The catholic tastes of Coloradans is shown by the itemized list of merchandise loaded on one mule train of fourteen wagons: "Coffee,

15 *Rocky Mountain News* (November 21, 28, 1860; May 2, 1861); *Nebraska City News*, (November 3, 1860).
16 Hafen, *Wildman Letters; ibid.,* "Supplies and Market Prices," *loc. cit.,* 136–42.
17 November 30, 1864.

sugar, brandy peaches, pickles, pineapple, peaches, strawberries, boots and shoes, boxes of mock turtle, one box of azumea [?], one box of drumfings [?], tomatoes, corn, salmon, oysters, huckleberries, a box of liquor, ten kegs of butter, ten kegs of liquor, prunes, paper, Worcestershire sauce, a barrel of ink, tea, starch, lozenges and Succotash."[18]

Very early, machinery became an important item of freight. The two steam-powered sawmills brought in during 1859 seem to have been the first load of machinery. A sawmill brought in during the next year weighed 5,000 pounds and was drawn by five yoke of oxen.[19] The miners soon found that the placer deposits were comparatively small but that some of the veins of gold ore could be worked with comparatively simple equipment. They began to import stamp mills to crush the rock. At first these mills were small affairs of about three stamps with pestles weighing only seventy-five to one hundred pounds each. As the mine shafts were driven deeper, the ore became more difficult to work, and larger and heavier mills were imported. The Fairfield Quartz Mill was described as a steam-powered six-stamper, and the Rock Island Mill as a ponderous machine with fifteen stampers, each weighing 503 pounds and driven by a fifty-horsepower steam engine. The report continued, saying that it would require fifty yoke of oxen to haul the mill and rations for the crew. In 1868 it was reported that a mine operator was tearing down an eight-stamp mill that used wooden stems and was replacing it with a twelve-iron-stem mill, the stamps of which weighed 750 pounds apiece.[20] A particularly heavy, clumsy load was a 4,000-pound fire- and burglar-proof safe delivered by Jones and Cartwright to Denver in 1860.[21]

[18] Forbes Parkhill, "There's Gold in Them Thar Files," *Denver Westerners Monthly Roundup*, Vol. VII (May, 1951).

[19] Hafen, *Wildman Letters*, 128; *Daily Times* (April 18, 1859); *Rocky Mountain News* (June 20, 1860).

[20] E. H. N. Patterson, "Chalk Marks of Overland Travel Pike Peakward," *Spectator* (Oquawka, Illinois) (April 19–September 19, 1860); Central City *Colorado Herald* (April 30, 1868).

[21] *Rocky Mountain News* (September 27, 1860).

By 1865 one Denver house received 127,000 pounds of freight, largely small machines and hardware—corn shellers, corn grinders, hay and straw cutters, iron, tin, nails, steel, plows, stoves, cedar buckets and tubs. Later the *News* pointed out that the high cost of transportation over 650 miles of the plains to Denver made the mining of gold three times as expensive as it would be in the East. Heavy machinery had to pay $.15 to $.20 per pound, and a single boiler might cost $1,500.00 in freight alone. A box of pills costing $.50 could be had in the States for $.06 by the gross, and a yard of $.40 cloth, in the States, cost $1.25 in Denver. The paper went on to say: "The railroad is an economic necessity."[22]

There was no tariff set by government to control the charges made by the freighters. The only controls were those exerted by time, distance, costs, and competition. These factors resulted in a fair degree of standardization at eight to ten cents a pound.[23] The contract between R. M. Bradford and Russell, Majors and Waddell specified that the company would charge Bradford $.10 per pound for freighting. John M. Lee, writing to a Kansas City forwarding and commission house in 1859, said that he would take all the freight he could get at $.10 a pound. One freighter hauled a load of fire brick for a desulphuring plant at Black Hawk at the rate of $1.00 for each eight- to ten-pound brick.[24]

Volume as well as weight was a controlling factor. It cost the freighter as much to move a bulky but light load as it did to move a compact, heavy load, and he sought the most economical use of his equipment. As a result there was a differential established: flour, $.09; tobacco, $.12½; sugar, $.13½; bacon, $.15; dry goods, $.15; crackers, $.17; whisky, $.18; glass, $.19½; trunks, $.25; and furniture, $.30 to $.31. Winter rates were 50 per cent higher. Hiram

22 *Ibid.* (September 25, October 16, 17, 1865).

23 Receipt, Jones and Cartwright, Pike's Peak, Leavenworth Transportation Line, June 6, 1861, in Cabanne, Suber, and Tesson Papers, in Teller Papers, University of Colorado Libraries.

24 Hafen, *Wildman Letters*, 130; Thomas T. Cornforth, "Early Colorado Days," (ed. by Albert B. Sanford), *Colorado Magazine*, Vol. I (September, 1924), 25–67.

Burton, Denver commission merchant, paid $1001.20 freight on a shipment of 11,574 pounds from Atchison, Kansas.[25]

In 1860 the *News* reported: "freights from Omaha are only eight cents being two cents cheaper per pound than from any other point." It was reported that in 1862 competition was so sharp that freighters accepted contracts at $.05 cents per pound and that the Indian troubles of 1864 made large contracts available to Denver, Camp Collins, and Fort Laramie at $.10 a pound and to Fort Halleck and Fort Sanders at $.12 to $.14 a pound. However, other freighters at the same time were getting $.20 per pound to Denver. A piano from the Missouri River cost $200.00 in freight alone. However, this was not all dead loss: about a year later the piano and $200.00 bought fifteen city lots which, in a few years, were sold for $15,000.00.[26]

The Civil War, followed by the Indian war of 1864–65, brought an increase in the freight rates. In 1865, Martin B. Hayes contracted with Kip and Buell Gold Mining and Tunnelling Company of New York to deliver two boilers, a flywheel, and an upright standard, a total weight of 17,572 pounds, to Central City, Colorado, at the rate of $.18 a pound. Hayes at once turned around and subcontracted the job to Michael Savelle of Atchison, Kansas, for $.12 per pound. Delivery was to be made within fifty days and in good order, Indian and war risks excepted.[27]

At the beginning of the Indian war in July the *News* reported a great many huge prairie schooners rolling through the streets all day but added, "There is a good deal of speculation in groceries and prices rule high." The paper then went on to surmise that the war was over; "we do not believe there is a particle of danger to travellers at the present." Augustus Wildman, brother of Thomas, wrote in May, 1865, that teams were arriving in large numbers so there would

[25] Root and Connelley, *Overland Stage*, 303; H. Burton, Receiving Book, CSHS.

[26] *Rocky Mountain News* (May 30, 1860); Fulton, "Freighting and Staging in Early Days," *loc. cit.*, 261–64; "Colorado Territorial Days," *The Trail*, Vol. I (October, 1908), 6–11.

[27] Memorandum, M. B. Hayes and Kip Buell, May 8, 1865; Certificate of Weights by Agent of Butterfield Overland Express; Memorandum, M. B. Hayes and Michael Savelle, May 24, 1865, in Teller Papers, University of Colorado Libraries.

be plenty of provisions and that prices would be at their old level, which was high enough. He added that if the Indians held the road all summer, "they might as well give them the country for good." That this nearly happened is clear from his letter, written in September, stating that the Indian war kept prices so high that only the best mines paid for the working. Three months later he wrote that, in addition to Indian troubles, recent grasshopper plagues had ruined local crops, making the city completely dependent on the East for everything.[28] Following the war period there was a sharp decline in the cost of teams and wagons; as a result, the cost of freighting dropped from a high of about $.25 cents to about $.12½ per pound.

When the freighter took delivery of a consignment of goods at one of the Missouri River towns, he accepted responsibility for the goods, with a number of exceptions. The following may be taken as a typical contract:

CHIVINGTON MULE TRAIN

J. ASHTON   J. W. TAIT

Ashton & Tait

Forwarding & Commission Merchants, General Steamboat Agents & dealers in Dry Goods & Groceries, on the Levee, Nebraska City, N. T.

Freight Contract

Received of Ashton & Tait the following described Packages, apparently in Good order, (Contents and Value unknown) Consigned and Marked in the Margin, to be transported & delivered in like Good order to the Consignee or owner (unavoidable accidents and dangers of the plains only excepted) unto L. M. Freas at Denver City Colorado Territory, the owner or assignee paying freight for said Goods at the rate of Twenty cents (20ᶜ) per pound and charges on their arrival. It is agreed and is a part of this contract that I will not be responsible for leakage of liquors, breakage of Glass or Queensware, the injury or breaking of looking Glasses, Glass show cases, Picture frames, stove castings or hollow ware, nor for injury to

28 *Rocky Mountain News* (July 27, 1864); Hafen, *Wildman Letters*, 318, 322, 324.

hidden contents of Packages, nor for loss of Weight or otherwise of Grain or Coffee or Rice in tierces, nor for the decay of perishable articles, nor of Nuts in bags, or Lemons or oranges in boxes, unless covered by canvass [*sic*].

In witness whereof I have affirmed to thru Bills of Lading, all of this date and tenor, one of which being accomplished the other to stand void. Dated at Nebraska City, the 30th day of January 1865.[29]

Legal complications were not unknown to the freighter. A. E. and C. E. Tilton were freighters from the Missouri River to Denver. On July 7, 1862, they accepted a shipment of 6,930 pounds of merchandise from H. D. Hull and Company of St. Joseph, Missouri, consigned to Tootle and Leach of Denver. When the goods reached Denver it was found that they were not what had been ordered, and the consignee refused to pay the freight bill of $554.40. The merchandise was put in storage and a suit filed on behalf of the shippers against the freighter. The Tiltons sued out a writ of replevin on most of the merchandise, on which freight charges of $445.28 were due, and Tootle and Leach replevined the remainder.[30]

Henry M. Porter, a Denver merchant who ran his own trains to stock his store, sold 100 four-yoke ox teams and wagons in 1866, to J. M. Chivington and O. A. Willard for about $100,000, to be paid for by hauling 1,000,000 pounds of freight from Atchison at $.10 per pound. On the first trip Chivington and Willard loaded half the train with Porter's goods and half with the freight of others, in order to earn money with which to pay the teamsters. The teamsters had to replevy the goods in order to get their pay, as no arrangements had been made to pay them. On the return trip the train went to North Platte, instead of to Atchison, and Porter received word, from the telegraph operator at North Platte, that Chivington and Willard had contracted with Wells, Fargo and Company to haul government supplies, with all the wagons, to the army posts in the Northwest. Porter posted to North Platte and found the train loaded. Chivington disappeared but his son-in-law, Pollock, claimed

29 Case Number 695, District Court, Arapahoe County, Colorado Territory.
30 Parkhill, *Law Goes West*, 64.

that he had bought the train from Chivington and Willard. There was much legal trouble and finally Wells, Fargo and Company bought the entire train, paying Porter $80,000 and settling with two others who had claims against the freighters.[31]

When Thomas M. Chivington, son of Colonel J. M. Chivington, failed to deliver some $5,000 worth of goods to L. M. Freas, the latter brought suit in the Territorial District Court. Unfortunately the court records do not indicate any reason for Chivington's failure to make delivery. The suit was canceled when Chivington was drowned in the North Platte on June 22, 1866, while trying to get the ferry back in operation.[32]

The collapse of Butterfield's Overland Despatch scattered troubles throughout Colorado as well as in Utah. A New York official of a Colorado mining company reported in July, 1865, that a shipment of "Stuff" had not been delivered the previous fall because it had never left Kansas City but it would start right way. The 20,000 pounds were thought to comprise one large and two small steam engines. The Colorado agent was instructed to let Butterfield make delivery, and, once having possession, the company would make a claim for damages suffered by the delay in delivery. The New Yorker went on, "The fact is we have been shamefully used by these freighters & must make them pay for it." Butterfield claimed that the delay was due to the subcontractor having been robbed of $600 while purchasing cattle in the spring. As the New Yorker said, "Now what's this to us."[33]

On the other hand, Butterfield was successful in a suit against the Sterling City Gold and Silver Mining and Tunnelling Company. Butterfield had contracted to deliver some 100,000 pounds of machinery at Sterling City by April 1, 1865, "if possible for ox teams to travel safely on the plains." The rate was $.13 per pound to Denver plus $.04 additional to the destination. Butterfield Over-

[31] Porter, *Autobiography*, 34; *Rocky Mountain News* (April 19, 1866).

[32] *Nebraska City News* (July 7, 1866).

[33] Jas. Stringer, New York, to W. N. Dickerson, Black Hawk City, Colorado, July 22, 1865, in Fisk Mining Company papers, Teller Papers, University of Colorado Libraries.

land Despatch claimed that by November, 1865, they had delivered 63,489 pounds to Sterling City and 5,000 to Denver. In August, 1866, another 24,501 pounds had reached Sterling City, and in July, 1867, the final 4,000 pounds had been delivered in Denver. Butter-field sued for an unpaid balance of the freight bill amounting to $5,902.00 and won a judgment. There was no mention in the case of damages caused by the two-year delay in delivery. Butterfield's failure also resulted in the filing in Denver of some dozen suits for money due for labor or services.[34]

Although Denver, almost from the first, was the distributing point for the goods needed in the mountains, a good deal of freight was delivered directly from the Missouri River to Central City, Black Hawk, and other mining camps. In August, 1860, the *Rocky Mountain News* noted that Jones and Cartwright's train number eleven was the first one for the season that had not passed on into the mountains to discharge a portion of its freight. In September it said: "A fleet of thirteen prairie schooners arrived at their dock to-day in Nevada Gulch, with goods for Lightner, Street and Co. who are opening a new store in that vicinity." In the same month it reported that Jones and Cartwright's train number twelve had passed through Denver on its way out of the mountains. Two months later it noted that stores in Central City and Gregory Gulch had received large stocks of flour, bacon, fruits, nails, tobacco, and liquor. In 1862, Cyrus Morton hauled blasting powder directly to Black Hawk, and in the next year Thomas T. Cornforth hauled the first steam boiler into Rollinsville, Colorado, going directly from the Missouri Valley in forty-two days. In one month in 1863 the proprietor of the Gay House on the road to Central City reported that 157 loads of hay and 165 loads of freight, drawn by 1,282 oxen and 224 horses and mules, had passed his place. In May, 1868, the

34 Parkhill, *Law Goes West*, 145, 149.
35 *Rocky Mountain News*, (August 30, September 8, 19, November 21, 1860); Charles N. Hart, "Reminiscences of the Early West," *Colorado Magazine*, Vol. XV (November, 1938), 209–17; Lynn I. Perrigo, "Life in Central City, Colorado, as Revealed by the *Register*," M.A. Thesis, University of Colorado, 1934.

Nye Freight Forwarding Company of Cheyenne, Wyoming, made four shipments directly to Central City that totaled over twenty tons.[35] The additional charge for freighting to the mines was usually $.01½ to $.03 per pound, the same as the rate from Denver.

Denver had certain advantages over the more remote settlements of the Mountain West. For one thing, the distance from the Missouri River was shorter and ox trains could make two, or even three, round trips in a single season, while mule trains could make three or four. As early as 1860 the train of Baily and Dunn pulled into Kansas City in mid-July, having been gone a little over two months on the first trip. This was in spite of a two-week layover in Denver and an extra ten days on the way home to rest the cattle. Within two weeks they had loaded and started out again—12 wagons, 124 head of oxen, and 53,000 pounds of freight, including dry goods, clothing, boots and shoes, hardware, tinware, queen's wear, groceries, and provisions. As the freighting business became more firmly established and the number of road ranches increased, freighters began to extend the freighting season. In March, 1866, the *Nebraska City News* reported that H. M. Hook, "Old Beaver," had reached town, that he had missed only twenty-seven days during the year, and that he was loading out for Bannock, Montana. In December of the same year it was reported that Hawley and White's mule train, Henry Sheldon, wagonmaster, had arrived from Denver, completing the fourth round trip since March 24—4,800 miles without losing a mule. R. M. Rolfe stated that in the mid-1860's the rate for ox freight was $1.00 per hundred pounds for each one hundred miles, where two trips per year were possible, and that the winter rate to Denver was $.10 to $.12 per pound.[36]

Another advantage offered to the high plains freighter was the location of Denver, approximately halfway between Salt Lake City and the Missouri Valley. By the time Denver was founded, the settlement in the Great Salt Lake Valley was well established and was

---

[36] *Journal of Commerce* (July 17, August 9, 1860); *Nebraska City News* (March 16, December 22, 1866); R. M. Rolfe, "Overland Freighting Business," *loc. cit.*

producing more farm produce than was needed for immediate consumption. In October, 1860, Miller and Russell brought to Denver from Salt Lake a train of twenty-seven wagons loaded with produce, causing the *Rocky Mountain News* to remark, "Utah is becoming quite important as a supply point for the gold regions, and we are pleased to see the above firm taking the initial step for opening a trade." One twenty-wagon train brought to Denver 1,000 dozen eggs, 700 sacks of flour at 100 pounds each, 3,000 pounds of fresh butter, 200 bushels of oats, 170 bushels of barley, and 100 bushels of onions. The flour, oats, and barley sold at $.12 a pound, the butter at $.40 a pound, the onions at $6.00 a bushel, and the eggs for $.40 per dozen. Members of this train reported that, on the road, they had passed 7 trains of 25 wagons with 4,000 sacks of flour and 2,500 bushels of oats and barley.[37] The hauling to Denver gave the Salt Lake freighter a pay load for about half of his return trip to the Missouri, an otherwise empty trip. A good deal of produce was also transported to Denver by the Mormons of Salt Lake.

Some idea of the volume of freighting into Denver and its rate of growth can be obtained from the statistics published in *Merchants' Magazine*, which made no claim for the completeness of its figures, for the year 1860:

	Pounds
Atchison, Kansas	3,250,681
Nebraska City, Nebraska	5,496,000
Leavenworth City, Kansas	4,927,590
Omaha, Nebraska	713,000
Total	14,387,271

The above figures do not include any part of over 1,500,000 pounds from St. Joseph, Missouri, "To the Pike's Peak Gold Regions, Utah, and Way Points." Nor is there any mention of minor river ports such as Brownsville and Plattsmouth, Nebraska. In 1866 the Committee on Resources of Colorado reported to the Chairman of the

---

[37] *Rocky Mountain News* (October 31, 1860); *Nebraska City News* (November 3, 1860).

Railroad Committee at Denver that the annual imports of Colorado were:

	Pounds
Provisions and groceries	40,000,000
Clothing	4,000,000
Hardware, building material, tools, and farm implements	10,000,000
Moving families	5,000,000
Machinery	15,000,000
Government stores	20,000,000
Grain	10,000,000
Total	104,000,000

at rates ranging from $.08 to $.30 per pound. Of the total freighted into Denver in 1860, Jones and Cartwright with 24 trains, 624 wagons, and Alexander Majors with 32 trains, 632 wagons, carried over half of the goods.[38]

Not all the freighting into Denver was conducted by large organized companies. A considerable weight was carried by speculating immigrants. As late as February, 1865, Captain Eugene Ware met two Germans, who spoke not a word of English, traveling toward Denver with a single wagon. They had loaded the wagon with canned oysters and poured water over the load. The water froze and Ware found the oysters as fresh as though just out of salt water. He bought two cans for $5.00, and some of his enlisted men also bought. Through an interpreter, the German told him that west of Fort Kearny they had traveled only at night for fear of robbers. When asked if they were not afraid of the Indians, their response was a simple, "Es macht nicht aus," and on they went toward the gold fields.[39]

It may not be considered freighting, in the strictest sense of the term, but one speculator developed a novel plan. He bought up a flock of turkeys in Iowa and Missouri, loaded a six-mule wagon with

38 "Commerce of the Prairies," *Merchants' Magazine*, Vol. XLIV (January, 1862), 42; *Rocky Mountain News* (June 9, 1866).
39 Ware, *Indian War of 1864*, 149.

shelled corn, and, with two boys for drovers, marched his birds to Denver. With a following wind, the birds could make about twenty-five miles in a day, but they had trouble in a head wind. Most of the way, the turkeys lived off the land, eating grasshoppers. When live feed was scarce, they were fed corn. As the *People's Press* said, "This is a novel method of transporting poultry."[40]

The potentialities of freighting as a business venture are well illustrated by the experience of James Creighton, who freighted to Denver in 1860. On his first trip he used 2 2-horse wagons; on his second trip he had 5 or 6 small ox teams; and on his third and final trip for the year he used 17 large wagons and over 100 yoke of oxen. As the *Rocky Mountain News* said, "Pretty good progress for one season." James Ralston Porter entered the freighting business in 1860, when a drought ruined his farm near Plattsmouth, Nebraska. He started with 3 farm wagons and 3 yoke of oxen. By plowing his profits back into his business, by 1864 he had 36 wagons with 6 yoke of oxen each. In the following year he formed a profit-sharing company, J. R. Porter and Company. Porter found 36 wagons, 432 oxen, and 40 men plus riding stock to be an uneconomical operating unit: "I found 26 wagons was the extent of economy." In 1865, Porter bought up 130 surplus army mules and started a mule train of 22 wagons. J. R. Porter and Company was dissolved in 1868. On the other hand, J. E. Zalinger had just pulled into Denver with his last load of freight when it was swept away by the flood of May 20, 1864. It was reported that Mr. Zalinger gave up freighting and settled down to farming.[41]

From early spring to early fall the streets of Denver presented a lively sight, with big freight wagons moving up and down or parked in front of the stores to unload. In October, 1860, the *News* reported that within the past week forty-five heavily loaded wagons had ar-

---

[40] *Semi-Weekly Peoples' Press* (April 27, 1863); Niel M. Clark, "When the Turkeys Walked," *American Heritage*, Vol. XV (December, 1963), 92.

[41] *Rocky Mountain News* (November 13, 1860); "Life of James Ralston Porter," unpublished manuscript, NSHS; Ida L. Uchill, *Pioneers, Peddlers, and Tsadikim*, 34.

rived from Salt Lake, enough to swell the total to seventy-five, and another train of twenty-three was expected daily. In a single day in 1865 three trains totaling seventy-one wagons rolled into Denver. During the freighting season hardly a week passed that the *Rocky Mountain News* did not take note of the arrival of the wagon trains. In fact, on one occasion, it apologized for having omitted mention of an arrival in its previous issue.[42] As an example of the interest, consider the following from the *News*:

> For several days past, the large freight trains that have wintered in and around the city, have been preparing for their spring departure. This morning they began moving, and at intervals throughout the day, long lines of "Prairie Schooners," have been wending their way eastward through the streets. Like steamers pulling out of their winter harbor all is life and bustle among the moving throng. A dweller on the Mississippi, or the Hudson, can hardly dream of the Commerce of the Plains.

In April, 1862, the paper, in urging its subscribers to get their advertisements in, waxed positively lyrical:

> The winter is past, the flowers appear on the earth, the time of the singing of birds is come and the sound of the teamster's whip will shortly be heard through our streets.[43]

Since most freighters might be in Denver for several days making their deliveries, they needed some place that would serve as a temporary headquarters. The most famous caravansary was the Elephant Corral. Built in 1859, it had an adobe wall 8 feet high and 2 feet thick, loopholed for rifles. Included in the complex were a hotel, the Denver House, a gambling saloon, and stables. The Mammoth Corral had a bunkhouse with a capacity of 20 or so and a cookstove for the use of transients. The McNasser Corral, in 1866, occupied a full half-block, with stalls for 160 horses and barns for 50 more. "A good cook house for freighter and emigrants is also

---

42 *Rocky Mountain News* (October 22, 1860; September 7, 1865).
43 *Ibid.* (March 27, 1861; April 5, 1862).

within the enclosure, where they can prepare their own meals, and thus avoid great expense."[44]

There were, from time to time, certain drawbacks in all this activity. In 1860 one of Miller and Russell's heavy wagons broke through the Ferry Street Bridge, but there was "little damage done." Three years later the Ute Peace Delegation loaded a wagon with treaty goods in Denver, but "the oxen not being city broke, got scared at something and ran the wagon against the drugstore." The store had just opened for business. "Oh, such a crash of bottles and glass you have never heard. Out came the wild-eyed proprietors and we nearly had to shoot them to keep them from licking us." Apparently the United States government eventually paid for the damage.[45] Besides damage to property, the presence of a body of teamsters led to breaking of the peace. The *Weekly Denver Gazette* in 1867 reported a fight between a freighter and one of his hands: "Both suffered considerably about the *os frontis*." Their meeting was adjourned to Judge Kent's office, where the freighter paid both fines.[46]

When word of the proposed transcontinental railroad reached Denver, there was great rejoicing. Wildman wrote that, with a railroad in prospect, "the country has a bright future." As the railroads stretched their rails westward, the distance to be covered by the wagons shortened. In May, 1867, the *Rocky Mountain News* commented that business was unusually dull that year since the preparations for freighting were not as necessary nor as early as they had been the year before. Instead of 600 miles of travel and heavy hauling, "we have less than 300 miles and even this is rapidly lessening." By fall the distance would not exceed 150 miles.[47] It was a great blow to the hopes of Denver when the Union Pacific announced

[44] Data on the Elephant Corral, typescript, CSHS; *Denver Post* (March 16, 1919); *Rocky Mountain News* (February 20, 1861; December 26, 1866).

[45] *Rocky Mountain News* (December 16, 1860); Finis E. Downing, "With the Ute Peace Delegation of 1863, Across the Plains, and at Conejos," *Colorado Magazine*, Vol. XXII (September, 1945), 193–205.

[46] *Weekly Denver Gazette* (August 7, 1867).

[47] Hafen, *Wildman Letters*, 322; *Rocky Mountain News* (April 28, 1869).

that it was going through Cheyenne, Wyoming, rather than through Berthoud Pass. Much of Denver moved north. Some merchants even tore down their stores and moved them to Cheyenne. As a result of this bypassing, one Union Pacific official remarked that Denver was too dead to bury. By April, 1869, the advance of the Kansas Pacific from Kansas City directly toward Denver had cut the freighting time to less than half.[48] In June, 1870, the rails of the Denver Pacific connected Denver to the Union Pacific at Cheyenne, and in August of the same year the Kansas Pacific completed Denver's direct rail connection with the East.

Governor Frank Hall of Colorado, in his message of December 3, 1867, well expressed his state's indebtedness to the freighters:

> In past years these supplies were transported in wagons from the Missouri River, a distance of more than six hundred miles, exposed during the greater part of the journey to the destructive and murderous attacks of the savages of the plains involving such losses as would have been fatal to the occupation of the country, had our people been less determined or our resources less abundant. The history of America no where else records such a steady increase of wealth and population under such peculiarly trying and disadvantageous circumstances.[49]

Had it not been for the high plains wagon-freighter, the development of Colorado and Denver would have been delayed for at least a decade, if not much longer. With their reliance on water for processing the gold ore, the mines were most active from the spring thaw until the first hard freeze of winter. This was just the period in which most of the supplies were brought in by the freighter. If the miners had had to return each summer to the Missouri Valley for a new stock of food and supplies, the amount of gold produced would have been greatly reduced, with far-reaching effects on the national economy.

The mining communities of Colorado were consumers rather

---

48 David Lavender, *The Big Divide*, 54; *Rocky Mountain News* (April 28, 1869).
49 *House Journal of the Legislative Assembly of the Territory of Colorado; Seventh Session.*

than producers, except for gold, which could not be eaten, drunk, or worn. They had to rely on the States for eveything from buttons to boilers, from shoes to shovels. The mining camps were essentially transient in nature; when a vein ran out, the miners moved on, and this unsettled nature of the communities discouraged the establishment of manufacturing or agriculture pursuits in a terrain that was fundamentally poorly adapted to such activities.

CHAPTER X

MONTANA GOLD

Gold was discovered in the mountains of western Montana, then part of the Territory of Idaho, in 1852, but the deposits apparently were too small to create any excitement. Sporadic prospecting continued until 1862, when the first paying strike was made on Grasshopper Creek at Bannock in the extreme southwestern corner of the present state. The winter of 1862–63 found 373 men and 37 women in and near Bannock, 37 men and 2 women in and around Fort Benton, then an Indian trading post some forty-five miles below the Great Falls of the Missouri, and 69 men and 8 women in Missoula County, west of the mountains—a total population of 479 men and 47 women.[1] In 1863 gold was found in Alder Gulch, where Virginia City sprang up. It was estimated that the population of Bannock had grown to between 2,000 and 3,000, and Virginia City was thought to have about 10,000 persons by the end of the year. In the following year the strike was made in Last Chance Gulch, where the city of Helena grew up almost overnight, with an estimated population of 10,000 to 15,000 souls. By 1865 the estimated population of the Territory of Montana was thought to be 120,000.

The Montana gold strike was made in one of the most isolated sections of the Mountain West. Bannock and Virginia City, some fifty miles to the east, were, as the crow flies, 300 miles from Salt Lake City, 900 miles from Omaha, 500 miles from Portland, 350 miles from navigation on the Columbia River, and 150 miles from

---

[1] Daniel S. Tuttle, *Reminiscences of a Missionary Bishop*, 120.

Fort Benton. There was neither agriculture nor industry in Montana to support this burgeoning population; everything eaten, worn, and used had to be imported.

Despite their isolation, the Montana gold fields had one great advantage over the older gold camps. They had three, even four, potential lines of supply. In 1860 the Mullan Road had been opened by the United States government, from Fort Benton on the Missouri to Walla Walla, Washington, a distance of 624 miles. This road was planned and laid out primarily as a military road for the movement of supplies and troops, and secondarily as an emigrant route. Despite the fact that the government had, by 1863, spent $230,000 on the road, it was used very little by the army or by emigrants; it was not maintained and soon fell into disrepair. So bad was the condition of the road that even pack train operators complained of the difficulty of taking heavy trains through the western half.[2] This western half of the Mullan Road served as a supply line to Montana from the navigable waters of the Columbia River.

A second supply line ran north from Salt Lake City along the valley of the Malad River, thence to Fort Hall, Idaho, on the Snake River. It crossed the Continental Divide through 6,800-foot-high Monida Pass and across the Big Hole Basin to the mining camps. By the time the mines were open in Montana, Utah had developed an exportable surplus of agricultural products. The third, and shortest, overland haul was the supply line from Fort Benton at the head of navigation on the Missouri River, through Prickly Pear Canyon to Helena and on south and west to Bannock and Virginia City. A fourth line, with a number of variants, ran from California to Montana. This line was not very important in the over-all picture of wagon freighting into Montana.

The first three routes all had their drawbacks. The lines from Walla Walla and Salt Lake were closed during the winter months

2 William S. Greever, *The Bonanza West: The Story of the Western Mining Rushes; 1848–1900; Daily Times* (March 16, 1858); Oscar O. Winther, *The Great Northwest; A History*, 231; W. Turrentine Jackson, *Wagon Roads West*, 277; Helena *Montana Post* (July 10, 24, 1868).

by deep snow in the mountains. The line from Fort Benton was controlled by the stages of water in the Missouri River, which in good years allowed steamers to reach Fort Benton during only about three months in the year.

Very shortly after the establishment of the Montana gold camps, an intense rivalry sprang up between Portland, Oregon, and St. Louis, Missouri, for the Montana trade. As the Idaho mining camps, established between 1860 and 1863, at Florence and in the Boise Basin, had been supplied almost entirely by pack train from the Columbia River, it was natural that the Oregon merchants should seek to extend their trade another 150 miles or so eastward to the new mines. The poor condition of the Mullan Road was early recognized as a handicap to trade from the west. In 1866 the *Montana Radiator* expressed the hope that the territorial legislature would take over the road, reopen and maintain it. The paper pointed out that merchants in Portland paid less for freight, by sea, from New York than did St. Louis merchants, by rail, from the same point. Six months later the paper stated that it was satisfied that the expenditure of $20,000 would make the Mullan Road passable for heavy wagons the year round. A year later the *Helena Herald* reported an Oregon merchant as saying that his state could lay goods down in Montana cheaper than via St. Louis, if the Mullan Road should be opened for wagons. He said that freight from New York to St. Louis was $70 per ton compared to $23 per ton from New York to Portland. The distance from St. Louis to Helena was given as 2,000 miles, while from Portland it was only 750 miles. The merchant added that $75,000 would take care of the road from Walla Walla, and wagons could make two or three trips per season.[3]

Barring a good wagon road, pack trains were the only means of transportation that could be used, and they were expensive. In general, only goods of small bulk and weight and high value could pay for the pack freight charge of sixteen to twenty-five cents per pound. The *Helena Weekly Herald* in June, 1868, listed the load of one

[3] Helena *Montana Radiator* (March 31, October 12, 1866); *Helena Herald* (June 12, 1867).

such pack train: wines, liquor, Havana cigars, blankets of excellent grade, hydraulic ducking of every grade and size, number-one white shirts, and ready-made clothing. A week later the paper reported the arrival of choice goods direct from China. There was some movement of heavy goods, at a price. The press for the *Montana Radiator* was "cut in two" and packed from Lewiston, Idaho. The largest piece weighed 560 pounds, and the freight charge on the whole press was sixty cents per pound. At least one pool table was freighted in by slinging the table between two animals.[4]

An average pack train of forty to fifty mules could be handled by four or five men for an average day's march of twenty-five miles. At two hundred to three hundred pounds per mule, this would be the equivalent of about two wagonloads. Besides having to be unloaded every night and reloaded every morning, the mules could not forage for themselves in the mountains so a certain amount of grain had to be carried, cutting down on the pay load. Because of the uncertainty of the mountain weather, the muleteers had to build shelters for their animals at various points along the trail.[5]

During the packing season of 1865 some 100 trains brought an estimated 750 tons of freight into Montana from the Columbia River with a total value of $1,440,000, on which freight charge was $240,000. The freight rates for that season were given as:

To Montana From	per pound
Walla Walla, Washington, by pack	15–16¢
San Francisco, California, by wagon	15–20¢
Omaha, Nebraska, by wagon	25¢
St. Louis, by steamer to Benton, 15–20¢	
Benton to Helena, by wagon, 5¢	20–25¢

By the time steamer freight from Portland to Walla Walla was added, the rates from Portland, San Francisco, and St. Louis seem to have been fairly competitive.[6] Nevertheless, all the pack trains in

[4] *Helena Weekly Herald* (October 31, 1867; June 4, 11, 1868).

[5] Oscar O. Winther, *The Old Oregon Country; A History of Frontier Trade, Transportation, and Travel*, 231; Barsness, *Gold Camp*, 109.

[6] Arthur L. Throckmorton, *Oregon Argonauts; Merchant Adventurers on the Western Frontier*, 269.

operation just could not carry enough for a population of over 100,000 persons. In the same year Albert D. Richardson estimated that 20 per cent of Montana's freight came from Oregon and California, 20 per cent came overland via Kansas and Nebraska, and the remaining 60 per cent came through the river port of Fort Benton. When preparing a memorial to be presented to Congress, the territorial legislature received an estimate that, from January 1 to November 15, 6,000 mules had left Walla Walla and the Columbia loaded with freight for Montana.[7]

The one great advantage enjoyed by the packers over the wagon freighters was their ability to reach the Montana towns earlier in the spring than could wagons from Fort Benton. The Helena papers usually reported the arrival of pack trains from the west at about the same time as the wagon trains were leaving Helena for Fort Benton, to await the arrival of the season's first steamer from St. Louis. In 1866 the *Montana Post* expected delivery by pack train two to three months earlier than by river.

The *Montana Post*, in 1868, summed up the whole problem of trading to the east or west when it said:

> One thing is certain pack trains, or other land travel, cannot compete with water navigation. Slow as steamer travel up the Missouri, the prices for goods and freight from the east are in currency, and from the west invariably in gold coin and on credit of at least thirty days shorter time than merchandise is bought in New York, St. Louis or Chicago. . . . California can not come up to the eastern merchants in supplying the Montana trade.[8]

The difference between one dollar in gold and one dollar in currency was vital to western businessmen in the 1860's. Gold was at a premium, and at one time it took four dollars in currency to equal one dollar in gold dust. A man who could buy for currency and sell for gold was in the way to realize a handsome profit.

As in Colorado, traders appeared in Montana as if by magic. As Rodman Paul said, the merchants, packers, teamsters, stage lines,

7 Winther, *Old Oregon Country*, 194.
8 *Montana Post* (June 16, 1868).

and express companies quickly appeared in each new mining camp, "arriving coincidentally with the speculators and promoters, but well after the saloon keepers and gamblers."[9]

The mobility of the speculator is illustrated by an old New Mexico freighter who started, in 1862, for the Salmon River diggings in Idaho. En route, his men heard of the strike at Grasshopper Creek and threatened to quit if the boss did not change his plans. The owner compromised; he returned to Salt Lake City to collect information about the new gold field. Based on this information, he rolled into Bannack where he sold fifty loads of merchandise "at higher figures, perhaps, than such articles, in such quantities, had ever been disposed of before."[10]

Alert Salt Lake City merchants began at once to ship farm produce to the new towns. J. Woodmansee and Brother took the first wagon train into Bannack on September 8, 1862. When the original discoverers of Alder Gulch returned to Bannack, they feasted on "Salt Lake eggs, ham, potatoes, everything."[11] A large proportion of the foodstuffs for Montana came from Utah, especially flour which, for the first six years, sold for $20 to $50 per hundred-pound sack. It has been estimated that in 1866 more than $1,000,000 worth of flour was freighted from Utah to Montana. It was not until 1869 that flour produced in Montana reached a volume that began to meet the needs of the home market.[12]

In August, 1863, Cyrus Morton sold his claim in Montana and bought ten yoke of oxen and three heavy wagons. He went to Salt Lake City and loaded up with flour, plus a barrel of sauerkraut, a firkin of fresh butter, and some apples. On his return, he went into Bannack, instead of Virginia City, because a large amount of flour

9 *Mining Frontiers*, 2.
10 *Historical Sketch and Essay on the Resources of Montana, Including a Business Directory of the Metropolis*, 49.
11 S. P. Bassett and Joseph Magee, *Montana Publishing Company's Statistical Almanac of 1869*; Robert G. Athearn, *High Country Empire*, 85.
12 W. A. Clark, "Centennial Address," *Contributions*, MHS, Vol. II (1896), 54; Throckmorton, *Oregon Argonauts*, 273; L. Kay Edrington, "A Study of Early Utah-Montana Trade, Transportation, and Communications, 1847–1881," M.A. Thesis. Brigham Young University (1959), 113.

was en route to Virginia City and the territorial legislature was about to meet in Bannack. A recent arrival at Bannack City wrote to a friend in Colorado, in 1864, advising him to load almost anything for Montana. He reported that flour was selling at $34.00 per sack, bacon was selling for $.80 a pound, coffee and sugar for $1.00 a pound, nails at $.50 a pound, shovels and picks for $8.00 and $9.00 each, respectively. If a man could get to Virginia City before the big loads began to arrive from Fort Benton, he could get $.45 a pound for flour. If he was two weeks behind the others, it was worth only $.15.[13]

In the winter of 1864 a number of wagon trains from Salt Lake City that had started north late in the season were snowed in along the Snake River and lost all their oxen. By the following spring a shortage of provisions developed in Virginia City. The price of flour skyrocketed to more than $1.00 per pound; bacon, the same; and sugar, to $.85. As a result of the exorbitant prices, there developed in April what has been called a flour riot. Actually an armed but orderly force of citizens searched the town, seizing all flour in the hands of merchants and issuing notes at $27.00 per hundredweight for Salt Lake flour and $36.00 per hundredweight for States flour. The flour was issued at the rate of twelve pounds to each single man, twenty-four pounds to each married man, and more to families with children. A notice was placed in the *Montana Post* ordering all flour to be sold for $27.00 to $36.00 in the future. On the day following the seizure the merchants were paid for their flour at the prescribed rates.[14]

Alexander Toponce, who had left Salt Lake City in November, was one of those snowed in. He moved some of his flour into Virginia City by pack train, paying $20.00 per hundred pounds in freight. He made two such trips before his wagons could move. The stranded wagons began to arrive in May and prices dropped to their

13 George M. Brown, Bannack City, to David Henderson, April 16, 1864, Teller Papers, University of Colorado Libraries; Barsness, *Gold Camp*, 110.

14 Granville Stuart, *Forty Years on the Frontier*, II, 28; Dorothy M. Johnson, "Flour Famine in Alder Gulch," *Montana*, Vol. VII (January, 1957), 18–27.

usual levels, flour selling at $30.00 to $40.00. During the flour famine most of the common boarding houses posted the following notice: "Board with bread at meals, $32; Board without bread, $22; Board with bread *at dinner*, $25." One freighter was paid $5,000 in "good clean gold-dust," in 1865, for freighting five wagonloads from Salt Lake City to Helena.[15]

In general, speculative freight from Salt Lake City supplied Virginia City in 1863 and 1864. Later the merchants began to buy in the East, and by 1866 the professional freighter had taken over most of the hauling job. An expert freighter could make the trip from Salt Lake City in fourteen days, but the usual time was three weeks. A freighter who wanted to fight the spring mud and risk being snowbound in the fall could make four round trips in a season. Allowing time for loading the wagons and for a few drunken sprees by the drivers, most freighters could manage only three round trips. In the spring the freighter was hard to get along with; he would charge $.15 to $.20 a pound for freight that he would be glad to handle a month later at $.10 per pound. Not all speculators made a killing. In the spring of 1866, when flour was selling in Virginia City for $125.00 per sack, a man loaded a train of eleven four-mule wagons with flour for which he paid $15.00 a sack. He paid the freighter $12.50 a sack for transportation. The train left Corinne, Utah, on March 1 and reached Virginia City in twenty-five days, only to find that a load of flour from Fort Benton had knocked the price of flour down to $18.00 per sack.[16]

Not all the freight that moved north from the Salt Lake Valley originated in that region. A comparatively small amount of wagon freight originated at San Francisco and Los Angeles. In 1866 the *Deseret News* of Salt Lake City noted the passage of trains from California bound for Montana. The San Francisco Chamber of Commerce, in the same year, published figures that showed the

[15] Harold E. Briggs, *Frontiers of the Northwest*, 66; Toponce, *Reminiscences*, 88–89; Emerson Hough, "A Study in Transportation," *Century*, Vol. LXIII (December, 1901), 212; Trexler, "Missouri-Montana Highways," *loc. cit.*, 151.
[16] Barsness, *Gold Camp*, 111–12; Brown, *Fort Hall*, 352.

problem faced by their merchants in trying to break into the Montana trade:

Route from San Francisco	Distance in miles	Cost per Ton
Owyhee—Snake river—Helena	1190	$345
Portland—Snake river—Lewiston—Helena	1338	320
Portland—Wallula—Helena	1283	275
Portland—White Bluffs—Helena	1370	270[17]

In the year following the gold strike at Helena, trains began to roll out from the Missouri Valley. Captain F. B. Kercheval, his son J. K. Kercheval, Joseph Kinney, and Thomas Tootle moved 46 wagons, drawn by 220 yoke of oxen, to Virginia City and opened the wholesale grocery house of Kercheval, Kinney and Company.[18] A party of emigrants with 5 4-yoke wagons loaded with 3,000 to 3,500 pounds of freight each made the trip in 5 months, losing 1 yoke of oxen from each wagon. They were paid $.25 per pound for their freighting. Eugene Munn delivered the complete stock for a drugstore, plus a quantity of liquor, at Virginia City. He received $.28 a pound for the 1,400-mile haul from Kansas City, Missouri.[19]

According to the Kansas City *Journal of Commerce*, in 1864 it took 70 days for a mule train to make the trip from Kansas City to Bannack or Virginia City, Idaho. For an ox train to make the same trip required 90 to 100 days. Machinery for the gold mines was an important part of the freight that went from the Missouri Valley by wagon. In 1865 a train of 6-mule wagons left Atchison, Kansas, with 150,000 pounds of machinery on which the freight charge was $.22½ per pound.[20]

In the next year a train of 52 wagons, with 235 yoke of oxen, left Nebraska City on June 20. In the load were 81 tons of machinery, including two boilers belonging to a Pennsylvania mining company

---

[17] Salt Lake City *Deseret News* (May 17, 1866); Winther, *Old Oregon Country*, 221.

[18] *History of Buchanan County, Missouri*, 792.

[19] Trexler, "Missouri-Montana Highways," *loc. cit.*, 151; Munn, "Early Freighting and Claim Club Days," *loc. cit.*, 314.

[20] *Journal of Commerce* (March 15, 1864); Root and Connelley, *Overland Stage*, 399.

that was operating a mine in Montana. There were also 5 wagon-loads of provisions. In crossing the South Platte at Julesburg, Colorado, 1 boiler was taken through the water and quicksand by employing 26 yoke of cattle and 15 drivers; the other by 48 yoke and 21 drivers. Most of the drivers were greenhorns, and this probably accounts for the frequent upsets that plagued the train. At one point both boiler wagons tipped over; two weeks later one of the boilers went over again; and three weeks later the same boiler tipped over once more. One wagon loaded with 4,000 pounds of machinery upset. The "pan wagon" must have been hexed: it upset three times and broke down once. The train finally reached Virginia City on October 4, after covering 1,115 miles in 107 days. This was one of the few professional freighting trains that used the Bozeman Trail, and it got through without any trouble from the Indians.[21]

In the first few years of the Montana trade many freighters sold their outfits in Montana. For one reason, there were plenty of men in the Missouri Valley and in Salt Lake City who wanted to work their way to Montana, but there were very few who wanted to come out. In addition, there was no pay load coming out. On the other hand, some freighters preferred to keep their stock and equipment. The *Nebraska City News*, on February 10, 1866, noted the return of a train of fifteen four-mule wagons from Virginia City with its mules in fine condition.

By far the most important line of supply for the mining towns of Montana was from St. Louis, Missouri, to Fort Benton, Montana, by river steamer and thence by wagon. As early as 1854, P. Chouteau and Company, owners of Fort Benton, were operating wagons in the Indian trade. By 1862 the chief interest shifted from the Indian trade to transportation and merchandising for the mines and to government contract freighting. In that year two steamers had to

[21] Thomas A. Creigh, "From Nebraska City to Montana, 1866," *NH*, Vol. XXIV (September, 1948), 208–37. (Apparently the term "pan wagon" refers to the wagon carrying the amalgamation pan used in processing ore. Such pans were up to five feet in diameter and eight feet in height, making a clumsy, top-heavy load. Arthur F. Taggert, *Handbook of Mineral Dressing*, 14–20.)

discharge their freight on the open prairie as there was no store-house space available.[22]

The fluctuations in Fort Benton's importance as a river port can be traced through a study of the arrivals of the river steamers. In 1859 there was only one such arrival, but by 1867 there were thirty-nine. After the completion of the first transcontinental railroad in 1869, arrivals dropped off to six in 1871. The completion of the Northwestern Railroad to Council Bluffs, Iowa, in 1867 had short-ened the steamer trip from Hannibal, Missouri, then the northern-most railhead on the Missouri River, to Fort Benton by about 150 miles. More important for Fort Benton was the completion of the Northern Pacific Railroad to Bismarck, North Dakota, in 1873, a saving of an additional 400 miles, or so, of river travel. From Bis-marck, a steamer could make four round trips per year to Benton.

The completion of the Northern Pacific to Helena in 1883 sealed the fate of Benton as the river port for the Montana gold fields. In that year there were only fourteen arrivals. From 1865 to 1881 the earliest date of arrival at Fort Benton was April 29, 1878, while the mean arrival date was May 14. It is small wonder that the pack trains from the Columbia River could reach the Montana markets before the wagon trains from Fort Benton.[23]

Like the river ports far to the southeast in Missouri, Kansas, and Nebraska, Fort Benton was a lively place during the freighting season. Cyrus Morton noted a polyglot population of Americans, French, and Indians, "with plenty of half-breed Indians who gener-ally inherited all the meanness of a no-account white man on one side and a lousy squaw on the other." In 1875 a party of bullwhack-ers "got on a big whiskey brave and very foolishly attempted to take possession of the town." The sheriff and his deputy were enjoying the sleep of newlywed men so the bullwhackers had things their own way for a while. They marched up and down Front Street

---

[22] John B. Ritch (ed.), "Fort Benton Journal," *Contributions*, MHS, Vol. X (1940), 1–99.

[23] T. C. Powers and Brothers, "Steam Boat Arrivals at Fort Benton" *loc. cit.*; Hakola, "Samuel T. Hauser," *loc. cit.*, 125–26.

whooping and yelling, kicked in the front doors of a couple of houses, and broke a number of windows. Finally the sheriff and deputy awoke and, with the aid of several able-bodied citizens, seized four of the troublemakers. Next morning they were taken before Justice Sanborn, who "relieved them of all their loose change."[24]

Freighting from Fort Benton to the Montana gold fields began as early as 1862 when Frank Worden's train came in for a load of freight. Prior to about 1865 the freighters could name their own price, usually about $.10 a pound, in gold, for the haul of 150 miles to Helena. By the next year the business had drawn so many people that it was estimated that 2,500 men, 3,000 teams, and 20,000 oxen and mules were employed in freighting out of Fort Benton, moving 6,000 tons of freight valued at $6,000,000. This competition drove the cost of freighting down to $.04 per pound on seasonal contracts. Special trips to haul the first goods to arrive at the port for the annual race to the early market might get $.05½ to $.06 per pound.[25]

The profits of a freighter often relied on the skill of the agent at Fort Benton. The notebook of S. C. Ashby, agent for Garrison and Wyatt, is revealing:

> On large lots of frghts. say of 150 tons or more we are willing to go as low as 1½ from B to H [Benton to Helena?] but talk and hold out for 1¾ or 1.80 Contact [sic] to move 50 tons upon arrival & the balance in 50 ton lots in 20 days—the above is for 3 trips.
>
> If any large shippers have 200 or 250 Tons come to Benton—we are willing to drop as low as 1.37½ to 1.25 if nothing else will catch it above that—This is with a distinct understanding that the Shipper is willing to ship in 50 ton lots & ship every 20 days or thereabouts by the same train.
>
> When you talk to Freighters as to the prospect of the price of FRGHT never come under 1.80 & up to 2¢ from Benton—

24 Morton, *Autobiography*, 26; *Fort Benton Record* (June 16, 1876).

25 James Harkness, "Diary of James Harkness of the Firm of LaBarge, Harkness, and Company of St. Louis to Fort Benton . . . in 1862," *Contributions*, MHS, Vol. II (1896), 351; *Montana Post* (September 29, 1866); Oscar O. Winther, "The Place of Transportation in the Early History of the Pacific Northwest," *Pacific Historical Review*, Vol. II (December, 1942), 391; Briggs, *Frontiers of the Northwest*, 60; *Helena Herald* (April 25, 1867).

Small lots of 25 tons or a little less—ask 1¾ to 2¢ to be governed
by the time the shipper wants his goods forwarded—if the Shipper
in these little lots claims that his goods must come upon arrival—be
stiff at 2¢

If any of those small shippers had a reasonable amount of Frght
& were willing to have it come about the third trip you can then go
as low as 1.60 to 1.50 but do as much better as you can All of the
Benton Frghts mentioned—Storage & Handling is included—[26]

The thirty-one steamers that reached Fort Benton in 1866 landed
4,441 tons of freight. Mining machinery was an important item, as
the heavy machinery could be handled better by steamer than by
bull trains. In September, 1867, the *Helena Weekly Herald* reported that there were then 32 quartz mills in the territory and
more were being set up. One mill had thirty stamps. A month later
the paper reported the opening of the Helena Foundry, which was
importing coal a distance of 2,000 miles from Pennsylvania as the
local coal was not good for iron work. In 1866, Samuel T. Hauser
shipped $36,000 worth of machines to the town of Argenta for the
St. Louis and Montana Mining Company. The cost of getting the
machinery to the mines was often as great as the initial cost.[27]

Fort Benton had its disadvantages as a river port. In seasons of
low water it was not unusual for freighters to go 200 to 250 miles
downstream to pick up loads, or parts of loads, of steamers that
could not negotiate the rapids. Freight might come up the river in
forty-five days, but, on the other hand, it might take as long as two
years in transit. In 1865 low water in the Missouri forced some
steamers to unload at the trading post of Major F. D. Pease, near
the mouth of the Yellowstone River, about 400 miles downstream
from Fort Benton.[28]

Charles M. Broadwater took several trains of the Diamond R

26 "Rules and Regulations for Freighting," copied from Ashby Notebook, typescript
in MHS.
27 *Helena Herald*, Supplement (March 14, 1867); *Helena Herald*, (September 26,
October 24, 1867); Hakola, "Samuel T. Hauser," *loc. cit.*, 45.
28 Montana News Association insert for the week of October 30, 1922, in *Bynum
Herald* (Montana) (n.d.); *Miles City American* (Montana) (March 14, 1921).

Company to Pease's fort to pick up the freight. On this trip he conceived the idea of developing a landing place below Fort Benton which would be accessible earlier in the spring and later in the fall. The town of Carroll, named for one of the partners of the Diamond R freighting company, was started about sixty miles above the mouth of the Musselshell River. It never was a great threat to Benton as the wagon road to Helena led through the Judith Basin, a favorite hunting ground of several Indian tribes who harrassed the wagon trains constantly. Carroll faded in the 1870's and was finally abandoned in 1874. The *Benton Record* was happy to report in June, 1875, that goods from Carroll to Helena had been cached in the Badlands for ten months. The paper also urged Congress to expend $7,400 to improve navigation between Carroll and Benton. Over 250,000 pounds of freight had to be picked up at Cow Island and Fort Peck.[29]

On June 16, 1866, the *Montana Radiator* noted that of the ten steamers that came up the river in 1864, only four reached Fort Benton, that in the next year only four out of twenty boats made it all the way, and that some of the goods still had not reached the mining camps. In 1869, while reporting that the water in the Missouri was six inches lower than the previous year, the *Montana Post* commented that more men and teams would be needed to bring in the freight. "What ever is steamboat man's loss is the teamster's gain."[30]

The forwarding and commission business at Fort Benton never supplanted, though it greatly exceeded, the business of trading with the Indians. There was a steady influx of hides, skins, and furs, as well as wool and ores of copper and silver, for shipment to eastern refineries. In May, 1868, it was reported that, by actual count, 725 wagons were at Benton or on the road to that place. With a capacity of 5,000 pounds per wagon, it was thought that there would not be good loads for more than two-thirds of the wagons. Apparently the local ranchers had turned out in force with 1 or 2 wagons and con-

---

[29] *Benton Record* (Montana) (May 15, August 21, 28, September 25, 1875).
[30] *Montana Radiator* (June 16, 1866); *Montana Post* (May 7, 1869).

solidated into trains of 10 to 20 wagons for protection and mutual assistance.[31]

In the early 1870's, Fort Benton entered on some bad times. The fur trade began to die out, the gold fields of Montana were playing out, the depression of 1873 affected business, and the completion of the Union Pacific Railroad took a lot of business from the town. In 1871 only six steamers reached the head of navigation. Relief for the businessmen of Benton came from an unexpected source. In 1874 the Canadian Northwest Mounted Police reached the Whoop-up country of southern Alberta and Saskatchewan. With the arrival of the police there came law and order and a great increase in the demand for goods. In addition, the police posts drew most of their supplies—clothing, provisions, and forage—through Fort Benton. In 1875, I. G. Baker and Company of Fort Benton hauled at least 307,443 pounds to Fort McLeod and 223,990 pounds to the post at Cypress Mountains, while T. C. Power and Brother delivered another 82,771 pounds to Fort McLeod.[32]

So important was the Canadian business that T. C. Power organized a bonded line from Chicago, Duluth, and St. Paul via Bismarck, Dakota Territory, and Fort Benton to Forts McLeod and Walsh and return. Previously some Fort Benton traders, operating in Canada, had to purchase their goods in Winnepeg and freight them 700 miles across the Canadian plains. From Fort Benton to Fort McLeod was a distance of 200 miles and to Fort Edmonton, 500 miles, with a good road, good grass, and plenty of water.[33]

The Canadian business did not entirely replace the trade with the Montana mines and the posts of the United States Army. In June, 1875, 1,200 tons of freight had already arrived, and Vawter had forwarded 76,500 pounds by small trains, while T. C. Power and Company had forwarded 408,539 pounds by single wagons and trains ranging from 10 to 32 wagons. Of the total forwarded by Power, 312,703 pounds were destined for Helena alone. The *Record*

---

[31] *Fort Benton Record* (July 24, 1875); *Montana Post* (May 22, 29, 1868).
[32] *Fort Benton Record* (May 1–December 18, 1875).
[33] *Ibid.* (June 20, 1876).

remarked, "Benton is just now crowded with mule and ox teams. Freighters are loading as fast as competent clerks can examine and check the goods."[34]

Unlike Colorado, Montana had some exports. Copper ore that assayed more than 30 per cent metal could be shipped to eastern refineries at a profit. The lack of proper reduction facilities and technical know-how prevented the development of local refineries. In 1867 copper ore could be shipped from the mines to New York for $35 per ton, and 50 per cent ore delivered in Boston, New York, or Baltimore was worth $250 a ton. One shipment in that year, of six tons of carbonates and oxides, yielded 50 to 60 per cent pure copper. In 1873 a Diamond R train loaded 40,000 pounds of silver ore for shipment east for reduction. Some $50,000 worth of hides and wool were shipped east in 1868, and thousands of pounds of wool were lost for lack of a local market.[35]

The advance of the transcontinental railroad led to a shift of base by many of the Montana wagon-freighters. As early as August, 1868, the *Montana Post* noted the departure of a train of twenty-four wagons and another of thirteen for Benton, "Dakota Territory," on the line of the Union Pacific. The trip down would take about six weeks, and the freight rate on the return trip would be the "usual" ten cents per pound. In October the paper noted the arrival of Bards and Wyatt's train of fifty-six wagons from the railroad and commented, "This is the commencement of an extensive trade with the States through this means of transportation, and will prove of incalculable benefit to the laboring class of our Territory."[36]

When the Golden Spike was driven on May 10, 1869, the town of Corinne, Utah, on the northern shore of Great Salt Lake at the mouth of the Malad River, became the chief transshipment point from rail to wagon. In July, 1869, it was noted that the railroad freight warehouses, though capacious, were crammed with goods

---

[34] *Ibid.*
[35] *Helena Weekly Herald* (September 5, 19, 1867; September 4, 1873); *Deseret News* (May 20, 1868).
[36] *Montana Post* (August 7, October 30, 1868).

for Montana. In May of the following year Creighton and Munro shipped from Corinne, in the week ending May 14, a total of 276,138 pounds as follows:

Idaho City, Idaho Territory	—14,272 pounds
Fort Hall, Idaho Territory	—28,220 pounds
Salmon City, Idaho Territory	—67,800 pounds
Rock Bay, Idaho Territory	—21,000 pounds
Deer Lodge, Montana	—12,960 pounds
Blackfoot, Montana	— 4,780 pounds
Helena, Montana	—51,580 pounds
Virginia City, Montana	—75,526 pounds[37]

By July the *Corinne Reporter* was complaining that business was dull; the Diamond R, the largest freighter, had loaded out only 100,000 pounds. The paper hoped for an improvement with the fall business. In June and July, 1872, Diamond R alone sent three trains from Corinne: one with 60,000 pounds, a bull train with 140,000 pounds, and a mule train with over 60,000 pounds.[38] According to a government report, the Union Pacific Railroad shipped to Montana:

Year	Pounds
1869	1,125,960—partial year
1870	6,898,732
1871	7,501,280
1872	6,129,644
1873	about 6,000,000—year of financial panic.[39]

The Overland Freight Line, better known from its trade mark ◈, a capital R in a diamond, as Diamond R, was the biggest and best-advertised wagon-freighting company in the Northwest. There were Diamond R hotels, saloons, and dance halls in Helena and along the routes used by the company. Many bullwhackers and mule skinners had Diamond R tattooed on some part of their bodies.

---

[37] *Cheyenne Leader* (Wyoming) (July 29, 1869); *Helena Daily Herald* (May 18, 1870).

[38] *Helena Daily Herald* (July 14, 1870); *Helena Weekly Herald* (July 18, 1872).

[39] William A. Jones, Report upon the Reconnaisance of Northwestern Wyoming, *House Exec. Doc. No. 285*, 43 Cong., 1 sess. (Serial 1615), 57.

The brand was also stamped on every blue-painted wagon, canvas cover, wagon bow, harness, saddle, and animal owned by the company. A huge Diamond R, visible for several miles, in the "highest style of decorative art," was mounted on the company's warehouse in Corinne. As one early settler said, the company was practically "the whole thing in this section of the country from '76 to '81."[40]

The company was first organized in 1863 by Captain Nick Wall, a steamboat captain, and John J. Roe under the name of John J. Roe and Company; hence, the R in the trade-mark. The old firm sold out in 1868 to E. G. Maclay, George Steele, and Matthew Carroll, and the new company organized under the name of E. G. Maclay and Company. At the time of the sale, the Diamond R owned 116 wagons and 700 oxen, valued at $75,000, and employed 70 men. In the following year Charles A. Broadwater, who had been one of the company's wagonmasters, bought into the firm. At the height of its career the company had an Eastern General Manager in New York and contracting offices in New York, Boston, and Philadelphia, Chicago, St. Louis, and St. Paul.[41]

The Diamond R is credited with bringing the first piano and first church bell to Helena, the first church organ to Bozeman, and the first silks to any point in the state. Broadwater offered to haul a fire engine from Corinne or Fort Benton to Helena, free of charge. In April, 1875, the company moved the records and equipment of the territorial government from Virginia City to Helena. The company provided a large part of Colonel John Gibbon's wagon train in the Sioux campaign of 1876, and it was one of their employees who brought out the first word of Custer's Massacre.[42] Hugh Kirkendall, general superintendent, was in charge of the wagon train that

40 Butte *Anaconda Standard* (Montana) (December 16, 1900); *Helena Independent* (March 1, 1937); *Helena Daily Herald* (June 27, 1870); "James Boyd Hubbell" Biographical Sketches, MHS.

41 Matthew Carroll, An Account of the "Diamond R" Freighting Company, typescript, MHS; Mark H. Brown and W. R. Felton, *The Frontier Years*, 178.

42 Muriel S. Wolle, *Montana Pay Dirt*, 75; *Great Falls Tribune* (Montana) (November 30, 1958).

transported Colonel Gibbon's infantry in the pursuit of Chief Joseph from Fort Missoula to the Big Hole Basin.

The Diamond R grew by absorbing rival companies. In 1870 it took over the Rocky Mountain Dispatch Company that had been operating out of Ogden, Utah, some fifty miles farther from Montana than Corinne. In the following year it consolidated with Hugh Kirkendall's Fast Freight and Express to form the largest combination of capital invested in transportation in Montana. The consolidation was expected to guarantee uniform rates, more prompt delivery, and faster time on the road.[43]

Other monopolistic practices were not unknown to the operators of Diamond R. In 1873, E. G. Maclay and Company signed an agreement with the Northern Pacific Railroad Company. Maclay was to build a wagon road from the mouth of "Muscle Shell [*sic*] or Little Rocky River (as may be found most practicable)." Maclay was to put on wagons and teams to haul all goods delivered to them for points in Montana by the boats of, or employed by, the Northern Pacific Railroad at 50 per cent of the rate from St. Paul to those points. Maclay was to establish offices and give through contracts at Chicago, St. Louis, and New York and to withdraw his business, agents, and teams from Corinne and Logan. Maclay was to use his influence to get business, originating in the east for the Northern Pacific, except government business. The railroad was to pay Maclay $40,000.00 as a bonus for constructing the road and to use its influence to get a mail contract for Maclay from Bismarck to Helena via Musselshell. Both parties agreed not to give rates to rivals below specified figures. This agreement between Diamond R and the Northern Pacific apparently violated a prior agreement with the Utah Northern Railroad Company, as Maclay paid $2,500.00 for a release and rebated $218.14 to the railroad and sold them his warehouse in Corinne.[44]

[43] *Helena Daily Herald* (May 28, 1870); Virginia City *The Montanian* (April 20, July 27, 1871).
[44] Memorandum of Agreement, E. G. Maclay and Co. and Northern Pacific Rail

In 1878 the *Ogden Freeman* reported that there were 140 wagons at Dunnville, the temporary terminal of the Ogden and Northern Railroad, which had come in from Idaho and Montana on fair promises of E. G. Maclay and Company. On arriving at Dunnville the company agent offered $.02 per pound for the round trip of 600 to 800 miles. When the freighters objected and said that they would do no more business with Maclay, the agent insisted that they bind themselves to make three trips in the season. It was also reported that a large number of immigrants had bought through tickets in the East to go on the "Diamond R Line," and on reaching the railroad terminal they found no accommodations.[45]

Matt Carroll said that the average charge from Benton to Helena, over the four-year period from 1866 to 1870, was just under $.03 per pound and that steamer freight from St. Louis through to Helena was $.10 a pound, plus an insurance charge of 3½ per cent on first-class steamers. From 1870 to 1874 the average freight charge for the 465 miles from Corinne to Helena was about $.04¼ per pound.[46]

Maclay's agreement with the Northern Pacific Railroad apparently did not hold very long, although the railroad paid Maclay the $40,000.00 for building the road. In April, 1878, Maclay contracted with H. C. Niebold of Butte to transport all freight between April 14 and September 15, 1878, from Chicago to the terminal of the Utah Northern. Rates from Omaha were to be $.25 per hundred pounds lower than rates from Chicago and St. Louis. When the railroad extended north of Bear River Crossing and established a new terminal, the through rate per hundred pounds was to be reduced by 9/10 to 65/100 of a cent for each mile of team freighting saved.

Not all Diamond R freighting was done in their own wagons. In 1874, C. W. Thrailkill moved 14,994 pounds from Carroll and 3,120 pounds from Badlands under subcontract at a rate of $.17 per

Road, September 2, 1873; Release of E. G. Maclay and Co. by Utah Northern Rail Road Company, November 21, 1873, in Diamond R Papers MHS.
45 *Ogden Freeman* (Utah) (May 21, 1878).
46 Carroll, "Account," MHS.

pound. Three years later Carroll accepted an offer of a train of 6 teams, 2 wagons and 6 yoke of oxen per team, with a capacity of 48,000 pounds to haul government supplies. The Diamond R was to pay $7.00 a day, "for each and every day the teams are in condition for service as herein provided until discharged." One freighter wrote from Canon City, Colorado, saying that business was dull and inquiring whether Maclay could give steady employment to a number of teams on his line.[47]

In the late 1870's, Diamond R began to fall apart. Steele left the company in June, 1873; Carroll left in June, 1879; and Maclay left in June, 1881. Broadwater, in association with James Hubbell of St. Paul who had, in 1865, been one of the men who bought out the American Fur Company, and A. H. Wilder, also of St. Paul, carried on for some time as the Diamond B.[48]

Montana freighting was no profession for the faint of heart or the slow of mind. In 1865, Alexander Toponce bought an outfit of 40 wagons and 505 head of oxen for $40,000.00. He left Fort Benton on December 1 for Fort Union, where he bought a lot of government supplies. His train was wintered in on the Quaking Asp and the stock was all lost. Toponce went in to Helena and bought 300 head of new oxen which the Indians ran off on the return trip to the wagons. On reaching the wagon camp, Toponce found that it had been swept away by a flood. He had started this venture with $75,000.00 in gold dust and the outfit; on returning to Helena in June, he lacked $18.00 of settling with his men, but he still had his old mule. He went into Salt Lake City and bought a new outfit of 26 wagons and 4 yoke of oxen per wagon, all on credit, plus $1,000.00 worth of supplies. A full load of freight for Virginia City at $.12 a pound, plus the sale of the outfit, netted him $15,000.00 in gold.[49]

It was Toponce who said, "Some of the business men of those

---

47 Contract, E. G. Maclay and Co. and H. C. Niebold, April 14, 1878, Diamond R Papers, MHS.

48 Diamond R Journal; Paul McCormick, Tongue River, Montana, to M. Carroll and Co., July 23, 1879; David Wood and Co., Canon City, Colorado, to E. G. Maclay, July 23, 1879, in Diamond R Papers, MHS.

49 Carroll, "Account," MHS.

early days in Montana were as crooked as a dog's hind leg and had all kinds of schemes for beating the freighters." He went on to cite the case of a shipment of 500 sacks of sugar destined for Kleinschmidt Brothers of Helena. The sacks were billed at 100 pounds each, but Toponce's wagonmaster noted that they seemed to be overweight. On passing through Benton, Toponce bought a platform scales and a number of seamless sacks. At the first noon halt all bags were weighed and found to tip the scales at 120 pounds. The sacks were opened and the surplus sugar put in the new sacks, reducing the old sacks to 101 pounds. On reaching Helena, the wagons were unloaded one at a time and the freight collected. When Toponce announced that that was all, Kleinschmidt noticed the extra sacks and claimed them. Toponce showed the bill of lading that called for 50,000 pounds of sugar. After a sharp argument, Kleinschmidt paid $.50 a pound for the extra ninety-five sacks but always considered that he had been robbed.[50]

By comparison, Edward H. Edwards, a businessman of Helena, wrote, in 1867: "... with all our losses we have held our own pretty well. Our losses occurred on our freighting operation . . . [with] great reluctance I consented to go into that . . . business."[51]

The hazards that the freighter had to meet were many and varied. In 1877 a train of twelve-horse wagons was struggling through heavy sand near Camas Creek in southern Idaho when it met a drunken prospector with two burros. The prospector stopped and offered a drink to the wagonmaster. One of the burros shook itself with a great clatter of pots and pans, and the other let out a resounding bray. One wagon string stampeded for half a mile and stopped only when the wagon was hub-deep in sand, and then the horses squealed and bucked until exhausted. It took forty-eight horses and all hands with shovels to get the lead wagon free.[52]

A mixed blessing to the freighter was the enthusiasm of the Mon-

[50] Toponce, *Reminiscences*, 117–39; see also clipping from *The Mineral Independent* (October 10, 1932) in Freighting File, MHS.
[51] Toponce, *Reminiscences*, 91–92.
[52] Harry Sinclair Drago and Phyllis Mott, "The Wagon Road to Virginia City," *Brand Book*, New York Westerners, Vol. IX, (1962), 1–3.

tana territorial legislature for chartering road and bridge companies. It granted thirty-four such charters in all, with a great variety of charges allowed. A bridge on the Big Hole River could charge $5.00 per wagon with one span and $1.00 for each additional span. The Bozeman City and Fort Laramie Road Company, with rights to the Montana end of the Bozeman Trail, could charge $2.00 for each wagon with one span and $1.00 for each additional span at each tollgate, and they had a tollgate every forty miles. One franchise even covered the government-built Mullan Road. It was estimated that the tollgate at the mouth of Ruby Canyon, on the road to Corinne, cleared $50,000.00 in three years.[53]

Probably much of this was the purest kind of legalized piracy, but in one case a road company seems to have been justified. Between Fort Benton and Helena the road passed through Prickly Pear Canyon, where, in a two- or three-mile stretch, the road crossed the creek twenty-seven times and then went over two steep slopes. A traveler in 1862 noted that all work done on the Mullan Road had washed away, and four trains were stopped by one of the slopes. Eventually all hands turned to and built a log trestle roadway. Next day the wagons had to be slid down the reverse slope. A toll road was chartered through the canyon, and, though the toll was $10.00 per wagon, there was a marked saving in time. In 1868, King and Gillette, owners of the road, announced a reduction in tolls and invited freighters to come by for round-trip passes. A train from Helena to Corinne and return paid as much as $40.00 in tolls.[54]

The law and its enforcement also raised problems for the freighter. In 1866 it appeared that the United States Revenue Collector was still trying to collect a 2½ per cent tax six months after the law had been repealed. In May of the following year all freighters were held liable for a special $10.00 tax as "express carriers." The definition read, " . . . every person, firm or company engaged in the carrying or delivery of money, valuable papers, *or any article for pay*, or

53 "Freighting in the Early Days in Montana," *Big Timber Pioneer* (Montana) (n.d.), in Freighting File, MHS.
54 Barsness, *Gold Camp*, 116–20.

doing an express business . . . shall be regarded as express carriers."[55]

Wagon-freighting in Montana had certain characteristics that made it distinctive when compared to the earlier days along the Santa Fe and Overland trails. Though the Indian menace was still present, it was not as acute along the trails from Fort Benton and Salt Lake City. Only the short-lived Bozeman Trail and the wagon road from Carroll ran through favorite hunting grounds of the Indians. This resulted in smaller trains. In the second place, the use of two or three wagons hitched in tandem and drawn by a single team became the favored method of operation. Will H. Sutherlin, writing in 1899, said that the firm of Sutherlin Brothers sent a train of four wagons to Benton in April, 1866. With work cattle costing $130 to $160 per yoke, they could afford no more. The wagons were hitched in pairs, each pair drawn by five or six yoke of oxen. He said, "This was the first train of the kind to go on the road, a view to economy caused its invention." The system was widely copied, some freighters going to four wagons having nine to twelve yoke per team, with a capacity of 16,000 to 20,000 pounds. Eight to ten teams might make a train with one driver per team, a wagon boss, and a night herder. With drivers earning $50 a month or more, plus board, this savings of about 50 per cent in the size of the payroll was a marked economy.[56]

The uncertainty of life in Montana and the dependence of her people on the wagon trains was early recognized. In 1868 the *Montana Post* remarked that the same scarcity of goods that existed in the spring would return before another boating season opened on the Missouri River. Nails had gone up to one dollar per pound in currency, and other prices had been equally "frightful." The paper went on with a touch of braggadocio, "And such is the trade of Helena, the metropolis of the mountains, the great city of the new Northwest, a town but three and a half years old."[57]

---

[55] *Montana Radiator* (January 27, 1866); *Montana Post* (May 14, 1868); Harkness, "Diary," *loc. cit.*, 351–52; Briggs, *Frontiers of the Northwest*, 64.

[56] *Helena Herald* (May 9, 1867; November 29, 1866).

[57] Robert Vaughn, *Then and Now*, 113–14; Unidentified clipping in Freighting

In the summer of 1871 groceries were getting short in Helena and prices were rising. A schoolboy, sent out to search for a stray cow, spotted an approaching bull train. He dashed back with the news, and the schoolmaster dismissed school in celebration. It seems that the bullwhackers had gone on a spree in Corinne and refused to leave. Finally, after losing a month, the wagonmaster put a barrel of whisky in one of the wagons and got the train out of town. Until the whisky was consumed, the train moved rather slowly.[58]

The high cost of freighting had a direct impact on the tastes of early Montanans. J. H. Beadle explained this when he noted that a freight charge of fifteen to forty cents a pound made the difference between grades of the same article comparatively much less than in the east.

> When the miner or mountaineer used foreign luxuries at all, he used only the best quality; for freight was no more on that than on the worst. The difference between crushed white sugar at twenty cents, and common brown at ten, was all important to the Eastern family, but when one added thirty cents a pound for freight, and one hundred per cent. for dealer's profits, the difference was not worth calculating about away up in Montana.[59]

Bishop Daniel S. Tuttle remarked that Mrs. Tuttle "Had yet to learn that the mountain people would have the best of everything regardless of expense."

It was the railroad that finally spelled the doom of the long-haul wagon-freighter in Montana. The first line to penetrate the territory was the Utah and Northern, a subsidiary of the Union Pacific Railroad, which reached Butte in 1880. It followed very closely the wagon road north from Great Salt Lake. Three years later the Northern Pacific was also completed to Butte, ending the river traffic to the mines.

Despite her isolation, the territory of Montana enjoyed a steady

File, MHS; Robert G. Athearn (ed.), "From Illinois to Montana in 1866; The Diary of Perry A. Burgess," *Pacific Northwest Quarterly*, Vol. XLI (January, 1950), 63.
58 *Helena Independent* (March 1, 1937).
59 *Undeveloped West*, 98.

growth prior to the coming of the railroads, thanks to the wagon-freighter and the connection he provided between the river steamers and the transcontinental railroad and the mining towns. This growth made available to the nation a steady flow of much-needed precious and base metals during the last years of the Civil War and during the immediately following years in which the great national debt, incurred during the war, was liquidated.

Of the various lines of supply for the Montana mines before 1869, by far the most important was that by steamer to Fort Benton and thence by wagon to the chief mining camps. From 1865, when this route really began to operate, until 1869, when the first transcontinental railroad was completed, there were 137 steamer arrivals at Fort Benton. At what seems to be a fair average of 200 tons per steamer, this amounts to 27,400 tons of supplies, equipment, and machinery, only a small part of which was destined for Canada. It would appear that the pack trains from Washington and Oregon never exceeded by much the 750 tons reported in 1865, the year before the supply line via Fort Benton swung into full operation. Richardson's estimate that 20 per cent of Montana's freight came across the plains through Kansas and Nebraska was also made before the river line was in full operation.

Once the Union Pacific was completed to Promontory, Utah, there was a great change in the traffic pattern. In 1871 the railroad reported some 3,751 tons of freight for Montana, and in the same year there were only six steamboat arrivals at Fort Benton, probably carrying 1,200 tons.

CHAPTER XI

UNCLE SAM: CUSTOMER

THE MEXICAN WAR of 1846–48 presented the United States Army with a problem unique in its history: the continuous support of several thousand troops in garrisons eight to nine hundred miles from the nearest supply depot, across an uninhabited expanse of land having no navigable rivers and in regions where agriculture was limited or non-existent. Previous military penetrations of the Trans-Mississippi West, like that of Lieutenant Zebulon M. Pike in 1806–1807, Major Bennett Riley's escort of the Santa Fe traders in 1829, and Colonel Henry Dodge's march in 1835 to overawe the Plains Indians, had all been affairs of a few months. Supplies for the trip were carried by the expeditions.

Prior to the war the ten frontier posts had stretched in a rough line from Fort Jesup, Louisiana, to Fort Snelling, Minnesota. Of the ten, five were located on navigable water and only Fort Scott, in southwestern Missouri, was as much as ninety miles from a steamer landing. Fort Washita, in the Chickasaw country near the Red River, alone, had to depend on the interior for all its supplies, and it was only eighty-five miles from a supply depot. The other posts could draw heavily on the surrounding countryside for a large part of their supplies, especially forage for horses and mules. In addition, all subsistence stores were delivered at the posts by contractors.[1]

---

[1] Report of the Secretary of War, *Sen. Exec. Doc. No. 1,* 32 Cong., 1 sess. (Serial 611), 109; T. S. Jesup to C. M. Conrad, November 11, 1850, in Report of the Secretary of Treasury, *House Exec. Doc. No. 11,* 31 Cong., 2 sess. (Serial 597), 64; *Congressional Globe,* Vol. XXII, Pt. 1, 32 Cong., 1 sess. (March 20, 1852), 806–807; *ibid.,* Vol. XXIII, 31 Cong., 2 sess. (February 26, 1851). 703.

In the fertile lands of the Middle West the establishment of an army post was followed shortly by the appearance of a civilian community capable of providing much of the food needed by the garrison. A new post in the desert regions did not become the nucleus of a settlement. All heavy subsistence had to be purchased in a distant market and transported to such a remote post. As early as 1845, Colonel Stephen Watts Kearny, one of the army's best frontiersmen, recommended against the establishment of Fort Laramie because of the expense of maintaining the post. He presented an idea that was to recur over and over again in official reports: rather than establish fixed posts in the Far West, he would mount a summer campaign from the Missouri Valley every two or three years to impress the Plains Indians.[2]

During the war with Mexico, Colonel Kearny's "Army of the West" and its reinforcements, 3,300 strong, had been supplied by army-operated wagon trains. The quartermaster at Fort Leavenworth, alone, purchased 459 horses, 3,658 mules, 14,904 oxen, 1,556 wagons, and 516 pack saddles for the cavalry, artillery, and transportation. These purchases were made after the departure of the annual Santa Fe caravan, some 400 wagons strong.[3]

Inexperience marked the whole operation. Wagons were dispatched in trains of twenty-five or thirty from Fort Leavenworth, with no regard to the march of detachments of the army. No escorts were provided. As a result, the Indians drove off many oxen, robbed the trains, and killed some of the teamsters. Many of the drivers were utter greenhorns who had rushed west to enlist and, on finding enlistments closed, had hired on as teamsters at $30 a month and found. Lieutenant J. W. Abert complained that the drivers seemed to be insubordinate and that they mishandled both cattle and wagons. Near Santa Fe he saw many carcasses of oxen, and along the trail he found that the grass, needed for forage for the animals, had been burned off through carelessness. He also reported that trains

2 Report of the Secretary of War, *Sen. Exec. Doc. No. 5*, 34 Cong., 3 sess. (Serial 876), 6; Report of S. W. Kearny of March . . . 1845, *Sen. Exec. Doc. No. 1*, 29 Cong., 1 sess. (Serial 470), 212.

of supplies needed in Santa Fe were halted at Bent's Fort because the drivers claimed that their articles of agreement did not call for them to proceed farther.[4] Francis Parkman noted in his journal on September 14 that the "Waggoneers proved a very disorderly set, and quite set at defiance the authority of Brown, the master waggoner." Thomas Fitzpatrick, Indian agent for the Upper Platte and Arkansas, reporting an Indian attack on a government train in June, 1847, in which all the oxen were lost, commented, "Therefore, by the imbecility and bad management of the party, over twenty more wagons, with their necessary accoutrements, were added to the freight losses sustained by the government on that road, and from like causes."[5]

Ignorance of the weather conditions caused additional trouble. In February, 1847, a man returning from Santa Fe encountered two or three trains that were held up by the weather and were short of rations, though they had not yet reached the Arkansas River. Lieutenant Colonel William Gilpin estimated the losses to the Indians in the summer of 1847 as 47 Americans killed, 330 wagons destroyed, and 6,500 head of cattle plundered, mostly from government trains.[6] In May, 1847, the acting quartermaster at Santa Fe complained to General Jesup, the quartermaster general, that private trains had arrived more than a month earlier and added, "I cannot possibly imagine any reason for the detention of public trains." Lieutenant Colonel Philip St. George Cooke remarked, "The greatest expense of this invasion, possibly, will be found in the matter of transportation."[7]

3 John T. Hughes, *Doniphan's Expedition*, 6.

4 Walker D. Wyman, "Military Phase of Santa Fe Freighting," *KHQ*, Vol. L (November, 1932), 418; Report of J. W. Abert of His Examination of New Mexico . . . 1846–47, *House Exec. Doc. No. 41*, 30 Cong., 1 sess. (Serial 517), 513, 534.

5 Thomas Fitzpatrick, Report as an Indian Agent, Upper Platte and Arkansas, *Sen. Exec. Doc. No. 1*, 30 Cong., 1 sess. (Serial 537). (This report by the Commissioner of Indian Affairs is not included in bound volumes. Available on Southwestern Mircofilm A141.)

6 *Niles Register* (March 6, 1847); Gilpin to Jones, August 1, 1848, in Report of the Secretary of War, *House Exec. Doc. No. 1*, 30 Cong., 2 sess., (Serial 537), 136.

7 W. M. D. McKissack to Jesup, July 5, 1847, in Report of the Secretary of War, *House Exec. Doc. No. 1*, 30 Cong., 2 sess. (Serial 537), 220; Philip St. G. Cooke, *Conquest of New Mexico and California*, 27.

With the establishment of permanent posts in New Mexico, the Quartermaster Department of the Army had to arrange for forwarding supplies from Fort Leavenworth, the main depot for the army in the West. The unfortunate wartime experience led the army to give consideration to contracting for the movement of supplies to New Mexico and to the two newly established posts on the Overland Trail, Forts Kearny and Laramie, 310 and 637 miles respectively from Fort Leavenworth.[8]

During the winter of 1847–48 there was considerable correspondence between Captain Langdon C. Easton, quartermaster at Fort Leavenworth, and Quartermaster General Thomas S. Jesup in Washington. Captain Easton submitted an estimate of the cost to the government of hauling the supplies in its own wagons, as follows:

5 Yoke of Oxen	at 50.00	$250.00
1 Wagon		170.00
2 Wagon Covers	at 7.50	15.00
5 Ox Bows	at 2.50	12.50
4 Ox Chains	at 2.50	10.00
1 Teamster for 5 months	at 25.00	125.00
Extra Yoke, chains, axletrees, coupling poles, etc., etc.		10.00
Total expense of one wagon that will transport 4,000 pounds		592.50
What it will cost the Dept. to transport one pound to Santa Fe		14¾¢

Finally it was decided to experiment with contract freighting. Easton was instructed to accept no bids above fourteen cents and for not more than 200,000 pounds, the remainder to be sent by public wagons. This was later modified by telegraphic instructions to allow an additional contract for hauling those supplies for which government wagons were not available. On May 18, 1848, Captain Easton signed a contract with James Brown of Independence, Missouri, to transport an unspecified amount of government stores from Fort

8 *Congressional Globe*, Vol. XXI, Pt. 2, 31 Cong., 1 sess. (September 25, 1850), 1967.

Leavenworth to Santa Fe at eleven and three-quarters cents per pound.

Some of the provisions of this contract are of interest in view of the troubles that were to arise later between the army and freighters. All goods were to be turned over to Brown prior to August 15, and delivery in Santa Fe was to be accomplished within sixty-five days "unless unavoidably detained." All equipment used by Brown was to be subject to inspection and rejection if found to be unfit. No train of less than fifty wagons and fifty-five well-armed and well-equipped hands to be used. " . . . said James Brown shall transport all the above-mentioned stores in good strong and substantial wagons, each wagon having two covers of good strong osnaberg, not be be overloaded and an adequate team of good work oxen." In addition, Brown was to take all spare government ox wagons, not to exceed 120, with covers, yokes, chains, tar buckets, etc., at the original cost to the government at Fort Leavenworth. Under this contract Brown hauled approximately 200,000 pounds and received $23,000 in payment. The contract was later modified to give Brown some wagons on credit, to be settled out of the proceeds of the contract.[9]

In the following year Brown entered into partnership with William H. Russell to freight supplies from Fort Leavenworth to Santa Fe at $9.88 per hundred pounds, with an additional 5 per cent allowance for bacon. Other contracts were let for hauling stores from Lavaca, Texas, to Austin at the rate of $1.75 per hundred, from Fort Leavenworth to Fort Laramie at $8.91 per hundred, and from Fort Leavenworth to Fort Kearny at $.06 per pound, with a 5 per cent allowance for bacon.[10]

9 Jesup to Easton, January 11, February 16, 1848; Jesup to MacRee, March 22, 1848, Letter Book, Office of the Quartermaster General [hereinafter referred to as OQMG], XL; Easton to Jesup, Februray 9, 25, 1848, OQMG, Consolidated File, Leavenworth, Easton, Box 73; Telegram, Jesup to MacRee, April 20, 1848, Letter Book, OQMG, XL; Contract, Easton with James Brown, May 18, 1848, RG 217, NA; Contracts under Authority of the War Department, *House Exec. Doc. No. 38*, 31 Cong., 1 sess. (Serial 576), 12.

10 Contracts under Authority of the War Department, *House Exec. Doc. No. 38*, 31 Cong., 1 sess. (Serial 576), 12.

The Quartermaster General reported in late 1849 that he had paid $133,000.00 on contracts for transportation to Santa Fe, Fort Kearny, and Fort Laramie. Some idea of the army's problem may be gained from the fact that the cost of a ration (one day's food for one man) on the Atlantic Coast was $.12½; in Texas it was $.19, and in New Mexico, $.42.

Cost of Transportation	Pork	Flour per bbl.
Nearer posts in interior of Texas	$ 8.00	$ 5.30
Santa Fe–Las Vegas, N.M.	32.00	21.30
Taos, Albuquerque, Paso del Norte	41.60	27.56
Elizario, Texas; Dona Ana, N.M.	48.00	31.80

On the old frontier line the cost of foraging one horse was $55.00 per year; on the Rio Grande and in all Texas it was $189.00; in Oregon and along the route, $335.00. In 1844 the total cost of transportation for the army, by all means, was less than $120,000.00, but for the year ending June 30, 1850, this figure had risen to $1,900,000.00.[11]

In the late summer of 1850 an urgent need for additional supplies arose in Santa Fe, probably as a result of Indian troubles. The post quartermaster at Fort Leavenworth advertised for bids. David Waldo, who had already made one trip to Fort Laramie with nineteen wagons, received a contract for 150,000 pounds at $.14⅓ per pound. The firm of Brown, Russell and Company, formed by James Brown, William H. Russell, and John S. Jones, received a contract for 600,000 pounds at the same rate. Between September 14 and October 4, Brown, Russell and Company sent out four trains of thirty wagons each, organized in two caravans. Brown led one caravan with Charles O. Jones, brother of John S., as assistant. Waldo's

---

[11] Report of the Quartermaster General [hereinafter referred to as QMG], 1849, *House Exec. Doc. No. 5*, 31 Cong., 1 sess. (Serial 569), 195; *Congressional Globe*, Vol. XXIII, 31 Cong., 2 sess., 704 and Appendix (December 2, 1850), 9; Report of the Secretary of War, 1850, *Sen. Exec. Doc. No. 1, Pt. 2*, 31 Cong., 2 sess. (Serial 587), 5; Jessup to Conrad, Report of the Secretary of the Treasury, *House Exec. Doc. No. 11* (Serial 597), 64.

two trains, totaling sixty-six wagons, with 308,000 pounds of freight, followed close behind.[12]

Forty-five miles short of Santa Fe the trains were caught in a blizzard and corralled. Brown pushed ahead into Santa Fe to report the delay. The commanding officer, faced by a shortage of anti-scorbutics, ordered Brown to bring in his trains, threatening to bring them in himself, at the contractor's expense, if Brown failed to comply with the order. This was in spite of the fact that the contract set no deadline for delivery because of the uncertainty of the weather. Brown fell sick and died in Santa Fe, and Charles O. Jones decided to comply with the order. He spent upwards of $14,000 in the purchase of forage and the hire of extra men and teams to bring in the trains. Waldo kept his trains in corral and arrived in Santa Fe shortly after the Brown, Russell and Company trains.[13]

Four years later William H. Russell presented a memorial to Congress asking reimbursement for losses sustained and services rendered. On the settlement of James Brown's estate, the loss appeared to be just under $40,000; in addition to the $14,000 spent by Charles O. Jones, all animals with the trains had been lost. The Committee on Claims of the House of Representatives recommended payment of $38,000, and the House concurred on the grounds that the commanding officer at Santa Fe had exceeded his authority.[14]

In 1858, "Davis [*sic*] Waldo" petitioned Congress for relief because of losses suffered during the same storm, namely 800 head of oxen at $25 each, sixty wagons complete at $150 each, and extraordinary expenses of $20,000, total $49,000. Waldo did not claim that the government had any legal liability, but as the conductor of the train had no control over events, the government was bound in equity and good conscience to make good his loss. The memorial

12 Report of the Secretary of the Treasury Showing Receipts and Expenditures for the Fiscal Year Ending June 30, 1853, *House Exec. Doc. No. 11*, 31 Cong., 2 sess. (Serial 597), 22.

13 *Congressional Globe*, Vol. XXVIII, Pt. 3, 33 Cong., 1 sess. (July 15, 1854), 1751.

14 Memorial of William B. Russell, *House Exec. Doc. No. 59*, 33 Cong., 1 sess. (Serial 742); *Congressional Globe*, Vol. XXVIII, Pt. 3, 33 Cong., 1 sess. (July 25, 1854), 1861.

was rejected by the Committee of Military Affairs on the grounds that the loss was one which men in that business must be prepared to face.[15]

The expression "Uncle Sugar" may not have been known in the 1850's, but some freighters seemed to know the idea behind the term. In 1851 the quartermaster at St. Louis advertised for bids for the transportation of stores to the western posts, indicating a minimum tonnage for each post. Joseph Clymer prepared a train of 30 wagons and 192 yoke of oxen and then was notified that there were no goods for him to carry. The Court of Claims held that the advertisement was no part of the contract. Clymer memorialized Congress, and the Committee on Claims felt that payment of $15,670 should be made to Clymer because the government did not provide the freight.[16]

In 1851 the surviving partners of Brown, Russell and Company carried on as Jones and Russell, contracting to haul supplies to Albuquerque and Santa Fe for $9.50 and $8.50 per hundred pounds, the contract to run for two years. Later in the same year the company took another contract for Las Vegas, Moro, and Reyado, New Mexico.

The Quartermaster General, in his report for 1851, pointed out that half of the army of 10,538 men was stationed on the remote frontier or on the Pacific Coast. In New Mexico alone there were seven posts garrisoned by 1,459 officers and men who had to be supplied with everything. The distances involved were given as follows:

From	To	Miles
Indianola, Texas —Fort Worth		420
Indianola, Texas —El Paso		803
Fort Leavenworth—Fort Union, N.M.		728
Fort Leavenworth—Santa Fe		821
Fort Leavenworth—Fort Laramie		637

15 Daniel Waldo & Co., Committee of Military Affairs. *House Rpt. No. 56,* 35 Cong., 2 sess. (Serial 1018).

16 Claim of Joseph Clymer, Report of Committee on Claims, *Sen. Rpt. No. 305,* 35 Cong., 1 sess. (Serial 939).

General Winfield Scott recommended that Fort Atkinson on the Arkansas and Forts Kearny and Laramie on the Platte be abandoned. He renewed Colonel Kearny's idea of six years previous—substituting summer marches by large columns to overawe the Plains Indians.[17]

If Captain Easton's figures were correct, the army was getting a bargain in its contract freighting. The professionals were doing the job for about two-thirds the price that it would have cost in government trains. Even so, economy of operation was always the watchword. In 1849 the quartermaster at Fort Leavenworth noted that it cost $9.98 per hundred pounds to ship supplies as far as Santa Fe and estimated that it would cost as much more to forward the stores from Santa Fe to El Paso. He asked, "Would it not be cheaper to convey supplies on the Rio Grande by Kell [*sic*] Boats from the head of Steam Boat navigation to El Paso?" The post quartermaster reported to General Jesup in 1850 that to maintain one hundred six-mule teams would cost the government $8,241.70 per month for a full year, and the wagons would be usable for only seven of the twelve months. He added that if iron-axle wagons were used, the maintenance cost would be reduced. He enclosed a detailed breakdown of the cost, which included the following figures:

120	Teamsters	@ $25.00 per month
2	Wagonmasters	@ $60.00 per month
4	Asst. Wagonmasters	@ $35.00 per month
1	Blacksmith	@ $50.00 per month
1	Wheelwright	@ $50.00 per month
	Subsistence for teamsters	
	for seven month	$3,584.00
	Forage for the winter	$11,165.40.

To reduce the cost of transporting supplies to the western posts, General Orders Number One, January 8, 1851, directed attempts at cultivation on the frontier posts with emphasis on grain for forage

[17] Report of the Secretary of War, *Sen. Exec. Doc. No. 1*, 32 Cong., 1 sess. (Serial 611), 109; Report of Winfield Scott, *Sen. Exec. Doc. No. 1*, 32 Cong., 1 sess. (Serial 611), 203.

and bread and on long forage (hay). Any surplus was to be sold to other posts or at St. Louis, and the profits were to be applied to the purchase of seeds and tools and to hire Indian labor. The results were only hopeful at best because of the constant activity of the troops on other projects, such as the construction of barracks. In this same year an experimental column was sent out under Captain S. G. French to determine whether it would be cheaper to supply Santa Fe by government train from the Gulf of Mexico. It was concluded that the old route from Fort Leavenworth was the cheaper route and that contract freighting was the cheaper method.[18]

In an attempt to reduce the cost of freighting in the Southwest, Jefferson Davis, Secretary of War in 1853, introduced camels and dromedaries to test their value and adaptability to the country. The first tests with a herd of thirty-six camels showed promise. Secretary of War John B. Floyd, Davis' successor, recommended the purchase of one thousand animals. The Civil War diverted attention from the project, and after the war the extension of the railroads across the plains put an end to the experiment.[19]

Another step in the direction of economy was the reduction of losses incurred in shipment. Better packaging of stores was a recurring recommendation of the Quartermaster Department inspectors. In 1851, Colonel Thomas Swords suggested that bacon and hard bread be packed in barrels weighing 230 and 130 pounds, respectively. He also recommended that little bread be sent, rather flour, which was easier to handle and which the troops could prepare themselves. Eight years later Russell, Majors and Waddell pointed out the Navy Department finding that flour in sacks was more subject to damage, especially in warm humid climates, than was

[18] Ogden to Jesup, June 9, 1849, December 21, 1850, RG 93, NA; Report of Winfield Scott, 1851, Sen. Exec. Doc. 1, 32 Cong., 1 sess. (Serial 611), 164; Report of the Secretary of War, 1852, Sen. Exec. Doc. No. 1, Pt. 2 (Serial 659), 4; Report of QMG, 1851, Sen. Exec. Doc. No. 1, 32 Cong., 1 sess. (Serial 611), 211–22, 227–35.

[19] Report of the Secretary of War, 1853, Sen. Exec. Doc. No. 1, Pt. 2, 33 Cong., 1 sess. (Serial 691), 25; ibid., 1855, Sen. Exec. Doc. No. 1, Pt. 2, 34 Cong., 1 sess. (Serial 811), 9; Message from the President, Sen. Exec. Doc. No. 5, 34 Cong., 3 sess. (Serial 875), 22–23; ibid., House Exec. Doc. No. 2, 35 Cong., 2 sess. (Serial 997), 4; Congressional Globe, Vol. XXI, 31 Cong., 1 sess., passim.

flour packed in barrels. As, under government contract, the freighter was responsible for shrinkage but not for leakage it was a common occurrence, if rain blew up a day or two from the destination, for the covers to blow off wagons loaded with corn. By the same sign, barrels of whisky arrived only half full.[20]

Barely three years after the first contract was signed, professional freighting for the army had become big business. During the fiscal year ending June 30, 1851, 15 contractors using 626 wagons hauled 3,131,175 pounds of supplies from Fort Leavenworth at a cost to the government of $2,094,408.51. The interest in farming at the frontier posts is understandable when one considers that, of the more than $2,000,000.00 spent for transportation, $1,287,327.91 went for the freighting of forage. New Mexico alone took 452 wagonloads of supplies, Fort Kearny 43, and Fort Laramie 47. Some of the contractors had less than 10 wagons, but David Waldo and Brown and Russell dominated the business, sending out 124 and 219 wagons respectively. As volume increased and competition became keener, the contract rates per hundred pounds decreased:

Year	Fort Kearny	Fort Laramie	Santa Fe
1849	$6.00	$8.91	$9.98
1852	3.80	6.80	8.59

Also a differential in rates began to appear based on the season of the year in which a trip was begun. The contract of Russell, Majors and Waddell of 1858 illustrates this on the Overland Trail:

Month	Fort Kearny	Fort Laramie	Salt Lake City
Jan.–Feb.	$3.55	$3.55	$4.00
March	2.90	2.90	2.90
April	2.00	2.00	1.80
May–July	1.35	1.35	1.80
Aug.	1.50	1.70	1.80
Sept.	2.00	2.00	2.20
Oct.	2.90	3.00	3.00
Nov.–Dec.	4.00	4.50	4.50

20 *Congressional Globe*, Vol. XXIV, Pt. 1, 32 Cong., 1 sess. (March 22, 1852), 816; Russell, Majors and Waddell to Jesup, March 22, 1859, RG 93, NA; Blair, *History of Johnson County, Missouri*, 68.

In 1860 the season rates, in dollars per hundred pounds, to Fort Union were:

Jan. Feb.	Mar.	Apr.	May	June July	Aug.	Sept.– Dec.
1.60	1.50	1.45	1.40	1.44	1.50	1.60[21]

Until 1855 contract freighting was a matter of open competition with a number of contractors involved. On December 28, 1854, William H. Russell, Alexander Majors, and William B. Waddell signed a two-year agreement to engage in "the buying and selling of goods, wares and mechandise and also in a general trading in stock, wagons, teams and such other things used in the outfitting of persons, teams, or trains across the plains or elsewhere and also in freighting goods or freight for government or others." In the following March, under the name of Majors and Russell, the company signed a two-year contract which gave it a monopoly of army freighting west of the Missouri River. With Leavenworth City, Kansas, as headquarters, the firm built offices, warehouses, a blacksmith and a wagon shop, a store to outfit its employees, and a packing plant to supply meat for its trains. The firm hired 1,700 men, including 25 wagonmasters and a like number of assistants, 40 to 50 stock tenders, and 20 to 30 cooks. They bought 7,500 oxen and in May began loading 20 trains totaling 500 wagons. The equipment represented an investment of $360,000 to $400,000 and the company went heavily into debt, a load that it never cleared. The profits for 1855 were set by Alexander Majors at $150,000.[22]

All went well with the big company until June 19, 1857. On that day Captain Thomas L. Brent, quartermaster at Fort Leavenworth, served notice on Majors and Russell that, in addition to the supplies already on the way to the frontier posts, they would be required to haul about 3,000,000 pounds of stores for the Utah Expedition.

[21] Report of Winfield Scott, *Sen. Exec. Doc. No. 1*, 32 Cong., 1 sess. (Serial 611), 110, 295–97; Contracts—Utah Expedition, *House Exec. Doc. No. 99*, 35 Cong., 1 sess. (Serial 958), 4; Contracts of the War Department, *House Exec. Doc. No. 47*, 36 Cong., 2 sess. (Serial 1099), 9.

[22] Settle and Settle, *Empire on Wheels*, 14–30; Contracts—War Department . . . for 1855, *House Exec. Doc. No. 17*, 34 Cong., 1 sess. (Serial 851), 9.

Russell objected that the season was late, that their trains were already on the road, and that the additional task would ruin the firm. Brent insisted, saying that he did not believe that the government would let the company suffer loss. Russell finally accepted the job but, unfortunately, did not insist on a new contract. Majors, the operating head of the company, set to work to collect the additional equipment. He found that wagons would cost more, that the price of oxen had risen by 25 per cent, and wages had risen by 50 per cent. Eventually men and equipment sufficient to move 4,525,913 pounds of supplies were collected.

The first two trains of Majors and Russell reached South Pass late in August. Because of hostile action by the Mormons, all trains were halted near Green River, Wyoming. On the night of October 4 a party of Mormons under Major Lot Smith captured three of the trains. After releasing the teamsters, including one William F. Cody, to return to the States, Smith burned the wagons with 300,000 pounds of supplies. Vacillation on the part of the commander of the advance guard, burning of the range grass by the Mormons, and raids that drove off 1,400 oxen and some mules soon put the contractor's trains in a bad position. When the army finally went into winter quarters near Fort Bridger, only enough oxen were left to move one train at a time. Eventually 375 wagons were brought in. The final loss to the company was estimated at $494,553.01.

The discovery of several boxes marked dry goods, consigned to the Mormon authorities, but actually containing gunpowder, in Majors and Russell wagons threatened a scandal. It was explained that the firm had received four wagonloads of goods from a commission house in Leavenworth for delivery in Utah. These four wagons had been attached to one of the trains hauling government supplies. Neither the army nor the company had inspected the contents of the boxes, and there was no charge to the army for these four wagons.[23]

---

[23] Settle and Settle, *Empire on Wheels*, 26–95; Norman F. Furniss, *The Mormon Conflict*, 134; Russell to Jesup, April 15, 1858, Correspondence of the Quartermaster, Fort Leavenworth, RG 92, NA.

Not discouraged by the unfortunate experiences of 1857, the partners reorganized as Russell, Majors and Waddell and signed a new contract to freight to the frontier posts and to the army in Utah. This contract authorized a new starting point north of Fort Leavenworth, and Nebraska City was chosen. Here new corrals, warehouses, and offices were built. Majors subcontracted twenty-five to forty-eight trainloads, thus relieving the company of an investment of up to half a million dollars.[24]

According to the *Deseret News* of March 30, 1859, the bookkeeper of Russell, Majors and Waddell had given the following statistics for the previous year:

Item	Number	Disbursements
Trains	146	
Wagons	4,796	$ 767,000
Oxen	46,720	1,645,000
Chains	38,680	70,000
Yokes	24,090	60,000
Mules	4,380	152,000
Wagon sheets		49,000
Merchandise		500,000
Freight		125,000
Pay of clerks, mechanics, etc.		948,090
Men with trains	4,380	
Men not with trains	300	

All might have gone well if the partners had stuck to freighting, a business they knew well, but they became involved in stagecoaching, a string of retail stores, and finally in the Pony Express. Besides overextension, plain bad luck added to their complications. In the late summer of 1859 a herd of 3,500 head of cattle were started for California from Salt Lake. The herd was wintered in by a blizzard in Ruby Valley, Nevada, and by spring there were only 300 survivors. The estimated loss was $150,000. By the close of 1859, Russell, Majors and Waddell was actually bankrupt. They did receive the contract for the New Mexico posts in 1860 and by September 20 had

24 Russell, Majors and Waddell to Jesup, June 2, 1858, RG 93, NA.

sent out 837 wagons with 5,007,686 pounds of stores. Even this contract was a costly venture as the army did not deliver the stores to the firm in May and June, as customary, but waited until August and September; meanwhile, payroll costs were mounting. In addition, payment for this shipment would not be received until six months after many obligations would fall due.[25]

In late 1860 the scandal of the "Floyd Acceptances" and the Indian bonds broke. Secretary of War John B. Floyd had been issuing notes stating the sums due to the firm for work performed, but the total of the notes soon exceeded the amount due to the company. Russell used the notes as collateral for loans from banks. When trouble over the acceptances threatened, a clerk in the Interior Department, a relative of Floyd's, gave Russell some $870,000 worth of Indian trust bonds with which to retire the notes. Apparently Russell used the bonds to float more loans. The clerk's conscience began to bother him, and he reported his act to Secretary of the Interior Jacob Thompson. Immediately a major scandal broke: Russell went to jail and his company went to the wall.[26]

As the clouds of financial disaster darkened over the head of Russell, Majors and Waddell, the army took steps to assure a continuous flow of stores to its frontier posts. A contract was drawn with Irwin, Jackman and Company under which they would take over in case Russell, Majors and Waddell failed to fulfill the contract of April 11, 1860. For the three years 1861–63, Irwin, Jackman and Company enjoyed a monopoly of army freighting.

To simplify the paperwork, the army designated three routes for its freighting, aside from Texas. Route One ran from Fort Leavenworth to Salt Lake City and Fort Hall, Idaho; Route Two from Leavenworth to Fort Union, New Mexico; and Route Three from Fort Union to posts in New Mexico and Arizona. In 1864 confusion arose over the bidding. One firm bid on Routes One and Two but was low bidder only on Route One. All bids on Route Three were

25 Settle and Settle, *Empire on Wheels*, 26–95; *Daily Times* (November 2, 1860).

26 Settle and Settle, *Empire on Wheels*, 76–102; *Journal of Commerce* (January 29, February 6, 1861); Abstracted Indian Bonds, *House Exec. Doc.* and *Supplemental Rpt. No. 78*, 36 Cong., 1 sess. (Serial 1105).

thrown out as being too high, and new bids were called for. The low bidder on Route Two offered to take Route One for the same rate. Alexander Caldwell, unsuccessful bidder on One and Two, claimed that the successful bidder would not be able to fulfill the contract.[27]

Opinion within the army varied as to the efficiency of contract freighting. Captain Charles Thomas, assistant quartermaster general, reported to General Jesup in 1857 that he had investigated the whole subject of army transportation from Fort Leavenworth and concluded that the army could not do its own freighting at less cost than the offer of Majors and Russell. To even match the cost, the army would have to take steps at once to buy wagons and animals and to build stables. " . . . if this be done and a law enacted authorizing a corps of wagon masters with enlisted teamsters there is a bare possibility of the labor being performed for a less sum than that proposed."[28]

On the other hand, in 1865, Colonel Joseph A. Potter, a quartermaster at Fort Leavenworth, said that delays and damages "arising from careless mode of shipment and want of proper care, will be in great measure avoided by using nothing but government trains." He went on to point out that penalties against the contractor for lost or damaged supplies did not get the supplies to the frontier posts on time. He claimed that seldom were supplies lost from government trains and that contractors were slow by comparison, as the contracts specified only a delivery date late in the fall. A year later Brigadier General James F. Rusling, inspector for the Quartermaster's Department, reported, "Contractors by the pound . . . are reported as doing the work faithfully." From Fort Morgan, Colorado Territory, he wrote that he had passed a train "and its marching condition was admirable. I have seen no better nor more ship-shape trains in the army or elsewhere." From Fort Bridger he

27 Contracts—War Department for the Year 1861, *House Exec. Doc. No. 101*, 37 Cong., 2 sess. (Serial 1136), 4; Transportation of Military Supplies from Fort Leavenworth Westward, *Sen. Exec. Doc. No. 31*, 38 Cong., 2 sess. (Serial 1209).

28 Thomas to Jesup, September 21, 1857, RG 93, NA.

reported that it was generally held to be impractical to supply that post from the West Coast.[29]

To the freighter who contracted at so much per hundred pounds per hundred miles, exact knowledge of distances was very important. In 1856 freighting from Fort Union to Albuquerque was based on a distance of 160 miles. After a couple of trips over the road hauling 800,000 pounds, "Uncle Dick" Wootton was sure that the distance was greater. He requested that the road be surveyed and offered to pay the expense if the measurement did not show the distance to be over 160 miles. The survey showed the distance to be 162½ miles. The extra 2½ miles made a difference of several hundred dollars in the amount collected by "Uncle Dick."[30]

The Civil War seems to have had little effect on the movement of government stores to the frontier posts. In mid–1861, Irwin, Jackman, and Company moved their depot from Kansas City to Leavenworth City because of what the Leavenworth *Daily Times* called the disloyalty of the former city. By March, 1863, the troubles in Kansas were under sufficient control that government trains were once again operating out of Kansas City. Most of the successful raids by Confederate guerillas seem to have hit army-operated trains rather than contractors' trains. The Indian War of 1864 had more effect. In July of that year the supplies for Fort Union, New Mexico, were landed at Nebraska City, instead of at Fort Leavenworth. Poteet and Company loaded out 125 wagons at 6,000 pounds each, with these supplies.[31]

The end of the Civil War saw active work begun on the transcontinental railroads. The fiscal year ending June 30, 1866, saw the first use of railroads west of the Missouri River for the transportation of military supplies. The rails out of Omaha shortened the wagon haul by 398 miles, and those out of Kansas City saved 215

[29] J. A. Potter to M. C. Meigs, September 15, 1865, in Report of the Secretary of War, *House Exec. Doc. No. 1*, 39 Cong., 1 sess. (Serial 1249), 848; Inspection by Generals Rusling and Hazen, *House Exec. Doc. No. 45*, 39 Cong., 2 sess. (Serial 1289), 11, 37, 49.

[30] Conard, *"Uncle Dick" Wootton*, 355.

[31] *Daily Times* (June 7, 1861, October 5, 1864); *Journal of Commerce* (May 17, 1862; May 1, 1863).

miles. General Rusling recommended that, for the summer of 1867, temporary depots be established at the termini of the railroads with canvas, lumber, teams, and employees as in field operations.[32]

The extension of the railroads eased but did not end the army's transportation problem. General William Tecumseh Sherman stated the problem very clearly in his report of 1869:

> The Quartermaster . . . department is more affected by the scattered condition of the troops, and the peculiar sterile character of the country in which they are kept, than any other. If the army could be concentrated and quartered in the region of supplies, the expenses could be kept down to a comparatively small sum; or if we had, as in former years, a single line of frontier a little in advance of the settlements, the same or similar would be the result; but now, from the nature of the case, our troops are scattered by companies to posts in the most inhospitable parts of the continent, to which every article of food, forage, clothing, ammunition, etc., must be hauled in wagons hundreds of miles at great cost.

For the year ending March 31, 1870, there was no contract for freighting on Route Number One because the transcontinental railroad had been completed. On Route Number Two the contracts were let from the end-of-track of the Eastern Division of the Union Pacific Railroad at rates lower than in the previous year.[33]

In 1870, General John Pope, commanding the Department of the Missouri, proposed to take advantage of the rails by closing Fort Larned, fifty-five miles from the rails, Fort Dodge, ninety miles from the line, and Fort Harker. He would concentrate the garrisons at Fort Hays, Kansas, which was situated on the railroad. He also proposed replacing Forts Wallace, Lyons, and Reynolds with a new post near Cedar Point or River Bend, Kansas. These steps would reduce the cost of transportation and enhance the morale of the

---

32 Report of the QMG, 1867, *House Exec. Doc. No. 1, Pt. 1*, 40 Cong., 2 sess. (Serial 1324), 533; Inspection by Generals Rusling and Hazen, *House Exec. Doc. No. 45*, 39 Cong., 2 sess. (Serial 1289), 8–9.

33 Report of W. T. Sherman, *House Exec. Doc. No. 1, Pt. 2*, 41 Cong., 3 sess. (Serial 1446); Report of the QMG, *House Exec. Doc. No. 1, Pt. 2*, 41 Cong., 2 sess. (Serial 1412), 213.

A wagon train loaded with supplies for the building of the Union
Pacific Railroad in Echo Canyon, Utah. The grade of the railroad
is shown at right.

Packing a reluctant mule on the Washburn-Doane Expedition,
Yellowstone Park.

Courtesy Historical Society of Montana, Helena

Pack mule ore team ready to leave Nellie Mine above Telluride, Colorado, in the 1890's.

Courtesy Denver Public Library Western Collection

A wagon train arrives in Bridge Street, Helena, in 1865.

Courtesy Historical Society of Montana, Helena

"The Sentinel," an oil painting by Frederic Remington.

Courtesy Remington Art Memorial, Ogdensburg, New York

"The Jerk Line," an oil painting by Charles M. Russell.

Courtesy C. M. Russell Gallery, Great Falls, Montana

"The Wagon Boss" supervises his train, in this drawing by Charles
M. Russell. Russell identified the train as a Diamond R outfit of
the 1870's.

"The Bullwhacker," as portrayed by Charles M. Russell.

Courtesy The Great Falls (Montana) Tribune Company

troops. The savings in wagon transport offered by the railroads is shown by the average rates from April 1 to October 1 from points on the Kansas Pacific Railroad to posts in Kansas, Colorado, Indian Territory, Texas, and to Fort Union, New Mexico:

1867–68	$1.28	per 100 lbs. per 100 miles
1868–69	$1.29	
1869–70	$1.15½	
1870–71	$1.08	

A typical year's supplies hauled in contractor's wagons is shown in the report of the Quartermaster General for 1876:

Subsistence	9,951,548 pounds
Quartermaster	16,511,949
Ordnance	1,515,808
Medical	245,272
Miscellaneous	1,928,618
Total	30,153,195[34]

With the shortening of the wagon hauls and a general pacification of the Indians in many parts of the country, large wagon trains of twenty-five or more wagons were no longer needed for self-protection, and the number of eager contractors grew. In 1877 the longest haul was 348 miles from Fort Union to Fort Bayard, New Mexico. In the following year the quartermaster reported that seventy contracts had been drawn to move only 26,559 tons of supplies.[35]

The army did not rely on the contractor for all of its transportation requirements. The supply trains which accompanied the columns of troops on the march or on campaign were operated by the quartermaster officer of the column. Most of the personnel of these trains were civilian employees of the War Department. An Act of Congress of 1838 set the pay of forage and wagonmasters at $40 per

[34] Report of John Pope, Department of the Missouri, *House Exec. Doc. No. 1, Pt. 2,* 41 Cong., 3 sess. (Serial 1446), 11–13; Report of the QMG, *House Exec. Doc. No. 1, Pt. 2,* 41 Cong., 3 sess. (Serial 1446), 152; Report of the QMG, 1876, *House Exec. Doc. No. 1, Pt. 2,* 44 Cong., 2 sess. (Serial 1742), 120.

[35] Abstract of Contracts by the Quartermaster's Department, *House Exec. Doc. No. 1, Pt. 2,* 45 Cong., 2 sess. (Serial 1794), 304; Report of the QMG, *House Exec. Doc. No. 1, Pt. 2,* 45 Cong., 3 sess. (Serial 1843), 252.

month, three rations, and forage for one horse. It also specified that they were to have no interest in any wagon or other means of transportation employed by the United States nor in the purchase or sale of property by or for the United States.[36] This was at a time when wagonmasters working for commercial freighters were getting $100 per month and found.

An ever-recurring theme in the problem of the army-operated transport was civilians versus enlisted men for drivers. In 1847 the quartermaster recommended the enlistment of a portion of the necessary mechanics, teamsters, and laborers because such men had to be paid high wages and to be transported to their place of work; few would engage for more than six months and very few would extend. It was estimated that enlistment of such specialists would reduce the cost of labor fully one-third and more than double the efficiency of the department. Two years later he again urged enlistment because of the lack of proper legal control by the army officers over the civilian teamsters, leading to bad performance.[37] In 1851 the suggestion was made to raise the strength of the frontier companies from seventy-five to one hundred men and to give extra pay to those detailed as drivers. The matter was brought up again in 1859, and ten years later President U. S. Grant ordered the discharge of all civilian teamsters and their replacement with enlisted men. Once more the matter came up in 1875 when the Secretary of War reported that soldiers were being detailed as drivers without any knowledge of the work and against their will. As a result the animals were overworked, maltreated, and neglected. He recommended the enlistment of a regular body of teamsters and pointed to the German army's transport service which was organized into battalions and companies.[38]

Typical of the problem of the civilian teamster was that faced by

36 *Statutes at Large*, V, 257–58.
37 Report of the QMG, 1847, *Sen. Exec. Doc. No. 1*, 30 Cong., 1 sess. (Serial 503), 548; *ibid.*, 1849, *House Exec. Doc. No. 5*, 31 Cong., 1 sess. (Serial 569), 195.
38 Report of the QMG, 1851, *Sen. Exec. Doc. No. 1*, 32 Cong., 1 sess. (Serial 611), 112; Report of the Secretary of War, 1859, *Sen. Exec. Doc. No. 2*, 36 Cong., 1 sess. (Serial 1024), 6; *ibid.*, 1875, *House Exec. Doc. No. 1*, Pt. 2, 44 Cong., 1 sess. (Serial 1674), 7.

the regimental quartermaster of the Fifth Infantry en route to Utah in 1857. He left Fort Leavenworth with over 100 6-mule teams, 5 wagonmasters, 4 assistants, and about 160 drivers. The men had been hastily collected from all trades and occupations; many were induced to sign up as a means of getting transportation to California. Most had never driven before and had to break young, wild mules, resulting in many dead or crippled animals. Discipline became a serious problem and led the lieutenant to recommend the enlistment of a nucleus of teamsters. In 1861, Congress granted permission to the Quartermaster Department to add as many master wagoners as the President might deem necessary with the rank, pay, and allowances of sergeants of cavalry. Wagoners were to have the pay and allowances of corporals of cavalry.[39] This would not have settled the problem of discipline, as these men were not to be enlisted but were to hold "comparable" or "Mex" rank.

Percival G. Lowe, after a five-year enlistment in the Dragoons, took his discharge as a first sergeant and went to work at Fort Leavenworth as a wagonmaster. One of his first actions was to discharge the whole crew of a train, including the wagonmaster, for drunkenness and inefficiency. Many of those fired found jobs with Russell, Majors and Waddell and, according to Lowe, "were the cause of strikes, mutinies and loss to their employers." Lowe remarked that government trains had more discipline than contractor's trains, as the former had a sprinkling of former soldiers and the man in charge had been in the army. Despite this, he admitted that contractors often accomplished the job better than the government would have done, but their business was so large that it left room for leaks and defective management.

Lowe's first major job as a government wagonmaster came in the fall of 1858. The winter clothing for the troops in Utah arrived at the depot too late to go on the contractor's trains. Three trains of 26 wagons were organized under Lowe and sent out loaded with 342 boxes and 910 bales. Lowe was ordered to report on such con-

---

[39] Report of the Secretary of War, 1857, *House Exec. Doc. No. 2, Pt. 2*, 35 Cong., 2 sess. (Serial 998), 47; *Congressional Globe*, 37 Cong., 1 sess. (July 12, 1861), 84.

tractor's trains as he might meet on the trail. He reported that, in general, the trains were in good shape but that at the Little Blue he had found a train, half of whose men were sick, in charge of the wagonmaster whom he had discharged just a few months before. Of Russell, Majors and Waddell, he said that it was a wonderful organization. While a few of their wagonmasters were not fit for their jobs, most of them were "the salt of the earth" as far as freighting was concerned, "possessing unusual courage, perseverance, good judgment, and business ability, and remarkable in the management of men."

When General Grenville M. Dodge reported on the Powder River campaign of 1865, he complained that the contract for freighting was not closed in Washington until May 1 and that the contractors were given until December to make the deliveries. This delay nearly ruined his operations north of Fort Laramie as the troops were delayed four to six weeks, waiting for supplies that had been en route for two to three months. " . . . we had finally to haul supplies for General Connor's columns by government trains from Fort Kearny and Cottonwood before they could move."[40]

Delays in closing the contracts were not always chargeable to army red tape. In 1860 the two low bidders on Route Three pleaded various difficulties and refused to close. The quartermaster at Fort Leavenworth noted that the bids all seemed to be in the same handwriting. In 1873 the low bid to posts in North Texas and the western parts of Indian Territory was rejected because it specified shipment via the Atchison, Topeka and Santa Fe Railroad. When it came time to sign, the next two lowest bidders had gone out of business because of the long delay.[41]

Not only was there trouble between the contractors and the pencil pushers, but, from time to time, unpleasantness arose between the troops and the bullwhackers. In front of the bar in the sutler's store

[40] OR, Series 1, XLVIII, 335–36.
[41] John Armor to Van Vliet, April 11, 1860; George W. Chrisman to Van Vliet, April 12, 1860; Abstract of Bids Received by Van Vliet; Van Vliet to Jesup, April 14, 1860, Russell, Majors and Waddell Correspondence, RG 93, NA; Report of the QMG, 1874, House Exec. Doc. No. 1, Pt. 2, 43 Cong., 2 sess. (Serial 1635), 172.

at Fort Fetterman, a white line was painted on the floor to separate the officers' and enlisted men's drinking area. The teamsters were expected to keep out of the officers' area and took this discrimination to heart. Bill Hooker spent three days in the guardhouse on bread and water, for crossing a forbidden part of the parade ground to get a close look at the first Gatling gun sent west of the Missouri. One teamster was spread-eagled on a cannon for some offense against military protocol. In this case the teamsters got their revenge: they so barbered the tail of the commanding officer's horse that a parade had to be canceled.[42]

The army was not the only department of the government that had business with the contract freighter. The Bureau of Indian Affairs, under both the War Department and the Department of the Interior, had need for his services. As early as 1833 the War Department estimated that it would cost $9,500 to transport and distribute the Indian annuities for the following year. In the same year the Indian agents were notified that, when the Indians so desired, they could take all or part of the annuity in goods instead of cash. The agents were to buy the goods on contract and have them transported to the point of distribution "at the sole expense of the contractor, and kept there at his risk until delivered by the proper officers to the Indians." Thomas Fitzpatrick, agent for the Upper Platte and Arkansas, in 1849, bought $5,000.00 worth of goods and arranged for their transportation to Bent's Fort at $.06 per pound; from there to the North Fork of the Platte or to Fort Laramie, any remaining goods were to be transported at $.03 per pound.[43]

Four years later Fitzpatrick reported that the goods were so late arriving at the depot that he could not solicit bids, and so he had arranged with "a responsible person" to transport the goods at the same cost as the last two years. In 1855 the Indian Bureau reported

---

42 William Francis Hooker, *Bullwhacker*, 48–50.
43 Report from the Office of Indian Affairs, *Sen. Exec. Doc. No. 1*, 23 Cong., 1 sess. (Serial 238), 187; Regulations Concerning Payment of Annuities, Report of Commissioner of Indian Affairs, *House Exec. Doc. No. 2*, 23 Cong., 2 sess. (Serial 587), 51; Thomas Fitzpatrick to D. D. Mitchell, September 24, 1850, in Report of Commissioner of Indian Affairs, *Sen. Exec. Doc. No. 1*, 31 Cong., 2 sess. (Serial 587), 51.

that it had cost $21,043.59 to transport the gifts and annuity goods to the Indians of the "Prairie and Mountain Tribes," plus $3,643.05 for the balance of the goods for 1853.[44]

Agent R. C. Miller accompanied the train of goods to Bent's Fort in 1857. On arrival he found that the Indians had not yet collected for the distribution. The freighter would not stay until they came in, and so Miller had to rent the fort for storage and safekeeping of the goods. The delivery of the goods could be fraught with difficulty. In 1861 the agent for the Upper Platte told the Indians that he would deliver the goods to the Indians' camps. As the next year's trains rolled westward, Chief High Bear and his band stopped the train and demanded two wagonloads of goods. When the wagonmaster demurred, the Indians stripped the covers from the wagons and began to help themselves. The wagonboss carefully explained that there had been a change of agents and that the plan of delivery to the camps had been disapproved. The Indians accepted the explanation and came in to Fort Laramie to receive their goods.[45] This was one of those ticklish situations which could easily have erupted into violence.

The threat of hostilities by the Sioux, in 1871, caused the Interior Department to order that the supplies for the Whetstone Agency, Dakota Territory, be detained in Cheyenne. Other Indians refused to escort the train across the Sioux Reservation, and a request for a military escort was refused for fear that its appearance would set off an Indian war. The freight contractor, Dwight J. McCann, had already loaded his wagons. There were no storage facilities available in Cheyenne so McCann had to hire men to guard the supplies on the wagons. McCann sought relief from Congress for the extra expense to the amount of $19,000.00, which was approved.[46]

[44] Report of the Commissioner of Indian Affairs, *Sen. Exec. Doc. No. 1, Pt. 1,* 33 Cong., 1 sess. (Serial 690), 350; Report of the Second Auditor . . . Accounts for the Benefit of the Indians, *Sen. Exec. Doc. 19,* 34 Cong., 1 sess. (Serial 815), 18.

[45] Leroy R. Hafen, *Relations with the Plains Indians,* 35; Report of the Commissioner of Indian Affairs, 1863, *House Exec. Doc. No. 1, Pt. 2,* 37 Cong., 3 sess. (Serial 1157), 274.

[46] Transportation of Indian Goods from Cheyenne to Sioux, *House Rpt. No. 417,* 43 Cong., 1 sess. (Serial 1624).

When the Red Cloud Agency was moved in midsummer of 1873, the Board of Indian Commissioners allowed only $9,377.00 out of $11,658.00 claimed by McCann for freighting. The contract specified a distance of 132 miles and a rate of $1.20 per hundred pounds per hundred miles. The Commissioners allowed only an additional 80 miles because of the move—the straight-line distance. McCann insisted that, to avoid deep sand and to find water, he had had to travel an additional 100 miles. McCann also pointed out that there were no facilities at the old location for the lightening of loads and temporary storage of goods; as a result the loads had to be reduced from 7,000 pounds to 5,500 to 6,000 for the entire trip.[47]

As the army was heavily involved in freighting already, an agreement was reached in 1869 between the War and Interior Departments under which the Army Quartermaster would transport supplies for the Indian Service in the Indian territory, the costs being refunded by the Interior Department. The contractors were not always as co-operative as they might be. Captain Henry E. Alvord, commissioner to the Kiowas, complained that in 1872 the contractor for flour and bacon hauled nothing but flour, ignoring the agent's request for bacon. He also reported that the contractor for sugar and coffee did the same thing. From the Crow Agency came the complaint that goods which were supposed to arrive on September 1 did not arrive until February 9, except for tobacco which did not arrive for another four months. The Commissioner of Indian Affairs received word, in 1875, that the Arapahoes were on short rations though the goods had lain in depots and cars for months while the contractor freighted for other parties.[48]

At times the Indian Bureau, as well as the army, felt the hand of

---

47 Contracts, Purchases, and Expenditures for the Indian Service, *House Exec. Doc. No. 123*, 43 Cong., 1 sess. (Serial 1608), 36–39; Investigation on the Conduct of Indian Affairs, *House Rpt. No. 778*, 43 Cong., 1 sess. (Serial 1627).

48 Report of the Secretary of War for 1869, *House Exec. Doc. No. 1, Pt. 2*, 41 Cong., 2 sess. (Serial 1412), 4; Report of Commissioner to the Kiowas . . . October 10, 1872; F. D. Pease, Agent for Crow Indians, September 1, 1872, in Report of the Secretary of the Interior, 1872, *House Exec. Doc. No. 1, Pt. 5*, 42 Cong., 1 sess. (Serial 1560), 531, 662; Report of the Commissioner of Indian Affairs, 1874, *House Exec. Doc. No. 1, Pt. 5*, 44 Cong., 1 sess. (Serial 1680), 546.

an economy-minded Congress. In 1874 it was pointed out that for the fiscal years 1873 and 1874 the $150,000 appropriated for transportation and distribution of goods to the Sioux had been barely enough. For the current year, only half that amount had been appropriated.[49]

As one step toward civilizing the Indians and making them self-sufficient, the agent to the Cheyennes and Arapahoes organized the Cheyenne-Arapahoe Transportation Company. In 1877 two trips were made to Wichita, Kansas, bringing back 65,000 pounds on the first trip. The agent noted that it was necessary to issue at least one wagon to each band so that there would be no complaints about one band hauling for another. In the following year, for the first time, the company brought the annuity to the agency on time. The cost and expenses were $6,150.20, and in four trips they hauled 318,433 pounds of goods.

Possibly as a result of the success with the Cheyenne-Arapahoe Transportation Company, the same plan was applied to the Sioux in 1878. The agent reported that bids for $47,500 had been rejected and $4,000 had been spent on equipment. The operation was a success, compared to the losses of past years, when white contractors had done the freighting; "Employes and teamsters lived off the flour, sugar, bacon and coffee transported by them." The Indians, on the other hand, brought the goods through intact.[50]

Some of the contractors apparently did not take kindly to this competition and burned off the grass between Rosebud Landing and Rosebud Agency. One former mule skinner commented that when, in 1881, the Shoshonis were "compelled" to do their own freighting, as part of a government economy streak, each four-pony, three-inch wagon carried one thousand pounds and required two Indians to drive. The Indians often laid over en route to hunt, and the wagon boss, a white man, had no control over his teamsters.

---

[49] Sioux Agencies, *House Exec. Doc. No. 35*, 43 Cong., 2 sess. (Serial 1644).

[50] John D. Miles to William Nicholson, August 31, 1877, in Report of the Commissioner of Indian Affairs, *House Exec. Doc. No. 1, Pt. 5*, 45 Cong., 2 sess. (Serial 1800), 479; Miles to Commissioner, *ibid.*, *House Exec. Doc. No. 1, Pt. 5*, 45 Cong., 3 sess. (Serial 1850), 462, 553.

"You can form your own opinion as to the saving realized by the Government. We freighters called it all bunk."[51]

Since many of the tribes continued to take their annuity in specie, and since their animals fed only on range grass, the transportation requirements of the Indian Bureau never reached the proportions of those of the army. In 1864 the Indian department advertised for bids for the transportation of only 165 tons of goods from Atchison, Kansas. As the plan of feeding, rather than fighting, the Indians grew in popularity, there was some increase in the amount of goods to be hauled. In 1871 some 80 railroad cars of goods arrived at Cheyenne, and the city felt some beneficial effects in its business. Five years later advertisements appeared for bids to transport 1,000,000 pounds of goods to the Red Cloud and Spotted Tail agencies.[52]

There can be no doubt that the United States government was the single largest customer of the high plains freighter and that, in general, the government got good and cheap service. As a reporter of the New York *Times* remarked in 1866, "Experience shows that Uncle Sam had better trust to private enterprise whenever he can, because individuals, as a rule, always do more and work cheaper than corporate bodies, the body politic especially."[53]

It would be too much to say that without the professional freighter, the United States Army and Indian Bureau would not have been able to fulfill their missions on the western frontier. But in view of the experience of the Mexican War and the constant pressure from Congress for economy, it seems fair to say that both sections of the federal government would have been sadly hampered in their operations. If the army had had to do all its own hauling, it would have had to increase its strength by several hundreds of men, and over-all strength, not ability to perform its mission, has, since time immemorial, been the yardstick that Congress has applied to

51 Report of the Commissioner of Indian Affairs, *House Exec. Doc. No. 1, Pt. 5,* 45 Congress., 3 sess. (Serial 1850); T. S. Garrett, "Some Recollections of an Old Freighter," *Annals of Wyoming,* III (July, 1925), 86–93.

52 Nebraska City *Daily Press* (March 19, 1864); *Cheyenne Daily Leader* (July 17, 21, 1871; November 3, 5, 1876).

53 (August 22, 1866).

the military establishment. The comparison of the American and German systems was entirely invalid in the face of radically different conditions of distance, climate, compulsory military service, and the condition of roads, or rather lack of them, in the Trans-Mississippi West.

Frederick L. Paxson rather oversimplified things when he said that Kearny's wagon trains in 1846 blazed a new trail for the wagon-freighter. It is true that the occupation of New Mexico and the establishment of Forts Kearny and Laramie brought the professional freighter to the fore and ended the period of the merchant-freighter, and that the stock and equipment accumulated to meet the needs of government could be easily converted or expanded to meet the needs of the civilian customer.

CHAPTER XII

MR. LO

GREAT DIFFERENCES in philosophy, economy, and civilization had kept relations between the white man and the North American Indian in a state of more or less perpetual tension since the Indian outbreaks of early colonial times. These variances were bound to cause clashes between the wagon-freighter and the Indians of the Great Plains. To the Plains Indians, the taking of scalps and stealing of horses by trickery, treachery, or overwhelming odds seems to have been a combination of religious duty and major sport. These activities were never appreciated by the white man when they were practiced on him.

The Plains Indians, though by some rated as the world's finest natural warriors, never committed themselves to hostilities unless they had an overwhelming advantage of numbers or surprise—preferably, both—on their side. When such an advantage was absent, the Indian simply turned aside or professed friendship, content to wait for a more advantageous time. Augustus Storrs, who captained a Santa Fe caravan in 1824, said that Indians bent on robbery were always willing to compromise when they found that their plan might cost too much in lives. The "Wagon Box Fight" of 1867, near Fort Phil Kearney in present-day Wyoming, was one of the very few cases in which the Indians mounted successive attacks in the face of heavy losses. Here the surprise was on the side of the soldiers; the Sioux did not know that the troops had recently been equipped with the new breech-loading Springfield rifle. They kept waiting for the usual pause in the fire that, until now, had come when the soldiers had to reload their muzzle-loaders. A well-armed, alert party of white men usually could traverse the plains with no more than the petty annoyance of hit-and-run raids or attempts to stampede their animals.

Not all the troubles were chargeable to the Indians. Many white men of the frontier displayed a crass ignorance of Indian philosophy and social customs. This ignorance was often compounded by downright carelessness. In 1826 two members of a party, returning from Santa Fe, wandered away from camp and lay down to take a nap. They were both killed with their own guns by a band of roving Pawnees. A few days later the traders opened fire on a group of six or seven Indians, without making any effort to determine their connection with the death of the two whites. All but one of the Indians were killed. The rest of the band from which the slain Indians had come followed the traders to the Arkansas and stole nearly one thousand head of horses and mules. The enraged Indians then turned their attention to a following party of traders, killed one, and ran off all their animals.[1]

A party of twelve men, having only four guns among them, was visited by a band of Indians, possibly Arapahoes, in 1828. At first the Indians professed friendship, but on seeing the defenseless condition of the traders, demanded a horse for each of the braves. The traders immediately granted this request. Finding the pickings so easy, the Indians promptly returned and demanded a second mount for each of them. When this request was also met, the Indians mounted their new horses and drove off the whole herd of nearly five hundred animals.[2]

The troubles of 1828 led the government, in the following summer, to order Major Bennett Riley, with four companies of the Sixth Infantry, 170 men, to escort the Santa Fe caravan as far as the Arkansas River. After the caravan had crossed the river by some six or seven miles it was attacked and one trader was killed. Riley at

---

1 Kate L. Gregg (ed.), *The Road to Santa Fe*, 231.
2 Gregg, *Commerce of the Prairies*, 17–19.

once crossed the river into Mexican territory and joined the caravan. The blowing of reveille in the camp next morning forewarned the Indians and there was no further attack. Riley's column suffered some ten or a dozen casualties inflicted by the Indians on couriers, herders, or small parties of discharged soldiers returning to the States.[3] This was the first important encounter between the United States Army and the Indians of the high plains. It also marked the introduction of oxen to high plains freighting.

In 1831 the Superintendent of Indian Affairs said that the safety of a Santa Fe party depended principally on the material composing it. If the party was made up of mature men of great prudence and firmness, with some knowledge of Indian character, there was little to fear, " . . . but if on the contrary, the party is composed of raw young men, not only ignorant of Indians, but destitute of a common knowledge of mankind, and above all, if signs of fear are exhibited by them in presence of Indians they may encounter, their destruction is certain."[4] In general, this statement remained valid until the Indians no longer presented a menace to the white man. A train staffed by well-armed, disciplined teamsters seldom was seriously attacked by the Indians. They might be harrassed by sudden charges to test their mettle; attempts might be made to run off their stock; but the Indian had no stomach for a stand-up fight.

In avoiding trouble, quick thinking and steady nerves were essential. In the 1860's an Indian and his wife approached a wagon train and the scout gave some water to them. The woman responded to this courtesy by spitting some of the water in the scout's face. Reacting instinctively, the white man reached for his gun. Luckily one of the drivers who was near seized the scout from behind and held him until the Indians rode away. In 1863, on Nine-Mile Ridge some seventy-five miles west of Fort Larned, a band of starving Indians approached a train that was preparing to camp for the night

3 Major Bennett Riley's Report of Escort Duty, November 22, 1829, *American State Papers, Military Affairs,* IV, 277; Henry P. Beers, "Military Protection of the Santa Fe Trail to 1843," *NMHR,* Vol. XII (April, 1937), 116.

4 Report of the Secretary of War Concerning the Fur Trade, and Inland Commerce to Mexico, *Sen. Exec. Doc. No. 90,* 22 Cong., 1 sess. (Serial 213), 32.

and begged for food. The wagonmaster refused to feed them. As the wagons were being corralled one nearly tipped over, and the nervous, frightened driver shot and killed one of the Indians. The Indians withdrew but returned before daylight and killed all but one of the train crew. The survivor claimed that there would have been no trouble if the wagonmaster had given the Indians some food.[5]

Plain curiosity on the part of the Indians could become irksome to the traveler on the plains, building tensions that might erupt into violence. Trying to prepare a meal, the cook of one train was bothered beyond endurance by some Indians who crowded around to watch. The cook decided to put on an act. He grabbed the long stick he had been using to poke the fire, rolled around on the ground, and then began to belabor the fire. "Never before or since have coals and ashes been scattered as then without an explosion," reported a witness. The Indians scattered also, and when another member of the crew tapped his head several times and pointed to the cook, the Indians understood that that one was weak in the head and thereafter kept a safe distance.[6]

One large group of travelers on the plains who were little bothered by the Indians were the Mormons. Captain Eugene Ware said, "There was a sort of Masonic understanding between the Indians and the Mormons which we never understood." The *Deseret News* of Salt Lake City blamed most of the trouble with the Indians on carelessness, wandering away from camp, or relaxed vigilance. "A moderate sized train or party of determined, vigilant and well armed men might travel across the plains in comparative safety." An occasional Quaker appeared among the high plains wagonfreighters, and, even in the worst of the Indian troubles, these persons were free of harrassment. "Mr. [John B.] Russell boasted of the superiority of the Quaker faith in quelling the riotous red man."[7]

[5] Independence *The Examiner* (Missouri) (June 7, 1929), clipping in Jackson County Historical Association, Independence, Missouri; Ryus, *Second William Penn*, 16; William E. Unrau, "History of Fort Larned," *KHQ*, Vol. XXIII (Autumn, 1957), 257–80.

[6] Withers (ed.), "Experiences of Lewis Bissell Dougherty," *loc. cit.*, 552.

[7] *Deseret News* (September 6, 1865); Obituary, John B. Russell, *The Trail*, Vol. VI (September, 1913), 27.

The inability of Major Riley's infantrymen to pursue mounted Indians who attacked his herds led Congress, imbued with the militia idea, to authorize the raising of a battalion of mounted volunteer rangers, six hundred strong. Enlistments were to be for one year, unless sooner discharged. In 1832 and 1833 companies of rangers escorted the Santa Fe traders to the Arkansas. Complaints soon arose that the ranger companies were too large and did not have sufficient officers for effective control. It was pointed out that the one-year enlistments were inefficient and that the Battalion cost about $150,000 per year more than would a regiment of dragoons. In 1833, Congress authorized the formation of a regiment of dragoons, and in the following year Captain Clifton Wharton's company of dragoons performed the escort duty.[8] This was the last military escort for the Santa Fe traders which was directed against the Plains Indians. The escort of 1843 was sent out to protect the caravan from Texan freebooters.

The escorts seem to have been fairly effective. In 1831, Alphonso Wetmore, a Santa Fe trader, reported that the whole number of lives lost until that year was eight, and that since 1828 the losses had been inconsiderable. Three years after the last escort, the train of Bent, St. Vrain and Company was attacked by the Pawnees, while en route to Santa Fe, with the loss of one man killed, three wounded, and animals and merchandise lost. George Bent entered a claim in Congress for $3,271.00, which included:

40 pieces domestics, 1,299½ yards	@	50¢ per yard
38 pair brogans	@	$3.00 per pair
6 pieces calico, 180 yards	@	75¢ per yard
1 piece scarlet cloth, 36 yards	@	$5.00 per yard
9 mules and saddles	@	$75.00 each
3 horses and saddles	@	$100.00 each
15 pounds coffee	@	$1.00 per pound
25 pounds sugar	@	50¢ per pound
10 reams paper	@	$10.00 per ream

8 Otis E. Young, "United States Mounted Ranger Battalion," *MVHR*, Vol. XLI (December, 1954), 463–68; Military Establishment, Report of the Secretary of War, *Sen. Exec. Doc. No. 6*, 22 Cong., 2 sess. (Serial 233), 13.

The Committee on Claims rejected the claim on the grounds that the attack had taken place on Mexican soil and therefore the United States government was not liable.[9]

Of all the tribes who appeared along the Santa Fe Trail, the Comanches were the greatest troublemakers. Colonel Henry Dodge, an army officer of wide experience with the Plains Indians, said, "Where all are such magnificent thieves, it is difficult to decide which of the plains tribes deserves the palm for stealing. The Indians themselves give it to the Comanche." On the night of August 5, 1864, two trains, one American, the other Mexican, camped close together for mutual protection on Pawnee Fork. During the night a small group of Kiowas and Comanches crawled through the camp of the Mexican train and into the corral of the other train. The Americans had grazed their mules before sunset and had then driven them into the corral for the night. The American wagonmaster, one DeLong, a man with fourteen years' experience on the plains, stationed two guards at the openings of the corral. Despite these precautions, the Indians got among the mules and stampeded them out through the lower opening, overrunning the guards, smashing wagons, and overturning everything in their way. As soon as the mules had cleared the corral, mounted Indians appeared to keep them running. Ninety-three mules were lost in this one raid.[10]

The Mexican War was a great boon to the Plains Indians. Since many of the experienced drivers of the Santa Fe caravans had enlisted in the army, the army's supply trains were manned by greenhorns who defied all efforts to bring them under any discipline. As a result, they were an easy prey for the marauding Indians. In November, 1846, the Pawnees attacked a supply train of twenty-

[9] Alphonso Wetmore's Report of Trade, Report of the Superintendent of Indian Affairs, 1831, Sen. Exec. Doc. No. 90, 22 Cong., 1 sess. (Serial 213); Bent, St. Vrain and Co., House Rpt. No. 194, 28 Cong., 2 sess. (Serial 468).

[10] Webb, Great Plains, 66; James H. Carleton to Matthew Steck, October 29, 1864, Condition of the Indian Tribes, Sen. Rpt. No. 156, 39 Cong., 1 sess. (Serial 1279), 205; Journal of Commerce (August 28, 1864); OR, XLI, 320.

eight wagons. They killed 1 man, wounded several, and drove off all but 7 of the 160 mules in the train.[11]

The Commissioner of Indian Affairs in 1847 claimed that, except possibly for the "mischievous Pawnees," it was not known that any Indians, over which the Indian Bureau had any control, were involved in the attacks of the previous year. He did admit that property, probably taken from the trains, had been found in the possession of two or three tribes who were drawing annuities, but the Indians claimed to have obtained them in trade with other tribes. All but the Pawnees surrendered such goods cheerfully, but with the Pawnees, force had to be used. He also said that the impression prevailed that it was the Comanches who had made the attacks, and possibly some were made by white renegades, either American or Mexican. At the same time, the superintendent at St. Louis recommended that guns, theoretically for hunting, not be included in the annuity payments, and that traders be forbidden to sell them, as the Pawnees and Osages received them and then traded them to the Comanches.[12]

The year 1847 witnessed the heaviest attack by the Southern Plains Indians against the Santa Fe Trail. On June 25 the Comanches struck a train returning from Santa Fe and ran off and killed all the oxen. On June 26, 2 outbound trains under the escort of a company of the First Dragoons reached the same area on Coon Creek and were attacked. Lieutenant John Love, commanding the escort, sent 25 men to help the immobilized train. They were soon surrounded by blanket-waving Indians who stampeded the Dragoons' horses. In this engagement 5 soldiers were killed and 6 were wounded, as were 4 teamsters, most of the oxen of 2 trains were run off, and the Dragoons lost about 20 horses. Colonel William Gilpin, writing from Fort Mann in August, 1848, estimated the losses of the previous year as 47 Americans killed, 330 wagons destroyed, and 6,500 head of cattle run off. He said that the greater part of the

[11] Thomas Swords to Jesup, July 12, 1846, Correspondence with Russell, Majors, and Waddell, OQMG, NA; Garrard, *Wah-to-yah*, 43.
[12] Report of the Commissioner of Indian Affairs, *Sen. Exec. Doc. No. 1*, 30 Cong., 1 sess. (Serial 503), 743; Report of the St. Louis Superintendency, *ibid.*, 832.

losses had been sustained by government trains and pointed out that, "No resting places, depots, or points of security exist between Council Grove and Vegas, a bleak stretch of 600 miles. There is no timber, fuel is scanty, and grass is scarce." He remarked that, in addition to government stores, the wagons carried loads of costly merchandise for the cities of Mexico and that the trade was growing rapidly. "It is a great stigma upon the home department of our government that a few piratical savages are allowed to menace with destruction all passengers for the space of six hundred miles."[13]

The years immediately following the Mexican War were marked by several isolated attacks on the wagon trains along the Santa Fe Trail. In 1848, Bent, St. Vrain and Company's train beat off an attack by Comanches and killed Chief Red Arm in the process. In the following year J. M. White and his family and employees were all killed by Indians. In 1851 and 1852, Colonel Edwin V. Sumner sent patrols from Fort Union to the Arkansas over the Cimarron Cutoff, but by 1854 the mounted portion of the garrison of Fort Union was down to one understrength company and the system of patrols was abandoned. The caravans would have to take care of themselves, which they generally were quite capable of doing.[14]

In 1852, Thomas Fitzpatrick, Indian agent, negotiated a treaty with the Kiowas, Comanches, and Kiowa-Apaches that brought a couple of years of comparative peace to the trail. Then the Indians began levying tributes of sugar, coffee, and other goods from the Santa Fe trains. Even the less warlike tribes began to cause trouble. In 1853 the Commissioner of Indian Affairs reported that the Kansas Indians were adept at stealing and that from their location near the Santa Fe Trail they annoyed passing wagon trains. He added, "Complaints are loud against these Indians, not only from the white people who pass through their country, but from all the

13 New York *Weekly Tribune* (August 7, 1847); Cragin Collection, Pioneer Museum, Colorado Springs, VIII, 85; Headquarters, Battalion of Missouri Volunteers . . . Fort Mann, August 1, 1848, in Report of the Secretary of War, *Sen. Exec. Doc. No. 1*, 30 Cong., 1 sess. (Serial 503), 136–40.

14 George Bird Grinnell, "Bent's Old Fort," *Collections, KSHS*, Vol. XV (1923–25), 27, 54; Wyman, "Freighting, A Big Business," *loc. cit.*, 19–20; Utley, "Fort Union," *loc. cit.*, 22–23; Steere, "Fort Union," *loc. cit.*, 19.

neighboring tribes." In the following year the agent for the Upper Platte and Arkansas reported that every train that passed that year had suffered some annoyance from the Indians and that the Osages in particular "had regular stations where they demand toll of all passing." He noted on the other hand that the Kiowas and Comanches had committed no depredations.[15]

While the Santa Fe Trail was the scene of almost continuous skirmishing between the wagon-freighter and the Indian from the beginning, the Overland Trail was comparatively quiet for a number of years. The murder of Bull Bear, a tyrannous but effective leader of the Oglala Sioux, about 1841, by other chiefs of the tribe, produced a sort of civic anarchy and military decline among the Oglalas. They were so busy repelling attacks by their Indian enemies the Pawnees, Crows, Shoshonis, Arapahoes, and Cheyennes that they paid little attention to the Oregon migration which had really opened with the "Great Migration" of 1843.

With the growth of travel on the Overland Trail, Oregon emigration, Mormon emigration, and the California Gold Rush, it appeared essential to come to some sort of an understanding with the Northern Plains Indians. In September, 1851, Thomas Fitzpatrick negotiated the Treaty of Fort Laramie with the Arapahoes, Cheyennes, Sioux, Assiniboins, Shoshonis, Arikaras, Gros Ventres, and Crows. Under the terms of the treaty, the United States was to pay $50,000 a year for fifty years in return for unmolested travel through the northern plains and the right to build roads and the forts to protect them. Although the United States Senate refused to ratify the treaty, all was relatively quiet along the Overland until 1854. In that year a hotheaded, inexperienced young "shavetail," Lieutenant John Lawrence Grattan, was killed, along with thirty soldiers, while trying to arrest a Sioux suspected of killing a cow belonging to a passing Mormon train. The Grattan Massacre set off a series of raids along the trail. In the following year Colonel Wil-

15 Report of the Commissioner of Indian Affairs, *Sen. Exec. Doc. No. 1, Pt. 1,* 33 Cong., 1 sess. (Serial 690), 248; Report of John W. Whitfield in Report of the Commissioner of Indian Affairs, *Sen. Exec. Doc. No. 1, Pt. 1,* 33 Cong., 2 sess. (Serial 746), 298–99.

liam S. Harney administered a stinging defeat to the Sioux at Ash Hollow which brought peace to the trail for a year or so.

By 1857 the Northern Plains Indians were on the warpath. Two small trains belonging to Russell and Waddell, totaling about sixteen wagons, camped within sight of each other, were attacked by a band of Cheyennes. One man was killed, one was severely wounded, and the wagons were burned. Another train was harrassed as it moved west of Fort Kearny. Finally, on the divide between the North and South Platte rivers, the Indians cut the train in two and surrounded the rear portion. Most of the weapons were in the last wagon. Oliver P. Goodwin, the wagonmaster, had been at the head of the column when the trouble struck. After distributing what weapons were available in the forward wagons, Goodwin rode to the rear. He found a band of some fifteen Cheyenne warriors under Chief White Crow attacking the wagons. Riding forward, Goodwin fired at the Indians and broke the arm of the chief, whereupon the Indians withdrew.[16] One factor that may have kept the Indians along the Overland Trail more or less quiet was the heavy travel over the trail. Emigrants to California, Oregon, and Utah must have numbered in the thousands every year, in addition to the trains of the wagon-freighters.

Fortunately for the United States, the Plains Indians did not take advantage of the reduction of army strength in the West during the first years of the Civil War. However, in 1864 a vicious war broke out across the plains. Irked by a series of raids on wagon trains and eastern Colorado ranches, Colonel John Chivington and his Colorado Volunteers fell on a camp of Southern Cheyennes and Arapahoes at Sand Creek. The Indians thought that they were under the protection of the United States flag which flew in front of the chief's tipi. The soldiers killed men, women, and children and showed a savagery which fully matched that of any of the Indians. This Sand Creek Massacre set the whole plains afire. Attacks on the trains occurred on Walnut Creek, on the Little Blue, on the Cimarron

---

[16] *Kansas City Enterprise* (August 22, 1857); Clipping dated 1907, Dawson Scrapbooks, CSHS.

Cutoff, near Fort Larned, and in the vicinity of Denver. The train of the James brothers was attacked in August, 1864, eleven wagons were burned, and two of the brothers were killed.[17]

In June, 1864, General Robert D. Mitchell, commanding the District of Nebraska, ordered all wagons halted at Cottonwood, formed into trains, and forwarded under military escort. Since there were not enough troops on the plains to escort all the stagecoaches and wagon trains, veritable log jams soon built up. On a tour of inspection, the General found almost three miles of wagons awaiting escort. He massed all the Denver-bound wagons into a single train and sent it off. The General and his escort convoyed the rest to Fort Laramie.[18]

All escort duty was heartily disliked by the troops, but duty with an ox train was the worst. The rate of travel of a bull train kept the escort at a slow walk. Since the movements of the train were controlled by the availability of grass, the troopers often had to be content with warm water from the kegs. Loose tires, cracked yokes, and other mishaps meant delays that put an additional strain on the escort commander. Mule-train escort was not as tedious because of the faster rate of march, but the Indian's desire for mules meant that larger escorts had to be provided. General James H. Carleton, commanding the Department of New Mexico, sent Colonel Christopher Carson out onto the plains to talk with the Kiowas, Comanches, and Cheyennes. He wrote to Carson, "Tell them this, they must not think to stop the commerce of the plains, nor must they imagine that we are going to keep up escorts with the trains. We do this now until we learn whether they will behave or not. If they will not, we will end the matter by a war which will remove any further necessity for escorts." Concern for the welfare of the freighters was felt in

---

[17] Massacre of Cheyenne Indians, Report of the Joint Committee on the Conduct of the War, *Sen. Rpt. No. 142, Pt. 3*, 38 Cong., 2 sess. (Serial 1214); *OR*, XLI, 320; St. Joseph *Winners of the West* (Missouri) (May, 1924); *Journal of Commerce* (July 2, 27, 30, September 10, 1864); *Daily Times* (August 17, 1864); Lynn I. Perrigo, "Major Hal Sayr's Diary of the Sand Creek Massacre," *Colorado Magazine*, Vol. XV (March, 1938), 41–57; James B. Thompson, "Crossing the Plains in 1864," *Sons of Colorado*, Vol. II (March, 1908), 3–8.

[18] "Indian War of 1864," *Overland News* (November, December, 1957).

the river ports. Practically every traveler, fresh from the plains, was queried concerning conditions along the trail and the status of the trains they had met. In late September, 1864, J. D. McCann reported that the road ranches between Latham, Colorado, and Kearney, Nebraska, were mostly deserted, that flour was selling for fifty cents a pound and bacon for a dollar a pound—when they could be found. He added that, despite the troubles, most trains were in good shape.[19]

Some freighters preferred to take care of themselves. Thomas Cornforth of Denver said that his trains always traveled well prepared for trouble with the best weapons available, and though the Indians attacked several times, they soon learned to leave those trains alone. Some went so far as to say, "God preserve us from the soldiers, we can take care of the Indians ourselves."[20] One wagonmaster related that the Indians would prepare an ambush by mounting two men on one horse, wrapped in a single blanket. On reaching the spot selected for the ambush, one brave would drop off while the other rode on as though nothing had happened. This action was repeated until all was ready. One of the drivers on this particular train, named "Whiskey Bill," would collect four or five other hardy souls and stalk the ambush, often killing and scalping as many as four Indians in one ambush. One impatient Montana-bound emigrant who was working his way as a bullwhacker, when told that his party would have to await the arrival of a government train before moving past Fort Laramie, cried, "Emigrants have to protect U.S. troops." A week later his wagonmaster was chased back to the train by some Cheyennes, and the train had to corral for two hours.[21]

Late in 1864 the army fired the prairie grass over a three-hundred-mile front, from west of Denver to Fort Kearny. Driven by a northwest wind, the fire reached the Arkansas in three days and even

19 Carleton to Carson, May 4, 1865, in Condition of the Indian Tribes, *Sen. Rpt. No. 156*, 39 Cong., 2 sess. (Serial 1279).

20 Thomas T. Cornforth, "Early Colorado Days," (ed. by Albert B. Sanford), *Colorado Magazine*, Vol. I (September, 1924) 251–57; *Daily Times* (March 23, 1865).

21 *Atchison Daily Globe* (Kansas) (July 16, 1894); Creigh, "From Nebraska City to Montana, 1866," *loc. cit.*, 28.

crossed into the Texas Panhandle. The fire burned off the grass on which the Indians fed their horses and drove most of the game out of the country. The fire, in conjunction with General Mitchell's winter campaign which drove the Indians out of their winter camp in the Big Timbers on the Republican River, practically cleared the land between the Platte and Arkansas rivers of Indians.[22] The effects were felt in Denver in the following spring when the wagon trains began to roll again with their accustomed freedom. The high prices that had ruled for over a year dropped by fully 30 per cent.

The Southern Cheyennes, who were estimated as being 1,500 strong, in moving out of the desolated area to join their cousins the Northern Cheyennes, struck Julesburg, Colorado, in January and February, 1865. Outside Gillette's Ranch, some nine miles west of Fort Sedgwick, they found eight heavy wagons loaded with bottled liquors bound for Denver. After an all-night orgy they burned Julesburg and moved off to the north, driving all the cattle that they had rounded up and the wagons that they had managed to hitch up. When the garrison at Fort Sedgwick, one under-strength company of cavalry plus about fifty civilians, was able to move out from behind the walls of the fort, they found scattered out on the plains twenty-four large wagons loaded chiefly with mining machinery. On a large cast-iron wheel were the words "Go To Hell" recently done with charcoal. The fugitives from Gillette's Ranch reported an Indian wearing a hat, blanket cape, and high-top cavalry boots, who carried a rifled musket of the new United States pattern, and who shouted swearwords in English. Captain Ware thought that he might be an Indian from one of the "civilized" tribes of the Indian Territory sent out by the Confederacy to stir up the Plains Indians.[23]

Clearing the area between the Platte and Arkansas rivers did not by any means end the Indian problems along the trails. In May, 1865, the *Daily Times* of Leavenworth reported, "Last Tuesday our beloved red brethren broke loose again, and demonstrated their perfect readiness for another treaty." Scattered attacks continued. Clark and Brothers lost to the Indians in 1865:

[22] Ware, *Indian War of 1864*, 354–57.   [23] *Ibid.*, 377–78.

85 oxen	$9,350.00
1 mule	150.00
1 saddle	20.00
1 revolver	25.00
1 spur	2.00
Total	$9,547.00

The United States Court of Claims allowed the bill, but payment was not made until 1898. When General William Tecumseh Sherman made an inspection trip along the Overland Trail from Omaha to the northeastern Colorado in 1866, he found everything apparently peaceful despite the complaints of officials and bloodthirsty reports in the newspapers. He concluded that, "as usual I find the size of Indian stampedes and scares diminishes as I approach their location."[24] It was entirely a matter of judgment concerning what was big and important and what was not—a matter of whose ox was gored.

In late July a wagon train loaded with telegraph wire for Salt Lake City was harrassed by Indians near Julesburg. The hostiles drew up in a line across the trail and, when the train tried to go around the line, opened fire with bows and arrows. The teamsters drove them off with rifle fire. A train returning from Santa Fe was hit next year some twenty-five miles from Fort Zarah by a band that was said to be led by Charley Bent, half-blood son of Colonel Bent. One man was killed and fifty-five mules were run off.[25] Brigadier General H. H. Heath reported from Fort Kearny in November, 1865, that he had pursued and fought twice with the Indians who had burned some trains and killed some whites near Alkali on October 20 and 28. In 1867 a train was attacked by the Sioux five times between Julesburg and Fort Phil Kearny.[26]

[24] Daily Times (May 3, 1865); H. T. Clarke, "Freighting—Denver and Black Hills," loc. cit., 303; Athearn, William Tecumseh Sherman, 64.

[25] Rocky Mountain News (August 1, 1866); Leavenworth Daily Conservative (Kansas) (July 19, 1867).

[26] Letter, H. H. Heath, November 12, 1865, Omaha Nebraska Republican (November 13, 1865); Jesse Brown, "The Freighter in Early Days," Annals of Wyoming, Vol. XIX (July, 1947), 112–16.

Typical of the Indian problem was the experience of one man who left Omaha for Custer City, South Dakota, in May, 1876. At Sydney, Nebraska, he saw in the *Omaha Bee* an account of the rumored massacre of his party and promptly wired his father to assure him of the falsity of the rumor. Indians had followed their train all the way, but there had been no trouble with them.[27]

The army maintained the system of organized convoys throughout 1867. A register of trains passing through Fort Sedgwick was kept from February 1 to September 28. It showed that 124 trains had passed going east or west. These trains contained 3,074 wagons, 4,587 men, 556 women, 587 children, and employed 5,738 mules, 11,096 oxen, and 1,062 horses. Unfortunately the record is not as complete or consistent as one could wish. There was no attempt to distinguish between emigrant and freight trains. The destination of all trains was not noted, and many trains gave their destination as Fort Laramie, the next check point on the trail, when they apparently were going beyond. Certainly that post did not require the loads of 395 wagons. By considering, rather arbitrarily, the proportion of men, women, and children to the number of wagons it would appear that about 105 of the 124 trains were freight trains. A few that originated in the west appear twice on the register—eastward bound to the railhead and later westward bound with their loads.[28]

The formation of the convoys meant delays in the movement of the wagons, and many westerners became impatient. The *Transcript* of Golden City, Colorado, said in January, 1867:

It is the veriest humbug to compel small freighters to organize coming this way at Junction [now Fort Morgan, Colorado], for nothing of the kind is required at this end of the road and single teams are continually going down the road in perfect safety. . . . teams of Western Transportation Co. & Overland Co. are allowed to pass but the unfortunate freighter, who is obliged to spend his money for hay & grain, is compelled to lay over at every post until

27 Henry Homan, letters, *Omaha Bee* (Nebraska) (May 8, 12, June 17, 1876).
28 Consolidated Report of Trains passing Fort Sedgwick, Colorado Territory, Report of the Secretary of War, 1868, *House Exec. Doc. No. 1*, 40 Cong., 1 sess. (Serial 1324), 62–64.

30 men are gathered, often a long time at this season of the year. The system is an unmitigated humbug & should be abolished.[29]

It does not require much imagination to visualize the uproar that would have arisen if the Indians had struck a few wagons and the army had taken no steps for their protection.

The mission of the freighter was to get his load through intact and in the best possible time. Often discretion was the better part of valor. In 1863 a train was warned that the Indians were having a big powwow at Fort Zarah so they slipped quietly past at night without any shouting or cracking of whips. The teamsters were cheered by the sound of the Indians' yelling, as the more noise they made, the less chance there would be that they would hear the wagons.[30]

The Indian economy, based as it was on grazing and hunting, precluded any sustained military effort. That the Indians nearly closed the Overland Trail for six weeks in 1864 was due to the accidental timing of scattered raids by small bands rather than to a sustained, organized operation. Because of the scattered nature of these raids, a number of freighters could report that they had never had a fight with the Indians. The opening of the Bozeman Trail in 1863 set off the one sustained campaign mounted by the Plains Indians, and though they lost the war, they won this campaign. To protect the trail, the army, in 1866, established three posts, Forts Reno, Phil Kearny, and C. F. Smith, but could not provide enough troops to keep the Indians away from the trail.

In the summer of 1866, Hugh Kirkendall decided to take a train loaded with merchandise for Montana over the Bozeman Trail. The train was attacked at Brown's Spring, barely thirty miles north of Fort Fetterman on the North Platte. From there on they had a running fight with the Indians until within forty miles of Fort Phil Kearny, a distance of some seventy miles. The soldiers could send no help because of the small size of the garrisons. Another train was hit ten miles south of Fort Reno but lost no lives. On reaching Fort Phil Kearny, this train was required to camp five miles from the

[29] Golden City *Transcript* (Colorado) (January 2, 1867).
[30] T. C. Hall, "Personal Recollections," *loc. cit.*, 55.

post, in order to save the range grass for the animals of the garrison. They were told not to proceed, but during the night they sneaked away. Twenty-seven freighters were armed with new Remington breechloaders while the troops were still carrying the old-style Springfield. It was claimed that the Indians feared the freighters more than they did three hundred soldiers. By traveling only at night, the train got through to Helena, suffering only three daylight attacks when the wagons were tightly corralled.[31]

In September, 1867, General C. C. Augur reported that as early as February the Indians had begun a series of raids along the Montana route and gradually extended them to all roads in his command. He said, "It is more in the nature of disconnected raids for stealing animals and getting other plunder than of a systematic and permanent war." Of the Bozeman Trail he said that the troops were able to keep it open only for their own supplies and that they had to fight almost daily to secure their supplies of wood and hay. "It has been unsafe as an emigrant road, though much required, and has not been used at all for that purpose."[32]

Though the Bozeman Trail saved three or four hundred miles over the route via Salt Lake Valley and Fort Hall, few freighters were willing to risk a clash with the Sioux and most took the longer road. As a result of a peace conference held at Fort Laramie in the spring of 1868, the army withdrew its ineffective garrisons from Forts Reno, Phil Kearny, and C. F. Smith and the trail was closed. Even the closing of the trail was accompanied by harrassment. A wagon train loaded with quartermaster supplies purchased at a surplus sale at Fort C. F. Smith had one man killed as he rode along some six hundred yards in advance of the wagons. A Diamond R train, on its way to C. F. Smith, lost six of its best horses when Indians cut their picket ropes under the guns of Fort Ellis.[33]

As the struggle against the advance of the white man went on, the Plains Indian began to develop a certain amount of co-ordination

---

31 Grace R. Hebard and E. A. Brininstool, *Bozeman Trail*, I, 227–29.
32 Report of C. C. Auger, September 30, 1867, in Report of the Secretary of War, *House Exec. Doc. No. 1*, 40 Cong., 1 sess. (Serial 1324), 58.
33 *Montana Post* (July 31, August 14, 1868).

and system in his fighting. For two successive days in 1867 a bull train loaded with corn for Denver was attacked by a war party of sixty to seventy-five Indians to the west of Fort Wallace in western Kansas. It was reported: "The Indians were very cool and deliberate in their conduct, and showed a method and determination in their movements, that is an entirely new feature in their warfare." A month later it was reported that a war party of Sioux, Cheyennes, and Arapahoes attacking a wagon train 160 miles west of Fort Harker were armed with Bogy, Spencer, and Sharp's rifles and Enfield muskets and had plenty of ammunition.[34]

The Indians' greatest weakness in opposing the white men was a lack of social conscience and discipline. The Cheyennes seemed to have the least sense of social responsibility and the Arapahoes were next. For respecting treaty obligations, the pioneers placed the Brûlé Sioux at the head of the northwestern tribes. When some braves raided the Platte Valley in violation of an informal treaty, Bad Wound, O-way-see-cha, burned all their property and killed all their horses. In 1866, Chief Spotted Tail returned to the wagon-master of a train, near Fort Mitchell, five stray oxen. The Indians had killed three oxen before finding the owner, and Spotted Tail made those guilty pay for the animals with three ponies and a buffalo robe. After the closing of the Bozeman Trail, Chief Red Cloud with a following of three hundred warriors met a train of thirty wagons on the Bighorn River. Red Cloud announced that they would take no scalps but intended to take what they wanted from the wagons. The Indians helped themselves freely, but the chief refused the demand of his braves for at least one scalp.[35]

The individualism of the Indians, even in battle, is shown by the ease with which they could be distracted. In October, 1865, a train of some twenty wagons was attacked between Julesburg and Denver. The men secured themselves in a near-by house built of a mixture of adobe and gravel. When the Indians discovered whisky in the wagons they forgot about the teamsters, who took advantage of the

[34] *Leavenworth Daily Conservative* (July 11, August 7, 1867).
[35] Ware, *Indian War of 1864*, 146, 274–75; *Omaha Daily Republican* (July 17, 1866); *Deseret News* (September 16, 1868).

distraction to escape. Returning next day with some troops, the owner found the wagons burned and the oxen slaughtered. One particular Indian showed unusual tenacity. In 1856 a teamster insulted him in some way and the brave followed the train with a gun for days. As a result, the driver had to be hidden in the wagons for the entire trip.[36]

Apparently the Comanches tried a form of crude blackmail in 1864 in an attempt to cause friction between Americans and Mexicans. They captured a train manned by a mixed crew at the Lower Cimarron Springs. The Indians took out the five Americans in the crew and shot them but allowed the Mexicans to go unharmed. Mexican-manned trains were considered, at least by the Americans, to be easier pickings for Indians bound on thievery.[37]

On the Northern Plains it was the Sioux who caused the most trouble for the freighter. An attempt was made in the early 1860's to open a wagon road from Minnesota directly west to Montana and Oregon. In 1862, 1863, and 1864, Captain James L. Fisk commanded the military escort for parties of emigrants. The third expedition was attacked and scattered by the Sioux, and the elements returned to Fort Rice on the Missouri River in North Dakota. After this the government withdrew support from Fisk's route.[38]

Another attempt was made in 1863 to open a road along a somewhat similar line. Congress appropriated $100,000 for construction of a wagon road from the Missouri in the vicinity of Sioux City, Iowa, to Virginia City, Montana. Colonel John A. Sawyers set out with a train of 85 wagons escorted by 143 volunteer soldiers. The train ran into trouble with hostile Indians, and General Patrick E. Connor, who was then engaged in the Powder River campaign, had to detach troops to strengthen Sawyers' inadequate escort. It was alleged that the government wagons carried some $20,000 worth

---

36 P. P. Gomer, "Freighting on the Plains in the 60's," related by Alva Gomer, *The Trail*, Vol. III (July, 1910), 5–8; McGee, "Early Days in the West," *loc. cit.*, 13.

37 Carleton to Steck, October 29, 1864, Condition of the Indian Tribes, *Sen. Rpt. No. 156*, 39 Cong., 2 sess (Serial 1279), 205; T. C. Hall, "Personal Recollections," *loc. cit.*, 55.

38 Merrill G. Burlingame, *The Montana Frontier*, 134–35.

of goods belonging to Sawyers' former partners, with which they planned to open a branch store in Virginia City.[39]

The trails from Fort Benton to Helena and into southern Canada passed to the north of the favored hunting grounds of the Sioux, but freighters were subject to sporadic annoyance by other tribes of the northern plains. In September, 1877, the wagonmaster of a train of ten wagons belonging to I. G. Baker and Company came in to Fort Benton and reported that his train had been captured on Milk River by a large band of Bloods, Piegans, and Gros Ventres, that two teamsters had been killed and the wagons burned. Major Guido Ilges, with three soldiers and a party of volunteers, rode out to the scene and found the remaining teamsters and wagons intact. A few Indians had been seen but not a shot had been fired. In fact there were only two guns in the train. This was apparently a case of pure cowardice. Later in the month the *Fort Benton Record* complained that, when the route from Carroll was opened, two companies of soldiers had been sent from Fort Shaw to protect the Diamond R interests. Even when the approach of the Nez Percés was announced, no soldiers were sent to Benton. "The Powers that be of course know why this was thus, but common folk can only suspect an African in the woodpile."[40] It should be noted that the road from Carroll to Helena ran through the Judith Basin, a favorite hunting ground of various Indian tribes, and was under constant attack.

An unusual turn of affairs occurred in 1868, when a freighter from Fort Peck to Helena was joined by a band of about three hundred Blood Indians. The Indians wanted protection from the Sioux. The Indians camped some distance from the wagon train, and here the Sioux struck, running off all but twenty old horses. The freighter provided transportation for the children and old folks for some days. Two Jewish merchants had been traveling with the train in their own buggy but became impatient and pushed ahead on their own. A day or so later, during an Indian scare, they abandoned the buggy and rode into Benton on the horses, reporting the

---

[39] Drago and Mott, "Edwards Letters," *loc. cit.*, 1–3, 16.
[40] *Fort Benton Record* (September 7, 28, 1877).

train to have been burned. I. G. Baker immediately rounded up twenty-five men and rode to the rescue of the train.[41] On such materials were built many of the newspaper accounts of Indian atrocities.

Only when their trails passed through country that was not particularly desirable to the Indians were the freighters comparatively free of raids and attacks by hostiles. Such was the case of the wagon road from the Great Salt Lake Basin to the Montana mines. In 1863, Alexander Toponce came across a train belonging to Livingstone and Bell of Salt Lake City that was on its way to Bannack, Montana. It had been under attack, above Fort Hall, for eight days. Otherwise, this trail seems to have been peaceful. It is small wonder that the professional freighter preferred to travel the extra distance involved —some 400 miles—rather than use the Bozeman Trail.

While the railroads spelled the end of the long-haul wagon-freighting business, the railroads themselves were not entirely free of Indian troubles. In 1867 a railroad train was attacked by Indians near Plum Creek, Nebraska, and about $20,000 worth of goods were destroyed.

Unpleasant though they were to those who suffered them, who lost their stock and equipment, who lost their lives, the depredations of the Plains Indians had little effect on the business of high plains wagon-freighting. The communities of the Mountain West continued to grow and to get the food, clothing, and supplies they needed. The closing of the Overland Trail in 1864 came about by accident rather than by design and lasted for only six weeks, though it was a critical six weeks, right at the height of the normal freighting season.

A well-organized, well-armed train under an experienced wagonmaster and with a cadre of experienced, disciplined teamsters had little to fear from the Indians. T. H. McGee said that in twelve years of freighting on the plains he never lost a man to the Indians, though he had a number of clashes with them.[42] In general, it was the small, poorly armed trains manned by inexperienced personnel that ran into serious trouble and suffered the heaviest losses.

41 Edward Swan, "Edward Swan, Pioneer," *Pony Express Courier* (1943–44), MHS.
42 "Early Days in the West," *loc. cit.*, 15.

CHAPTER XIII

THE SHORTENING HAUL

The year 1865 marked the beginning of the end for the High Plains wagon-freighter. It was the year in which construction began in earnest on the first transcontinental railroad.

Railroads had long been one of the great dreams of the westerner, who realized how fragile and expensive were his transportation links to his main sources of supply in the States. As early as 1820 the idea had been advanced of linking the Missouri and Columbia rivers by a railroad. The matter again received considerable attention in the 1840's. Finally, in 1852, Congress passed the Pacific Railroad Survey Act under which the Army's Topographical Engineers ran a series of surveys from the Mississippi-Missouri Valley to the Pacific Coast, seeking the best route for a transcontinental railroad. Further action by the government was blocked by sectional rivalry in Congress until the Southern members withdrew in 1861. In the next year Congress passed the first act under which the national government agreed to give financial assistance to private enterprise to build a railroad to the Pacific Coast.

While Congress debated the matter of a transcontinental line, private enterprise had undertaken to lay rails from the Mississippi to the Missouri. The Hannibal and St. Joseph Railroad, the first of these links, was completed in 1859. Other fine plans for the extension of the nation's rail net were ruined or postponed by the financial panic of 1857. The railhead at St. Joseph had an immediate effect on the relative importance of the Missouri River towns as eastern terminals of high plains wagon-freighting. Atchison, Kansas, was now barely thirty-five miles down river from the end of the rails, instead of some five hundred miles upstream from the rails at St. Louis. When the ice went out of the river in the spring, freight could reach Atchison and Leavenworth City, another thirty-five miles downstream, much earlier than it could from St. Louis.

The annual report for 1860 of the Parkville and Grand River Railroad Company of Missouri pointed out that the money invested in wagon-freighting would build a lot of railroad. It presented the following figures in support of its argument:

	Source			Cost	
	Register, S. M.				
	Hays Co.	Unknown	Total	Unit	Total
Place	Council Grove, Kan.	Manhattan, Kan., etc.			
Period	Apr. 24–Oct. 1	Apr. 15–Oct. 10			
Number of					
Men	3,519	7,560	11,079		$3,220,000
Wagons	2,667	4,975	7,642	$125	954,000
Horses	478	980	1,458	100	145,800
Mules	5,819	7,897	13,716	130	1,782,080
Oxen	22,738	43,762	66,500	33	2,194,500
Tons, frght.	6,819	13,422	20,241		
Total cost					$8,295,880[1]

Unfortunately, in advancing the same argument, the *Daily Times* of Leavenworth, quoting from the Westport *Border Star*, published quite different figures from the register of S. M. Hays and Company, as follows:

Men	2,400				[corrected]
Wagons	1,827	@	$200	$365,400	[$365,400]
Horses	429		150	647,500	[64,350]
Oxen	15,714		50	785,700	[785,700]
Mules	5,316		150	807,400	[797,400]

[1] John D. Cruise, "Early Days on the Union Pacific," *Collections*, KSHS, Vol. XI (1909–10), 533n.

Carriages	67	250	16,750	[16,750]
Tons frght	9,608			
		Total	2,627,300	[2,029,600]

The article went on to say that when incidentals were added it would bring the total to $3,500,000, enough to build 350 miles of railroad at $10,000 per mile.[2] It is impossible now to determine who was to blame for the various arithmetical errors in these figures.

The *American Railway Times* reported the capital invested in wagon-freighting for wages, stock, equipment, and rations during the year 1860 as being $5,545,900. This figure would place the business in the top dozen industries in the nation from the point of view of capital invested—between printing and carpet manufacture.[3]

By the beginning of 1865 there was a total of 35,085 miles of railroad track in the United States, but only 3,272 miles of this total was located west of the Mississippi and none of it west of the Missouri, except for a few very short lines on the Pacific Coast.

The official ground-breaking ceremony for the Union Pacific Railroad took place in Omaha, Nebraska, on December 2, 1863, but little work was done for eighteen months. Material had to be brought in by river steamer as there was no rail connection to the east. It was not until December, 1867, that a temporary bridge was put in. This bridge went out with the first spring flood, and the Union Pacific had to rely on a car ferry or on tracks laid on the ice in the river. The first track out of Omaha toward the west was laid on July 10, 1865.

In 1866 the town of Kearney, Nebraska, was the western terminal of the Union Pacific. Plans made by forwarding houses to operate out of Kearney were foiled by high water in the Platte River. The town was located on the north bank of the river, and wagons could not reach the Overland Trail on the south bank. As a result, most freighting was conducted from St. Joseph and other Missouri River towns. Because the population of the territories had been

[2] *Daily Times* (February 8, 1860).
[3] *Manufactures of the United States in 1860 . . . Eighth Census.*

growing steadily, freighting from the Missouri Valley reached its crest in 1866.[4]

By the summer of 1867 the rails had reached North Platte, Nebraska, the first of a succession of famous, or infamous, "Hell on Wheels" towns. The population was estimated at 3,000 persons, and it was reported that 15,000 tons of government freight had piled up awaiting wagon transportation. It was also reported that at one time there were 1,200 wagons and 800 teamsters in camp on the near-by prairie. To the wagon-freighter, North Platte offered the advantage that two round trips to Fort Laramie could be made in a single season. When the rails were completed into Julesburg, Colorado, so much of the population of North Platte moved to the new terminal that only 16 votes were cast in an election to bring the county seat to North Platte.[5]

Julesburg's growth was as spectacular as North Platte's collapse. In June there were resident in the town 40 men and 1 woman, but by the end of July the population was some 3,000 and building lots were selling for $1,000. Nearly 100 wagonloads of pine lumber were brought in from Denver, and the army quartermaster built five large warehouses, each holding upwards of 300 tons of supplies. Eight trains, totaling 236 wagons, were loaded out with government supplies for posts in Montana and Dakota, and some 12 or 13 trains of private freight left for Denver, Salt Lake City, and Virginia City in July, 1867.[6]

As the end of track moved westward, so did the lumber and canvas towns—Sidney, Nebraska, and Cheyenne, Wyoming. The latter became the main transshipment point for Denver and the Colorado mining towns, until the Denver Pacific Railroad started laying their tracks to Denver. In May, 1868, the end of track was at Laramie, Wyoming, and the *Frontier Index* reported that mule and ox trains were pouring into Laramie City from the Missouri and from the

---

4 *Rocky Mountain News* (October 25, 1866); Dick, *Vanguards of the Frontier*, 342.

5 Brown, "Freighter in Early Days," *loc. cit.*, 113; Dick, *Sod-House Frontier*, 357; Edwin L. Sabin, *Building the Pacific Railway*, 255–57.

6 Julesburg *Frontier Index* (Colorado) (July 26, 1867) ; *Weekly Denver Gazette* (July 24, 1867).

far west to load for Salt Lake City, Virginia City, and Helena. The paper said, "Laramie is like unto a bee hive." Most of the "Hell on Wheels" towns left some trace as railroad division points or agricultural or ranching supply points, but a few, such as Benton City, Wyoming, disappeared so completely that there is now no certainty of their exact locations. One traveler said that Benton City was fourteen miles east of Rawlins' Springs, but no more exact location for it is known.[7]

Beyond Benton City the terminal was successively at Bryan and Green River in Wyoming and Wasatch and Corinne in Utah. Corinne became the transshipment point for the mining camps of southeastern Idaho and western Montana and apparently was just as wild as the rest. A correspondent for the *Cincinnati Commercial* noted that the town had nineteen saloons, two dance houses, and eighty *nymphes du pave*. The *Ogden Freeman*, which waged a long fight against the facts of geography to make Ogden, Utah, the center of a large net of wagon and stage routes, commented that Corinne was blessed with "a hard crowd, such as tramps, cut-throats, second-class gamblers, etc." It also noted that a riot had occurred during a temperance meeting.[8] For some time wagon-freighters did operate out of Ogden, but that city lay some fifty miles farther away from the Montana mines than did Corinne. The latter city lost the Montana trade when the Utah Northern rails intersected the Montana trail at the Snake River.

With the driving of the Golden Spike at Promontory Summit, Utah, on May 10, 1869, linking the lines of the Union Pacific and Central Pacific railroads, the nation had its first rail connection between the Atlantic and Pacific coasts. These events did not, by any means, bring an end to wagon-freighting. The western pioneers—prospectors, miners, saloonkeepers, and merchants—had not waited on the rails but had pushed out into the more remote regions. To protect the advanced settlements, the army had to locate new posts

[7] Laramie City *Frontier Index* (Wyoming) (May 22, 1868); Beadle, *Undeveloped West*, 103.

[8] Beadle, *Undeveloped West*, 120; *Ogden Freeman* (Utah) (September 12, October 6, 1867; January 1, 1878).

in the same remote areas. Indian reservations were located as far as possible from white settlements. All these required the services of the wagon-freighter.

The Union Pacific was not the only railroad leading westward from the Missouri Valley. The Union Pacific, Eastern Division, later renamed the Kansas Pacific, completed a line from Kansas City, Missouri, to Lawrence, Kansas, in December, 1864, a distance of some 35 miles or two to three days' march for a bull train. The *Rocky Mountain News* of Denver noted that the opening of this line all the way from St. Louis cut about 130 miles off the Smoky Hill route and should give preference to that road. It went on to say that it was expected that the line would be completed to Manhattan, Kansas, 100 miles this side of Missouri, by November 1. Actually the rails only got as far as Topeka in the following year, an advance of 20 miles. Many freighters now picked up their loads at the new terminal while others continued to go back to Lawrence. A correspondent of the *New York Tribune* said, "I was amazed at the extent of the freight business across the Plains; yet I am told that it has somewhat fallen off this season. I have seen at least two thousand wagons between Lawrence and this place [Junction City]." He reported that ox trains were arriving from Denver in twenty-seven days and expected to make three round trips in the season of 1866.[9]

Sixty miles beyond Topeka, Junction City became the next terminal. In mid-1866 the short-lived Butterfield Overland Despatch gave the town a boost. They sent out a construction train to build a road to Denver and later dispatched 150,000 pounds to Denver and other Colorado points. The freighting business promised to be so big that a town meeting was called in March, 1867, to discuss the problem of a better road up Lyons Creek.[10]

During 1867, Salina and Ellsworth were successively railroad terminals. In the following year Hays City was the end of track. One traveler remembered, "Hays City by lamplight was remarkably live-

[9] *Rocky Mountain News* (September 18, 1865); Bayard Taylor, *Colorado: A Summer Trip*, 6–18.

[10] George A. Root, "Ferries in Kansas," *KHQ*, III (February, 1934), 15; Oscar O. Winther, *The Transportation Frontier; Trans-Mississippi West, 1865–1890*, 20.

ly and not very moral." The streets were lighted by lights from the saloons, decorated by gaily dressed, made-up dancing women and crowded with Mexicans from Santa Fe. The large warehouses along the railroad track were packed with wool awaiting shipment east and with merchandise for Santa Fe. The *Hays City Advance* reported that for five miles along the creek, prairie schooners were packed as close as steamers at a Mississippi levee.[11]

Beyond Hays City, Coyote was the terminal for a few months in the spring of 1868, and in the next year the terminal moved on to Sheridan, Kansas, almost on the Colorado state line. One wagonmaster claimed the record for a trip from Sheridan to Denver, a distance of 230 miles, of 11½ days. He admitted that in order to set the record he had to make 3 marches per day, but the feat was noted in all the territorial papers. He used 18 teams of 10 to 12 yoke of oxen drawing 2 wagons in tandem carrying 10,000 to 12,000 pounds of freight. The crew was composed of the wagonmaster, an assistant, 18 drivers, a day herder, and a night herder. The cook drove the lead wagon and received extra pay.[12]

In 1870 the terminal moved on to Kit Carson, Colorado, and the line was completed into Denver in August, a little over a month after the Denver Pacific Railroad had completed a connecting line to the Union Pacific at Cheyenne. While Kit Carson was not the end of the track for very long, it remained the primary transshipment point for the Santa Fe trade until 1873. One newly arrived traveler at Kit Carson remarked that to a tenderfoot it was a strange sight to see every grown man with two six-shooters at his belt.[13]

While the Kansas Pacific had been building westward across central Kansas, a competitor had been pushing westward along the valley of the Arkansas River. In 1873 the Atchison, Topeka and Santa Fe Railroad reached Granada, Colorado, just west of the

<hr>

[11] William E. Webb, *Buffalo Land*, 142; Central City *Daily Colorado Herald* (May 25, 1868).

[12] Denver *Daily Colorado Tribune* (May 12, 24, 1868); Homer W. Wheeler, *The Frontier Trail; Or, From Cowboy to Colonel*, 26–27.

[13] P. G. Scott to Miss Boach, Rocky Ford, Colorado, July 16, 1921, Pickett Papers, University of Colorado Libraries.

Kansas line. From here the newcomer threatened to take over the Santa Fe trade. The Kansas Pacific at once countered the threat by building a branch line to West Las Animas on the Arkansas River about fifty miles west of Granada. West Las Animas and Granada competed for the New Mexico trade until 1875 when both lines pushed west to La Junta, Colorado. Las Animas grew overnight to a fair-sized, wood-built town: several general stores, two lumber yards whose goods were largely freighted in from the Colorado mountains, three restaurants, two hotels, a number of residences, and several saloons, two of which had dance-hall connections. In addition there were two forwarding houses, Kihlberg and Bartels and Prowers and Hough. Despite the size of the town, it was still on the frontier. It was located close to the customary range of the hostile Kiowas and Comanches, who were not crushed until the Red River War of 1874–75. Meanwhile, the clerks of Prowers and Hough worked with their rifles close at hand. With the completion of the Atchison, Topeka and Santa Fe into Granada, two forwarding houses, Chick, Brown and Company and Otero, Seller and Company had moved there from Kit Carson to take advantage of the shortened overland haul.[14]

At La Junta the Kansas Pacific withdrew from the race, and Atchison, Topeka and Santa Fe pushed its tracks into Pueblo in early 1876. Here it connected with the Denver and Rio Grande's line from Denver to El Moro near Trinidad at the foot of Raton Pass. Two years later the Atchison, Topeka and Santa Fe laid its own lines to Trinidad and in the following year, having surmounted Raton Pass, moved its terminal to Otero and then to Las Vegas, New Mexico. On February 9, 1880, the rails reached Santa Fe.

The westward advance of the railroads changed the pattern of wagon-freighting. Forwarding and commission houses kept up with the movement of the railroads. Woolworth and Barton Overland Transportation Company advertised, "Having Portable Warehouses on line of each road [Union Pacific and Union Pacific, East-

[14] P. G. Scott, personal statement, Pickett Papers, University of Colorado Libraries.

ern Division], we shall move west as fast as the roads are open." The Nye Forwarding Company operated out of Julesburg, Colorado, and Cheyenne, Wyoming, on the line of the Union Pacific and out of Sheridan, Kansas, on the line of the Kansas Pacific. From Sheridan they claimed to be able to forward freight to Colorado, New Mexico, and Arizona faster than from Cheyenne. From Cheyenne they promised a daily freight line to Denver and Central City, and their first wagons reached Central City in 29½ hours. This time seems to have been exceptional; the Northern Freighting Company that was controlled by Nye advertised a daily fast-freight line from Cheyenne and set the time to Denver at 36 hours. On May 22, Nye forwarded for the merchants of Central City 35,097 pounds of merchandise and for those of Denver 16,935 pounds, and 6 days later he moved another 8,998 pounds for Central City.[15] The charge for freighting from Cheyenne to Central City varied from $.02 to $.03¼ per pound. The charge varied with the season. In April, 1867, Elias Smith charged $.06½ per pound from North Platte, Nebraska, to Denver, a distance of about 270 miles, plus $.02 a pound from Denver to Central City. In December of the same year another freighter charged $.03½ on a shipment of 1,430 pounds from Cheyenne to Black Hawk, Colorado, a distance of some 140 miles. It was a general rule of thumb that one railroad freight car load was equal to three wagonloads.[16]

The shortened distances from the railheads meant a shorter turn-around time for the wagon-freighter and a smaller initial investment. As early as June, 1867, with the Union Pacific completed to Julesburg, the *Daily Colorado Tribune* noted that now, instead of 600 to 700 miles of hauling, the distance from Denver to the rails was something less than 200 miles, "consequently those forty or fifty wagon trains are things of the past, the freighting business is now being done by mule or horse train instead of oxen." This made for quicker trips and allowed a longer season for the arrival of

15 *Denver Daily* (March 12, 1867); *Daily Colorado Tribune* (December 21, 1867); *Daily Colorado Tribune* (May 26, 1868); *Daily Colorado Herald* (May 26, June 2, 1868).
16 H. M. Orahood Papers, Box No. 3, University of Colorado Libraries; Pamphlet 355/40, CSHS.

goods. Two months later the same paper noted that merchants no longer had to buy six months' or a year's supplies at a time; they could buy in smaller quantities and oftener. When the railhead was at Las Animas, Pat Shanley's train made the trip to Silver City, New Mexico, with 38,000 pounds of freight, including 32,000 pounds of mining machinery, in less than two months.[17]

As the railroads advanced, the once-empty plains behind them began to fill up with settlers, and important transshipment points developed. In 1873, when the lines of the Atchison, Topeka and Santa Fe reached Wichita, Kansas, that town became an important transshipment point. Supplies for the Indian agencies and military posts in the Indian Territory went out from this point. As much as 5,000,000 pounds a year was handled by regular freighters and by local farmers with idle teams.[18]

The settlement of the plains country also meant an increase in the return loads for the freighter. In addition to wool from New Mexico, there appeared wool from the San Luis Valley of southern Colorado. In 1868, 80,000 pounds of vegetables were hauled out of Denver for Cheyenne and eastern markets. In the following year Londoner and Brother of Denver shipped out a large lot of groceries and provisions, including 10,000 pounds of cabbage, to the railhead at Sheridan. At the same time they were receiving four wagonloads, mostly sugar and coffee, from the rails at Cheyenne.[19] As the farming frontier advanced and local flouring mills were set up, flour began to disappear as one of the largest items on the manifest of the wagon-freighter.

Interest in the advance of the rails was intense throughout the west. In June, 1868, the *Colorado Chieftain* of Pueblo pointed out that, as late as May 9, a train of the Union Pacific was delayed by snow at Cheyenne. The paper stated that it was unwise to subsidize railroads farther north and that a line through Santa Fe would have

---

17 *Daily Colorado Tribune* (June 27, September 5, 1867); *Las Animas Leader* (Colorado) (February 13, 1874).

18 Richard Sheridan, *An Economic History, 1500–1900.*

19 Pueblo *Colorado Chieftain* (May 13, 24, 1869); *Daily Colorado Tribune* (October 16, 1868; October 5, 1869).

certain definite advantages. It was soon found that the rails did not answer all the problems of the West. In November, 1869, a wholesale house in Omaha had to send its regrets over a delay in shipping a new supply of "Winter Lard Oil" because the goods were "delayed on the other side of the river."[20]

The *Daily Colorado Herald* of Central City reported on the cost of shipping a buggy from Chicago to Central City. According to the railroad, the buggy and its boxing weighed 750 pounds, but according to the freighter who brought it from Cheyenne, it weighed only 630 pounds. In addition, the total freight bill was $130.16—Chicago to Omaha, $24.39; Omaha to Cheyenne, $86.63; by wagon to Central City, $19.14. The paper noted that, taking the highest figure for weight, the buggy could have been delivered, before the day of railroads, for $37.50 by ox train or $75.00 by fast freight. "There is something about this railroad freight business which we cannot exactly understand. One of our citizens had a car load of freight brought through for less money than was paid for this buggy." Fourteen months before Denver had its own rail connection to the east the *Rocky Mountain News* was complaining that the rates charged by the western railroads were too high, and the paper supported a bill presented in Congress by Representative Cadwalader C. Washburn of Wisconsin to regulate the Pacific railroads.[21] This was a fight that was to go on for many and many a year.

Problems that plagued the freighter and his customer, in the earlier days of wagon-freighting, continued to crop up. In 1874 the *Trinidad Enterprise* reported that newspapers in New Mexico had temporarily suspended publication because the unreliable schedules of the wagons had brought on a paper shortage. This same trouble had plagued the *Deseret News* of Salt Lake City and the *Rocky Mountain News* of Denver some years earlier. In November, 1879, the Las Vegas, New Mexico, *Optic* carried a story to the effect that a couple of freight teams which had been dispatched to Santa

---

[20] *Colorado Chieftain* (June 11, 1868).

[21] Walcott and Co., Omaha, Nebraska, to Fonda and Furnald, November 21, 1869, H. M. Orahood Papers, Box No. 3, University of Colorado Libraries.

Fe had been gambled away by the driver. The owner had recovered all but one set of harness, and, while he had not caught up with the driver, he was still looking for him.[22]

The opening of the silver mines around Silver City, New Mexico, in the 1870's, kept the wagon-freighter employed, hauling mining machinery as well as general merchandise for the miners. As early as May, 1873, a train of 25 wagons belonging to the Silver City Mining Company of Chicago was noted passing through Las Animas, and it was reported that there were 25 tons of machinery still at Sargent, Kansas, some 60 miles to the east, which would soon be on the way. Six years later the *Optic* noted that 9 carloads of machinery were due in Las Vegas in a few days. A month later the same paper reported that George Lail was loading 40 wagons with 150,000 pounds of mining machinery for the Massachusetts and New Mexico Mining Company of Silver City. At the same time Otero, Seller and Company was receiving carload lots of copper from Clifton, Arizona, for shipment to the east.[23]

In the face of the changing conditions, some freighters gave up the business and turned to other employment. Charles Raber, who had been freighting and trading to Santa Fe for six years, sold his outfit when the Kansas Pacific line extended beyond Fort Harker, Kansas, in 1868.[24] The more or less orderly withdrawal westward of the wagon-freighter before the advance of the railroads was suddenly reversed for a short time in the 1870's and early 1880's by the gold rush into the Black Hills of South Dakota.

Prospectors had examined the Black Hills very early, but the first paying strike was not made until 1874 when General George A. Custer led a column into the area on reconnaissance. At the time the area was part of the Sioux Reservation and was supposed to be closed to white men. The army did its best, with a handful of men,

22 *Daily Colorado Herald* (May 11, 1868); *Rocky Mountain News* (April 9, 1868); *Congressional Globe*, Appendix, 40 Cong., 2 sess., 299.

23 *Trinidad Enterprise* (Colorado) (October 17, 1874); Las Vegas *Optic* (New Mexico) (January 22, 1880).

24 *Las Animas Leader* (May 30, 1873); *Optic* (November 13, December 11, 13, 1879; January 22, 1880).

to keep prospectors out, or to drive out those who had entered. The effort was a failure, and it has been estimated that as many as ten to fifteen thousand men spent the winter of 1875–76 in the Hills, despite the hostility of the Sioux. After negotiating a new treaty with the Indians, the government opened the area to prospecting and settlement on February 28, 1877. The first bull train into the Black Hills seems to have been one from Cheyenne, Wyoming, in the winter of 1875–76. Fred Evans of Sioux City, Iowa, was caught by the army and his first train destroyed for illegal entry.[25]

Because of the extreme hostility of the Sioux, large parties were required to assure safe passage across northeastern Wyoming. One train out of Fort Laramie, belonging to several owners, consisted of fourteen bull teams of six or seven yoke each, pulling big freight wagons with trailers. There were fifty-five men in the outfit: wagon bosses, bullwhackers, miners, and prospectors. Despite the strength of the party, this train was attacked twice by Indians who tried to stampede the oxen, apparently for the beef they represented.[26]

The experience of the mining camps of the Black Hills was similar to that of the early days of the other mining camps of the west. Before the big freighting outfits were organized, flour was selling in Deadwood Gulch for sixty dollars per one hundred pounds. In the fall of 1876 it was plentiful at nine dollars a hundred. For a brief period in the spring of 1877, when the roads were nearly impassable, the price went up to thirty-five dollars. One of the earliest loads into the Black Hills was a sawmill which required six ox teams for its transportation.[27]

Great rivalry sprang up among the various supply towns—Sidney, Nebraska, and Cheyenne, Wyoming, on the line of the Union Pacific; Bismarck, North Dakota, on the line of the Northern Pacific; and the steamer landing at Pierre, South Dakota. Several Omaha merchants, seeking a short cut to the Hills, paid a handsome bonus to H. T. Clarke to build a bridge across the Platte at a point

[25] Raber, "Personal Recollections of Life," *loc. cit.,* 340.
[26] Newcastle *News Letter-Journal* (Wyoming), Half-Century Anniversary Edition (August 17, 1939); Lass, *History of Steamboating on the Upper Missouri,* 133–34.
[27] *News Letter-Journal* (August 17, 1939).

about 40 miles north of Sidney, Nebraska. The bridge, some 2,000 feet long, was completed on June 6, 1876, and there was a great traffic jam as a throng of freighters who had been waiting for several days tried to rush their trains across. The toll was $2.00 for two draft animals, wagon, and driver and $.50 for each additional animal. The usual train consisted of 20 wagons with trailers, drawn by 5 yoke of oxen and followed by a 2-horse cook-wagon.[28] Thus, an average train would pay a toll of $140.00 to $150.00.

A merchant-freighter from Omaha sold his goods in Custer City so as to make $.10 per pound freight, "all around." He went on to say that he knew he could do better at Deadwood, where they were paying $.05 to $.06 per pound for freight from Custer. "They are wanting parties to haul quartz from here [Custer City] to Sidney now, so a man can freight both ways."[29]

The principal freighting lines from Fort Pierre to the Black Hills were the Merchants Line, owned by Downer T. Bramble of Yankton, South Dakota, and the Evans Line of Fred Evans. In 1879, after the Black Hills were legally opened, Evans hauled five thousand tons of freight into the Hills, using approximately two hundred wagons. In the same year Bramble and Miller hauled about the same amount. A reporter of the *Bismarck Tribune* ascribed the increase of freighting from Bismarck in 1879 to an increase in the shipping of mining machinery that formerly had gone through Sidney, Nebraska. By 1880, Bramble and Miller employed three hundred men and two thousand oxen. The capacity of each of their trains was seven hundred tons, and a round trip required one month. By August of that year the company had forwarded four thousand tons and expected one thousand more for that season.[30]

The total amount of freight received in the Black Hills after 1877 was said to have been at least 4,000,000 pounds per year. A good

28 Jesse Brown and A. M. Willard, *The Black Hills Trails* (ed. by John T. Milek), 64; *Cheyenne Daily Leader* (January 11, 1876).

29 H. T. Clarke, "Freighting—Denver and Black Hills," *loc. cit.*, 305–306; Alfred R. Sorenson, "Western Pioneer Transportation, in Its Various Forms," Omaha *World Herald* (July 10, 1927).

30 Henry Homan, "Letters," *Omaha Bee* (May 8, 12, June 17, 1876).

proportion of this amount was hauled by "farmer outfits" during the winter months when men and animals were not needed on the farms. One freighter, fully awake to the needs of a young mining town, bought up a load of cats in Cheyenne, paying twenty-five cents each, and sold them on the street in Deadwood for from ten to twenty-five dollars apiece.[31]

A typical outfit of these later days of wagon-freighting was described as three wagons coupled together, drawn by ten yoke of oxen. The "lead" wagon was loaded with 7,000 pounds of freight; the "swing" wagon carried 5,000 pounds; and the "trail" wagon, 3,000 pounds. In good weather such an outfit would cover 12 to 15 miles per day and in bad weather, about 5. Special wagons had to be built to carry machinery for the Homestake Mine—an engine bed that weighed 16,000 pounds and a cogwheel made in two parts, each of which weighed 11,000 pounds. The movement of these very heavy loads had to wait until the fall of the year when the ground was dried out and gave support to the wagons.[32]

The decline of freighting in other parts of the West brought many outfits into the Black Hills area, and the competition drove rates down from four to five cents per pound to about one cent. A number of freighters formed the "Bull Union" and went on strike for higher rates, but the strike was not successful. Freighting to the Black Hills remained fairly profitable until about 1886, the year in which the railroad finally reached Rapid City, South Dakota, at the eastern edge of the Black Hills. When Charley Zabel decided to withdraw from the freighting business, his eighteen wagons were almost a total loss, and when he sold his work cattle for beef, he got back about half of their original cost.[33]

While wagon-freighting had been vital to the development and early growth of the Mountain West, the capacity of the entire industry was limited. As early as 1866, General John Pope, command-

---

[31] Lass, *History of Steamboating*, 133–34; Briggs, "Early Freight and Stage Lines," *North Dakota Historical Quarterly*, Vol. III (July, 1929), 245.

[32] Briggs, *Frontiers of the Northwest*, 387–88; Dick, *Vanguards of the Frontier*, 362.

[33] Charley Zabel, "Freighting in to Deadwood," *Frontier Times*, Vol. XXXVII (June-July, 1963), 6–9, 52–54.

ing the Department of the Missouri, pointed out that the population of the Mountain West was so great that means of supply other than wagons was needed. He thought that the mining regions would never produce enough food and so they would have to rely on the farming communities of the Missouri and Mississippi Valleys. All the trains in use could not haul enough supplies during the summer months to supply the mining camps for a full year. As a result, many freighters continued to operate during the winter. This defiance of the elements filled the military hospitals along the Overland Trail with frozen and frostbitten teamsters and emigrants; much stock was lost to the weather; and many wagons were left standing in the snow.[34]

The railroads provided faster transportation and year-round service, despite an occasional delay caused by floods and blizzards. As already noted, the western merchants did not have to tie up their capital for such long periods and so could turn it over more frequently. Lower transportation costs and more efficient use of capital meant lower living costs for the inhabitants. The effect of the completion of one railroad connection is well illustrated by the growth of Denver. In 1870, the year in which the rails reached the city, the population was 4,749, and ten years later it was 35,629.[35]

Completion of the transcontinental lines was greeted with enthusiasm by local freighters because the railroads stimulated settlement and supplies had to be distributed from the rails to towns and ranches.[36]

Thus, as has happened over and over again in American history, a large and vital industry had to give way to a more efficient means of performing the same essential function.

[34] *Ibid.*

[35] Report of John Pope, February 25, 1866, *House Exec. Doc. No. 76,* 39 Cong., 1 sess. (Serial 1263), 2–3.

[36] Oscar O. Winther, "The Persistence of Horse-Drawn Transportation in the Trans-Mississippi West, 1865–1900," in *Probing the American West* (ed. by K. Ross Toole, *et al.*), 47.

CHAPTER XIV

END OF THE TRAIL

THE COMPLETION of the first skeleton railroad network in the Far West was marked by the driving of the Golden Spike in 1869, the rail connection of Denver with the Missouri Valley in the following year, and the arrival of rails in Santa Fe, New Mexico, and Butte, Montana, in 1880. This did not bring an end to wagon-freighting. Goods still had to be distributed from the rails to the out-of-the-way towns and settlements.

In 1866, Douglas, Wyoming, was supplied by wagons drawn by 14 to 16 horses or mules from the end of the Fremont, Elkhorn and Missouri Railroad (now the Chicago and Northwestern). This was a 6-day haul. Other freighters hauled from the Union Pacific at Rock River, Wyoming, a distance of 90 to 100 miles, at $.03 to $.05 a pound, a trip that took 7 to 10 days.[1] It was not until 1926 that C. W. Wardle replaced wagons with trucks on the 125-mile route from Price to Vernal in Utah—a trip that took 16 to 20 days with a load of 7,000 to 8,500 pounds of merchandise or gilsonite (asphalt) ore, and on which the freighter cleared about $50.00 per day.[2] As late as 1908, the agents of a mining company in Mogollon, New Mexico, had to scour the countryside for teams from the local farmers and ranchers to move a large shipment of mining machinery from the railhead at Silver City.[3]

[1] Bert Wagner, "Reminiscences of the Early Days of Douglas," *Quarterly Bulletin,* Historical Department, State of Wyoming, Vol. II (April 15, 1925), 64.
[2] Jerry Brosnan, "You Just Kept Going," *Tribune* (Salt Lake City) (May 16, 1948).
[3] H. A. Hoover, *Early Days in the Mogollons,* 29.

The completion of the rail net did mean the end of the big freighting company. Distribution from the railroads could be handled by small one-man outfits, operating one, two, or three teams. In 1880 the army quartermaster made sixty-two contracts for wagon transportation to move 34,428 tons of supplies at a cost of $853,007.45. The Arizona posts were being supplied from the line of the Southern Pacific Railroad from Tucson, Benson, Maricopa, or Whipple Depot.[4] This should be compared to the late 1850's when Russell, Majors and Waddell had a monopoly for several years of government freighting on the high plains.

A later historian had this to say about the role of the wagon-freighter:

> Important and spectacular as was the service of the stage-coach and the pony express in carrying the mails, a service more vital to the existence of the Indian agencies, the military posts, and the settlements in the plains and mountain regions was that rendered by the prosaic, slow-moving freight wagons.[5]

The wagon-freighter played a vital role in the development of a huge sector of the United States. Much of the economic growth of the Missouri Valley was directly dependent on the wagon-freighter. All the equipment, draft animals, and rations for the crews were either locally produced or handled by commission merchants in the river towns. While only a relatively small portion of the train crews returned to the Missouri towns, those teamsters who did spent most of their wages on new clothes and on a good time.

The economic effect of wagon-freighting even spread beyond the Missouri—to the Shlutter wagon works in Jackson, Michigan, to the Studebaker works in South Bend, Indiana, and to the cattle ranges of Texas whence came many of the longhorn oxen. The machine works of Chicago and other industrial cities sent a portion of their products across the plains by wagon, and even advertised machines specially adapted to wagon transport.

[4] Report of the Quartermaster General, *House Exec. Doc. No. 1, Pt. 2*, 47 Cong., 1 sess. (Serial 2010), 222, 368.
[5] D. E. Clark, *The West in American History*, 518.

Moving the freight from St. Louis and from St. Joseph to the various terminals of wagon-freighting gave employment to a large portion of the fleet of river steamers and their crews. The storage of the goods in the river towns required the building of large warehouses, mostly with local materials and by local labor. In every town there were forwarding and commission houses which made a profit from handling the goods that went out and came in by the wagons. These business houses gave employment to staffs of clerks and warehousemen whose wages all swelled the volume of business.

The *American Railway Times* in January, 1861, reported the high plains freighting industry for the previous year as follows:

Exports and Imports:

New Mexico, at about	$3,000,000
The Pike's Peak gold regions	6,000,000
Utah	500,000
The Indian trade	1,000,000
Total	$10,500,000

Capital employed:

Wages of 11,000 teamsters average $75 per month			825,000
844 horses	@	$125	105,500
7574 mules	@	125	946,750
65,950 oxen	@	35	2,308,250
6922 wagons, including covers yokes, chains, etc.	@	150	1,038,300
Provisions for the men			250,000
		Total	$5,473,800

Adding the value of the exports and imports to the capital invested, the *Railway Times* figured the value of the freighting industry to be at least $16,000,000 and estimated that there was probably another $5,000,000 represented by freighters not regularly in the business and by goods hauled by emigrants.[6]

In the early days of the Santa Fe trade the gold and silver brought in by the traders had an important effect on the Missouri economy.

[6] (January 19, 1861).

Later, when the traders had blotted up the available supply of specie and bullion, wool and then copper took the place of the precious metals. At the western end of the great wagon routes the effects of high plains wagon-freighting were even more marked. In New Mexico the Santa Fe traders made possible, through more regular service and lower prices, a higher standard of living. It would seem only just to say that the influence of the merchant-freighter was in large part responsible for the relatively peaceful acquisition of New Mexico in 1846.

Without the assistance of the merchant-freighter, the attempt to colonize the Great Salt Lake Basin might well have failed. The colonists of the mid-nineteenth century were accustomed to, and demanded more finished goods than had the colonists of the early seventeenth century. Attempts to achieve self-sufficiency generally failed. The efforts of the Mormons to replace the merchant-freighter with church-operated stores, supplied by church-operated wagon trains, met only a small part of the needs of the community. Without a stream of goods from the East, the community might well have found itself in a condition not much better than that of the native Digger Indians. Largely because of the wagon-freighter, and despite the opposition of the Mormon church, Salt Lake City became the entrepôt, and source of much agricultural produce, for the whole intermountain west, even before the completion of the transcontinental railroad.

The mining communities of Colorado and Montana produced a great flood of gold that was urgently needed by the Union government during the Civil War, to sustain the war effort, and after the war for the payment of war debts. Without the wagon-freighter the flow of gold would have been reduced to a trickle, as the miners would have had to use much of the summer season, the best time of year for mining operations, to return to the Missouri Valley to replenish their supplies.

The wagon-freighters provided a means by which a man without stagecoach fare could walk all, or part, of his way to the New Eldorado of California, Colorado, or Montana. At times they provided the means for a whole family to move west in exchange for the labor of the head of the house. Some accepted the responsibility of escorting greenhorns who owned their own outfits across the plains in the face of a hostile nature and several tribes of hostile Indians.

It was the worn-out cattle of the bull trains, revived and fattened on prairie grass, that have been credited with being the basis on which the high plains cattle industry was built.

"Manifest Destiny" and "Westward the Course of Empire" were ringing phrases, but it was the lowly wagon-freighter who carried the lifeblood of great movements to the west.

BIBLIOGRAPHY

THERE is no single work, or group of works, that presents an over-all study of wagon-freighting across the high plains from the time the first wagons were taken to Santa Fe in 1822 until the railroads reached New Mexico and Montana in the early 1880's. Two books deal with the great firm of Russell, Majors and Waddell: Alexander Majors, *Seventy Years on the Frontier*, and Raymond W. and Mary L. Settle, *Empire on Wheels*. Unfortunately, only about 25 per cent of each deals with freighting operations, the rest being devoted to stagecoaching and the Pony Express.

A number of unpublished monographs dealing with specific phases of the industry have been written: Walker D. Wyman, "The Missouri River Towns in the Westward Movement," Dwight Bennett Newton, "Techniques of Overland Freighting in the Trans-Missouri West," George L. Strebel, "Freighting Between the Missouri River and Utah, 1847-1869," and Carla Elizabeth Neuhaus, "Transportation to Colorado, 1858-1869." In addition, there are a number of theses and dissertations that are peripheral to the subject.

A few contemporary published writings devote a good deal of attention to freighting: Josiah Gregg, *Commerce of the Prairies*; J. H. Beadle, *The Undeveloped West*; William Chandless, *A Visit to Salt Lake City*; and William Henry Jackson, *Time Exposure*. These works report the personal experiences of the authors as team-sters. In addition, there are some thirty or forty reminiscences written from ten to forty years after the events, mostly as articles in his-

297

torical periodicals. After one has read six or seven of these accounts there is little that is new, except for isolated experiences.

The contemporary western newspapers contain much information in the form of short notices and an occasional article of some length dealing with some phase or period of the industry. From time to time eastern journals carried articles—*Merchants' Magazine, Niles Register, New York Tribune,* or *American Railway Times.*

The greatest lack of reference material is in original manuscript form—account books, business correspondence, and journals of men actually engaged in the business. The Huntington Library has a collection of records of Russell, Majors and Waddell. There are some business records of the Diamond R company in the Historical Society of Montana, but they do not present a complete picture of the company's operations.

Altogether, the contemporary newspapers have proved to be the most prolific source. Some city directories were useful, but others had little or nothing of value.

1. MANUSCRIPT MATERIALS

Arbor Lodge (Nebraska City, Nebraska).

Church Historian's Office, Church of Jesus Christ of Latter-day Saints (Salt Lake City).

Account Book, Livingstone and Kincaid in Account with Governor Brigham Young.

Journal History.

Pass Book, B. Young and Council in Account with Livingstone and Kincaid.

Colorado State Historical Society (Denver).

H. Burton Account Books.

Data on the Elephant Corral, typescript.

J. S. Hoy Manuscript. (Copy in University of Colorado Libraries, Boulder).

District Court Records (Denver).

Bibliography

Historical Department, State of Wyoming (Cheyenne).
 Carter Account Books.
 Freighting and Transportation Folder—Miscellaneous File.
 John Hunton Papers.
Historical Society of Montana (Helena).
 S. C. Ashby Papers.
 Diamond R Papers.
 Manuscript File.
Huntington Library (San Marino, California).
 Russell, Majors and Waddell Papers.
Jackson County Historical Society (Independence, Missouri).
 David Waldo Papers.
Mexican Archives of New Mexico, State Records Center and Archives (Santa Fe).
National Archives (Washington, D.C.).
 Records of the Department of State.
  Consular Despatches, Santa Fe, 1830–46.
 Records of the War Department.
  Consolidated Correspondence File, Office of the Quartermaster General.
  Correspondence of the Depot Quartermaster, Fort Leavenworth, 1845–1900.
  Letter Book, Office of the Quartermaster General.
  Register of Wagon Trains Passing Fort Sedgewick, Colorado.
  Special File of Correspondence Concerning Russell, Majors and Waddell.
Nebraska State Historical Society (Lincoln).
 Biographical Notes.
 "An Early Freight Train" by Lita Mary Simon. [Unpublished manuscript, 1926 (4 pp.).]
 Letters of Francis Withee, Stella, Nebraska, 1899–1900. [Handwritten and typed copies (16 pp.).]
 "The Life of James Ralston Porter." [Unpublished manuscript (autobiographical) (23 pp., n.d.).]
 Sorenson Papers.

New Mexico Highlands University (Las Vegas).
Arrott Collection. [A collection of typescript copies of papers from the National Archives pertaining to Fort Union, New Mexico.]
Old Jail Museum (Independence, Missouri).
Account Book, unidentified blacksmith shop.
Pioneer Museum (Colorado Springs).
Cragin Collection. [This is a collection of twenty-eight note-books of notes and reminiscences, apparently taken for a projected history.]
State Historical Society of Missouri (Columbia, Missouri).
Letter Book of Ben Holladay's St. Joseph to Denver Freighting Line, January-July, 1864. [This is the letter book of the Denver agent of Holladay's stage line.]
University of Colorado Libraries (Boulder).
Colonel William Carey Brown Papers. Includes 4 vols. of *Winners of the West*.
DeBusk Manuscript Collection.
J. S. Hoy Manuscript, copy.
H. M. Orahood Papers.
H. L. Pickett Collection.
Teller Papers.
Clinton M. Tyler Papers.
Weston Public Library (Weston, Missouri).
Journal of Egbert Railley, typescript copy.

2. GOVERNMENT DOCUMENTS

I. *Congressional Documents*

Abstracted Indian Bonds. *House Executive Document No. 78; Supplemental Report No. 78*, 36 Cong., 1 sess. (Serial 1105).
American State Papers, Foreign Affairs, VI.
American State Papers, Military Affairs, III–V.
Annual Reports of the Commissioner of Indian Affairs, 1824–80.
[Until 1848, these reports were appended to the Report of the

Secretary of War; thereafter, to that of the Secretary of the Interior.]

Annual Reports of the General Commanding the Army, 1866–80.

Annual Reports of the Lieutenant General Commanding, 1864–65.

Annual Reports of the Major General Commanding, 1826–63.

Annual Reports of the Quartermaster General, 1826–80.

Annual Reports of the Secretary of the Interior, 1849–80.

Annual Reports of the Secretary of War, 1823–80.

Answers of Augustus Storrs of Missouri to Certain Queries . . . Propounded by the Hon. Mr. Benton, *Senate Document No. 7*, 18 Cong., 2 sess. (Serial 108).

Bent, St. Vrain and Co., Reports of Committees, *House Report No. 194*, 28 Cong., 2 sess. (Serial 468).

Claim of Joseph Clymer, Report of Committee on Claims, *Senate Report No. 305*, 35 Cong., 1 sess. (Serial 939).

Condition of the Indian Tribes, Report of Joint Special Committee, *Senate Report No. 156*, 39 Cong., 2 sess. (Serial 1279).

Contracts Made by the Quartermaster's Department, *House Executive Document No. 28*, 39 Cong., 2 sess. (Serial 1289).

Contracts, Purchases, and Expenditures for the Indian Service, *House Executive Document No. 123*, 43 Cong., 1 sess. (Serial 1608).

Contracts of the War Department for 1860, *House Executive Document No. 47*, 36 Cong., 2 sess. (Serial 1099).

Contracts Under Authority of the War Department, *House Executive Document No. 38*, 31 Cong., 1 sess. (Serial 576).

Contracts—Utah Expedition, *House Executive Document No. 99*, 35 Cong., 1 sess. (Serial 958).

Contracts—War Department . . . for 1855, *House Executive Document No. 17*, 34 Cong., 1 sess. (Serial 851).

Contracts—War Department for the Year 1861, *House Executive Document No. 101*, 37 Cong., 2 sess. (Serial 1136).

Daniel [David] Waldo and Co., Committee of Military Affairs, *House Report No. 56*, 35 Cong., 2 sess. (Serial 1018).

Exploration and Survey of the Valley of the Great Salt Lake of Utah ... by Howard Stansbury, Captain Corps of Topographical Engineers, *Senate Executive Document No. 3*, 32 Cong., Spec. sess. (Serial 608).

Heitman, Francis B. Historical Register and Dictionary of the United States Army, *House Document No. 446*, 57 Cong., 2 sess. (Serial 4535–36).

Indian Goods from Cheyenne to Sioux, Transportation of, 1871, *House Report No. 417*, 43 Cong., 1 sess. (Serial 1624).

Inspection by Generals Rusling and Hazen, *House Executive Document No. 45*, 39 Cong., 2 sess. (Serial 1289).

Investigation on the Conduct of Indian Affairs, *House Report No. 778*, 43 Cong., 2 sess. (Serial 1627).

Letter, Thomas Fitzpatrick, Bent's Fort, to Commissioner of Indian Affairs, September 18, 1837. [Supposed to be appended to Report of Commissioner of Indian Affairs but not included in bound volumes of House or Senate Documents. See Wagner-Camp No. 133 and Lost Cause Press microcard.]

Letter, Quartermaster General Thomas S. Jesup to C. M. Conrad, Secretary of War, November 11, 1850, in Report of the Secretary of the Treasury Showing Receipts and Expenditures for Fiscal Year Ending June 30, 1850, *House Executive Document No. 11*, 31 Cong., 2 sess. (Serial 597).

Letter, Maj. Gen. Thomas S. Jesup, Quartermaster General, upon the Cost of Transporting Troops and Supplies to California, Oregon, New Mexico, etc., in Report of the Secretary of War Communicating the Several Pacific Railroad Explorations, *House Executive Document No. 129*, 33 Cong., 1 sess. (Serial 736–38).

Massacre of Cheyenne Indians, Report of the Joint Committee on the Conduct of the War, *Senate Report No. 142, Part 3*, 38 Cong., 2 sess. (Serial 1214).

Memorial of William B. Russell, *House Executive Document No. 59*, 33 Cong., 1 sess. (Serial 742).

Message from the President, *Senate Executive Document No. 5*, 34 Cong., 3 sess. (Serial 875).

Raymond, Rossiter W. Statistics of Mines and Mining in the States and Territories West of the Rocky Mountains, *House Executive Document No. 207,* 41 Cong., 1 sess. (Serial 1424).

Report of Brig. Gen. Henry Atkinson, Expedition up the Missouri, *House Executive Document No. 117,* 19 Cong., 1 sess. (Serial 136).

Report of Captain W. F. Raynolds' Exploration of the Yellowstone Done 1859, *Senate Executive Document No. 77,* 40 Cong., 1 sess. (Serial 1317).

Report of General John Pope, February 26, 1866, *House Executive Document No. 16,* 39 Cong., 1 sess. (Serial 1263).

Report of Lieut. J. W. Abert of His Examination of New Mexico in the Years 1846–47, *House Executive Document No. 41,* 30 Cong., 1 sess. (Serial 517).

Report of Lieut. W. H. Emory, Notes of a Military Reconnoissance from Fort Leavenworth in Missouri to San Diego in California, *House Executive Document No. 41,* 30 Cong., 1 sess. (Serial 517).

Report of the Second Auditor of the Treasury . . . Accounts for Benefit of the Indians, for the Fiscal Year Ending June 30, 1855, *Senate Executive Document No. 19,* 34 Cong., 1 sess. (Serial 815).

Report of the Secretary of the Interior, *House Executive Document No. 2,* 35 Cong., 2 sess. (Serial 997).

Report of the Secretary of War Concerning the Fur Trade, and Inland Trade to Mexico, *Senate Executive Document No. 90,* 22 Cong., 1 sess. (Serial 213).

Sioux Agencies, *House Executive Document No. 35,* 43 Cong., 2 sess. (Serial 1644).

Transportation of Military Supplies from Fort Leavenworth Westward, *Senate Executive Document No. 31,* 38 Cong., 2 sess. (Serial 1209).

II. General Government Documents

Annual Report of the Director of the Mint to the Secretary of the Treasury for the fiscal year Ending June 30, 1881. Washington, Government Printing Office, 1881.

Army Regulations, 1857.

Browne, J. Ross, and James W. Taylor. *Reports upon the Mineral Resources of the United States.* Washington, Government Printing Office, 1867.

Bureau of the Census.

Compendium of the Ninth Census. Washington, Government Printing Office, 1872.

Manufactures of the United States in 1860 . . . Eighth Census. Washington, Government Printing Office, 1865.

Population of the United States in 1860 . . . Eighth Census. Washington, Government Printing Office, 1864.

Report of the Superintendent of the Census for December 1, 1852. Washington, Robert Armstrong, 1853.

Statistics of the Population of the United States at the Tenth Census. Washington, Government Printing Office, 1883. [Also in *House Miscellaneous Document No. 42,* 47 Cong., 2 sess. (Serial 2129).]

Congressional Globe (1850–61).

House Journal of the Legislative Assembly of the Territory of Colorado; Seventh Session. Central City, David C. Collier, 1868.

Official Records of the War of the Rebellion. 4 series, 128 vols. Washington, Government Printing Office, 1880–1901.

Owen, Richard E., and E. T. Cox. *Report on the Mines of New Mexico.* Washington, Government Printing Office, 1865.

Risch, Erna. *Quartermaster Support of the Army; A History of the Corps, 1775–1939.* Washington, Quartermaster Historian's Office, Office of the Quartermaster General, 1962.

Taylor, James W. *Report of James W. Taylor on the Mineral Resources of the United States East of the Rocky Mountains.* Washington, Government Printing Office, 1868.

United States Statutes at Large.

Upton, Emory. *The Military Policy of the United States.* Washington, Government Printing Office, 1904.

3. *Newspapers*

Central City Register, Colorado (1862–72).

Bibliography

Cheyenne Leader, Wyoming (1867–80).

Colorado Chieftain, Pueblo (1868–73).

Colorado Chronicle, Trinidad (1870–80). [Scattered issues in De-Busk Collection, Trinidad State Junior College.]

Council Grove Press, Kansas (1859–65).

Daily Colorado Herald, Central City (1868).

Daily Colorado Tribune, Denver (1867–71).

Daily Missouri Democrat, St. Louis (1853–73).

Daily Times, Leavenworth, Kansas (1857–67).

Denver Daily, Colorado (1867).

Deseret News, Salt Lake City, Utah (1850–80).

Fort Benton Record, Montana (1875–80).

Freedom's Champion, Atchison, Kansas (1858–69).

Frontier Index, Knight, Wyoming (1867–68). [Published in several towns at railhead of Union Pacific Railroad; incomplete file.]

Helena Herald, Montana (1866–80).

Journal of Commerce, Kansas City, Missouri (1858–65).

Kansas City Enterprise, Missouri (1854–57).

Kansas Herald of Freedom, Lawrence (1854–55).

Kansas Press, Cottonwood Falls, Kansas (1859).

Las Animas Leader, Colorado (1873–80).

Lawrence Republican, Kansas (1857–62).

Leavenworth Daily Conservative, Kansas (1867–68).

Leavenworth Times, Kansas (1859–66).

Montana Post, Helena (1864–69).

Montana Radiator, Helena (1865–66).

Nebraska Advertiser, Brownville (1856–70).

Nebraska City News, Nebraska (1857–67).

Nebraska Herald, Plattsmouth (1865–71).

Nebraska Republican, Omaha (1865–66).

Niles Register, Washington, D. C. (1822–49).

Ogden Freeman, Utah (1876–77).

Omaha Daily Republican, Nebraska (1858–80).

Optic, Las Vegas, New Mexico (1879–80).

Palladium, Bellvue, Nebraska (1854–55).

Peoples' Press, Nebraska City, Nebraska (1859–64).

The Plains, Fort Larned, Kansas (November 25, 1865). [Copy of the only issue of this soldier-edited newspaper at Fort Larned.]

Pueblo Chieftain, Colorado (1872–80).

Rocky Mountain Herald, Denver, Colorado (1868–69).

Rocky Mountain News, Denver, Colorado (1860–80).

St. Louis Weekly Reveille, Missouri (1844–46).

Spirit of the West, Nebraska City, Nebraska (April 6, 1859). [Only one issue in Nebraska State Historical Society.]

Squatter Sovereign, Atchison, Kansas (1855–57).

Trinidad Enterprise, Colorado (1870–80).

Valley Tan, Salt Lake City, Utah (1858–60).

Weekly Denver Gazette, Colorado (1865–69).

Weekly Reveille, St. Louis, Missouri (1845–46).

Winners of the West, St. Joseph, Missouri (1923–27).

4. Theses and Dissertations

Blomstrom, Robert Lowell. "The Economics of the Fur Trade of the West, 1800–1840." Ph.D. Dissertation, University of Colorado, 1961.

Briggs, Harold E. "The Settlement and Economic Development of the Territory of Dakota." M.A. Thesis, University of Iowa, 1931.

Crawford, Thelma. "Transportation Across the Great Plains, 1849–1865." M.A. Thesis, University of Oklahoma, 1921.

Crook, John G. "The Development of Early Industry and Trade in Utah." M.A. Thesis, University of Utah, 1926.

Edrington, L. Kay. "A Study of Early Utah-Montana Trade, Transportation, and Communications, 1847–1881." M.A. Thesis, Brigham Young University, 1959.

Hakola, John W. "Samuel T. Hauser and the Economic Development of Montana." Ph.D. Dissertation, Indiana University, 1961.

Jameson, Jesse H. "Corinne; A Study of a Freight Transfer Point in the Montana Trade, 1869 to 1878." M.A. Thesis, University of Utah, 1951.

Bibliography

Neuhaus, Carla Elizabeth. "Transportation to Colorado, 1858–1869." M.A. Thesis, University of Colorado, 1928.

Newton, Dwight Bennett. "Techniques of Overland Freighting in the Trans-Missouri West." M.A. Thesis, University of Kansas City, 1942.

Olson, Lawrence E. "The Mining Frontier of South Dakota." M.A. Thesis, University of Iowa, 1931.

Perrigo, Lynn I. "Life in Central City, Colorado, as Revealed by the *Register*." M.A. Thesis, University of Colorado, 1934.

Strebel, George L. "Freighting Between the Missouri River and Utah, 1847–1869. M.A. Thesis, Brigham Young University, 1954.

Unrau, William E. "The Role of the Indian Agent in the Settlement of the South-Central Plains, 1861–1868." Ph.D. Dissertation, University of Colorado, 1963.

Welty, Raymond L. "The Western Army Frontier, 1860–1870." Ph.D. Dissertation, State University of Iowa, 1924.

Wyman, Walker D. "The Missouri River Towns in the Westward Movement." Ph.D. Dissertation, State University of Iowa, 1935.

5. Unpublished Manuscripts

Steere, Edward. "Fort Union: Its Economic and Military History." National Park Service, Fort Union National Monument, New Mexico.

Utley, Robert M. "Fort Union and the Santa Fe Trail." National Park Service, Fort Union National Monument, New Mexico.

6. Books and Pamphlets

Abbey, James. *California; A Trip Across the Plains in the Spring of 1850*. New Albany, Indiana, Kent & Norman, and J. K. Nunemacher, 1850.

Alter, J. Cecil. *Utah: The Storied Domain*. 3 vols. Chicago, The American Historical Society, 1932.

Arrington, Leonard J. *Great Basin Kingdom; An Economic History of the Latter-day Saints*. Cambridge, Harvard University Press, 1953.

Ashton, Wendell. *Voice in the West: Biography of a Pioneer Newspaper.* New York, Duell, Sloan & Pearce, 1950.

Athearn, Robert G. *High Country Empire.* New York, McGraw-Hill Co., 1960.

———. *William Tecumseh Sherman and the Settlement of the West.* Norman, University of Oklahoma Press, 1956.

Barnes, Demas. *From the Atlantic to the Pacific, Overland.* New York, D. Van Nostrand, 1866.

Barney, Libeus. *Early-Day Letters from Auraria.* Denver, Ludditt Press, n.d.

Barsness, Larry. *Gold Camp: Alder Gulch and Virginia City, Montana.* New York, Hastings House, 1962.

Bartlett, John Russell. *Personal Narrative of Explorations.* 2 vols. New York, B. Appleton, 1854.

Bassett, S. P., and Joseph Magee. *Montana Publishing Company's Statistical Almanac of 1869.* Helena, Montana Publishing Company, 1869.

Beadle, J. H. *The Undeveloped West.* Philadelphia, National Publishing Company, 1873.

Beal, Merrill D. *I Will Fight No More Forever.* Seattle, University of Washington Press, 1963.

Beckman, Peter. "The Overland Trade and Atchison's Beginnings," *Territorial Kansas.* Lawrence, University of Kansas Publications, Social Science Studies, 1954.

Bieber, Ralph P., (ed.). *Marching with the Army of the West.* Vol. V of *The Southwest Historical Series.* Glendale, Arthur H. Clark Co., 1936.

Binkley, William C. *The Expansionist Movement in Texas, 1836–1850.* Berkeley, University of California Press, 1925.

Birge, Julius Charles. *The Awaking of the Desert.* Boston, R. G. Badger, 1912.

Blair, Ed. *History of Johnson County, Missouri.* Lawrence, Kansas, Standard Publishing Co., 1915.

Bolton, Herbert Eugene. *Bolton and the Spanish Borderlands.* Ed.

by John Francis Bannon. Norman, University of Oklahoma Press, 1964.

Bowles, Samuel. *Our New West.* Hartford, Hartford Publishing Co., 1869.

Bratt, John. *Trails of Yesterday.* Lincoln, Nebraska, The University Publishing Co., 1921.

Briggs, Harold E. *Frontiers of the Northwest; A History of the Upper Missouri Valley.* New York, D. Appleton-Century Co., 1940.

Brown, Jennie Broughton. *Fort Hall on the Oregon Trail.* Caldwell, Idaho, Caxton Press, 1932.

Brown, Jesse, and A. M. Willard. *The Black Hills Trails.* Ed. by John T. Milek. Rapid City, South Dakota, Rapid City Journal Co., 1924.

Brown, Mark H., and W. R. Felton. *The Frontier Years.* New York, Henry Holt & Co., 1955.

Bruce, Robert. *Three Old Plainsmen.* New York, 1923.

Bryan, Jerry. *An Illinois Gold Hunter in the Black Hills: The Diary of Jerry Bryan, March 13 to August 20, 1876.* Springfield, Illinois State Historical Society, 1960.

Bryant, Edwin. *What I Saw in California.* New York, D. Appleton & Co., 1848.

Burlingame, Merrill G. *The Montana Frontier.* Helena, State Publishing Co., 1942.

Burton, Sir Richard Francis *The City of the Saints.* New York, Harper & Bros., 1862.

Carter, Kate B. (comp.). *Heart Throbs of the West, Official Organ of the Daughters of Utah Pioneers Central Company.* 12 vols. Salt Lake City, Daughters of Utah Pioneers, 1939–51.

———. *Our Pioneer Heritage.* 7 vols. Salt Lake City, Utah Printing Co., 1958–64.

Carvalho, S. N. *Incidents of Travel and Adventure in the Far West.* New York, Derby & Jackson, 1857.

Case, Theodore S. *History of Kansas City, Missouri.* Syracuse, New York, D. Mason and Co., 1888.

Chandless, William. *A Visit to Salt Lake City.* London, Smith, Elder & Co., 1857.

Chittenden, Hiram Martin. *The American Fur Trade of the Far West.* 2 vols. Stanford, Academic Reprints, 1954.

Clark, Charles M., M. D. *A Trip to Pikes Peak and Notes by the Way.* Chicago, S. P. Rounds Steam Book and Job Printing House, 1861.

Clark, D. E. *The West in American History.* New York, Thomas Y. Crowell Co., 1937.

Cleland, Robert Glass. *This Reckless Breed of Men.* New York, Alfred M. Knopf, 1950.

Cody, William F. *Life and Adventures of "Buffalo Bill."* Chicago, Stanton & Van Vliet, 1917.

Collins, Charles. *Collins' City Directory of Leavenworth, June, 1866.* Leavenworth, Author, 1866.

———. *Omaha Directory for 1866.* Omaha, Author, 1866.

Collins, Dennis. *The Indian's Last Fight or The Dull Knife Raid.* Girard, Kansas, Press of the Appeal to Reason, *ca.*1915.

Collins, John S. *Across the Plains in '64.* Omaha, National Printing Co., 1904.

Coman, Katherine. *Economic Beginnings of the Far West.* 2 vols. New York, Macmillan, 1912.

Conard, Howard Louis. *"Uncle Dick" Wootton.* Chicago, W. E. Dibble & Co., 1890; reprint by Long's College Book Co., 1950.

Connelley, William E. *History of Kansas: State and People.* 5 vols. Chicago, American Historical Society, 1928.

Cooke, Philip St. George. *Conquest of New Mexico and California.* New York, G. P. Putnam's Sons, 1878.

Creer, Leland Hargrave. *The Founding of an Empire; The Exploration and Colonization of Utah, 1776–1856.* Salt Lake City, Bookcraft, 1947.

Dale, Harrison Clifford (ed.). *The Ashley-Smith Explorations and the Discovery of a Central Route to the Pacific, 1822–1829.* Glendale, Arthur H. Clark Co., 1941.

Bibliography

Deatherage, C. P. *Early History of Greater Kansas City, Missouri and Kansas.* 2 vols. Kansas City, Interstate Publishing Co., 1927.

DeSmet, Pierre Jean. *New Indian Sketches.* New York, D. & J. Sadlier & Co., 1865.

De Voto, Bernard. *Across the Wide Missouri.* Boston, Houghton Mifflin, 1947.

———. *The Course of Empire.* Boston, Houghton Mifflin, 1952.

———. *The Year of Decision.* Boston, Houghton Mifflin, 1942.

Dick, Everett. *Sod-House Frontier.* New York, D. Appleton-Century Co., 1937.

———. *Vanguards of the Frontier.* New York, D. Appleton-Century Co., 1941.

Dickson, Albert Jerome. *Covered Wagon Days.* Cleveland, Arthur H. Clark, 1929.

Dixon, Olive K. *Life of "Billy" Dixon.* Dallas, Texas, Southwest Press, *ca.*1927.

Driggs, Howard Roscoe. *The Old West Speaks.* Englewood Cliffs, New Jersey, Prentice-Hall, 1956.

Duffus, Robert Luther. *Santa Fe Trail.* New York, Longmans, Green & Co., 1931.

Eggenhofer, Nick. *Wagons, Mules, and Men.* New York, Hastings House, 1961.

Farnham, Thomas Jefferson, *Travels in the Great Western Desert.* Vol. XXVIII of *Early Western Travels, 1748–1846,* ed. by Reuben Gold Thwaites. Cleveland, Arthur H. Clark Co., 1906.

Ficke, Charles August. *Memories of Fourscore Years.* Davenport, Iowa, Graphic Services Inc., 1930.

Fite, Emerson David. *Social and Industrial Conditions in the North During the Civil War.* New York, The Macmillan Co., 1910.

Frederick, James Vincent. *Ben Holladay, The Stagecoach King; A Chapter in the Development of Transcontinental Transportation.* Glendale, Arthur H. Clark Co., 1940.

Fritz, Percy Stanley. *Colorado; The Centennial State.* New York, Prentice-Hall Inc., 1941.

Furniss, Norman F. *The Mormon Conflict*. New Haven, Yale University Press, 1960.

Gardiner, Dorothy. *West of the River*. New York, Thomas Y. Crowell Co., 1941.

Garrard, Lewis H. *Wah-to-yah and the Taos Trail*. Vol. VI of *The Southwest Historical Series*, ed. by Ralph P. Bieber. Glendale, Arthur H. Clark, 1938.

Greeley, Horace. *An Overland Journey from New York to San Francisco in the Summer of 1859*. New York, C. M. Saxton, Barker & Co., 1860.

Greene, Max. *The Kanzas Region*. New York, Fowler and Wells, 1858.

Greever, William S. *The Bonanza West: The Story of the Western Mining Rushes, 1848–1900*. Norman, University of Oklahoma Press, 1963.

Gregg, Josiah. *Commerce of the Prairies*. Ed. by Max L. Moorhead. Norman, University of Oklahoma Press, 1954.

Gregg, Kate L. (ed.). *The Road to Santa Fe*. Albuquerque, University of New Mexico Press, 1952.

Hafen, Leroy R. *Colorado Gold Rush; Contemporary Letters and Reports, 1858–1859*. Glendale, Arthur H. Clark Co., 1941.

———. *Fort Laramie and the Pageant of the West*. Glendale, Arthur H. Clark Co., 1938.

———. *Relations with the Plains Indians, 1857–1861*. Glendale, Arthur H. Clark Co., 1959.

———. *Reports from Colorado: The Wildman Letters, 1859–1865, with Other Related Letters and Newspaper Reports, 1859*. Glendale, Arthur H. Clark Co., 1961.

———. *Western America*. New York, Prentice-Hall, Inc., 1941.

Harvey, Augustus Ford (ed.). *Sketches of the Early Days of Nebraska City, Nebraska Territory, 1854–60*. St. Louis, Western Insurance Review Book and Job Printing House, 1871.

Hebard, Grace Raymond. *Washakie, An Account of Indian Resistance*. Cleveland, Arthur H. Clark Co., 1930.

————, and E. A. Brininstool. *The Bozeman Trail.* 2 vols. Cleveland, Arthur H. Clark Co., 1922.

Hickman, W. Z. *History of Jackson County, Missouri.* Topeka, Historical Publishing Co., 1920.

Hieb, David L. *Fort Laramie National Monument, Wyoming.* Washington, 1954.

Historical Sketch and Essay on the Resources of Montana, Including a Business Directory of the Metropolis, Helena. Helena, Herald Book and Job Printing Office, 1868.

History of Buchanan County, Missouri. St. Joseph, Missouri, Union Historical Co., 1881.

History of Pettis County, Missouri. n.p.,n.d.

Hobbs, Captain James. *Wild Life in the Far West.* Hartford, Wiley, Waterman & Eaton, 1872.

Honig, Louis O. *Westport, Gateway to the Early West.* N.p., 1950.

Hooker, William Francis. *The Bullwhacker; Adventures of a Frontier Freighter.* Yonkers-on-Hudson, World Book Co., 1940.

————. *The Prairie Schooner.* Chicago, Saul Brothers, 1918.

Hoover, H. A. *Early Days in the Mogollons.* El Paso, Texas Western Press, 1958.

Hough, Emerson. *The Way to the West.* Indianapolis, The Bobbs-Merrill Co., 1903.

Howard, Joseph K. *Strange Empire; A Narrative of the Northwest.* New York, 1952.

Hughes, John T. *Doniphan's Expedition.* Cincinnati, U. P. James, 1850.

Hunter, Louis C. *Steamboats on the Western Rivers; An Economic and Technological History.* Cambridge, Harvard University Press, 1949.

Hunton, John. *John Hunton's Diary.* Ed. by L. G. Flannery. 5 vols. Laramie, Wyoming, Guide-Review, 1956–64.

Hutchinson, William T. *Cyrus Hall McCormick; Harvest, 1856–1884.* 2 vols. New York, D. Appleton-Century Co., 1935.

Hynes, William F. *Soldiers of the Frontier.* Denver, *ca.*1943.

Ingalls, Sheffield. *History of Atchison County, Kansas.* Lawrence, Kansas, Standard Publishing Co., 1916.

Irving, Washington. *The Adventures of Captain Bonneville, U.S.A., in the Rocky Mountains and the Far West.* Ed. by Edgeley W. Todd. Norman, University of Oklahoma Press, 1961.

Jackson, W. Turrentine. *Wagon Roads West.* Berkeley, University of California Press, 1952.

Jackson, William Henry. *Time Exposure.* New York, G. P. Putnam's Sons, 1940.

————. "Bullwhacking Across the Plains," *Told at the Explorers Club.* New York, Albert and Charles Boni, 1931.

Johnson, William. "Recollections of a Bullwhacker" in *History of Johnson County, Kansas,* by Ed Blair. Lawrence, Standard Publishing Co., 1915.

Jones, Daniel W. *Forty Years Among the Indians.* Salt Lake City, Juvenile Instructor Office, 1890.

Kansas City Directory and Reference Book with a Business Directory for 1867–8. Quincy, Illinois, Excelsior Book and Job Office, 1878.

Kennerdine, Thaddeus S. *California Revisited.* Doylestown, Pennsylvania, Doylestown Publishing Co., 1898.

————. *A California Tramp.* Philadelphia, Press of the Globe Printing House, 1888.

Kinsey, Howard Joseph. *Strange Empire; A Narrative of the Northwest.* New York, William Morrow & Co., 1952.

Kuykendall, William L. *Frontier Days.* N.p., J. M. and H. L. Kuykendall, 1917.

Larimer, William Henry Harrison. *Reminiscences of General William Larimer.* Lancaster, Pennsylvania, Press of the New Era Printing Co., 1918.

Lass, William E. *A History of Steamboating on the Upper Missouri.* Lincoln, University of Nebraska Press, 1962.

Lavender, David. *The Big Divide.* Garden City, New York, Doubleday, 1948.

Bibliography

Leavenworth City Directory and Business Mirror for 1865–66. Leavenworth, Braunhold & Crowell, 1865.

Little, J. A. *What I Saw on the Old Santa Fe Trail.* Plainfield, Indiana, The Friends Press, 1904.

Longstreet, Stephen. *A Century on Wheels: The Story of Studebaker, A History; 1852–1952.* New York, Henry Holt & Co., 1952.

Lowe, Percival Green. *Five Years a Dragoon.* Kansas City, F. Hudson Publishing Co., 1906; reprint, Norman, University of Oklahoma Press, 1965.

Lucia, Ellis. *The Saga of Ben Holladay.* New York, Hastings House, 1961.

McConnell, H. H. *Five Years a Cavalryman.* Jacksboro, Texas, J. N. Rogers & Co., 1889.

McCoy, Joseph G. *Historic Sketches of the Cattle Trade of the West and Southwest.* Vol. VIII of *The Southwest Historical Series,* ed. by Ralph P. Bieber. Glendale, Arthur H. Clark Co., 1940.

McCracken, Harold. *The Charles M. Russell Book.* Garden City, New York, Doubleday, 1957.

McReynolds, Edwin C. *Missouri: A History of the Crossroads State.* Norman, University of Oklahoma Press, 1962.

Magoffin, Susan Shelby. *Down the Trail to Santa Fe; The Diary of Susan Shelby Magoffin.* Ed. by Stella Drumm. New Haven, Yale University Press, 1926.

Majors, Alexander. *Seventy Years on the Frontier.* Chicago, Rand McNally & Co., 1893.

Maximilian, Prince of Wied. *Travels in the Interior of North America.* Trans. by Hannibal Evans Lloyd. Vols. XXII–XXIV of *Early Western Travels,* ed. by Reuben Gold Thwaites. 25 vols. Cleveland, Arthur H. Clark Co., 1905–1906.

Meline, James F. *2000 Miles on Horseback.* New York, Hurd & Houghton, 1867.

Miller, Nyle H., Edgar Langsdorf, and Robert W. Richmond. *Kansas in Newspapers.* Topeka, Kansas State Historical Society, 1963.

Miller, William. *Men in Business; Essays in the History of Entrepreneurship.* Cambridge, Harvard University Press, 1952.

Millet and Sloan. *Kansas City Business Directory and Mirror for 1865–66.* Kansas City, authors, 1866.

Moody, Dan W. *Life of a Rover.* Chicago, author, 1926.

Moorhead, Max L. *New Mexico's Royal Road.* Norman, University of Oklahoma Press, 1958.

Morgan, Dale L. (ed.). *Rand McNally's Pioneer Atlas of the West.* Chicago, Rand McNally & Co., 1946.

Morton, Cyrus. *Autobiography.* Omaha, Douglas Printing Co., 1895.

Mulder, William, and A. Russell Mortensen (eds.). *Among the Mormons; Historic Accounts by Contemporary Observers.* New York, Alfred A. Knopf, 1958.

Napton, W. B. *On the Santa Fe Trail in 1857.* Kansas City, Franklin Hudson Publishing Co., 1905.

Nye, Lt. Col. W. S. *Carbine and Lance: The Story of Old Fort Sill.* Norman, University of Oklahoma Press, 1943.

Parish, William J. *The Charles Ilfeld Company: A Study of the Rise and Decline of Mercantile Capitalism in New Mexico.* Cambridge, Harvard University Press, 1961.

Parkhill, Forbes. *The Law Goes West.* Denver, A. Swallow, *ca.*1956.

Parkman, Francis. *Journals.* Ed. by Mason Wade. 2 vols. New York, Harper & Bros., 1947.

Paul, Rodman Wilson. *Mining Frontiers of the Far West, 1848–1880.* New York, Holt, Rinehart and Winston, 1963.

Paxson, Frederick L. *The Last American Frontier.* New York, Macmillan, 1910.

Paxton, William. *Annals of Platte County, Missouri.* Kansas City, Hudson-Kimberly Publishing Co., 1897.

Pearson, Gustavus C. *Overland in 1849.* Ed. by Jessie H. Goodman. Los Angeles, 1961.

Pino, Pedro Bautista, *et al. Three New Mexico Chronicles.* Trans. by H. Bailey Carroll and J. Villasana Haggard. Albuquerque, The Quivera Society, 1942.

Porter, Henry M. *Autobiography; 1838–1932.* Denver, 1932.

Bibliography

Quigg, Matthew, *Atchison City Directory and Business Mirror for 1865*. Geo. A. Crofutt & Co., 1865.

Reinhart, Herman F. *The Golden Frontier: The Recollections of Herman F. Reinhart, 1801–69*. Ed. by Doyce B. Nunis. Austin, University of Texas Press, 1962.

Richardson, Albert D. *Beyond the Mississippi*. Hartford, American Publishing Co., 1869.

Richardson, Rupert Norval. *The Comanche Barrier to South Plains Settlement*. Glendale, Arthur H. Clark Co., 1933.

Ridings, Sam P. *The Chisholm Trail*. Guthrie, Oklahoma, Co-operative Publishing Co., 1936.

Root, Frank A., and William Elsey Connelley. *The Overland Stage to California*. Topeka, 1901; reprint by Long's College Book Co., 1950.

Rules and Regulations for the Government of Russell, Majors & Waddell Outfit. Nebraska City, Thomas Morton & Co., ca.1859.

Rusling, Brig. Gen. James T. *Across America or the Great West and the Pacific Coast*. New York, Sheldon & Co., 1874.

Russell, Marian. *Land of Enchantment; Memoirs of Marian Russell along the Santa Fe Trail*. Dictated to Mrs. Hal Russell; edited by Garnet M. Brayer. Evanston, Illinois, The Branding Iron Press, 1954.

Ryus, William H. *The Second William Penn; Treating with Indians on the Santa Fe Trail, 1860–66*. Kansas City, Frank T. Riley Publishing Co., 1913.

Sabin, Edwin Legrand. *Building the Pacific Railway*. Philadelphia, Lippincott, 1919.

———. *Kit Carson Days, 1809–1868*. 2 vols. New York, Press of the Pioneers, 1935.

Settle, Raymond W., and Mary L. Settle. *Empire on Wheels*. Stanford, Stanford University Press, 1949.

Sharp, Paul F. *Whoop-up Country*. Helena, Historical Society of Montana, 1955.

Sheridan, Richard. *An Economic History, 1500–1900*. Lawrence, Bureau of Business Research, University of Kansas, 1956.

Shinn, Jonathan. *Memoirs*. Greeley, Colorado, Weld County Democrat, 1890.

Sorenson, Alfred Rasmus. *History of Omaha*. Omaha, Gibson, Miller & Richardson, printers, 1889.

Spaulding, C. C. *Annals of the City of Kansas*. Kansas City, Van Horn & Abeel, 1858.

Spring, Agnes Wright. *A Bloomer Girl on Pike's Peak, 1858: Julia Archibald Holmes, First Woman to Climb Pike's Peak*. Denver, Western History Department, Denver Public Library, 1949.

Stuart, Granville. *Forty Years on the Frontier*. Ed. by Paul C. Phillips. 2 vols. Cleveland, Arthur H. Clark Co., 1925.

Stullken, G. *My Experiences on the Plains*. Wichita, Kansas, 1913.

Sunder, John E. (ed.). *Matt Field on the Santa Fe Trail*. Norman, University of Oklahoma Press, 1960.

Sutherland, James. *Atchison City Directory and Business Mirror for 1860–61*. Indianapolis, author, 1860.

———. *Kansas City Directory and Business Mirror for 1860–61*. Indianapolis, author, 1861.

Taggert, Arthur F. *Handbook of Mineral Dressing*. New York, John Wiley and Sons, 1945.

Taylor, Bayard. *Colorado: A Summer Trip*. New York, G. P. Putnam's Sons, 1867.

Throckmorton, Arthur L. *Oregon Argonauts; Merchant Adventurers on the Western Frontier*. Portland, Oregon Historical Society, 1961.

Thwaites, Reuben Gold, (ed.). *Original Journals of the Lewis and Clark Expeditions: 1804–1806*. 7 vols. New York, Dodd, Mead & Co., 1904–1905.

Toponce, Alexander. *Reminiscences of Alexander Toponce, Pioneer*. Salt Lake City, Century Printing Co., 1923.

Tullidge, Edward D. *History of Salt Lake City*. Salt Lake City, Star Publishing Co., 1886.

Turner, Frederick Jackson. *The Rise of the New West*. Vol. XIV of *The American Nation*, ed. by Albert B. Hart. 28 vols. New York, 1906.

Bibliography

Tuttle, Daniel S. *Reminiscences of a Missionary Bishop*. New York, Thomas Whittaker, 1906.

Twitchell, Ralph Emerson. *Old Santa Fe*. Santa Fe, New Mexican Publishing Corp., 1925.

Uchill, Ida Libert. *Pioneers, Peddlers, and Tsadikim*. Denver, Sage Books, 1957.

Utley, Robert M. *Fort Union, National Monument, New Mexico*. Washington, National Park Service, 1962.

Vaughn, Robert. *Then and Now*. Minneapolis, Tribune Printing Co., 1900.

Ware, Captain Eugene F. *The Indian War of 1864*. Lincoln, University of Nebraska Press, 1960.

Webb, James Josiah. *Adventures in the Santa Fe Trade, 1844–1847*. Vol. I of *Southwest Historical Series*. Ed. by Ralph P. Bieber. Glendale, Arthur H. Clark, 1931.

Webb, Walter Prescott. *The Great Plains*. New York, 1931.

Webb, William E. *Buffalo Land*. Philadelphia, Hubbard Bros., 1873.

Wheeler, Homer Webster. *The Frontier Trail; Or, From Cowboy to Colonel*. Los Angeles, Times-Mirror Press, 1923.

White, John. *Sketches from America*. London, Sampson, Low, Son and Marston, 1870.

Whitney, Orson F. *History of Utah*. 4 vols. Salt Lake City, George Q. Cannon & Sons, 1892.

Williams, R. H. *With the Border Ruffians: Memories of the Far West, 1852–1868*. Toronto, Musson Book Co., 1907.

Wilson, Richard Lush. *Short Ravelings from a Long Yarn*. Chicago, 1847; reprint by Fine Arts Press, Santa Ana, California, 1936.

Winther, Oscar Osborn. *The Great Northwest; A History*. New York, A. A. Knopf, 1947.

———. *The Old Oregon Country; A History of Frontier Trade, Transportation and Travel*. Stanford, Stanford University Press, 1950.

———. "The Persistence of Horse-Drawn Transportation in the Trans-Mississippi West, 1865–1900," in *Probing the American*

West. Ed. by K. Ross Toole *et al.* Santa Fe, Museum of New Mexico Press, 1962.

―――. *The Transportation Frontier; Trans-Mississippi West; 1865–1890.* New York, 1964.

Wislizenus, Adolphus. *Ein Ausflug nach den Felsen-gebirgen im jahre 1839.* St. Louis, Weber, 1840.

Wolle, Muriel Sibell. *Montana Pay Dirt.* Denver, Sage Books, 1963.

Woolworth, James M. *Nebraska in 1857.* Omaha, C. C. Woolworth, 1857.

Young, Harry [Sam]. *Hard Knocks.* Chicago, Laird & Lee, Inc., 1915.

7. PERIODICALS

Ainsworth, Newton, "The Old Santa Fe Trail in Johnson County, Kansas," *Collections*, Kansas State Historical Society, Vol. XI (1910), 456–63.

Allison, W. H. H. "Santa Fe in 1846," *Old Santa Fe*, Vol. II (April, 1915), 392–406.

Alter, Cecil J. "Travelogs," *Salt Lake Tribune* (Utah), 1922.

Anderson, Bernice Gibbs. "The Gentile City of Corinne," *Utah Historical Quarterly*, Vol. IX (July-October, 1941), 141–54.

Ashton, John. "History of Jack Stock and Mules in Missouri," *The Monthly Bulletin*, Missouri State Board of Agriculture, Vol. XXII (August, 1924).

Athearn, Robert G. "The Great Plains in Historical Perspective," *Montana, The Magazine of Western History*, Vol. VIII (January, 1958), 13–29.

Aull, James and Robert. "Letters of James and Robert Aull." Ed. by Ralph P. Bieber. *Collections*, Missouri Historical Society, Vol. V (June, 1928), 267–310.

Beckler, Marion. "He Could Crack a Bull-Whip," *Desert Magazine*, Vol. XIII (August, 1950), 27–29.

Becknell, Captain Thomas. "The Journals of Captain Thomas Becknell from Boone's Lick to Santa Fe, and from Santa Cruz to

Green River," *Missouri Historical Review*, Vol. IV (January, 1910), 65–84.

Beers, Henry P. "Military Protection of the Santa Fe Trail to 1843," *New Mexico Historical Review*, Vol. XII (April, 1937), 113–33.

Bemis, Edwin A. "Wagonmaster," *1952 Brand Book*, Denver, The Westerners.

Bernard, William R. "Westport and the Santa Fe Trade," *Transactions*, Kansas State Historical Society, Vol. IX (1905–1906), 552–65.

Bieber, Ralph P. "Some Aspects of the Santa Fe Trade; 1848–1880," *Missouri Historical Review*, Vol. XVIII (January, 1924), 158–66.

Bloom, Lansing. "Ledgers of a Santa Fe Trader," *El Palacio*, Vol. XIV (May 1, 1923), 133–36.

————. "From Lewisburg (Pa) to California," *New Mexico Historical Quarterly*, Vol. XX (January, 1945), 14–57.

Bott, Emily Ann O'Neal. "Joseph Murphy's Contribution to the Development of the West," *Missouri Historical Review*, Vol. XLVII (October, 1952), 18–28.

Bradley, Lt. "Affairs at Fort Benton from 1831 to 1869 from Lieut. Bradley's Journal," *Contributions*, Historical Society of Montana, Vol. III (1900), 201–87.

————. "Bradley Manuscript—Book II, Miscellaneous Events at Fort Benton," *Contributions*, Historical Society of Montana, Vol. VIII (1917), 127–96.

Briggs, Harold E. "Early Freight and Stage Lines in Dakota," *North Dakota Historical Quarterly*, Vol. III (July, 1929), 229–61.

————. "Pioneer River Transportation in Dakota," *North Dakota Historical Quarterly*, Vol. III (April, 1929), 159–82.

Britton, Wiley. "Pioneer Life in Southwest Missouri," *Missouri Historical Review*, Vol. XVI (October, 1921), 42–85; (January, 1922), 263–88; (April, 1922), 388–421; (July, 1922), 556–79.

Brosnan, Jerry. "You Just Kept Going," *Tribune* (Salt Lake City) (May 16, 1948).

Brown, Jesse. "The Freighter in Early Days," *Annals of Wyoming*, Vol. XIX (July, 1947), 112–16.

"Bullwhackers," *Montana*, Vol. III (Autumn, 1952), 31.

Burgess, Perry A. "From Illinois to Montana in 1866; The Diary of Perry A. Burgess." Ed. by Robert G. Athearn. *Pacific Northwest Quarterly*, Vol. XLI (January, 1950), 43–65.

Burns, Thomas F. "The Town of Wilmington and the Santa Fe Trail," *Collections*, Kansas State Historical Society, Vol. XI (1909–10), 597–99.

Caldwell, Alexander. "Address," *Publications*, Kansas State Historical Society, Vol. I (1886), 259–66.

Carroll, H. Bailey. "Steward A. Miller and the Snively Expedition of 1843," *Southwestern Historical Quarterly*, Vol. LIV (January, 1951), 261–86.

Case, Frank M. "Experiences on the Platte River Route in the Sixties," *Colorado Magazine*, Vol. V (August, 1928), 146–51.

Clark, Niel M. "When the Turkeys Walked," *American Heritage*, Vol. XV (December, 1963), 92–93.

Clark, W. A. "Centennial Adress," *Contributions*, Historical Society of Montana, Vol. II (1896), 45–60.

Clark, William. "A Trip Across the Plains in 1857," *Iowa Journal of History and Politics*, Vol. XX (April, 1922), 163–223.

Clarke, H. T. "Freighting—Denver and Black Hills," *Proceedings and Collections*, Nebraska State Historical Society, 2nd Series, Vol. V (1902), 299–312.

"Colorado Territorial Days," *The Trail*, Vol. I (October, 1908), 6–11.

Colyer, Julie Beehrer. "Freighting Across the Plains; True Experience of George W. Beehrer from His Diary and as Related to a Friend," *Montana*, Vol. XII (Autumn, 1962), 2–17.

"Commerce of the Prairies," *American Railway Times* (January 26, 1861).

"Commerce of the Prairies," *Merchants' Magazine and Commercial Review*, Vol. XLIV (January, 1862), 19–45.

Condron, H. David. "Knapheide Wagon Company; 1848–1943," *Journal of Economic History*, Vol. III (May, 1943), 32–41.

Connelley, William E. "A Journal of the Santa Fe Trail," *Missis-*

sippi Valley Historical Review, Vol. XII (June, 1925), 72–98; (September, 1925), 227–55.

Cornforth, Thomas T. "Early Colorado Days." Ed. by Albert B. Sanford. *Colorado Magazine*, Vol. I (September, 1924), 251–67.

"The Cotton Mission," *Utah Historical Quarterly*, Vol. XXIX (July, 1961), 201–21.

Coutant, [C. G.]. "Dwight Fisk, Early Freighter," *Annals of Wyoming*, Vol. IV (October, 1926), 305–308.

Cox, W. W. "Reminiscences of Early Days in Nebraska," *Transactions and Reports*, Nebraska State Historical Society, 1st Series, Vol. V (1893), 63–82.

Creigh, Thomas Alfred. "From Nebraska City to Montana, 1866: The Diary of Thomas Alfred Creigh." Ed. by James C. Olson, *Nebraska History*, Vol. XXIV (September, 1948), 208–37.

Crook, John. "Journal," *Utah Historical Quarterly*, Vol. VI (April, 1933), 51–62; (July, 1933), 110–112.

Cruise, John D. "Early Days on the Union Pacific," *Collections*, Kansas State Historical Society, Vol. XI (1909–10), 533n.

Darley, Rev. G. M., D. D. "The End-Gate of the Mess Wagon," *The Trail*, Vol. II (November, 1909), 17–18.

Dickinson, John P. "On a Government Survey in the Early 70's," *The Trail*, Vol. X (December, 1917), 14–22.

Downing, Finis E. "With the Ute Peace Delegation of 1863, Across the Plains, and at Conejos," *Colorado Magazine*, Vol. XXII (September, 1945), 193–205.

"Do You Know or Don't You?" *Missouri Historical Review*, Vol. XXXIV (October, 1939), 96.

Drago, Harry Sinclair, and Phyllis Mott. "The Edwards Letters and the Wagon Road to Virginia City," *New York Posse Brand Book*, The Westerners, Vol. IX (1962), 1–3, 16–19.

Dunham, Harold H. "Sidelights on Santa Fe Traders; 1839–1846," *1950 Brand Book*, Denver Posse, The Westerners.

Dunn, William. "Diary of William Dunn, Freighter," *Nebraska History*, Vol. IV (April-June, 1921), 31–32.

Edmondson, William. "Diary Kept by William Edmondson, of Oakloosa, While Crossing the Western Plains in 1850," *Annals of Iowa*, 3rd Series, Vol. VIII (October, 1908), 516–35.

Eldridge, S. W. "Recollections of Early Days in Kansas," *Publications*, Kansas State Historical Society, Vol. IX (1920), 11–26.

Ellsworth, Alonzo E. "Early Denver Business," *Denver Westerners Monthly Roundup*, Vol. VI (November, 1950), 1–13.

Espenschied, Lloyd. "Louis Espenschied and His Family," *Bulletin*, Missouri Historical Society, Vol. XVIII (January, 1962), 87–103.

Field, Edmund C. "A Wind Wagon," *Missouri Historical Review*, Vol. XXXI (October, 1936), 85.

Fletcher, Bob. "Smoke Signals," *Montana*, Vol. I (Summer, 1952), 41–45.

"Fort Larned, Larned, Kansas." Reprint from *Between the Lines*, employee magazine, Natural Gas Pipeline Co. of America.

"Freighting in 1866: Part of a Letter Written from the Interior of the Territory of Nebraska to the East, January 29, 1866," *Proceedings and Collections*, Nebraska State Historical Society, 2nd Series, Vol. I (1894–95), 47.

"Freighting on the Frontier," *Kansas Historical Quarterly*, Vol. XX (May, 1953), 452–54.

"Freighting to Denver," *Nebraska History*, Vol. XV (January–March, 1934), 121.

Fulton, William. "Freighting and Staging in Early Days," *Proceedings and Collections*, Nebraska State Historical Society, 2nd Series, Vol. V (1902), 261–64.

Garrett, T. S. "Some Recollections of an Old Freighter," *Annals of Wyoming*, Vol. III (July, 1925), 86–93.

Gomer, P. P. "Freighting on the Plains in the 60's," related by Alva Gomer, *The Trail*, Vol. III (July, 1910), 5–8.

Greene, J. Evarts. "The Santa Fe Trade: Its Route and Character," *American Antiquarian Society Proceedings*, New Series, Vol. V (1892–93), 324–41.

Grinnell, George Bird. "Bent's Old Fort and Its Builders," *Collections*, Kansas State Historical Society, Vol. XV (1923–25), 28–91.

Bibliography

Hadley, C. B. "The Plains War in 1865," *Proceedings and Collections*, Nebraska State Historical Society, 2nd Series, Vol. V (1902), 273–78.

Hafen, Leroy R. "Supplies and Market Prices in Pioneer Denver," *Colorado Magazine*, Vol. IV (August, 1927), 136–42.

Hall, T. C. "Personal Recollections of the Santa Fe Trail," *Kansas Magazine*, Vol. V (January, 1911), 49–55.

Harkness, James. "Diary of James Harkness of the Firm of LaBarge, Harkness, and Company of St. Louis to Fort Benton by the Missouri River and to Deer Lodge Valley and Return in 1862," *Contributions*, Historical Society of Montana, Vol. II (1896), 352–55.

Hart, Charles N. "Reminiscences of the Early West," *Colorado Magazine*, Vol. XV (November, 1938), 209–17.

Haygood, A. W. "The Freighting Business," *Annals of Wyoming*, Vol. III (July, 1925), 85–86.

Holt, R. D. "Old Texas Wagon Trains," *Frontier Times*, Vol. XXV (September, 1948), 269–72.

Homan, Henry. "Letters," *Omaha Bee* (May 8, 12, June 17, 1876).

Hooker, William F. "The Freight Train Wagon-Boss of the 1870's," *The Union Pacific Magazine*, Vol. IV (1925), 9–10.

Hough, Emerson. "A Study in Transportation: The Settlement of the West," *Century*, Vol. LXIII (November, 1901), 91–107; (December, 1901), 200–17; (January, 1902), 355–69.

"How Noted Old Freight Outfit, Diamond R, Came into Being as Biggest Firm in State Related," *Independent* (Helena) (March 1, 1937).

"Indian War of 1864," *Overland News* (November, December, 1957).

Irvine, J. B. (comp.). "A Steam Wagon Invented by an Early Resident of South Dakota," *South Dakota Historical Collections*, Vol. X (1930), 371–87.

Jackson, Clarence S. "Roll Out, Roll Out, The Bulls are Coming, William H. Jackson's Letter," *1954 Brand Book*, Denver Posse, The Westerners.

Jackson William H. "The Most Important Nebraska Highway—

Nebraska City–Fort Kearny–Denver Trail or 'Steam Wagon Road,' " *Nebraska History,* Vol. XIII (July-September, 1932), 137–59.

Johnson, Dorothy M. "Flour Famine in Alder Gulch," *Montana,* Vol. VII (January, 1957), 18–27.

Jones, Charles Irving. "William Kronig, New Mexico Pioneer, from His Memories of 1849–1860," *New Mexico Historical Review,* Vol. XIX (July, 1944), 185–224; (October, 1944), 271–311.

"Letters Home," *Nebraska History,* Vol. XVII (July-September, 1936), 156–61.

Lummis, Charles F. "Pioneer Transportation in America," *McClure's Magazine,* Vol. XXV (October, 1905), 561–73; Vol. XXVI (November, 1905), 81–94.

Lyon, Herman Robert. "Freighting in the '60's," *Proceedings and Collections,* Nebraska State Historical Society, 2nd Series, Vol. V (1902), 296–97.

McGee, T. H. "Early Days in the West," *Quarterly Bulletin of the Wyoming Historical Department,* Vol. I (April, 1924), 13–16. [Now *Annals of Wyoming*].

McKinnon, Bess. "The Toll Road over Raton Pass," *New Mexico Historical Review,* Vol. II (January, 1927), 83–89.

Maddox, Porter. "Freighting Reminiscences," *Proceedings and Collections,* Nebraska State Historical Society, 2nd Series, Vol. V (1902), 296–97.

Mallory, Samuel, "Overland to Pike's Peak with a Quartz Mill," *Colorado Magazine,* Vol. VIII (May, 1931), 108–15.

Mantor, Lyle E. "Stage Coach and Freighter Days at Fort Kearny," *Nebraska History,* Vol. XXIX (December, 1948), 324–38.

Mark Trey. "Jerk Line Jockey," *True West,* Vol. V (May-June, 1958), 22–23, 40–42.

Marvin, George P. "Bull-Whacking Days," *Proceedings and Collections,* Nebraska State Historical Society, 2nd Series, Vol. V (1902), 226–30.

Meek, C. P. (Dub). "C. P. Meek Drove First Bull Train into the

Black Hills," *News-Letter Journal* (Newcastle, Wyoming) (August 17, 1939).

———. "Bull Whacker Tells of 2nd Trip to Hills," *ibid.*

Milligan, E. W. "John Wesley Iliff," *Denver Westerners Monthly Roundup*, Vol. VI (August, 1950).

Moorhead, Max L. "Spanish Transportation in the Southwest; 1540–1846," *New Mexico Historical Review*, Vol. XXXII (April, 1957), 107–20.

Morton, Paul. "Early Freighting Days in the West," *Santa Fe Employees' Magazine*, Vol. III (August, 1909), 1013–16.

Munn, Eugene. "Early Freighting and Claim Club Days in Nebraska," *Proceedings and Collections*, Nebraska State Historical Society, 2nd Series, Vol. V (1902), 313–17.

"The New Mexico Wool Trade," *Merchants' Magazine and Commercial Review*, Vol. XLVII (October, 1862), 356–57.

Nickerson, H. G. "Early History of Fremont County," *Annals of Wyoming*, Vol. II (July 15, 1924), 1–13.

Obituary—Robert J. Spotswood. *The Trail*, Vol. II (May, 1910), 24.

Obituary—John B. Russell. *The Trail*, Vol. VI (September, 1913), 27.

An Old School Boy. "School Days in Early Denver," *The Trail*, Vol. III (August, 1910), 23–24.

Oviatt, Alton B. "Steamboat Traffic on the Upper Missouri River, 1859–1869," *Pacific Northwest Quarterly*, Vol. XL (April, 1949), 93–105.

Parkhill, Forbes. "There's Gold in Them Thar Files," *Denver Westerners Monthly Roundup*, Vol. VII (May, 1951).

Parsons, William B. "Pike's Peak Fourteen Years Ago," *Kansas Magazine*, Vol. I (June, 1872), 552–61.

Patterson, E. H. N. "Chalk Marks of Overland Travel Pike Peakward," *Spectator* (Oquawka, Illinois) (April 19–September 19, 1860), Southwest Microfilm No. A–291.

Peabody, Frances Clelland. "Across the Plains DeLuxe in 1865," *Colorado Magazine*, Vol. XVIII (March, 1941), 71–76.

Peck, Robert M. "Recollections of Early Times in Kansas Territory," *Transactions*, Kansas State Historical Society, Vol. VIII (1904), 484–507.

Perrigo, Lynn I. "Mayor Hal Sayr's Diary of the Sand Creek Massacre," *Colorado Magazine*, Vol. XV (March, 1938), 41–57.

Porter, Henry M. "Freighting and Merchandising in Early Denver," *Colorado Magazine*, Vol. VI (September, 1929), 171–73.

Powers, T. C., and Brothers. "Steam Boat Arrivals at Fort Benton," *Contributions*, Historical Society of Montana, Vol. I (1859–74), 280–87; Vol. III (1875–88), 351–58.

Raber, Charles. "Personal Recollections of Life on the Plains from 1860–1868," *Collections*, Kansas State Historical Society, Vol. XVI (1923–25), 315–40.

Remsburg, George J. "Gleaned from the Old Files," *The Trail*, Vol. XIX (July, 1926), 16–17.

Rice, William B. "Early Freighting on the Salt Lake–San Bernardino Trail," *Pacific Historical Review*, Vol. XI (March, 1942), 73–80.

Rickard, T. A. "The Chino Enterprise—I; History of the Region and the Beginning of Mining at Santa Rita," *Engineering and Mining Journal*, Vol. CXVI (November 3, 1923), 753–58; (November 10, 1923), 803–10.

Ritch, John B. (ed.). "Fort Benton Journal," *Contributions*, Historical Society of Montana, Vol. X (1940), 1–99.

Rivington, Tom. "Bull Train Boss Was Doughty Man," Cheyenne *Wyoming State Tribune* (August 17, 1932).

Roeschlaub, Robert S. "The Pioneer Trail," *Sons of Colorado*, Vol. I (May, 1907), 33–34.

Rolfe, R. M. "The Overland Freighting Business in the Early Sixties," *Kansas City Star* (December 31, 1899).

Root, George A. "Ferries in Kansas—Part II, Kansas River," *Kansas Historical Quarterly*, Vol. II (August, 1933), 251–93; (November, 1933), 343–76; Vol. III (February, 1934), 15–42.

Sagendorf, Andrew. "History of Auraria—Narrative of Andrew

Sagendorf," *Commonwealth Magazine* (Denver), Vol. I (April, 1889), 57–60.

Sampson, F. A. (ed.). "Santa Fe Trail: M. M. Marmaduke Journal," *Missouri Historical Review*, Vol. VI (October, 1911), 1–10.

Scott, P. G. "Diary of a Freighting Trip from Kit Carson to Trinidad in 1870," *Colorado Magazine*, Vol. VIII (July, 1931), 146–54.

———. "Pioneer Experiences in Southern Colorado," *Colorado Magazine*, Vol. IX (January, 1932), 21–25.

Settle, Raymond W. "Robert B. Bradford," *1954 Brand Book*, Denver Posse, The Westerners, 49–64.

———, and Mary Lund Settle. "The Early Careers of W. B. Waddell and W. H. Russell: Frontier Capitalists," *Kansas Historical Quarterly*, Vol. XXVI (Winter, 1960), 355–82.

———. "Napoleon of the West; Biography of William Hepburn Russell," *Annals of Wyoming*, Vol. XXXII (April, 1960), 5–47.

Sharp, Paul F. "Merchant Princes of the Plains," *Montana*, Vol. V (Winter, 1955), 2–20.

Sloan, William K. "Autobiography," *Annals of Wyoming*, Vol. IV (July, 1926), 235–64.

Sorenson, Alfred R. "Western Pioneer Transportation, in Its Various Forms," Omaha *World Herald* (July 10, 1927).

"A Stage Ride to Colorado," *Harper's Magazine*, Vol. XXXV (July, 1867), 137–50.

Standish, John K. "A Pioneer Freighter," *American Cattle Producer*, Vol. XXIX (March, 1948), 11–12, 30–31.

Stephens, F. F. "Missouri and the Santa Fe Trade," *Missouri Historical Review*, Vol. X (July, 1916), 223–62; Vol. XI (April-July, 1917), 289–312.

Swan, Edward. "Edward Swan, Pioneer," *Pony Express Courier* (1943–44).

Sydenham, Moses H. "Freighting Across the Plains in 1856; A Personal Experience," *Proceedings and Collections*, Nebraska State Historical Society, 2nd Series, Vol. I (1894–95), 164–84.

Thompson, James B. "Crossing the Plains in 1864," *Sons of Colorado*, Vol. II (March, 1908), 3–8.

Trexler, H. A. "Missouri-Montana Highways—I, The Missouri River Route." *Missouri Historical Review*, Vol. XII (January, 1918), 67–80;—"The Overland Route," Vol. XII (April, 1918), 145–62.

Tyson, T. K. "Freighting to Denver," *Proceedings and Collections*, Nebraska State Historical Society, 2nd Series, Vol. V (1902), 256–60.

Unrau, William Errol. "History of Fort Larned," *Kansas Historical Quarterly*, Vol. XXIII (Autumn, 1957), 257–80.

Utley, Robert M. "Kit Carson and the Adobe Walls Campaign," *The American West*, Vol. II (Winter, 1965), 4–11, 73–75.

Vanderwalker, George F. "The Bull-whacker or Prairie Sailor," *The Trail*, Vol. I (February, 1909), 26.

———. "Over the Santa Fe Trail in 1864," *The Trail*, Vol. II (June, 1909), 16–18.

Vasquez, Hiram. "Experiences at Fort Bridger, with the Shoshones and in Early Colorado," *Colorado Magazine*, Vol. VIII (May, 1931), 106–108.

Viles, Jonas. "Old Franklin: A Frontier Town of the Twenties," *Mississippi Valley Historical Review*, Vol. IX (March, 1923), 269–82.

Wagner, Bert. "Reminiscences of the Early Days of Douglas," *Quarterly Bulletin*, Historical Department, State of Wyoming, Vol. II (April 15, 1925), 64–66.

Ward, Colonel Samuel. "Diary of Colonel Samuel Ward, "*Contributions*, Historical Society of Montana, Vol. VIII (1917), 37–92.

Watkins, Albert. "History of Fort Kearney," *Collections*, Nebraska State Historical Society, Vol. XVI (1911), 227–67.

Watt, James W. "Experiences of a Packer in Washington Territory Mining Camps During the Sixties." Ed. by William S. Lewis. *Washington Historical Quarterly*, Vol. XIX (July, 1928), 207–13; Vol. XIX (October, 1928), 285–93; Vol. XX (January, 1929), 36–53.

Webb, James J. "The Papers of James J. Webb, Santa Fe Merchant,

1844–61." Ed. by Ralph P. Bieber. *University of Washington Studies*, Vol. XI, Humanistic Series No. 2 (1924), 255–305.

Webb, W. L. "Independence, Missouri, a Century Old," *Missouri Historical Review*, Vol. XXII (October, 1927), 30–50.

Webster, John Lee. "Address," *Collections*, Nebraska State Historical Society, Vol. XVI (1911), 47–65.

Wellman, Paul I. "The Silent Partner Who Made History and Lost Fortunes on the Great Plains," clipping, Scrapbook, Leavenworth Public Library.

Wilson, James W. "Reminiscences of Overland Days," *Sons of Colorado*, Vol. I (May, 1907), 3–6.

"Wind Wagon of Westport," *Missouri Historical Review*, Vol. XXV (April, 1931), 528–29.

Winther, Oscar Osborn. "The Place of Transportation in the Early History of the Pacific Northwest," *Pacific Historical Review*, Vol. II (December, 1942), 383–96.

Withers, Ethel Massie (ed.). "Experiences of Lewis Bissell Dougherty on the Oregon Trail," *Missouri Historical Review*, Vol. XXIV (April, 1930), 359–78.

Wood, Asa A. "Fort Benton's Part in the Development of the West," *Washington Historical Quarterly*, Vol. XX (July, 1929), 213–22.

Woody, Frank H. "How an Early Pioneer Came to Montana and the Privations Encountered on the Journey," *Contributions*, Historical Society of Montana, Vol. VII (1910), 138–64.

Wright, R. M. "Personal Reminiscences of Frontier Life in Southwest Kansas," *Transactions*, Kansas State Historical Society, Vol. VII (1902), 47–83.

Wyman, Walker D. "Bullwhacking: A Prosaic Profession Peculiar to the Great Plains," *New Mexico Historical Review*, Vol. VII (October, 1932), 297–310.

———. "Freighting: A Big Business on the Santa Fe Trail," *Kansas Historical Quarterly*, Vol. I (November, 1931), 17–27.

———. "Military Phase of Santa Fe Freighting, 1846–1865," *Kansas Historical Quarterly*, Vol. I (November, 1932), 415–28.

———. "Omaha, Frontier Depot and Prodigy of Council Bluffs," *Nebraska History*, Vol. XVII (July-September, 1936), 143–55.

Young, Otis E. "The United States Mounted Ranger Battalion; 1832–33," *Mississippi Valley Historical Review*, Vol. XLI (December, 1954), 463–88.

Zabel, Charley. "Freighting in to Deadwood," *Frontier Times*, Vol. XXXVII (June-July, 1963), 6–9, 52–54.

8. SCRAPBOOKS

Dawson Scrapbooks. Vols. XLVI–XLVII. Transportation, State Historical Society of Colorado, Denver.

Freighting Scrap Book. Historical Society of Montana, Helena.

Scrapbook. Atchison, Kansas, Public Library.

Scrapbook. Council Bluffs, Iowa, Public Library.

Scrapbook. Leavenworth, Kansas, Public Library.

Trails Clippings. Kansas State Historical Society, Topeka.

"Travelogs" by J. Cecil Alter from *Salt Lake Tribune*, Utah State Historical Society.

INDEX

Index

339

Index

Index

347

The Wagonmasters has been cast on the Linotype in eleven-point Baskerville, a weight-for-weight and curve-for-curve copy of John Baskerville's celebrated printing type. Modifications of the two-letter italic, to fit the needs of machine placement, have been performed sympathetically, with appreciation of the subtleties of the original.

This book is printed on paper bearing the watermark of the University of Oklahoma Press and is designed for an effective life of at least three hundred years.